GENDER <u>IN</u> HISTORY

Series editors:
Lynn Abrams, Cordelia Beattie, Pam Sharpe and Penny Summerfield

The expansion of research into the history of women and gender since the 1970s has changed the face of history. Using the insights of feminist theory and of historians of women, gender historians have explored the configuration in the past of gender identities and relations between the sexes. They have also investigated the history of sexuality and family relations, and analysed ideas and ideals of masculinity and femininity. Yet gender history has not abandoned the original, inspirational project of women's history: to recover and reveal the lived experience of women in the past and the present.

The series Gender in History provides a forum for these developments. Its historical coverage extends from the medieval to the modern periods, and its geographical scope encompasses not only Europe and North America but all corners of the globe. The series aims to investigate the social and cultural constructions of gender in historical sources, as well as the gendering of historical discourse itself. It embraces both detailed case studies of specific regions or periods, and broader treatments of major themes. Gender in History titles are designed to meet the needs of both scholars and students working in this dynamic area of historical research.

Being boys

MANCHESTER
1824

Manchester University Press

BEING BOYS
YOUTH, LEISURE AND IDENTITY
IN THE INTER-WAR YEARS

—— Melanie Tebbutt ——

Manchester University Press
Manchester and New York

distributed in the United States exclusively by Palgrave Macmillan

Published by Manchester University Press
Oxford Road, Manchester M13 9NR, UK
and Room 400, 175 Fifth Avenue, New York, NY 10010, USA
www.manchesteruniversitypress.co.uk

Distributed in the United States exclusively by Palgrave Macmillan
175 Fifth Avenue, New York,
NY 10010, USA

Distributed in Canada exclusively by UBC Press
University of British Columbia, 2029 West Mall,
Vancouver, BC, Canada V6T 1Z2

British Library Cataloguing-in-Publication Data
A catalogue record for this book is available from the British Library

Library of Congress Cataloging-in-Publication Data applied for

ISBN 978 0 7190 6613 9 hardback

First published 2012

Typeset by Servis Filmsetting Ltd, Stockport, Cheshire
Printed in Great Britain
by TJ International Ltd, Padstow

To my beloved sister, Alison

Contents

Illustrations

Abbreviations

BB   Boys' Brigade
ISTD   Imperial Society of Teachers of Dancing
NABC   National Association of Boys' Clubs

Preface and acknowledgements

This book has been a long time in the making and I have inevitably accumulated many personal debts while writing it. So many friends, colleagues, students and relatives have lived in proximity to it over the last few years that I am bound to overlook some, for which I can only apologise. The main absence in this list of thanks is my father, Les Tebbutt, who died in 1997. The mementos of his teen years in the 1930s which he left behind are the reasons this book has come into being, because among the personal effects he left were diaries written in the mid 1930s, when he was sixteen and seventeen. I had known about them before he died, and we had even looked through them together when he was in his seventies, although the writing was so densely packed that neither of us could make out much of what he had written. He put them aside, reserved about my reading them while he was still alive, yet happy for me to have them after he had 'passed on'. I'm not quite sure what I expected to find. There are no dramatic revelations, although they were written at a time when he was very keen to get a girlfriend, which perhaps accounts for his reticence. Family memory stops in a particular way with the death of a parent, and this opportunity to catch hold of his early life through his diaries helped shape my own growing interest in inter-war leisure and working-class youth. By the time I came to write this book, it seemed fitting that his diaries should also have their own place in it, since without their initial inspiration it would not have been written.

The diaries comprise two Boys' Brigade pocket diaries a few centimetres across in which, by dint of very small writing, Les managed to cram more than sixty thousand words. When he was looking back on his life in his seventies, work dominated his recollections of this period, yet the diaries barely mention it, apart from occasional references to when the boss was off sick, much disliked occasions when he had to sweep up and asides about ups and downs with a much older workmate. They appear to have been the mark of a particular youthful moment, because he did not keep similar records after he joined the RAF as an engineer in the war, or in his adult life, and their witness to his teen years obviously meant a great deal to him.[1] There are few references to work, but plenty to friends, relatives and the scuffles and negotiations of family life. Most of all, they describe what he did in his leisure time. Over the course of their two years, the style of writing changes from a large, rather childish hand at the beginning of 1936 to something much smaller, more cramped and perhaps more secretive as his attempts to get a girlfriend intensified. Les's emotional life has to be inferred from these matter-of-fact entries, a reserve attributable to many factors. Boys of Les's generation were not used to talking about, let alone writing about feelings and he was probably also aware that the diaries might be read by his older brothers. This absence, however, started me on a quest to discover more about the emotional lives of his working-class contemporaries, to find out how they negotiated the social and cultural changes of the inter-war years, and whether they were quite so cocksure as working-class boys of his age and generation have often been painted. The book that has emerged explores some of the expectations and stereotypes which were attached to working-class boys and young men in the inter-war years, but more importantly sets these against their own feelings of uncertainty as they encountered new social behaviours and experiences, or worried about measuring up to what was expected of them. *Being boys* is a book that has become something much broader than the family sources which were the original inspiration, but I hope their inclusion in it has helped to shape a distinctive and useful contribution to debates and narratives of working-class boys' lives in the 1920s and 1930s.

There are some formal thanks for the research support I have received, without which the book's completion would have been impossible. I owe special thanks to the AHRC, whose funding for research leave allowed me, finally, to finish the book. I am also grateful to Clive Archer of the Manchester European Research Institute at Manchester Metropolitan University, and to the Research Committee of the Department of History and Economic History at Manchester Metropolitan University. A British Academy small grant allowed me to complete research for chapters 1 and 2, while discussions with fellow members of the AHRC Landscape and Environment Network coordinated from the University of Sussex in 2006–8 contributed to Chapter 7. I am also grateful to the book's anonymous readers and Emma Brennan, my ever-patient editor at Manchester University Press.

Staff in the following libraries and archives have been unfailingly helpful: Manchester Local Studies Library, Manchester; Manchester Metropolitan University Library; Northamptonshire Central Library and Northamptonshire County Record Office; the Working-Class Movement Library, Salford; the Cinema Culture in 1930s Britain (CCINTB) Archive and the Centre for North-West Regional Studies, both at the University of Lancaster; the British Library; Bolton Central Library; the North West Film Archive at Manchester Metropolitan University; the John Rylands University Library, Manchester; the Greater Manchester County Record

Office; the Burnett Archive of Working Class Autobiographies, Brunel University.

Many colleagues have been supportive of my work as it has gradually turned into a publishable manuscript. I owe an immense debt to Pat Ayers for encouraging me to finish it and finally put it to rest. Her insights have been invaluable at it would have been a poorer book without her. John Walton has been unfailingly generous with his time, always ready to read and offer fresh insights and suggestions, including putting me in touch with Gary Cross, who so kindly read and commented on work from someone he has never met. My colleague Craig Horner, who has shared the various ups and downs through which this book has gone with unfailing good grace and humour, has brought his own hawk-eyes to bear on the manuscript. Martin Hewitt and Tony Adams have both been understanding heads of department. I am also grateful to the following who have shared ideas and references or offered encouragement and suggestions: Lou Kushnick and Patricia Kushnick, friends in the Ahmad Iqbal Ullah Race Relations Resource Centre at Manchester University, Lou Taylor, Marion Hewitt, Alan Kidd, Terry Wyke, Philip Lloyd, Sheila Rowbotham, Sally Solokoff, Suzanne Schwarz, Jean Turnbull, Colin Pooley, Janet Beer, John McHugh, Rob Colls, Anna Davin, Alistair Mutch, Gilly Gostick, Louise Willmot, Stephen Bowd, Neville Kirk, Alan Kahane, Laura Ugolini, Sarah Norris, Catherine Danks, Hilda Kean, Elizabeth Roberts, Heather Norris Nicholson, Rebecca Andrew, Anne-Marie Hughes, Liz Bracken, Chris Wrigley, Maggie Walsh, Mike Rose, Martin Doughty, Michael Bush, Inga Phillipo, Paula Moorhouse, Colin Eaton, Claire Grover, Jane Morgan, Antonia Forte, Dermot Healy and Richard Haines.

My family is at the heart of this book. My mother, sadly, is no longer here, but I know she would have enjoyed seeing it come to completion. Donald Rae, more than anyone, knows what it has involved and has never flagged in his support. The book was written as our own son, Alex, passed out of his teens and I hope that parts of it will remind him of his granddad, who was always so proud of him. Alex and Pooja Sitpura have made this book worthwhile in many different ways, as have my sister Alison, brother-in-law Kevin and niece Sarah. This book is for all of you, with love.

Melanie Tebbutt

Note

1 He also kept a diary in 1938 for just over nine months, and more sporadically, diaries in 1939, 1940 and 1941, before he went into the RAF.

Introduction

In 1936, my father, Les Tebbutt, was in his mid teens, living and working in the Midlands market and boot-making town of Northampton. He was a quiet, unassuming, working-class boy, strongly attached to his family and neighbourhood, independent, occasionally solitary, yet also one of the lads. He could be seen as one of those 'average steady-goers' whom historians have often overlooked or dismissed in favour of the more dramatic accounts of youth and adolescence that have dominated popular understanding of young people's lives.[1] It was Les's diffidence and the rich range of place-based leisure activities chronicled in his diaries, written in 1936 and 1937, when he was 16 and 17, that helped to turn me to less familiar aspects of being a boy and growing to adulthood in the inter-war years and led ultimately to this much broader examination of working-class boys and leisure. The humdrum routines and relationships which the diaries revealed were a multi-textured counterpoint to the exceptional behaviour and delinquency which have often marked the literature on working-class young men, whose offending (and offensive) potential has, since industrialisation, and especially during periods of rising social anxiety, exerted a peculiar fascination for social commentators.[2] Such preoccupations have helped to reinforce a largely masculine image of adolescence which also informs historical interpretations, although the past two decades have seen more works addressing the experiences of girls and young women.[3] One might ask why working-class boys and young men should feature yet again in a book such as this, given that they have already received so much attention, but *Being Boys* offers a different approach, using the diaries as a starting-point for a more detailed examination of the emotional experiences and often tentative self-making which are much less well known. It aims to contribute a fresh view of such youthful masculinities and leisure in the inter-war years, mediating between discourses and representations on the one hand, and the lived experiences and everyday trials of becoming and being a man on the other. This is an ambitious undertaking which inevitably omits many significant themes; the meanings of different types of sport, for example, and the 'vocabularies of masculinity' to which they gave rise deserve extended attention which is not possible here.[4] The book's emphases nevertheless offer a necessary challenge to those dominant stereotypes of 'youth in trouble' or 'youth as trouble' which have done so much to obscure the diversity of youthful masculinities.[5] It is in the hope of bringing more nuanced perspectives to these debates that *Being Boys* has been written.

Being a boy and becoming a man

We start with Les's diaries (Figure 1), which were kept together with other ephemera, including bills, letters from relatives and friends mentioned in the diaries, photographs and Boys' Brigade (BB) memorabilia. These keepsakes from his teens and early twenties survived in part because they had been packed up and stored away when he joined the RAF during the Second World War, although their survival was also testimony to a broader story of class-based traditions and practices whose disappearance was encapsulated by his personal mementoes.[6]

Les was born in 1919, and spent most of his working life in small engineering firms, as a fitter-welder. A Northamptonian 'born and bred', he was deeply rooted in the town, which had many family and personal associations, and towards the end of his life was deeply unsettled by the thought that ill-health might force him to leave it. He died in 1997, unexpectedly, in a Northern hospital, the dislocation from place which his death encapsulated capturing many of the broader social and cultural changes which had unsettled him towards the end of his life. The family and social networks of the neighbourhood in which he had grown up were long gone, casualties of fragmenting trends which made working-class communities of the sort that had shaped him seem increasingly meaningless.[7] A sense of how these changes had affected him was powerfully apparent as we sifted through the souvenirs of a lifetime, reminders of his rootedness and testimony to how he became, by default, the family's unacknowledged archivist.[8] There were patterns in the apparent disarray of 'bits and pieces' we sorted through after his death, all of which represented something slightly different. Some things kept for memory, others for use, a compelling mix of pragmatism and sentiment, testimony to the hoarding imperatives of a more materially deprived culture. Paper bags, string, old nails, representing sheer discomfort with waste, reminders of the persisting novelty of consumer culture for a generation born and raised before the Second World War, a need to preserve and maintain as much as to consume.[9] Les had also put aside tokens of 'special' events – weddings, holidays, tangible records of happy experiences, relationships and feelings, much of which related to his youth and family life in the 1930s.[10] Photographs, 'perhaps the most ubiquitous and insistent focus of nineteenth- and twentieth century memory' were well represented in what had been set aside.[11] Brownie Box cameras became widely

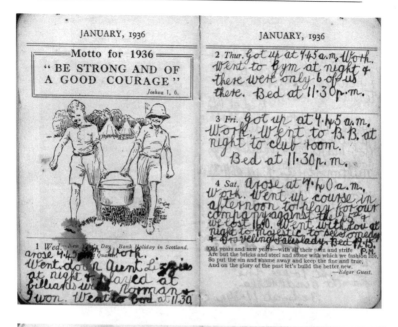

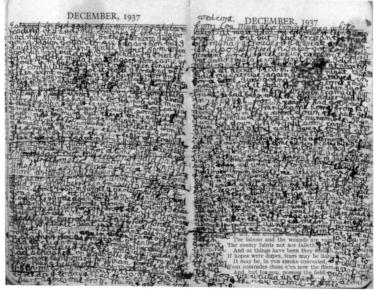

Figure 1 Diaries, 1936 and 1937

Figure 2 Practising with a new camera in the back yard. Les's younger sister, Gwen.

affordable in the 1920s and casual snapshots complemented the handful of more formal studio portraits of his family in the 1930s (Figure 2).

Besides photographs there were letters written to Les by his mother and brothers during the Second World War and Les's own diaries written in 1936 and 1937, when he was 16 and 17. The diaries revealed little about work experiences but much about friendship networks, leisure activities and the structure and strength of leisure routines, many of which helped to reinforce an attachment to the local and familiar. Entries, clearly bounded by the time of getting up and going to bed, appear to have been made daily, within a few days, or at the weekend.[12] Why did he write them? Perhaps there was a sense of time speeding up, of things being left behind. Possibly a desire to commemorate the changes of adolescence, lingering as he was at the edge of dependency and responsibility. Maybe the desire for private space in a crowded household where he shared an attic bedroom with his two older brothers.[13] Les had a strong sense of his working-class background and was strongly grounded in Northampton, where he grew up and spent most of his adult life. The diaries consequently provide a case-study of youthful leisure activities which is rather different from more familiar city-based ones.[14]

Northampton was smaller than the urban areas which have typically dominated interpretations of working-class youth and did not, for example, fall into Priestley's categories of nineteenth-century industrial England and the dole, the 'old England of the southern counties and the guide books' or the twentieth-century England of the Home Counties. The dust-jacket of the autobiography by Jeremy Seabrook, a much better-known Northampton boy, used a painting by Lowry called *Market Scene, Northern Town*, symptomatic of the Northern landscapes which dominated post-war representations of the 'traditional working-class community'.[15] It was, however, very misleading. Northampton was a Midlands market town and industrial centre, with a population of 92,341 in 1931,[16] lying 65 miles north-west of London. Its main industry was shoe making, with printing and engineering also important sectors of employment.[17] Trade unionism, strong in the boot and shoe trade, was weaker in the workshop conditions of many smaller local firms, where relations with the owner remained close.[18] About a quarter of Northampton's working population were registered unemployed in 1932, but conditions were not as bad as in the manufacturing centres of northern England and it was never classified as a depressed area. There was much run-down housing, but 'no real slums', and a reputation for environmental cleanliness was enhanced by many parks and green spaces.[19] There was little obvious residential segregation between town centre and suburbs, and a large lower-middle class comprised 22 per cent of the working population in 1931.[20] Northampton was 'small enough for everyone to keep track of a vast network of acquaintances, who had worked in the same factories, danced the veleta in the same *palais de danse*, and lay in the same cemetery on the outskirts'. Familiarity reflected in the leisure patterns of Les's youth.[21]

Les's family lived in a terraced house close to the town centre, and several aunts and uncles lived in Northampton or just outside it. Good bus routes criss-crossed the town to its outskirts, although most of the places Les visited were within relatively easy walking distance; many of the activities he describes took place within half a mile and a mile of his home.[22] His family had a fairly steady income in that all the children were earning and still at home. His father, a warehouseman in a local department store, earned about £2 a week, supplemented by his mother's charring jobs. Les was working as a tool-maker in a small boot and shoe tool manufacturer's near where he lived.[23] Both older brothers, Lou (21 when the diaries start) (Figures 3 and 4) and Frank (20), were working in boot and shoe factories, while their 14-year-old sister, Gwen, was in a box-making firm. Adults often forget the distance separating 'a fourteen year-old from a sixteen year old or younger sisters from elder brothers', and the age differences between his brothers and Les were important at this stage of their lives, when they had girlfriends, different interests and friendships, although this gap narrowed in their twenties, when they started to socialise together much more.[24] Gender clearly shaped the family's leisure patterns, with his sister spending more of her leisure time with her mother. They regularly went to the pictures and listened to radio plays together on Saturday evenings, although his father thought they were 'rubbish' and refused to listen. In 1937, while Les and his young fellow Boys Brigaders were at their annual camp on the east coast, Gwen, his mother and Aunt Lizzie went to the iconic northern seaside resort of Blackpool (Figure 5), having saved up through a holiday savings club, while Les's father stayed behind in Northampton.[25]

The age hierarchy was important in family life. Les's mother usually had his tea ready for him when he came in from work, but he had to wait behind his two elder brothers and sometimes his father for his turn to wash in the scullery before going out, when he often did a variety of errands for them (Figure 6). Les got on well with Lou, who took rather a fatherly interest in his youngest brother, occasionally treating him at the pictures and paying half of Les's entrance fee so they could go in the 'posh' shilling seats.[26] Relations with his middle brother, Frank, were often rather more fraught, however, as was illustrated by a squabble over the occupation of a particular chair when Les returned home from doing an errand for Lou:

> Got up at 7.20 a.m. Work. Stopped in at night until about 9.30 and then I went for a walk with Prince. I fetched some chips for some of Lou's Lyceum [*a cycling club*] who were up here for a meeting. When I got in Frank and I had a quarrel over the chair and he hit me in the eye and nearly gave me a black eye. Bed at 11.30 p.m. (Diary entry, Thursday, 10 September 1936)

The diaries reveal not only changing sibling relationships during adolescence but the shifting nature of friendships. The first half of 1936 involved much more hanging around with the 'gang' on the street where he lived or outside the local fish and chip shop, and taking part in many

Figure 3 Les's older brother Lou, 1937, aged 22

still childish activities such as 'heading' and 'stab', playing at the gas works, watching the circus arrive at the station or the construction of a new 'super-cinema'.[27] Much of this was pursued with a friend called Bill Darker, whom Les had known since infant school. They saw each other at least twice a week and sometimes five or six times, going to weekly performance at the, Hipp – a local variety theatre – and often to the cinema, although in his seventies, Bill insisted he had hardly ever gone to the pictures.[28] There were 76 diary references to Bill, until a dramatic

Figure 4 Les's brother Lou with his prize rabbits, which he kept in the family's back yard. Les often noted going on errands for his brother, to fetch 'green-stuff' to feed the rabbits. The family ate the rabbits during the war, when Lou was away in the army

falling-out in August 1936, a time when Les was still shifting between jobs:

> I had no work to do today so I stopped in bed till about 11.30 a.m. In the afternoon I stopped in and floored a bit more of the shed. [*Afterwards*] I went up to the chapel and helped Skipp [*the BB's Skipper*] and some of the boys to unload the trailer. [*Equipment that they had taken to camp.*] Afterwards I went for ride with Bob Maris. I fell out with Bill Darker tonight he knocked my bike and bust a spoke and cheeked mum. Bed at 11.30 p.m. (Tuesday, 11 August 1936)

The day after the quarrel, he wrote of going to the Hipp alone and seeing Bill but not speaking.

Figure 5 Les's mother, sister Gwen, relatives and neighbours outside their boarding house in Blackpool, 1937

> Got up at 7.15 a.m. Started work today. At night I went to the hipp by myself to see a musical comedy 'The Means Test' and I had to come through door lower down than the ordinary one because the decorators are in. I saw Bill Darker and Rodger Peach there but did not speak to them. Went to bed at 11.30 p.m. (Wednesday, 12 August 1936)

It must had been a big argument, because Les's recreational pattern changed abruptly over the months which followed, when he seemed to be 'mooching' about, on the edge of childish pursuits and more adult ones. He remained on the lookout for his friend in subsequent weeks, noting several occasions when he failed to see him, as in September, 'Bill Darker didn't come to the Hipp tonight because I didn't see him', and in November, 'I thought I would change my night for once and Bill Darker was there'. Thereafter, however, there is but one reference, to bumping into Bill with some other friends at the park after the annual carnival parade, and then losing them in the crowds. Diary references to friends reduced by a third in the three months after the quarrel and the autumn of 1936 also saw the loss of his regular Saturday evening cinema companion, his older brother Lou (who now had a new girlfriend), and the beginnings of the break-up of his BB year, as older boys started to drift away. The quarrel, insignificant enough in itself, suggests the flow of adolescent

Figure 6 Building a shed in the back garden. Diary entry, 1936: 'Stopped in afternoon and helped Frank put a new floor in the bicycle shed. Lou also started to build a shed for his rabbits.'

friendship, the street's function as a place where boys learned to deal with abuse from their peers and maintain personal and family honour, and not least, the powerful repercussions that insulting a friend's mother could have.[29] It also echoes remarks made a generation earlier by Charles Russell, pioneer of boys' clubs in Manchester, about the ease with which friendships between adolescent boys were often severed, inferring an emotional intensity more often associated with girls than with boys.

> You see, I arranged to meet him last Wednesday at half-past six, and he never turned up, and I know he *could* have done. Do you think I was going to stand that! Not me! So the next time I saw him I just walked past without noticing him, and we have not spoken since . . .
>
> Each is too proud to make it up, each often longs to. Both still attend regularly the same club, but, with the utmost coolness, pass each other and form part of a group with other boys; neither utters a word nor appears to recognise the presence of the friend, the 'chum' of yesterday and years before.[30]

Russell's account, like Les's diaries, does, however, place a misleading closure on such relationships, since despite this deep cooling in relations and Bill's disappearance from the diaries, they made up in their later teens and were still friends sixty years later.

Les's evening and weekend leisure activities were marked by distinctive weekly and seasonal patterns and structured by family expectations, meal times and a particular weekly order in which attendance at BB played a large part, particularly during the first eighteen months. BB membership gave a particular shape to his week. Attendance at a weekly drill parade and 10 o'clock Sunday morning Bible class was compulsory, and boys who missed three consecutive drills or Bible classes without good reason were liable to be expelled. The period between September 1935 and Easter Bank Holiday 1936 comprised a regular routine of drill practice with the BB on Monday evenings for a Drill Shield final in April, when a diary entry suggested his satisfaction: 'we won it easy'.[31] Tuesday evenings were at night school, where he studied English, Calculations and Science, eventually finishing the year's course with a session on 'morse signalling'.[32] On Wednesday evenings he usually went to the cinema or Hipp, a local variety theatre whose popularity suggests the persistence of older recreational forms among young people in smaller towns like Northampton.[33] Thursdays saw him back at the BB's gym, where much time was spent practising pyramids and club swinging for a company tableau and demonstration to families and friends. Les was keen, and took his club home to work on the routine (not easy in the cramped space) and won a gym prize, a book called *One Free Island*.[34] On Fridays he was in the Brigade's club room again, playing billiards, practising drill and gym, or taking part in table-tennis or skittle tournaments.

Saturday evenings were invariably spent at the cinema. Les, like many of his young contemporaries, regularly noted the names of the films he had seen, and their stars. The largest, most 'luxurious' cinema he frequented was the Savoy, an ABC 'super-cinema', often full, despite a seating capacity of nearly 2,000, and which he rarely frequented during the week. He failed to get in on his first visit soon after it had opened, and frequently had to wait so long to buy a seat that the programme had already started by the time he got in; he often ended up at one of the town's smaller, older (and cheaper) cinemas. One of these, about a mile from his home in an expanding suburban district at the edge of Northampton, eventually became one of his favourite Saturday evening destinations, reflecting friendships with local boys there whom he had got to know through the BB, and which provided useful opportunities to get to know girls away from the prying eyes of his own neighbourhood.

Les's diaries reveal a pattern common to the mid-adolescence of working-class boys, as they drew away from their families to spend more time with their peers. They also suggest, however, how home life continued to be an important element in this mix, as he chatted or quarrelled with the family and his brothers' girlfriends, or played games such as darts, bagatelle, crib or cards with them. There was cricket in the back yard with Lou or his Uncle Alf, who was living with them, table billiards with a cousin who lived near by, and Sunday visits to relatives or to one of his mother's old friends from her time in service (Figure 7).

There were also family outings on spring and summer bank holidays to Skegness, Yarmouth or Brighton, or to see the Blackpool illuminations.[35] When his mum was ill in bed, he practised his exercises in her room 'so she could see me while I did them'. On a snowy Saturday in December 1937, he and his brother Frank 'snowballed' some local girls and then went inside to sit around the fire singing carols with 'Mum, Gwen, Ivy and Uncle Alf'. They did the same at Christmas, and there were similar sing-songs around the piano at a friend's house.[36] On Boxing Day 1936 he put his uncle to bed, who had come home rather worse for wear.

> Got up about 1.30 p.m. Lay in bed reading. I then got ready and went with Dad up County Ground kick-off 2.30 p.m. to see the 'Cobblers' play 'Swindon' which we won by 4 goals to 0. After tea I fetched Dad a paper and then played at billiards first with Lou and then with dad. I lost all my games. Afterwards I went to the cinema-de-luxe by myself to see Eddie Cantor . . . Came out at about 10.20 p.m. so went for a

Figure 7 Visiting relatives when younger. Les is on the far right, next to his sister Gwen. His mother is at the back, third from the right

walk round the mayorhold district because they didn't come out of pubs till 11 p.m. Got home at about 11.15 p.m. Mum and Dad went down Aunt Lizzie's and I had to get uncle Alf to bed who was drunk. Bed at about 1.20 p.m.[37]

Les spent most of his leisure outside, but was not averse to staying in, especially in bad weather, when he played games of paper cricket, or more rarely paper football, recording many of the home-based activities which are often neglected in accounts of boys' teen years or hobby literature.[38] Sixteen- and seventeen-year-old boys were said to spend between 7 and 8 per cent of their weekday leisure time reading or listening to the radio, and such pastimes occupy a similar place in Les's diaries, especially during holiday lulls, quiet Sunday afternoons or when some other event like a company sports game had fallen through.[39] Indoor activities included not only reading but 'messing about doing nothing', playing patience, or doing jigsaw puzzles. He also listened to the radio, which was attracting large working-class audiences by the early 1930s.[40] Most British households had one by the middle of the decade, although poverty and unemployment made them virtually unknown in the poorest neighbourhoods.[41] The radio's arrival in Les's household was reflected in the souvenirs he saved, which included the first eight issues of D. C. Thomson's *Radio Review*, from November 1935, after the family bought a Portable H.M.V. Radio on hire purchase. Radios remained 'a symbol of relative affluence' until the late 1930s, and this one was only affordable because he and his siblings were all working.[42] (It was finally paid off in May 1937.[43])

In the 1920s, listening to the early 'cat's whisker' sets had been a solitary activity often dominated by boys in their teens.[44] Boys such as Joe Loftus's older brother, for example, had 'eagerly' followed the diagrams to make one, experimenting 'with all the latest developments', much like Thomas Waddicor's brother, who had followed an article in *Tit-Bits* in order to make a set which could tune into 2ZY, the British Broadcasting Company's station in Manchester.[45] The advent of valve receivers with loudspeakers, increasingly common from the early 1930s, transformed such solitary listening into a family event, although Les, like many other male contemporaries, continued to take charge of the novel technology, fixing it whenever it broke down. Letters Les received from his mother when he was away in the RAF during the war explained how they had decided to have the Relay because the wireless kept going wrong, 'and you are not here to see to it and none of us can't do it, so I think it is the best plan don't you it seems awful not to be able to have a bit of music'. (Relay, or subscription radio, was often a cheaper alternative to buying a radio in many working-class households.[46]) The popularity of dance music among both older and younger generations in the 1930s reflected the dominance of such shared listening habits, as well as boys' ability to take over radio tuning, once their fathers had gone out. As Les's mother lamented during the war, the house seemed terribly quiet without him: 'the wireless don't seem to get put on half so much now you are not here'. The family also acquired a gramophone in the 1930s, although Les only recorded listening to it twice, when the wireless was broken. Gramophones were similarly advertised as family-centred entertainment, with fathers usually hovering in command over it, although cosy domestic images of families listening together belied sibling and generational rivalries over who should manage the control knob – tensions which would become much more prominent in the teenage culture of the 1950s.[47]

Les's listening pattern, shared with many older listeners, included variety shows, light music, dance bands, concerts and sport, particularly national sporting commentaries.[48] He sometimes listened with the family, sometimes with a friend. He heard eleven sports broadcasts in 1936, including an England v. America ice hockey match, an England v. Scotland football match, the 'Arsenal v. Sheffield Cup Final' and the light heavyweight world boxing championship fight from Wembley between John Henry Lewis and Len Harvey. Too late for the pictures on

11 November 1936, he tuned in to an Armistice concert from the Albert Hall. Finally, at the year's end:

> Got up at 7.20 a.m. Work. At night I got ready and I got out my bike again and I went for a ride around the town . . . When I got back I put my bike up and then I sat up and listened in to the wireless as the new year came in. I heard a watch night service from London. Bed at about 12.15 a.m. Mam and the others went in to Mrs Galsworthy [*a neighbour*] to see it in.[49]

Once BB and his night class stopped after Easter, Les's leisure interests became less structured, with many more references to chatting or just watching the world go by: 'talking and messing around', hanging around the fish and chip or beer shop, going for bike rides, walking the dog around town or dropping in to see relatives. Cinema audiences were usually at their lowest in the summer months and, as in other working-class communities, it was common to range farther from home once the weather improved. With no expectation of having to be in by a set time, he and Bill Darker often stayed out as long as the light and weather permitted: 'You used to stay out for as long as you could. You'd either be sitting on steps, talking, that sort of thing.'[50] There were outdoors games, like cricket, in the back yard or parks, for the BB Cricket League. The parks also held many other attractions. Les and his friends often ended up there during the summer months, listening to the bands. Northampton was a 'pioneer' of Sunday band concerts, and the two park concerts held every Sunday drew large crowds of sometimes 10,000, which included many young people.[51] November's Bonfire night, when a park-based civic fireworks display was put on, also attracted many adolescents.[52] Another reason for the parks' popularity was their unsupervised opportunities to chat up girls; a typical summer Sunday in 1936 saw Les and a friend listening to the park band for much of the afternoon, going home for tea, and returning in the evening to speak 'to some girls most of night'.[53] Such moral support from friends was important because Les was rather a shy boy, who on one occasion noted how he had intended to get his photo taken but decided not to because he could not get anyone to go with him.[54] Another time, a friend invited him to a 'social', but on arriving 'I wouldn't go in it was only 3d. I was a bit shy. Elsie & two girls came & tried to persuade me to come but I wouldn't'.[55] This bashfulness was, perhaps, why he enjoyed the BB so much, because it helped him to build friendships with more confident boys who, as we shall see in Chapter 5, were important in mediating his transition to rather different leisure patterns as the more fixed routines of earlier adolescence started to fall away in 1937. Les's diaries not only suggest how his leisure behaviour gradually changed over their two years, but also reveal a pattern of adolescent leisure activities which were not discrete interests experienced in isolation from each other, but were more a mesh of informal and commercial, individual and collective, private and public, an uneven intermingling of 'old' and 'new', as the flow of family, friendships and local connections continued to lap over the growing autonomy of his leisure and social life.

Defining youth

Les was in his mid teens when he started these diaries, years generally seen as a key moment of working-class adolescence, the second most important after starting work at 14, although he and his contemporaries had little sense of a distinctive age-related identity. Wallace Brereton from Salford, for example, the same age as Les, recalled how 'the period known as adolescence had no special significance'. 'Judy Garland may well have sung "I'm just an in-between" but the expression had not caught on. One was either a schoolchild or a wage-earner, the division was as sharp as that.'[56] As Brereton suggests, the clearest and most significant transition for a working-class boy in the inter-war years was starting work full time, at 14.[57] It was synonymous with manliness, the acquisition of a weekly wage giving him 'a new valuation of himself, he is a wage-earner, he thinks himself a man'.[58]

> To be able to buy cigarettes and to spit. To cheek the foreman (at least once), to dream of the backchat you'll give the boss, to go to the pictures with your own money, to swagger in the monkey-parade with your own girl.[59]

Experiences of starting work were, of course, more varied, often more negative and subjectively uncertain than such bold statements suggest, for washing over such sharp transitions and continuing through the teens was the liminal status of adolescence, a borderland 'between sexual immaturity and sexual maturity', childhood and adulthood, in which starting work was only the most prominent of other social and cultural transitions whose significance varied considerably between individuals.[60]

Although boys such as Les, and Wallace Brereton, may have had little sense of being adolescent, a range of professionals were developing a strong sense of what adolescence should be, as had become increasingly apparent from the 1890s, when the term acquired a particular definition, identified with psychological changes which started with the biological transformations of puberty and ended with sexual maturity.[61] Psychologists, social scientists and educationalists increasingly regarded this phase as developmentally distinct and needing the stabilising guidance of 'experts', although its actual boundaries at either end of the age range were often rather vague.[62] The physical changes of puberty, for example, have many variations, historically and culturally, with the age of menarche progressively reducing over the course of the twentieth century in western societies, while the timing of puberty not only differs between individuals but also tends to occur later in boys than in girls.[63] The biology of puberty differs from the social and cultural transitions of adolescence, which in modern Britain have been constituted in particular ways by gender and class, ranging from entry into the worlds of work and marriage, to religious rituals and differing social, cultural and legal definitions. Contemporaries concerned with adolescence in the interwar period tended to focus on the ages between 12 or 13 and 18, although they too recognised the somewhat 'arbitrary' nature of such boundaries. The medical officer of Joseph Lucas Ltd. of Birmingham, for example, suggested that these years could 'for convenience' be regarded as covering from 14 to 21, although this 'limit' might be 'extended both ways', given that adolescence did not 'suddenly begin or end'.[64]

Being Boys is largely concerned with working-class young males from the time they left school at 14 until their early twenties, although the age range is occasionally pushed slightly back or forward, into the mid twenties. These young people are variously referred to as young men and 'boys', in much the same way that contemporaries often described young males who had left school but not yet entered their twenties.[65] Another broader term applied to those aged from 13 to 19 in this period, especially in the press, was the 'teens'.[66] The adjective 'teen-age' first appeared in the 1920s, in North America, although the noun 'teenager' was not commonly used in Britain until after the Second World War.[67] By contrast, youth, as a distinctive stage of life, tended to be defined more broadly, from the early teens to various points in the twenties. It also, more commonly than 'adolescent', referred not only to developmental boundaries but to a state of mind or set of attitudes which could be relevant to people much older than the age range conventionally applied to it; a fluid general meaning which strengthened over the course of the twentieth century, particularly after the First World War as the young were increasingly identified with progress, 'modernity', and hope for the future.[68]

Historians and the history of youth

The inter-war years were, until relatively recently, rather side-lined by historians of youth and adolescence. Pioneering studies in the 1970s, such as those by Joseph Kett on the United States and John Gillis on England and Germany, inspired by the student protests of the 1960s, and the new youth cultures and politics of the post-war period, were more preoccupied with mapping the origins and key moments of what seemed to be a striking new phenomenon than with dissecting its more low-key inter-war expressions. Kett focused on 1890–1920, when 'the era of the adolescent' came to prominence in Europe and America as adolescence was increasingly defined by narrow and specific psychological and moral parameters.[69] In Britain, Gillis and Frank Musgrove highlighted the significance of the reformed public schools and the rise of secondary education from the mid nineteenth century, which, in extending dependence on adults, had helped to focus attention on boys' behaviour and how to control it.[70] John Springhall's book *Coming of Age* also largely ignored the inter-war years, concentrating on the 'invention' of the adolescent between the 1880s and the 1900s and on post-war 'coming of age' with the advent of the teenager in the 1950s.[71] Stephen Humphries, in *Hooligans or Rebels?*, certainly examined inter-war youth, but largely from the point of view of misbehaviour, resistance and class conflict, while Harry Hendrick's *Images of Youth* focused on the political, economic and racial concerns which coalesced around working-class youth in the Edwardian period, highlighting worries about the 'boy labour problem' as labour-market changes coincided with the development of the new psychological discourses on adolescence already mentioned.[72] Hendrick, preoccupied with the notions of manliness which dominated contemporary accounts, largely ignored broader gender issues, paying little attention to related discourses on female employment. Michael Childs, who also took late-Victorian and Edwardian youth as his subject in *Labour's Apprentices*, again typically concentrated on young males and their work-place experiences.[73] Carol Dyhouse was unusual in the early 1980s in addressing the distinctive experiences of working-class and middle-class girls and young women, examining how they were socialised through schooling.[74]

Where these works on the history of youth centred on the periods before and after the two world wars, by the mid 1980s and 1990s, broader studies of inter-war poverty, gender and leisure were starting to highlight the diversity of working-class young people's daily lives and how these differed between young men and young women. Elizabeth Roberts's study of working-class women in Barrow, Preston and Lancaster located the leisure lives of young females in the context of their families, neighbourhoods and work.[75] Andrew Davies also highlighted the formative effects of both poverty and gender in the leisure experiences of working-class young people in Manchester and Salford, stressing the continuing importance of informal activities and family relationships despite the expansion of the commercialised leisure market.[76] Inter-war youth culture in England did not receive its first extended analysis, however, until David Fowler's *The First Teenagers*, which stressed the resilience of juvenile labour markets in some areas, where the increased purchasing power of 14- to 18-year olds encouraged greater cultural and social autonomy, helped by smaller families and better welfare provision.[77] Fowler's contribution in emphasising the distinctive aspects of inter-war youth culture was extended by Claire Langhamer, who explored the lives of working-class girls and young women as part of a broader study of women and leisure between the 1920s and the 1950s.[78] More recently, Selina Todd has demonstrated how the changing economic circumstances of young women in the inter-war years placed them at the forefront of many cultural changes, particularly in the 1930s, as radically changed employment patterns in retail and clerical work, the service sector and light manufacturing significantly influenced their behaviour and aspirations.[79] David M. Pomfret's work has also opened up a useful comparative urban-element dimension by contrasting age relations in Nottingham and Saint-Etienne, France between the 1890s and 1930s.[80]

Research such as Todd's suggests the readiness with which working-class young women adapted to inter-war consumer culture, unlike many of their male counterparts, whose cultural experiences retained, as Brad Beaven emphasises, considerable continuities with those of their fathers and an older generation of men.[81] These more recent studies have challenged earlier emphases on the homogeneity of youth culture by highlighting the significance of class, gender, poverty and locality in the formation of inter-war youth identities, themes which *Being Boys* aims to complement and extend.

Representing working-class young men

Late-Victorian and Edwardian assumptions about adolescence, class and masculinity are relevant to the inter-war years in that they help us to understand how post-war responses to working-class boys and young men were shaped and understood. The immense investigative attention devoted to working-class life from the 1880s revealed strongly independent neighbourhood cultures which challenged middle-class notions of privacy and respectability and played an important part in how the 'new' adolescence of the late nineteenth and early twentieth centuries was constructed. The rowdy street culture and precocity of 'working boys' greatly concerned many middle-class reformers, who believed that 'diseased and criminally' inclined working-class communities were a product of urban failure. Metaphors of age and ageing informed troubling juxtapositions of innocence and experience, as in the disturbingly precocious man-boy, symbol of eugenic fears and moral and social breakdown.[82] Both production and consumption informed worries about working-class boys and young men, whose disturbing economic independence, a result of the buoyant late-Victorian juvenile labour market, made them worryingly susceptible to the negative influences of popular culture.[83] By the 1890s, the youthful hooligan had become a symbol of urban failure, a sign of growing urban disorder and working-class antagonism.[84] The last three decades of the nineteenth century saw the norms of middle-class adolescence, 'conformity, self-denial and dependence', becoming the measure by which all youth were judged, as behaviour regarded as acceptable within working-class communities was redefined as not only immature but 'delinquent or psychopathic', ensuring that not only a minority but '*all* working-class youth' were perceived as 'problematic and at least potentially deviant'.[85] Such fears were exacerbated by the growth of socialism and the emergence of working-class political movements which not only fuelled fears of class conflict but reinforced middle-class concerns about the apparent vulnerability of working-class young men to political extremism and the need to turn them into loyal citizens.[86] These moral panics were precursors of a phenomenon which would inform public opinion about working-class young men throughout the twentieth century as the growing influence of the popular press regularly amplified their delinquency and anti-social activities.[87]

The late nineteenth and early twentieth centuries was also a period in which adolescence was being 'invented' by a range of middle-class reformers, moralists, youth workers and educationalists whose approaches received academic legitimacy in the works of the American psychologist G. Stanley Hall. Hall was key in transforming perceptions of adolescence into a distinctive and impressionable stage of disturbing emotional changes, offering a distinctly gendered interpretation of adolescent development, coinciding as it did with a period when expectations of masculine behaviour were becoming increasingly rigid.[88] In Britain, a 'rigorous' debate about 'the true attributes of manhood', which lasted until the Second World War, placed great emphasis upon the 'determined avoidance (especially by elite males) of all things "feminine"' and provided an important context for how working-class boys and young men were perceived in the inter-war years when, as we shall see, youth acquired a complex new significance as a touchstone for many social and cultural changes.[89] Not only did youth become a cipher for broader modernising trends in the 1920s and 1930s, but it also encapsulated many broader fears of national effeminacy as contemporaries focused on young women's economic and cultural visibility as consumers and workers in retail and clerical jobs, in service sector employment and in light manufacturing.[90] 'Modern', independent, active young women featured widely in the popular press of the inter-war period, where topics of interest to women were much more prominent than before the war, and the potential emasculation of working-class young men by these economic, social and cultural changes was a continuing concern amongst those who clung to pre-war models of masculinity.[91] The youth organiser S. F. Hatton observed in 1931, for example, how the contemporary 'young lad' had 'generally speaking, a "softer time" than he had say twenty years ago', and was consequently 'a little "softer" himself'.[92] Hatton used the 'word "softer" in the physical sense and not the mental', although many of his contemporaries also worried about such boys' emotional and psychological vulnerability to commercial entertainment such as the cinema.

Historians highlighting the often contradictory gender readjustments which took place after the First World War have been divided as to the extent to which 'traditional' notions of manliness were destabilised in this period, particularly in the 1920s, which were a time of considerable social and 'cultural confusion over gender and sexual identity'.[93] The literature on masculinities has tended to overlook the significance of generational and class differences, and the feminising implications of modernising trends have largely been assessed in relation to the 'emasculation' of middle- and upper middle-class young men. Less familiar in these debates is how pre-war notions of working-class young males were reconfigured in the 1920s as part of a more general redefinition of many pre-war values.[94] Working-class young men were, in fact, an important counterpoint to middle-class masculinity in contemporary 'critiques of modern youth', as was apparent in the boys' club movement, where some youth workers attempted to rework traditional notions of manliness through a nostalgic and conservative model based on pre-war public school ideals of 'traditional' manliness. The behaviour of working-class young men continued to cause disquiet in the 1920s, although the assumed hedonism of upper middle-class youth helped to undermine pre-war assumptions about deserving middle-class and undeserving working-class adolescence.[95] Indeed, the readiness of working-class young men to fight during the First World War, in challenging pre-war assumptions of their 'maladjustment', helped to inform some of the more progressive responses to male adolescents in the 1920s, which the book's first two chapters examine; sympathy towards even anti-social working-class boys persisted in the 1930s, when, despite recurring worries about delinquency, they were reinforced by concerns about the pernicious effects of youth unemployment.

The 'young' of the 1920s were seen as 'a more confident and restless race than their fathers', 'much more independent' and 'to a greater extent than previously ... their own arbiters' in deciding how they should 'spend their leisure and in distinguishing between right and wrong'.[96] As a result, many who worked with working-class young people found themselves having to revise their pre-war attitudes towards them. The Scouts, for example, recognised the advisability of a lighter hand with the post-war boy, who, unlike his pre-war equivalent, did not lend himself 'so easily to compulsion'.[97] The advent of mass democracy accentuated concerns about the responsibilities of citizenship, causing many who worked with the young to view their potential rather differently, women's acquisition of the vote reinforcing the desire to make young men more aware of their democratic responsibilities.[98] As the Russells' revised Lads' Clubs observed in 1932: 'times have changed. Boys have become more independent, more democratic in outlook, more "politically developed," and it is now advisable, if not necessary, to train them to undertake more genuine responsibility'.[99]

Boys, with fewer domestic 'duties' than girls and too much time on their hands, remained a particular worry in the inter-war years; one of the secrets of the Scout movement was said to be how it taught them 'to be busy'.[100] The expansion of commercialised opportunities for unsupervised leisure reinforced the dissonance between adult control and adolescent autonomy as the liminal years of 14 to 18 were seen 'more than any preceding period in his life' to make or mar the man that was to be.[101] Contemporary concerns about the difficulties of policing these years were reinforced by the waning influence of many traditional institutions.[102] Church and chapel going was declining, with attendance highest amongst Catholics and more usual in village than urban communities, and most of the large if dwindling number of children who attended Sunday schools stopping once they started work or not long afterwards.[103] Rowntree suggested that most young people regarded the social life of church and chapel as distinctly 'old-fashioned', preferring to flock 'to the entertainments now so lavishly provided in the form of cinemas, the music hall, and dance halls'.[104] The Catholic Truth Society lamented that its boys and girls were 'being sent out into a world infinitely more treacherous and subtle than anything with which their grandparents had to contend', although these perennial misgivings tended to underestimate the extent to which well-established moral codes and expectations continued to restrain behaviour.[105]

The dangerous years of 'apprentice' adulthood also assumed new significance as Hall's views became part of the official youth canon of educational, social and welfare services which increasingly sought to extend their control of working-class young people through institutional and advice frameworks designed to deal with the many 'anxieties' which now surrounded adolescence.[106] Developmental psychology saw adolescence as a time of emotional volatility and risk taking when the strengths of adult masculinity were appropriately tried and tested, but there was a fine line between freedom to experiment and the need for expert adult guidance through these troubled waters. Sea and river metaphors were often used to describe this time of life. The 'growing boy' of 14 was said to be 'like a ship at sea', veering in many contrary directions, 'influenced rather by feelings than by reason'.[107] The streets of big cities 'flowed' with the 'young stream of Life; a stream for good or evil' which could all too easily 'trickle away into lonely little pools of purposelessness'.[108] 'With the full sweep of unrelated passions, sex awakenings and adolescent mystification', the 14-year-old school leaver was 'plunged into the world of employment at the most critical years of his life'.[109] Concerns about these 'lost years' of early adolescence were reinforced by the lack of statistical information about school-leavers until they received insurance cards at 16.[110] Fourteen- to fifteen-year-olds were not entitled to benefit, did not register themselves for employment and did not enter the unemployment insurance scheme until 1934.[111] Once school stopped, so did 'all reliable information' about them, 'and after that the dark'.[112] From then until the age of 16 'no one' could 'make' a boy do anything. 'He is told to attend night school, but there is no Act in the country that can insist on his doing so. If, after a while, he leaves his job, no one in authority knows about it. There is no insurance, no unemployment benefit, no panel·doctor'.[113]

Work had been central to how working-class masculinities were shaped since the nineteenth century, and many publications in the 1930s were devoted to the problem of youth unemployment and dead-end jobs.[114] Unemployment defied the 'storm and stress' assumptions of adolescent psychology, undermining the 'adventurous spirit of youth', lowering ambitions and crushing the pride and self-esteem of having a regular wage.[115] Older working-class young men aged 18 to 25 caused particular disquiet because of their higher unemployment levels compared with boys in their early and mid teens. Twenty per cent of 18- to 25-year olds were out of work in the 1930s and youth unemployment averaged 10 per cent during the inter-war period, when it was particularly high in the distressed areas.[116] Lack of work and reliance on state benefits were seen as emasculating young men, sapping youthful 'vigour' at precisely the time when it should have been moving towards manhood. The potential militancy of the young was now less worrying than youth's political apathy. Unemployed young males were 'the citizens of tomorrow', yet 'years of idleness' sapped their energies and political interests, bringing 'acquiescence' and a 'feminised' passivity which made them 'emotionally more liable to become drifters'.[117] Many from 'better homes' were said to fall back upon their families in a prolonged adolescence which made them reluctant to take their own decisions, 'tied to the apron strings', 'afraid to move away'.[118]

Fears of national effeminacy, a recurring theme in the inter-war years, combined these fears of the emasculating effects of unemployment with unease about the 'feminising' effects of consumption.[119] In England, where distress was most pronounced in areas of mining and heavy manufacturing such as the North East and North West, social commentators such as Orwell and Priestley helped to fashion a gendered debate of two nations, a regional dichotomy of northern unemployed masculinity and prosperous 'feminised' service-based consumer industries in the Midlands and the South East.[120] The many opportunities for school-leavers and single young women in the expanding production-line industries of these regions transgressed ideas of the traditional male work ethic.[121] Undermining the wages and status of male industrial workers, they threatened 'working class masculinity' and encouraged fears that young men were being deskilled, losing the romanticised craft skills which most 'truly' expressed their manhood, and becoming more susceptible to feminised leisure interests and activities.[122]

Younger adolescents did, in fact, find it relatively easy to find short-term employment, since their cheap labour was very attractive to many employers and in high demand; even during the worst years of the Depression, many boys and girls had choice and autonomy in moving between jobs.[123] Gollan observed in 1937 how other than in the 'severely depressed areas', most young people who left school at 14 or 15 found it fairly easy to find employment, although many had very low aspirations.[124] Les had little difficulty finding work when he left school in 1933. His mother found him his first job, as a polisher with British Speedcraft, and his entry into the adult world was marked by what he carefully noted was his first diary, although its short jottings petered out after a few months. He changed jobs several times in this period, eventually finding work as a tool-maker, whose significance was recorded in his diary's end-notes, where he noted the date of starting what he later described as his first 'real' job, together with its first wage packet, which was twelve shillings. In London, where the development of light industry had accentuated the demand for boy labour, a 'lad' could 'throw up' his job 'at the slightest pretext and move, across the road perhaps, to another'.[125] Such young workers were continually moving around employers and it was 'not at all unusual' to find that a boy 'had half a dozen different jobs, all of the fetch and carry type, within a twelve month'.[126] It was only in their early twenties that the 'truly terrible' effects of unemployment pushed some 'hapless lads' to 'the edge of the abyss'.[127] (Issues of citizenship became more urgent at the age at 21, the legal age of adulthood.)

Concerns about dead-end employment underestimated, however, a significant movement between blind-alley and skilled jobs. Employers became liable for health and unemployment contributions when employees turned 16, and many sacked older teens in favour of younger and cheaper 14-year-olds.[128] Not only did many younger boys prefer higher wages to lower-waged jobs with training, but many transferred at 16 from dead-end jobs to apprenticeships, which were often difficult to secure before their mid teens, although such movement was only possible in regions where the demand for juvenile labour exceeded supply, as in Manchester.[129] It was far more difficult in areas of high unemployment and a large adult casual labour market of 'industrial nomads', such as Glasgow or Liverpool.[130]

Once in full-time employment, most working-class young people expected to contribute to household costs, frequently giving over their entire wage to their mothers, who handed back 'spends'. Family expectations of financial contributions from their children added particular strains. Roker and Crawford Scott, for example, described a 17-year-old, 'beaten at home and sent to look for work', who was so afraid to return that he 'walked to Southend and back in a vain search'.[131]

A *Daily Mirror* series aimed at finding whether youth was getting a 'square deal' suggested most young respondents kept a 'little more than a shilling or two a week for themselves. Just enough to go to the cinema on Saturday.'[132] There were considerable differences across the teen years, however, with the amount handed over tending to be greatest in the period after immediately starting work, between 14 and 15. Rowntree's 1930s survey of poverty in York found that only these youngest wage earners 'tipped' up their whole wage to their mothers, and that this amount declined as they entered their mid and late teens. On turning 16, it was common to hand over the equivalent of what they would have paid for board and lodgings if they had left home.[133] Other inter-war surveys revealed similar patterns of fixed household payments, although these often ignored differences between girls' and boys' contributions.[134] As many historians have pointed out, girls' family responsibilities were more onerous than those of their male peers, and where many boys eventually paid board for their lodgings and kept back the most of their pay, girls often carried on handing over their wages 'sometimes even up to their wedding day'.[135] Both girls and boys, nevertheless, usually retained a portion for their own 'personal use', and having their own earnings made many very resentful if parents tried to exert too much control over them.[136] These young wage earners were at the most affluent period of their life cycle, with a standard of living often higher than that of other family members, particularly from mid-teen adolescence, when many retained 50 per cent or even more of their earnings.[137]

By the inter-war years, the spending power of most working-class young people aged between 14 and 21 was greater than before the First World War, reflecting rising standards of living for the working class as a whole.[138] In York, 76.3 per cent of 15- to 25-year-olds were above the poverty line, compared with 60.9 per cent of 5- to 14-year-olds and 50.3 per cent of those aged between 1 and 4 years.[139] Increased purchasing power and a credit boom encouraged the rapid expansion of popular consumer culture in the 1930s. Contemporaries largely addressed the implications of these new leisure patterns for the future of young people as a male issue, mainly ignoring the needs and interests of young women until the Second World War.[140] Their greater concern was the susceptibility of 'impressionable' boys in their teens to the feminised 'values' and 'exhibitions of false emotion' encouraged by mass commercial culture, which threatened not only their adult masculinity but the future of mass democracy.

As this overview suggests, women and femininity were a defining presence in a period when the meanings and representation of masculinity were more mutable than before the First World War, although what implications these changes had for working-class boys and young men has rarely been considered in the existing literature.

Being boys

Negotiating areas of anxiety and vulnerability was difficult for boys as they grew to manhood, particularly given the clear boundaries which defined what was acceptably male, yet research has largely overlooked the uncertainties of self-esteem and confidence which contemporary expectations of masculinity often masked. *Being Boys* starts by examining how these expectations were redefined in the 1920s in the boys' club movement, which engaged in something of a rear-guard action to maintain ideals of pre-war manliness so comprehensively fractured in the war. Chapter 1 focuses on publications by several well-known youth workers who were also ex-combatants, to suggest the complex commemorative dimension to their work in boys' clubs, where ideas of citizenship, manhood and the rational use of leisure were distinctively fashioned not only by war memories and experiences but also by heightened post-war awareness of female 'otherness' as young women's social and economic visibility increased. The motivations of such writers offer an implicit commentary on older masculinities in the sense that their involvement with these boys suggests the deep emotional legacies of their war experiences and how these were 'contained' not only in writing but in social action of the sort described here.[141]

Chapter 2 further develops the themes of working-class boys and masculine expectations by examining the inter-war expansion of boys' clubs, which were significantly influenced by the determination to create a movement whose unifying mission was to turn 'ordinary' boys into 'masculine men'.[142] The boys' club movement was smaller than either the Scouts or BB, and its history has been relatively neglected, although boys' clubs were especially noted for their work in poor and disadvantaged areas and achieved national prominence in the inter-war years with the foundation, in 1925, of the National Association of Boys' Clubs (NABC).[143] Within the movement, understanding and empathy for their working-class members combined with a desire to reinvigorate masculine values. This shaped a mission whose resonance had broader national implications, given that this 'most truly working-class youth institution in terms of clientele' had an authority beyond its size, with many influential supporters contributing to educational and social welfare policy for adolescent males, locally and nationally.[144]

Chapter 3 moves away from middle-class representations of working-class boys and young men to compare and contrast anxieties and concerns which surrounded the clothed and unclothed male body. Male bodies had a powerful cultural resonance after the war, in rehabilitative initiatives and emerging consumer industries, preoccupations again often expressed in ways which spoke of insecurities about feminising influences upon masculinity and national 'character'.[145] By the 1930s, the physical power of the masses, from the Bolshevik Revolution to images of crowds at play, was informing a national iconography of controlled and disciplined youth, very visible in newsreel footage from the 1930s of the Scouts, BB, boys' clubs, and totalitarian youth movements in Germany and Italy.[146] At the same time, at an individual level, young men's physical sense of self was coming under the growing influence of visual forms and commercial leisure trends, bringing working-class young men into contact with new models of personal behaviour and social interaction which made many sensitive to style, fashion and appearance. This chapter examines how working-class young men mediated the feminised connotations of consumption in negotiating these new physical images and ways of performing masculinity. With the worst of the Depression receding, the 1930s became a pioneering decade for marketing initiatives aimed at young people, particularly young women, who were important consumers of leisure and very visible in the popular press, which was increasingly alert to their marketing potential.[147] The emergence of these sexualised images and new models of personal behaviour and social interaction have more usually been analysed in relation to young women's experiences. Their implications were, however, also apparent in young men's bodies and the male physique, since they helped to accentuate self-consciousness, and interest in physical self-improvement and in clothing and appearance, although this was carefully negotiated, given the weight of traditional masculine expectations.

Chapters 4 and 5 pursue the idea of this awakening of the senses expressed in more relaxed social and emotional codes by turning to the 'male world of feeling'. Historians have addressed the sexual behaviour of both heterosexual and homosexual youth in the inter-war years, but the emotional uncertainties of heterosexual young men have received little attention.[148] These chapters contest familiar representations of working-class young men as a largely insensitive subject by exploring how they negotiated the new models of behaviour, intimacy and social expectations which surrounded personal relationships. As Chapter 4 suggests, much social behaviour was more relaxed than before the First World War and the informalising trends of popular culture exposed generational fissures which were particularly apparent in concerns about the cinema's imaginative and sensual impact. Courtship and 'dating' were becoming 'private' acts of consumption, taking place away from family and neighbourhood venues, in public social spaces such as the cinema and dance hall. This distancing stimulated many adult concerns about their inability to supervise adequately young people's leisure, and produced much often ill-informed commentary about how young people's sexual lives were changing. What received less attention were shifting imaginative landscapes and the cinema's catalysing role for emotional tensions between individual and public expressions of masculinity, as the chapter suggests in its exploration of the responses which particular films evoked in some young men.

The social and cultural climate of the inter-war years inflected anxieties about relationships and changing social mores in new ways, and Chapter 5 continues this examination of how these changes affected the emotional landscapes of young men's lives by scrutinising how the 'male world' of youthful feeling was expressed through the advice columns of popular newspapers and magazines, which expanded significantly in the 1930s. The chapter samples letters from boys and young men to illustrate a complex interplay of discourse and mediated experience to help illustrate their responses to the period's informalising expectations and changing social relations.

In Chapters 6 and 7 we turn from representations, the body and feelings to questions of male movement, everyday social and recreational space and 'geographies of performance'.[149] Chapter 6 asks how youthful masculinities were performed, constructed and contested in sexualised leisure locales such as the dance hall – like letters to advice columnists, an expressive outlet more usually perceived in relation to young women. It traces the implications of how social dancing changed over the inter-war years, from that of the 1920s, which subverted traditional notions of male physicality, to the shaping effects of the sexualising modernity increasingly apparent in the 1930s. The exhibitions and inhibitions of these dance hall cultures reinforced and contested traditional gender expectations and assumptions.[150] Social dancing presented a disturbing 'otherness' of gender, race and class which challenged traditional notions of masculinity and Englishness, as was apparent in the dance profession's attempts to restrain the easy-going 'oppositional' spontaneity of dance styles in the 1920s with dignity and manly restraint.[151] Concerns about dancing reflected the same worries about eroding traditional values so apparent in the boys' club movement, and both moral and commercial interests sought to regulate it for their own reasons, although young men's relationship with social dancing was more varied than is often assumed.

Chapter 7 enters a very different performance space, that of the street and the part that the 'largely taken for granted world' of walking played in the formation of adolescent masculinity.[152] Working-class boys and young men enjoyed greater spatial freedoms than their female counterparts, but their occupation of street space was often depicted in very passive terms, as in cartoons from the late nineteenth century of scowling, slouching individuals, arms akimbo or hands in pockets, legs apart and a cigarette invariably drooping from the mouth.[153] Assumptions of street 'loitering' ignored the dynamic nature of young people's relationships with neighbourhoods and how 'hanging around', gossiping and watching the world go by helped to construct male social identity in relation both to their peers and adult society. The role of place in mediating boys' entry into the world of adults is usually seen in terms of neighbourhood territory and gangs. This chapter explores how walking and place-based leisure routines helped to fashion the streets and districts in which working-class boys grew up into a 'knowable' landscape, a *practiced* place' whose meanings during adolescence deepened and extended into distinctive topographical identities, reinforced by habit, familiarity and the casual rhythms of daily life.[154] Following studies of women's leisure which have been particularly adept at recognising the significance of the casual and familiar in everyday life, the chapter suggests how such everyday activities as walking and cycling help to form distinctive place-bound identities among working-class young men as repetitive, habitualised rhythms played their own part in shaping adolescent identity.[155]

Les's diaries weave through these chapters. Where the early ones explore how the masculinity of working-class young males was rhetorically constructed after the First World War, in relation to the boys' club movement, the diaries illustrate how, within the reassuring boundaries of the BB, a quiet boy like Les could become less reserved and shape a self-confident identity for himself more in keeping with his own needs than with those of the youth organisation to which he belonged. The diaries suggest the frequently pragmatic motivations of boys like Les who joined such organisations, and membership was used for their own ends and interests, subverting expected codes of discipline just as they actively engaged with commercial leisure.[156] The activities which the diaries describe and complement other, broader themes. Les was keen on keep fit and fitness and also made an effort at being fashionable, although this was largely at the behest of his older brother Frank, who was the real conduit for fashionable trends into the family. The dance hall is a notable omission from them. His brothers went dancing, as did his younger sister, who was a particular enthusiast, but Les did not really find his dancing feet until he joined the RAF during the war and experienced the leisure delights of Blackpool during training. Despite the growth of such commercial leisure alternatives in the 1930s, the diaries illustrate the continuing importance of informal leisure activities and illuminate interrelationships often bypassed in histories of leisure, an uneven blend of tradition and modernity as home, locality, family, friendship and leisure activities flowed into and across each other. They are testimony to the importance of seeing youth 'in individual terms', one version of many different adolescent realities which exemplifies both the growing social autonomy of adolescence and the 'private world and quiet times' of home and family relationships.[157] Les's leisure story, slipping in and out of the book's broader narrative, highlights the diversity and contingency of adolescent transition and the need to address individual as well as collective identities if we are to understand the personal sensitivities which also shaped working-class boys during this period.

Notes

1 Jon Savage, for example, takes a 'romantic' view which privileges the 'extraordinary' over the ordinary: J. Savage, *Teenage: The Creation of Youth, 1875–1945* (London: Chatto and Windus, 2007), pp. xvii–xviii.

2 There is an extensive historical literature on juvenile delinquency. See, for example: M. May, 'Innocence and experience: the evolution of the concept of juvenile delinquency in the mid nineteenth century', *Victorian Studies*, 17:1 (1973), 2–29; S. Magarey, 'The invention of juvenile delinquency in early nineteenth-century England', *Labour History* (Sydney), 34 (1978), 11–25; V. Bailey, *Delinquency and Citizenship: Reclaiming the Young Offender, 1914–1948* (Oxford: Clarendon, 1987); P. King and J. Noel, 'The origins of the problem of juvenile delinquency: the growth of juvenile prosecutions in London in the late eighteenth and early nineteenth centuries', *Criminal Justice History*, 14 (1993), 17–41; P. King, 'The rise of juvenile delinquency in England, 1780–1840: changing patterns of perception and prosecution', *Past and Present*, 160:1 (1998), 116–66; H. Shore, 'Cross coves, buzzers and general sorts of prigs: juvenile crime and the criminal "underworld" in the early nineteenth century', *British Journal of Criminology*, 39:1 (1999), 10–24; H. Shore, 'The trouble with boys: gender and the "invention" of the juvenile offender in the early nineteenth century', in M. Arnot and C. Usborne (eds), *Gender and Crime in Modern Europe* (London: UCL Press, 1999), pp. 75–92; H. Shore, *Artful Dodgers: Youth and Crime in Early Nineteenth-Century London* (Woodbridge: Boydell and Brewer, 1999); P. Cox and H. Shore, *Becoming Delinquent: British and European Youth, 1650–1930* (Aldershot: Ashgate, 2002). See also S. Humphries, *Hooligans or Rebels? An Oral History of Working-Class Childhood and Youth, 1889–1939* (Oxford: Basil Blackwell, 1981). Humphries's interpretation of youth indiscipline and delinquency, as a form of class conflict with the middle-class authorities which tried to control young people's behaviour, was influenced by contemporary sociological approaches to youth culture such as Stan Cohen's *Folk Devils and Moral Panics: The Creation of the Mods and Rockers* (London: MacGibbon and Kee, 1972); S. Hall and T. Jefferson (eds), *Resistance through Rituals: Youth Subcultures in Post-war Britain* (London: Hutchinson, 1976); D. Hebdige, *Subculture:*

The Meaning of Style (London: Methuen, 1979). Geoffrey Pearson also examined the history of negative stereotypes surrounding working-class young men in *Hooligan: A History of Respectable Fears* (London: Macmillan, 1983). See also G. Pearson, 'Perpetual novelty: a history of generational conflicts in Britain', in D. Dowe (ed.), *Jugendprotest und Generationenkonflict in Europa im 20. Jahrhundert: Deutschland, England, Frankreich und Italien im Vergleich* (Bonn: Verlag Neue Gesellschaft, 1986), pp. 165–77; P. Cohen, 'Historical perspectives on the youth question especially in Britain', in Dowe (ed.), *Jugendprotest*, pp. 241–59. For gangs, see A. Davies, 'Youth gangs, masculinity and violence in late Victorian Manchester and Salford', *Journal of Social History*, 32:2 (1998), 364–5; A. Davies, 'Street gangs, crime and policing in Glasgow in the 1930s: the case of the Beehive Boys', *Social History*, 23 (1998), 251–68; A. Davies, ' "These viragoes are no less cruel than the lads": young women, gangs and violence in late Victorian Manchester and Salford', *British Journal of Criminology*, 39:1, Special Issue (1999), 72–89. See also J. Springhall, *Youth, Popular Culture and Moral Panics: Penny Gaffs to Gangsta Rap, 1830–1966* (London: Macmillan Press, 1998); A. Davies, *The Gangs of Manchester: The Story of the Scuttlers, Britain's First Youth Cult* (Preston: Milo Books, 2008). For changing perceptions and experiences of crime in working-class communities, see R. Hood and K. Joyce, 'Three generations: oral testimonies on crime and social change in London's East End', *British Journal of Criminology*, 39:1, Special Issue (1999), 136–60; J. Davis, *Youth and the Condition of Britain: Images of Adolescent Conflict* (London: Athlone Press, 1990), p. 19; E. J. Yeo, ' "The boy is the father of the man": moral panic over working-class youth, 1850 to the present', *Labour History Review*, 69:2 (2004), 185–99; M. Mitterauer, *A History of Youth* (Oxford: Blackwell, 1986, 1992), p. 19.

3 E. Roberts, *A Woman's Place: An Oral History of Working-Class Women, 1890–1940* (Oxford: Basil Blackwell, 1984); A. Davies, *Leisure, Gender and Poverty* (Buckingham and Philadelphia: Open University Press, 1992); C. Langhamer, *Women's Leisure in England, 1920–1960* (Manchester: Manchester University Press, 2000); C. M. Parratt, *More than Mere Amusement: Working-Class Women's Leisure in England, 1750–1914* (New York: St. Martin's Press, 2001); S. Todd, *Young Women, Work and Family in England, 1918–1950* (Oxford: Oxford University Press, 2005).

4 Collins suggests few historians make more than a passing reference to sport when dealing with issues of masculinity and the body, or class and community: T. Collins, 'Review article: Work, rest and play: recent trends in the history of sport and leisure', *Journal of Contemporary History*, 42:2 (2007), 398; F. Mort, 'Boy's own? Masculinity, style and popular culture', in R. Chapman and J. Rutherford (eds), *Male Order: Unwrapping Masculinity* (London: Lawrence and Wishart, 1988, 1996), p. 197. Scholars such as Jeffery Hall, Richard Holt, Tony Mason, Martin Polley, Dave Russell and John Walton have pioneered work in this field, and much fine work on sport has been produced by De Montfort University's International Centre for Sports History and Culture.

5 G. Levi and J.-C. Schmitt (eds), *A History of Young People*, vol. 1: *Ancient and Medieval Rites of Passage*, trans. C. Naish (Cambridge, MA: Harvard University Press, 1997), p. 5.

6 L. Passerini, *Fascism in Popular Memory: The Cultural Experience of the Turin Working Class* (Cambridge: Cambridge University Press, 1987), p. 18.

7 R. Colls, 'When we lived in communities: working class culture and its critics', in R. Colls and R. Rodger (eds), *Cities of Ideas, Governance and Citizenship in Urban Britain, 1800–2000* (Aldershot: Ashgate, 2005), p. 24.

8 For discussion of the complex relationship between death, bereavement and the 'mnemonic potency' of 'materialised memories', see E. Hallam and J. Hockey, *Death, Memory and Material Culture* (Oxford: Berg 2001).

9 My thanks to Hilda Kean for generously sharing her unpublished paper 'London Stories'.

10 D. Lupton, *The Emotional Self* (London, 1989), pp. 144, 148, cited in Hallam and Hockey, *Death, Memory and Material Culture*, pp. 42–3; see, for example, H. Kean, 'East End stories: the chairs and the photographs', *International Journal of Heritage Studies*, 6:2 (2000), p. 126. Also R. Samuel, *Theatres of Memory: Past and Present in Contemporary Culture*, Vol. 1 (London, 1996).

11 E. Edwards, 'Photographs as object of memory', in M. Kwint, C. Breward and J. Aynsley (eds), *Material Memories: Design and Evocation* (Oxford: Berg, 1999), p. 221.

12 Humphries, *Hooligans or Rebels*; J. White, *The Worst Street in North London: Campbell Bunk, Islington, between the Wars* (London: Routledge and Kegan Paul, 1986); A. Davies, *Leisure, Gender and Poverty. Working Class Cultures in Salford and Manchester, 1900–1939* (Buckingham and Philadelphia: Open University Press, 1992); D. Fowler, *The First Teenagers. The Lifestyle of Young Wage Earners in Inter-war Britain* (London: The Woburn Press, 1995); B. Beaven *Leisure, Citizenship and Working-class Men in Britain* (Manchester: Manchester University Press, 2005). Most of these were based on Lancashire and London. Some of Humprhries's interviews were from Bristol. Beaven has developed a useful Midlands case-study of relatively affluent workers in inter-war Coventry.

13 For the complex relationship between death, bereavement and the 'mnemonic potency' of 'materialised memories', see Hallam and Hockey, *Death, Memory and Material Culture*.

14 Beaven highlights Coventry in *Leisure, Citizenship and Working-Class Men in Britain*. David Pomfret has contrasted Nottingham and Saint-Etienne: D. M. Pomfret, *Young People and the European City: Age Relations in Nottingham and Saint-Etienne, 1890–1949* (Aldershot: Ashgate, 2004).

15 J. Seabrook, *Mother and Son* (London: Victor Gollancz, 1979). Seabrook was born in 1939. C. Waters, 'Representations of everyday life: L. S. Lowry and the landscape of memory in post-war Britain', *Representations*, 65 Special Issue: New Perspectives in British Studies (1999), pp. 122–3. The town had fourteen parks and recreation grounds, comprising over 409 acres: A. L. Bowley and M. Hogg, *Has Poverty Diminished?* (London: P. S. King & Son Ltd., 1925), pp. 52, 54; *Northampton Official Handbook*, 1936.

16 *Census Report, 1931: classification of occupations* (London: HMSO, 1934).

17 R. Greenall, *A History of Northamptonshire and the Soke of Peterborough* (Chichester: Phillimore, 1979).

18 *Ibid.*, p. 157.

19 H. Barty-King, *Expanding Northampton* (London: Secker and Warburg, 1985), pp. 15–16; C. Brown, *Northampton 1935–1985: Shoe Town, New Town* (Chichester:

Phillimore, 1990), p. 144, citing NCBC Public Health Department Report re Working-Class Housing to the Ministry of Health (1930).

20 *Census of England and Wales, Report*, 1931.

21 J. Seabrook, 'The New Statesman essay – goodbye to provincial life', *New Statesman*, 129:18 (December 2000).

22 Bowley and Hogg, *Has Poverty Diminished?* p. 53.

23 He later became a fitter-welder.

24 J. Springhall, *Coming of Age: Adolescence in Britain, 1860–1960* (Dublin: Gill and Macmillan, 1986), p. 57.

25 Blackpool was Britain's most popular resort in the 1930s, with seven million visitors annually, and a range of regional accents was increasingly heard on its promenade by the late 1930s, including those of 'London, Northampton, Glasgow, and even Plymouth': G. Cross (ed.), *Worktowners at Blackpool: Mass-Observation and Popular Leisure in the 1930s* (London: Routledge, 1990), p. 231; J. K. Walton, *The British Seaside: Holidays and Resorts in the Twentieth Century* (Manchester: Manchester University Press, 2000), pp. 57–8, 61; J. K. Walton, *Blackpool* (Edinburgh: Edinburgh University Press, 1998), p. 102. S. Barton, *Working-Class Organisations and Popular Tourism, 1840–1970* (Manchester: Manchester University Press, 2005), p. 103. See also, J. K. Walton, *The Blackpool Landlady* (Manchester: Manchester University Press, 1979).

26 Unpublished diary of Les Tebbutt, hereafter 'Diary' (26 September 1936).

27 For the social significance of the fish and chip shop see J. K. Walton, *Fish and Chips and the British Working-Class, 1870–1940* (Leicester: Leicester University Press, 1994).

28 Interview with Bill Darker, Northampton, c. 2001.

29 A. Curtin and D. Linehan, 'Where the boys are: teenagers, masculinity and a sense of place', *Irish Geography*, 35:1 (2002), p. 71.

30 C. E. B. Russell and L. M. Russell, *Lads' Clubs: Their History, Organisation and Management* (London: A. & C. Black Ltd., 1932), p. 7.

31 'Diary', 22 April 1936.

32 Some 365,937 young people aged between 14 and 18 were attending evening classes, in 1936–37: 211,985 boys and 153,952 girls. Attendance tended to fall away as they got older; only 38 per cent were over 16. A. E. Morgan, *The Needs of Youth. A Report Made to King George's Jubilee Trust Fund* (Oxford: Oxford University Press, 1939), p. 13. Almost 29 per cent of boys aged between 14 and 16 attended some kind of evening school on Merseyside: D. C. Jones, *The Social Survey of Merseyside*, 3 vols (Liverpool: Liverpool University Press, 1934), vol. III, p. 218.

33 James and Moore found that young men and women wage earners in Hulme, Manchester spent a third of their weekday leisure at the cinema. H. E. O. James and F. T. Moore, 'Adolescent leisure in a working class district: Part II', *Occupational Psychology*, 18:1 (1944), 24–34. James and Moore were psychologists from Manchester University. Their investigation took place in the summer of 1939 and focused on the leisure pursuits of young people aged between 12 and 21. The survey was based on over 500 working-class adolescents who kept diaries of their leisure activities for one week during June/July 1939. The raw data was lost during the Second World War, but the study's conclusions survive in contemporary articles.

34 'Diary' (9 April 1936).

35 J. Stevenson, *British Society, 1914–45* (Harmondsworth: Penguin, 1984, 1990), p. 393.

Butlin's opened at Skegness in 1937 as the country's first purpose-built holiday camp.

36 'Diary' (4 December 1937).

37 *Ibid.* (26 December 1936). The Mayorhold was a poor working-class district

38 *The Social Survey of Merseyside* suggested that reading was popular among adolescents of both sexes. For boys, this fell only slightly after leaving school, from 53 per cent to 51.9 per cent. Comparable figures for girls were 57 per cent and 44.7 per cent, again reflecting expectations of helping in the home after work while in their early to mid teens. Jones, *Social Survey of Merseyside*, Vol. III, pp. 219–20.

39 J. Bourke, *Working-Class Cultures in Britain, 1890–1960: Gender, Class and Ethnicity* (London: Routledge, 1994), p. 81.

40 J. Baxendale, '". . . into another kind of life in which anything might happen . . .": Popular music and late modernity, 1910–1930', *Popular Music*, 14:2 (1995), 137–54. The number of households with radio licences rose from 30 per cent in 1930 to 71 per cent by 1939. There were significant regional variations in radio ownership and listening patterns. Radio ownership was 'densest' in London, the South East and Midlands and lower in the North: R. McKibbin, *Classes and Cultures: England, 1918–51* (Oxford: Oxford University Press, 1998), p. 457.

41 Baxendale, '". . . into another kind of life"', p. 142; Davies, *Leisure, Gender and Poverty*, p. 40.

42 M. Pegg, *Broadcasting and Society, 1918–1939* (London: Croom Helm, 1983), pp. 48–9. In 1940, out of 9 million licence holders, 4.2 million had incomes of between £2 10s and £4 a week. Two million licences were held by those earning less than £2 10s. On Merseyside in the early 1930s, scarcely more than a quarter of households had radio sets: Jones, *The Social Survey of Merseyside*, Vol. III, pp. 274–5.

43 Payment cards, Wm. H. Russell and Son, Leicester's Music Centre, 99 Granby Street, Leicester; Pegg, *Broadcasting and Society*, p. 47.

44 S. Moores, '"The box on the dresser": memories of early radio and everyday life', *Media, Culture, Society*, 10:23 (1988), p. 27.

45 J. Loftus, *Lee Side*, Burnett Archive of Working-Class Autobiographies, University of Brunel (hereafter, Burnett Archive), p. 34; T. Waddicor, *Memories of Hightown and Beyond*, Burnett Archive, pp. 13, 19.

46 Family letters (9 December 1942, 28 January 1943). A weekly rental charge linked subscribers to a central exchange by cable. They had a narrower range of programmes, which depended on what the exchange decided to broadcast, but reception was often better than on interference-prone 'normal' radio sets: Pegg, *Broadcasting and Society*, p. 58. A. Crisell, *Understanding Radio* (London: Methuen, 1986), p. 21.

47 W. Boddy, 'Archaeologies of electronic vision and the gendered spectator', *Screen*, 35:2 (1994). p. 111; J. J. Nott, *Music for the People: Popular Music and Dance in Interwar Britain* (Oxford: Oxford University Press, 2002), p. 38.

48 Stevenson, *British Society*, p. 409; R. Holt, *Sport and the British: A Modern History* (Oxford: Clarendon Press, 1989), pp. 311–14.

49 'Diary' (31 December 1936). Sheffield was Sheffield United.

50 Interview with Bill Darker, Northampton, 2001; C. Burt, *The Young Delinquent* (London: University of London Press, 1925, 1931), p. 176.

51 Bowley and Hogg, *Has Poverty Diminished?* p. 54.

52 *Life in Old Northampton* (Northampton: Northamptonshire Libraries, 1976), p. 91.

53 'Diary' (14 June 1936).

54 *Ibid.* (4 December 1937).

55 *Ibid.* (9 December 1937).

56 W. Brereton, *Salford Boy. The Illustrated Memories of Wallace Brereton* (Manchester: Neil Richardson, 1985; first published by Salford Local History Society, 1977), p. 45. The song was released in 1939 and ended with the verse, 'I hope and pray for the day when I'll be sweet sixteen, Then I won't have to be an in between'. International Lyrics Playground: http://lyricsplayground.com/index.html.

57 79.1 per cent of boys and 80.9 per cent of girls left school at, 14: *Education in 1935*, Cmnd. 5290 (HMSO, 1936), cited in J. Gollan, *Youth in British Industry: A Survey of Labour Conditions To-day* (London: Gollancz, 1937), p. 210. Many were still 'children barely on the threshold of adolescence', in height and 'physical maturity' resembling 'the twelve- or thirteen-year-olds of the sixties': N. Branson and M. Heinemann, *Britain in the Nineteen Thirties* (London: Weidenfeld and Nicolson, 1971), p. 198. Girls' entry into employment had fewer connotations of the adult world. They remained subject to greater parental control and their major rite of passage was marriage: S. Todd, 'Young women, work and leisure in inter-war England', *Historical Journal*, 49:3 (2005), p. 798.

58 S. F. Hatton, *London's Bad Boys* (London: Chapman & Hall Ltd., 1931), p. 31; A. E. Morgan, *Young Citizen* (Harmondsworth: Penguin, 1943), p. 19.

59 *Ibid.*

60 For how starting work altered the dynamics of family relationships, see B. Naughton, *On the Pig's Back* (Oxford: Oxford University Press, 1988), p. 122; Levi and Schmitt, *A History of Young People*, vol. 1, p. 2.

61 Adolescence, from the Latin verb *adolescere*, 'to grow up'. Contemporary dictionary definitions highlight the gendered character of a process 'ordinarily considered as extending from 14 to 25 in males, and from 12 to 21 in females': http://dictionary.oed.com (accessed September 2006).

62 Mitterauer, *History of Youth*, pp. 6–7.

63 B. A. Hanawalt, 'Historical descriptions and prescriptions for adolescence', *Journal of Family History*, 17:4 (1992), p. 343; J. Springhall, *Coming of Age*, p. 234; H. Hendrick, *Images of Youth: Age, Class and the Male Youth Problem, 1880–1920* (Oxford: Clarendon Press, 1990), p. 2. For more detailed discussion of these rates in relation to European history, see Mitterauer, *History of Youth*, pp. 2–6.

64 T. M. Ling, 'The abnormal and temperamental worker', *British Medical Journal*, 21 November 1936, p. 1021.

65 D. M. Pomfret, *Young People and the European City: Age Relations in Nottingham and Saint-Etienne, 1890–1940* (Aldershot: Ashgate, 2004), pp. 4–5.

66 Young people 'in their teens' were recognised in the seventeenth century: D. Fowler, *The First Teenagers*, pp. 2–3; Mitterauer, *History of Youth*, p. 14.

67 M. Abrams, *The Teenage Consumer* (London: London Press Exchange, 1959); B. Osgerby, 'From the roaring twenties to the swinging sixties: continuity and change in British youth culture, 1929–59', in B. Brivati and H. Jones (eds), *What Difference Did the War Make?* (Leicester: Leicester University Press, 1993), p. 83. The term 'youth

culture' was coined by Talcott Parsons in 1942: D. Fowler, *Youth Culture in Modern Britain, c. 1920–c. 1970* (London: Palgrave Macmillan, 2008), p. 1.

68 Contemporary sociologists associate youth not so much with chronological age as with transitions which may occur at 12, 16, 20, 30 or even older. Puuronen points out how 'the meaning of the concept "youth" may vary in each sociological youth study': V. Puuronen, 'Youth research at the beginning of the new millennium', in V. Puuronen (ed.), *Youth on the Threshold of the Third Millennium* (Joensuu: Karelian Institute, University of Joensuu, 2001), pp. 16, 28; L. Jackson, 'Childhood and youth', in H. G. Cocks and M. Houlbrook, *The Modern History of Sexuality* (Basingstoke: Palgrave Macmillan, 2006), p. 231.

69 J. Kett, *Rites of Passage: Adolescence in America, 1790 to the Present* (New York: Basic Books, 1977), p. 215.

70 J. Gillis, *Youth and History: Tradition and Change in European Age Relations, 1700–Present* (New York and London: Academic Press, 1974); F. Musgrove, *Youth and the Social Order* (Bloomington: Indiana University Press, 1964). See also A. Marwick, 'Youth in Britain, 1920–60: detachment and commitment', *Journal of Contemporary History*, 5:1 (1970), 37–45.

71 Springhall, *Coming of Age*.

72 Humphries, *Hooligans or Rebels?*; Hendrick, *Images of Youth*, p. 4.

73 M. Childs, *Labour's Apprentices: Working-Class Lads in Late Victorian and Edwardian England* (London: Hambledon Press, 1992).

74 C. Dyhouse, *Girls Growing Up in Late Victorian and Edwardian England* (London: Routledge and Kegan Paul, 1981). See also F. Hunt (ed.), *Lessons for Life: The Schooling of Girls and Women* (Oxford: Basil Blackwell, 1987). See also M. Gomersall, *Working-Class Girls in Nineteenth-Century England: Life, Work and Schooling* (Basingstoke: Macmillan, 1997).

75 Roberts, *A Woman's Place*. See also J. Sarsby, *Missuses and Mouldrunners: An Oral History of Women Pottery-Workers at Work and Home* (Milton Keynes: Open University Press, 1988).

76 A. Davies, *Leisure, Gender and Poverty*. See also White, *The Worst Street in North London*.

77 Fowler, *First Teenagers*. See also D. Fowler, 'Teenage consumers? Young wage-earners and leisure in Manchester, 1919–1939', in A. Davies and S. Fielding (eds), *Workers' Worlds: Culture and Communities in Manchester and Salford, 1880–1939* (Manchester: Manchester University Press, 1992), pp. 133–55.

78 Langhamer, *Women's Leisure*.

79 Todd, *Young Women*. See also S. Todd, '"Boisterous workers": young women, industrial rationalization and workplace militancy in inter-war rural England', *Labour History Review*, 68:3 (2003), 293–310; S. Todd, 'Young women, work and family in inter-war rural England', *Agricultural History Review*, 52:1 (2004), 83–98; S. Todd, 'Poverty and aspiration: young women's employment in inter-war England', *Twentieth Century British History*, 15:2 (2004), 119–42; S. Todd, 'Young women, work and leisure'. See also Fowler, *Youth Culture*, ch. 3, 'The flapper cult in inter-war Britain: media invention or the spark that ignited girl power?', pp. 59–71.

80 Pomfret, *Young People and the European City*.

81 Beaven, *Leisure, Citizenship*. See also White, *The Worst Street in North London*.

82 Humphries, *Hooligans or Rebels*, p. 11.

83 Springhall, *Coming of Age*, p. 8.

84 Similar considerations surfaced again during the inter-war years, when youthful hooligans were blamed for their involvement in the unemployment riots of the early 1930s: Beaven, *Leisure, Citizenship*, p. 115.

85 Hendrick, *Images of Youth*, p. 87; Davis, *Youth and the Condition of Britain*, p. 56; N. Lesko, *Act Your Age! A Cultural Construction of Adolescence* (New York and London: Routledge Falmer, 2001), p. 49.

86 Springhall, *Coming of Age*, p. 9; Beaven, *Leisure, Citizenship*, p. 163.

87 Pearson, *Hooligan*. Such press campaigns, particularly prominent after the Second World War, inspired Stanley Cohen's influential *Folk Devils and Moral Panics*.

88 G. S. Hall, *Adolescence: Its Psychology and Its Relations to Physiology, Anthropology, Sociology, Sex, Crime, Religion and Education*, 2 vols (London: Sidney Appleton, 1904).

89 C. Griffin, *Representations of Youth: The Study of Youth and Adolescence in Britain and America* (Cambridge: Polity Press, 1993), p. 12; J. Tosh, Review of J.A. Mangan and James Walvin (eds), *Manliness and Morality: Middle-Class Masculinity in Britain and America 1800–1940*, in *History Workshop Journal*, 29 (1990), p. 187.

90 Bingham, *Gender, Modernity and the Popular Press in Britain* (Oxford: Oxford University Press, 2004), p. 55; McKibbin, *Classes and Cultures*, p. 434; *The Advertiser's Annual and Convention Year Book, 1925–6* (London: Business Publications Ltd, 1926), p. 36. See also M. Pumphrey, 'The flapper, the housewife and the making of modernity', *Cultural Studies*, 1:2 (1987), 179–94; Langhamer, *Women's Leisure*, pp. 53–4; Griffin, *Representations of Youth*, p. 18; L. Hall, *Sex, Gender and Social Change in Britain since 1880* (London: Macmillan Press Ltd., 2000), p. 99; B. Melman, *Women and the Popular Imagination in the Twenties: Flappers and Nymphs* (New York: St. Martin's, 1988); M. Macdonald, *Representing Women: Myths of Femininity in the Popular Media* (London: Edward Arnold, 1995), p. 77. For localised working-class versions of the independent young woman worker see articles in the *Manchester Evening News* (5 February 1920), p. 4; (3 May 1920), p. 4; (6 May 1920), p. 3; (4 May 1925), p. 7.

91 A. Light, *Forever England: Femininity, Literature and Conservatism between the Wars* (London: Routledge, 1991); A. Bingham, *Gender, Modernity and the Popular Press in Britain* (Oxford: Oxford University Press, 2004).

92 Hatton, *London's Bad Boys*, p. 43.

93 L. Doan, 'Passing fashions: reading female masculinities in the 1920s', *Feminist Studies*, 24:3 (1998), pp. 665, 670.

94 Fowler, *Youth Culture*, pp. xiv, 38. Fowler argues that Rolf Gardiner played a key role in introducing the concept of 'youth culture' into British universities in the 1920s. In 1923, Gardiner became editor of the Cambridge undergraduate journal *Youth*, which he transformed into a 'vehicle' for promoting the concept of an 'international youth culture', unifying 18- to 25-year olds. Gardiner's emphasis contrasts with those of other undergraduate contemporaries who, unlike him, had fought in the war, and were more interested in 'theories and ideas about boys'. A group of such undergraduate war veterans at Oxford established a University Scout Club and a paper called *The Boy*, which aimed to link with similar university groups in Cambridge, Manchester and London, and was a precursor of the NABC journal, *The Boy*.

95 See, for example, D. J. Taylor, *Bright Young People: The Rise and Fall of a Generation, 1918–1940* (London: Vintage, 2008).

96 Beaven, *Leisure, Citizenship*, p. 1; S. B. Rowntree, *Poverty and Progress: A Second Social Survey of York* (London: Longmans, Green and Co., 1941: 1942), pp. 446–7.

97 C. E. B. Russell and L. M. Russell, *Lads' Clubs*, p. 123.

98 C. Cameron, A. Lush and G. Meara (eds), *Disinherited Youth* (Edinburgh: Carnegie United Kingdom Trust, 1943), p. 87; Morgan, *Young Citizen*, pp. 84–5; H. Llewellyn Smith (ed.), *The New Survey of London Life and Labour*, vol. IX, *Life and Leisure*, (London: P.S. King and Son Ltd., 1935), p. 47.

99 Russell and Russell, *Lads' Clubs*, p. 66.

100 *The Boy* (May 1924), p. 3.

101 Llewellyn Smith (ed.), *The New Survey*, vol. IX, p. 24; H. Secretan, *London below Bridges* (London: Geoffrey Bles, 1931), pp. 70–1.

102 R. White and J. Why, 'Youth agency and social context', *Journal of Sociology*, 34:3 (1998), p. 319. See also Griffin, *Representations of Youth*; Rowntree, *Poverty and Progress*, p. 350.

103 A. E. Morgan, *The Needs of Youth*, p. 273; A. H. Gray, *Sex Teaching* (London: National Sunday School Union, [1929]), p. 74; Jones, *Social Survey of Merseyside*, vol. III, p. 217.

104 Rowntree, *Poverty and Progress*, p. 447.

105 E. Dudley, *The Leakage: Cause and Remedy* (London: Catholic Truth Society, 1931), pp. 4, 11.

106 H. Cunningham, *The Invention of Childhood* (London: BBC Books, 2006), p. 208.

107 Secretan, *London below Bridges*, pp. 70–1; National Association of Boys' Clubs, *Fourteen to Eighteen: The Critical Years of Boyhood*, Annual Report, 1930–31, p. 6.

108 Hatton, *London's Bad Boys*, p. 49.

109 J. Butterworth, *Clubland* (London: The Epworth Press, 1932), p. 56.

110 *The Boy* (December 1929), p. 55.

111 Fowler, *First Teenagers*, pp. 8, 14–15; *The Boy* (October 1924), p. 10.

112 *The Boy* (October 1924), p. 10.

113 *The Boy* (December 1929), p. 58.

114 See, for example, Gollan, *Youth in British Industry*; H. Durant, *The Problem of Leisure* (London: George Routledge and Sons, 1938); W. F. Lestrange, *Wasted Lives* (London: George Routledge and Sons, 1936). See also M. Francis, 'The domestication of the male? Recent research on nineteenth and twentieth century British masculinity', *Historical Journal*, 45:3 (2002), 637–52; W. R. Garside, 'Juvenile unemployment statistics between the wars', *Bulletin of the Society for the Study of Labour History*, 33 (1976), 38–46; W. R. Garside, 'Juvenile unemployment and public policy between the wars', *Economic History Review*, 30:2 (1977), 322–39; D. K. Benjamin and L. A. Kochin, 'What went right in juvenile unemployment policy between the wars: a comment', *Economic History Review*, 32:4 (1979), 523–8; W. R. Garside, 'Juvenile unemployment between the wars: a rejoinder', *Economic History Review*, 32:4 (1979), 529–32; B. Eichengreen, 'Juvenile unemployment in twentieth-century Britain: the emergence of a problem', *Social Research*, 54:2 (1987), 273–301; W. R. Garside, 'Youth unemployment in twentieth-century Britain: protest, conflict and the labour market', in D. Dowe (ed.), *Jugendprotest und Generationenkonflikt in Europa im 20. Jahrhundert: Deutschland, England, Frankreich und Italien im Vergleich* (Bonn: Verlag Neue

Gesellschaft, 1986), pp. 75–81; K. Burgess, 'Youth unemployment policy during the 1930s', *Twentieth Century British History*, 6:1 (1995), 23–55; S. Alexander, 'Men's fears and women's work: responses to unemployment in London between the wars', *Gender and History*, 12: 2 (2000), 401–25.

115 Francis, 'The domestication of the male?'; Cameron, Lush and Meara, *Disinherited Youth*, pp. 69–70.

116 Davis, *Youth and the Condition of Britain*, pp. 73–4.

117 Cameron, Lush and Meara, *Disinherited Youth*, pp. 69–70, 79.

118 *Ibid.*, pp. 71, 80.

119 S. Brooke, 'A new world for women? Abortion law reform in Britain during the 1930s', *The American Historical Review*, 106:2 (2001), 431–59; Lestrange, *Wasted Lives*, p. 5.

120 See, for example, S. Alexander, 'Becoming a woman in London in the 1920s and 1930s', in D. Feldman and G. Stedman Jones (eds), *Metropolis London: Histories and Representations since 1800* (London: Routledge, 1989), pp. 245–71.

121 D. Baines and P. Johnson, 'In search of the "traditional" working class: social mobility and occupational continuity in inter-war London', *Economic History Review*, 52:4 (1999), 692–713.

122 Cameron, Lush and Meara, *Disinherited Youth*, p. 98.

123 Unemployment amongst young people aged between 14 and 17 (or 18) was about 150,000 at the beginning of the 1930s and 100,000 towards the end: Fowler, *First Teenagers*, pp. 27–9, 35.

124 Gollan, *Youth in British Industry*, pp. 226–7; Fowler, *First Teenagers*, pp. 14, 17, 24. The White Paper on the Children and Young Persons' Bill, published in 1932, highlighted the shortage of juvenile industrial labour due to the low wartime birth-rate: P. Roker and H. Crawford Scott, 'Juvenile unemployment in West Ham', *Economica* (16 March 1926), pp. 61, 64.

125 Morgan, *Needs of Youth*, p. 47.

126 Hatton, *London's Bad Boys*, p. 71.

127 Morgan, *Needs of Youth*, pp. 49–50.

128 *The Boy* (December 1929), p. 58.

129 Fowler, *First Teenagers*, pp. 8, 10, 22–3, 35–6.

130 Morgan, *Needs of Youth*, p. 51; Fowler, *First Teenagers*, p. 7. Roker and Crawford Scott highlighted similar problems in the casual labour market of West Ham, London, in 1926: Roker and Crawford Scott, 'Juvenile unemployment', pp. 58–77.

131 Roker and Crawford Scott, 'Juvenile unemployment', p. 65.

132 *Daily Mirror* (11 February 1939), p. 11.

133 Fowler, *First Teenagers*, p. 96.

134 Bowley and Hogg, *Has Poverty Diminished?* This 1920s survey included Northampton, Reading, Warrington, Bolton and Stanley. See also Jones, *The Social Survey of Merseyside*, Vol. II, pp. 30–2.

135 Langhamer, *Women's Leisure*, p. 102.

136 Davies, *Leisure, Gender and Poverty*, p. 83.

137 Fowler, *First Teenagers*, pp. 95–6.

138 Nott, *Music for the People*, pp. 2–3, 11, 36. The average weekly wage almost trebled between 1913 and 1938. The average working week shortened and more workers received holidays with pay (almost 42 per cent in 1938).

139 Rowntree, *Poverty and Progress*, p. 181.

140 For young women and leisure, see: P. Tinkler, *Constructing Girlhood: Popular Magazines for Girls Growing up in England, 1920–1950* (London: Taylor and Francis, 1995); P. Tinkler, 'Sexuality and citizenship; the state and girls' leisure provision in England, 1939–45', *Women's History Review*, 4:2 (1995), 193–217; P. Tinkler, 'English girls and the international dimensions of British citizenship in the 1940s', *European Journal of Women's Studies*, 8:1 (2001), 103–27; P. Tinkler, 'Cause for Concern: young women and leisure, 1930–1950', *Women's History Review*, 12:2 (2003), 233–60; P. Tinkler, 'An all-round education: the Board of Education's policy for the leisure-time training of girls, 1939–1950', *History of Education*, 23:4 (1994), 385–403; P. Tinkler, 'At your service: the nation's girlhood and the call to service in England, 1939–1950', *European Journal of Women's Studies*, 4 (2001), 353–77.

141 M. Roper, 'Between manliness and masculinity: the "war generation" and the psychology of fear in Britain, 1914–1950', *Journal of British Studies*, 44:2 (2005), p. 345.

142 Childs, *Labour's Apprentices*, p. 142.

143 John Springhall pioneered the history of British youth movements in works like *Youth, Empire and Society: British Youth Movements, 1860–1960* (Beckenham: Croom Helm, 1977); *Coming of Age; Sure and Steadfast: A History of the Boys' Brigade, 1883–1993* (London: Collins, 1983). See also J. Springhall, 'Lord Meath, youth and empire', *Journal of Contemporary History*, 5:4 (1970), 97–111; J. Springhall, 'The Boy Scouts, class and militarism in relation to British youth movements, 1908–30', *International Review of Social History*, 16 (1971), 121–58; J. Springhall, 'Young England, rise up and listen! The political dimensions of youth protest and generation conflict in Britain, 1919–1939', in D. Dowe (ed.), *Jugendprotest und Generationenkonflikt in Europa im 20. Jahrhundert: Deutschland, England, Frankreich und Italien im Vergleich* (Bonn: Verlag Neue Gesellschaft, 1986), pp. 151–63. Scouting has received considerable attention, particularly in relation to imperialism. See J. P. Hantover, 'The Boys Scouts and the validations of masculinity', *Journal of Social Issues*, 34:1 (1978), 184–95; Michael Blanch, 'Imperialism, nationalism and organised youth', in J. Clarke, C. Critcher and R. Johnson (eds), *Working Class Culture: Studies in History and Theory* (Birmingham: Centre for Cultural Studies, 1979); M. Rosenthal, *The Character Factory: Baden-Powell and the Origins of the Boy Scout Movement* (New York: Pantheon Press, 1986); M. Dedman, 'Baden-Powell, militarism, and the "invisible contributors" to the Boy Scout Scheme, 1904–1920', *Twentieth Century British History*, 4:3 (1993), 201–23; R. H. MacDonald, *Sons of the Empire: The Frontier and the Boy Scout Movement, 1890–1918* (Toronto: University of Toronto Press, 1993); S. Pyke, 'The popularity of nationalism in the early British Boy Scout movement', *Social History*, 23:3 (1998), 309–24; A. Warren, 'Citizens of the empire: Baden Powell, Scouts and Guides, and an imperial ideal', in J. Mackenzie (ed.), *Imperialism and Popular Culture* (Manchester: Manchester University Press, 1986); A. Warren, 'Sir Robert Baden-Powell, the Scout movement, and citizen-training in Britain, 1900–1920', *English Historical Review*, 101 (1986), 376–98; A. Warren, 'Popular manliness: Baden-Powell, scouting and the development of manly character', in J. A. Mangan and J. Walvin (eds), *Manliness and Morality*; A. Warren, 'Baden-Powell: a final comment', *English Historical Review*, 102:405 (1987), 948–50; A. Warren, 'Mothers for the empire? The Girl Guide Association in Britain, 1909–1939', in J. A. Mangan (ed.),

Making Imperial Mentalities: Socialisation and British Imperialism (Manchester: Manchester University Press, 1990), pp. 96–109; A. Warren, 'Sport, youth and gender in Britain, 1880–1940', in J. C. Binfield and J. Stevenson (eds), *Sport, Culture and Politics* (Sheffield: Sheffield Academic Press, 1993), pp. 49–71. For how scouting and guiding adapted to inter-war changes, see T. M. Proctor, *On My Honour: Guides and Scouts in Inter-war Britain* (Philadelphia: American Philosophical Society, 2002). See also T. M. Proctor, '(Uni)forming youth: girl guides and boy scouts in Britain, 1908–39', *History Workshop Journal*, 45 (1998), 103–34; T. M. Proctor, 'Scouts, Guides and the fashioning of empire, 1919–1939', in W. Parkins (ed.), *Fashioning the Body Politic: Gender, Dress, Citizenship* (Oxford: Berg, 2002), pp. 125–44; T. M. Proctor, '"Something for the Girls": Girl Guides and Emerging Youth Cultures, 1908–1939', in C. Benninghaus, M. J. Mayne, and B. Søland (eds), *Secret Gardens, Satanic Mills: Placing Girls in Modern European History* (Bloomington: Indiana University Press, 2005), pp. 239–53. Other articles on Guides include R. Voeltz, 'The antidote to "khaki fever"? The expansion of the British Girl Guides during the First World War', *Journal of Contemporary History*, 27 (1992), 627–38.

144   These influential boys' club supporters included Frederic George D'Aeth (1875–1940), a founder member of the NABC and 'pioneer' of a 'welfare society'. D'Aeth was associated with the Liverpool University Settlement movement and taught in the School of Social Work at Liverpool University. He moved to Liverpool in 1905, having been a curate in London's East End. In 1919, he became vice-chair of the National Council for Voluntary (later Social) Service, which he had helped to found: M. Simey, 'D'Aeth, Frederic George (1875–1940)', *Oxford Dictionary of National Biography* (Oxford: Oxford University Press, 2004), www.oxforddnb.com/view/article/54584 (accessed 9 February 2008). Robert Stanford Wood (1886–1963), also at the NABC's founding meeting, was a well-known civil servant, who was also a scout commissioner. He joined the Board of Education in 1911 as an inspector of schools and was Principal Private Secretary to the President of the Board of Education between 1926 and 1928. He made important contributions to post-Second World War education policy. See D. Crook, 'Wood, Sir Robert Stanford (1886–1963)', *Oxford Dictionary of National Biography* (Oxford: Oxford University Press, 2004) www.oxforddnb.com/view/article/37004 (accessed 9 February 2008).

145   A. Carden-Coyne, *Reconstructing the Body: Classicism, Modernism, and the First World War* (Oxford: Oxford University Press, 2009), pp. 10, 173.

146   See, for example, footage on British Universities Newsreel Database (BUND): *Universal News*, Issue No: 332, 'Boys' Brigade Jubilee' (14 September 1933); *Gaumont British News*, Issue No: 559, 'Boys Brigade Review at Glasgow' (8 May 1939); *British Paramount News*, Issue No: 538 '1,000 Scouts cheer King' (24 April 1936); *Universal News*, Issue No: 123 (14 September 1931), 'Homage to Il Duce', Inspection by Mussolini of 50,000 young fascists; *British Paramount News*, Issue No: 57 (15 September 1931), '50,000 Salute Il Duce. Young fascists greatest parade'. *Gaumont British News*, Issue No: 301 (16 November 1936), 'Soviet League of Youth Movement's Display in Moscow'. See also clips on the British Pathé website, www.britishpathe.com/.

147   Todd, 'Young women, work and leisure', p. 792; Bingham, *Gender, Modernity and the Popular Press*, p. 55.

148   S. Humphries, *A Secret World of Sex: Forbidden Fruit. The British Experience, 1900–*

1950 (London: Sidgwick and Jackson, 1988); M. Houlbrook, *Queer London: Perils and Pleasures of the Sexual Metropolis, 1918–1957* (Chicago: University of Chicago Press, 2005).

149   J. Butler, 'Performative acts and gender constitution: an essay in phenomenology and feminist theory', in S. E. Case (ed.), *Performing Feminisms: Feminist Critical Theory and Theatre* (Baltimore, MD: Johns Hopkins University Press, 1990). For the social significance of dance and mobility see S. Banes, *Dancing Women: Female Bodies on Stage* (London: Routledge, 1998); B. Browning, *Samba: Resistance in Motion* (Bloomington: Indiana University Press, 1995); R. Burt, *The Male Dancer: Bodies, Spectacle, Sexualities* (London: Routledge, 1995); A. C. Albright, *Choreographing Difference: The Body and Identity in Contemporary Dance* (Hanover, NH: Wesleyan University Press, 1997); B. Farnell, 'Ethno-graphics and the moving body', *Man*, 29:4 (1994), 929–74; S. Foster (ed.), *Corporealities: Dancing Knowledge, Culture and Power* (London: Routledge, 1996); M. Franko, *Dancing Modernism/Performing Politics* (Bloomington: Indiana University Press, 1995); J. L. Hanna, *Dance, Sex and Gender: Signs of Identity, Dominance and Desire* (Chicago: Chicago University Press, 1988); G. Morris, *Moving Words: Re-writing Dance* (London: Routledge, 1996); C. J. Novack, 'The body endeavours as cultural practices', in S. L. Foster (ed.), *Choreographing History* (Bloomington: Indiana University Press, 1995); S. A. Reed, 'The politics and poetics of dance', *Annual Review of Anthropology*, 27 (1998), 503–32; D. Williams, *Ten Lectures on the Theories of the Dance* (Metuchen, NJ: The Scarecrow Press, 1991).

150   B. S. Turner, 'Introduction. Bodily performance: on aura and reproductibility', *Body and Society*, 11:4 (2005), p. 5.

151   R. M. Vanderbeck, 'Masculinities and fieldwork: widening the discussion', *Gender, Place and Culture*, 12:4 (2005) 391; F. Mort, *Cultures of Consumption: Masculinities and Social Space in Late Twentieth-Century Britain* (London: Routledge, 1996).

152   T. Edensor, 'Walking in the British countryside: reflexivity, embodied practices and ways to escape', *Body and Society*, 6:81 (2000), p. 82.

153   K. Malone, 'Street life: youth, culture and competing uses of public space', *Environment and Urbanization*, 14:2 (2002), 157–68.

154   For the development of the outdoor movement, see H. Taylor, *A Claim on the Countryside: A History of the British Outdoor Movement* (Edinburgh: Keele University Press, 1997). For the complex relationship which many walkers had with local landscapes, see M. Tebbutt, 'Rambling and manly identity in Derbyshire's Dark Peak, 1880s–1920s', *Historical Journal*, 49:4 (2006), 1125–53.

155   M. E. Gardiner, *Critiques of Everyday Life* (London and New York: Routledge, 2000), pp. 2–3, 75. Davies, *Leisure, Gender and Poverty* is one of the few works to look at the continuing significance of more informal types of leisure activity in working-class communities.

156   For similar observations on such pragmatic motivations in the late Victorian and Edwardian period, see M. Childs, *Labour's Apprentices*, pp. 153–6.

157   Levi and Schmitt, *A History of Young People*, vol. 1, p. 5.

1

Looking at youth

Youth assumed an important metaphorical significance in the inter-war years, particularly in the early 1920s as nationalist, political, religious and military movements across Europe idealised young people as a force for change and moral regeneration, and educated and politicised youth gave literary vent to 'grievances' which helped to shape an 'unprecedented' opposition of 'the young' and 'the old'.[1] This chapter focuses on these generational issues and gender ambiguities by consider-ing the significance that the energy and vitality of working-class young boys and young men had for a number of influential middle-class youth workers who were also war veterans.[2] It takes as its subject the writings of several leading boys' club workers who were based in London. These works were published in the early 1930s and have often been cited in his-tories of inter-war youth culture, although with little explanation of the background and experiences which informed them. The chapter argues that shared war-time experiences had an important effect on how these writers conceptualised their relationships with the working-class young boys and young men with whom they continued to work in the post-war years. Before turning to this theme, however, it is necessary to consider the broader significance that the idea of youth assumed after the First World War.

Post-war reconstruction in Britain involved a complex negotiation of memory and forgetting, of mythologising those who had fallen whilst often turning away from the painful reality of the dead and the disabled 'whose wounded bodies belied aesthetic ideals of masculine beauty'.[3] The redefinition of 'gender identities' played an important part in these nego-tiations, particularly as represented in the contemporary press, which was particularly alert to examples of modernity and change, such as the emergence of the flapper and the 'modern woman', who was such a topic of popular discussion in the 1920s.[4] These new images helped to shape a feminised image of society which was reinforced by changes taking place in the social experiences of young women, who were at the forefront of the 'new modernism' of the 1920s.[5] Not only had a 'generation of men' been lost, but a surplus of women of childbearing age meant that by 1927 there were two million more women than men.[6] Whereas the roles and expectations of young men remained largely within traditional roles and expectations, the changes in young women's lives challenged pre-war masculinities at many levels, and contributed to the common inter-war belief that the 'sexes were converging', with the blurring of boundaries between masculine and feminine.[7]

Appalling death rates, shell shock, injury and mental breakdown introduced a disquieting vulnerability to notions of masculinity and rendered the hard emphases of late-Victorian and Edwardian manliness more ambivalent.[8] The strong anti-militaristic sentiments of the post-war years fed into new models of education and youth training. The pacifist woodcraft groups were established, while youth groups like the Church Lads' Brigade, in which military symbolism was important, declined, and many youth associations discouraged the 'unimaginative' use of drill.[9] The bold, martial heroism of the pre-war years was becoming something altogether more low key, a cheerful, 'domestic', commonsense endurance which would acquire further iconographic resonance during the Second World War.[10] Images of young men in the 1920s were often a delicate balance of sympathy and anxiety, which feminists such as Ethel Mannin thought was at the expense of young women, maintaining that young men's high jinks were afforded far greater toleration than the nonconformist behaviour of their female counterparts.[11]

> When young men get drunk and ride on the tops of taxicabs and knock off policemen's helmets, and create disturbances in music-halls, it is merely an exciting 'rag', and mothers smile tolerantly, murmuring: 'Boys will be boys'. Fathers remember their own young days and reflect that 'we are only young once'. But when a young woman lights up a cigarette in a railway carriage or wears her skirt above her knees – because girls will be girls, and that is the fashion, anyway – the generation old enough to know better gets annoyed.[12]

The 'infantile but precocious' flapper, with her bobbed hair, androgynous figure, fashions and risqué smoking was a far greater press draw. Her masquerade of boyishness, doing little to appropriate male power and authority, seemed to presage disturbing changes in gender relations.[13] Images of strong, healthy, 'boyish women' were frequently juxtaposed against the effeminate, emasculated masculinity of often upper-class intellectuals, whose narcissistic, 'languid' or 'affected' style suggested physical degeneracy, impotence or homosexuality.[14] Such representations of 'a muscular, healthy "new womanhood"' reinforced notions of 'a deformed, debilitated masculinity', for this youthful ebullience and physicality was in striking contrast to more sombre narratives of death, broken bodies and the post-war legacy of physical and mental disability.[15]

Boyishness, masculinity and boys' club workers

Boyishness was a key motif. It was self-consciously vaunted by many involved in post-war work with young people. It was thrust upon disabled veterans, who were discursively emasculated and homo-eroticised as 'soldier boys' in need of care and protection.[16] This 'dissonant conjunction of youthful manhood with the helplessness of childhood and the impotence of old age' 'troubled' many, not least because it brought into sharp focus the tensions of male victimhood and female affirmation.[17] The popular press readily exploited the infantilised plight of disabled ex-soldiers who had lost both their masculinity and 'full citizenship', quick to point out, with implications of castration, how a war which 'had destroyed one generation of men and had invalided . . . another' had 'simultaneously invigorated the younger generations of women'.[18]

In a population thirsty for renewal, the idea of youth as a state of mind rather than a chronological age invigorated pre-war ideas of grown men retaining their boyishness into adulthood and helped to give many involved in the education and training of working-class young males a new sense of purpose. Noted youth workers such as Baden-Powell, schooled in the late-Victorian and Edwardian periods, remained 'boy-men', 'permanent' whistlers 'addicted to an impossible dream of the persistence of male adolescence'.[19] Edwin Butterworth, a prominent inter-war club organiser, described as having a 'boyish heart', was typically almost taken for a boy himself at one social event: 'The fact is that Butterworth has triumphantly mistaken himself for a boy. If he has grown up in mind, his spirit is still fresh as primroses on a bank.'[20] The reference to Butterworth's boyish 'fresh' spirit is a reminder of the degenerate connotations of over-civilised adult manliness, whose energies were sapped by modern urban society. Boyishness had, since the late nineteenth century, allowed middle-class men to feel reconnected with an unadulterated manly essence whose meanings could be both savage and innocent.[21] The war, however, in tempering the appeal of boyish savagery, helped to accentuate the attractions of the irresponsible boy nature. Looking back on his war experiences from the vantage point of the 1960s, Charles Carrington, who had joined up at 17, realised that where he had once thought that the 'knowledge of adult problems' had made him very mature in his twenties, he now thought 'quite the contrary':

> The 1916 fixation had caught me and stunted my mental growth, so that even at ten years I was retarded and adolescent. I could not escape from the comradeship of the trenches which had become a mental internment camp, or should I say soldier's home.[22]

Carrington believed an important emotional need had been met 'by the necessity to exert the whole of one's strength in generous rivalry with one's friends'. Yet, musing later on his younger, war-time self, he also wondered whether the boy he had 're-discovered' through writing his recollections was 'anything more than a juvenile delinquent, whose characteristics were a longing for ganging-up with the other boys, a craving to demonstrate his manliness and a delight in anti-social violence'.[23]

Many believed the boundaries between those born before 1900 and those born after, who had no adult memories of the pre-war period, seemed to have hardened. In 1926, the Rev. John Christian Pringle, born in 1872 and then secretary of the Charity Organisation Society, mused on his involvement with boys' club work, which had first started in 1890.[24] Despite thirty-five years' experience, Pringle thought that his ideas on the subject had only clarified relatively recently, 'when I was too old to be a serious worker at it!'[25] Realisation of his earlier lack of understanding was influenced in part by new insights, from psychology, into children and young people and changing educational philosophies.[26] He now felt:

> deeply and remorsefully, the blasphemous fatuity of supposing that, because I cared for a thing, that was any reason under heaven why the boy should do so . . . [N]othing can save us, as we get older, from moving all the time *away from* the boy's outlook, the boy's problems, the boy's life . . . We must be masters of every paragraph of such a book as Burt's 'Young Delinquent', and . . . must have served an apprenticeship in all the departments of craftsmanship he describes, and a great many others.

Pringle's remarks are a reminder of how 'everyday' psychology was reaching a much broader audience by the inter-war years, providing 'new methods of healing those "nervous" ailments' thought to be 'the cause of so much eccentricity and inefficiency'. The psychology of adolescence was said to have 'revealed something of the true nature of delinquency and crime', and to have shown 'anew the inadequacy of the vengeful and deterrent conceptions of punishment'.[27] Yet there are glimpses, too, in Pringle's account of how this new comprehension also connected with other more personal impulses, particularly the post-war impact of loss and bereavement. As he explained:

> I was a very affectionate big brother to my own young brother. He never regarded me as anything but an interfering, officious ass. He grew to be an incomparably more effective man than myself, and died magnificently at Loos. I can only mourn him as I mourn my failure with all these other countless lads.[28]

The attitudes of those who, like Pringle, been drawn into boys' club work towards the end of the nineteenth century and in the Edwardian period, had been shaped by a particular context of masculinity. By the 1880s, the decade in which the BB was established, manliness had in many respects become synonymous with 'the toughest and most exclusive male attributes'. This idealisation of robust masculinity which reinforced men's 'monopoly on courage and stoicism' and denied their emotional vulnerability also informed satirical representation of lower middle-class males, between the 1870s and 1914, as overly domesticated and feminised.[29] The very public masculinity and 'homosocial camaraderie' of young working-class males consequently made a strong appeal to some middle-class youth workers in relationships which, although strongly status driven, were also described as developing a sense of shared identity as men.[30] Despite their faults, young working-class males, valued for their manly potential, in some respects manifested many of the independent qualities so important to middle-class masculinity.[31] The working-class boy's autonomy on starting work, for example, worried many contemporary commentators, yet could also exemplify the capacity to 'make one's own way in the world', so central to the manly ideal.[32] Similarly, the intense comradeship intrinsic to notions of the 'clubbable male' could be seen as mirrored in the gang relationships and street affiliations of working-class boys; the very fact that they were so frequently resistant to the strictures of Christian manliness adding, perhaps, to the manly challenges of working with them.[33]

Boys' clubs had, since their inception in the nineteenth century, been more successful than either the Scouts or BB in providing a focus for the 'rougher', most difficult to handle, working-class lads.[34] Boys' club workers were often conscious of walking a narrow line between gaining their confidence and appearing too 'soft', particularly given that membership tended to fluctuate and was frequently short term. The usual aim of such clubs was to offer leisure alternatives to boys who might otherwise have drifted into delinquency, yet identification with those in their charge led some middle-class workers to romanticise the exuberance and spontaneity of such 'lads' (albeit inflected by 'irrationality', exaggeration and 'feminine' sentimentality), which was so lacking in their own masculinity.[35] Joseph Kett observed of 'boys-workers' in the United States that 'successful encounters' with lower-class boys gave them 'new confidence in their own virility', and something similar may be observed among their British counterparts, particularly in the 1920s, at a time when their own manly character was often far from certain.[36] How such sympathies were invested with fresh conviction in the 1920s, as revulsion against the 'horrific waste' of young lives in the war also encouraged a broader relaxation of attitudes towards the anti-social behaviour of working-class young men, forms the subject of the next section.[37]

Understanding the 'hooligan'

Youth workers, educationalists and members of the judiciary expressed a sometimes 'surprising permissiveness' towards young male hooligans in the inter-war years and there was a generally low-key response 'towards crime and punishment'.[38] Greater understanding of and leniency towards youth offenders was reflected in an article in *The Boy*, journal of the NABC, which suggested that 'The diminution in juvenile crime reflected in the criminal statistics' owed much 'to a kindlier conception of justice'.[39] D. S. H., former housemaster of a Borstal institution, stressed the importance of more sympathetic approaches to juvenile offenders:

> Always trust a lad until he gives himself away and you are forced into taking action. Never let the fact that a lad has a sticky past influence you unduly. Run the risk of being let down where you have trusted, rather than be continually suspecting evil. It will pay in the long run. A word of encouragement at the right moment will do more to a tough case than any amount of punishment. In all cases of this description, avoid cheap sentimentality; come straight to the point; talk as man to man; and, above all be patient.[40]

Complex factors were responsible for these changed emphases. The expansion of child psychology and social welfare organisations in the late nineteenth and early twentieth centuries was attended by greater awareness of the emotional and physiological changes of adolescence, whose 'turbulence' was seen as making young people, and boys in particular, especially susceptible to hazardous external influences. Concerns about the damaging effects of urban life had been rising since the end of the nineteenth century, but the inter-war years saw growing appreciation of the influence that environmental factors had upon young people's behaviour. This was accentuated by the impact of high levels of unemployment in many working-class communities and growing concerns about young people's susceptibility to mass forms of commercialised leisure. Awareness of the need to address the emotional and intellectual development of children and adolescents was reinforced by progressive educational ideas which emphasised more informal, child-centred approaches under the influence of Freudian psychoanalysis and developmental psychology.[41] At the same time, 'new developments in the biological and social sciences', which attributed greater fluidity to 'sexuality and sex roles', reinforced efforts to maintain existing sexual distinctions and the pre-eminence of heterosexuality.[42]

Despite growing emphases upon social and environmental influences, adolescence was increasingly defined in psychological terms, as a specific and individual stage of development separate from that of adults and children, associated with uncertainty, turbulence and insecurity. These troubled definitions stemmed in large part from the work of the American psychologist G. Stanley Hall, who founded the child study movement in the United States and was the first psychologist to advance adolescence as a separate, universal stage of psychological development.[43] Hall's two-volume book *Adolescence: Its Psychology and Its Relations to Physiology, Anthropology, Sociology, Sex, Crime, Religion, and Education*, published in 1904, did much to popularise the concept of adolescence. His views influenced a range of other writers on both sides of the Atlantic, particularly by being repeated in works aimed at teachers and youth workers, and came to inform a range of policies and practices based on the 'notion of "adolescence"' as a difficult transitional phase when young people 'needed special guidance and discipline'.[44] As was suggested in the Introduction, Hall popularised a strongly gendered interpretation of adolescence which reflected many contemporary anxieties in American society: about feminism, women's economic and social advances, the emasculation of men and how best to encourage the more masculine upbringing of boys and young males.[45] Significantly, he gave scientific justification to rowdy behaviour as an essential developmental phase on the road to manhood. Male adolescence was constructed as a time of 'ambition, growth and challenge', when 'naturally' adventurous instincts had to be encouraged as part of striving for the self-knowledge of rational adulthood.[46] Hall's works reflected contemporary worries that 'masculine impulses' were too often repressed in middle-class boys who were 'victims of over-civilization and nervousness'.[47] (Tellingly, the *Daily Mail* described the Boyette's 'physique' as 'finer . . . than the average boy of her age'.[48]) Richmal Crompton's popular fictional hero, William Brown, vigorously asserted the adventurous instincts which middle-class society attempted to inhibit, readily identifying with 'uncivilised' others such as 'natives' and working-class boys, whose boisterous, anarchic independence seemed so much more appealing than the constrictions of his own middle-class family and school life.[49] Crompton's books were described as 'prodigiously popular' among boys aged between 12 and 14 in the inter-war years, and A. J. Jenkinson's study of boys' and girls' reading habits concluded that their popularity was quite suitable to this less mature stage of psychological development.[50]

The title of the NABC's journal, *The Boy*, also reflected this belief in the distinctiveness of the boy nature, which needed to be slowly nurtured to manhood rather than being exposed to the enervating influences of popular culture. One of its older writers bemoaned the changed tastes of younger readers. Those who had been brought up 'on Henty and the "B.O.P." [*Boys' Own Paper*] knew the joy of following the adventures of boys like ourselves, on whom we, consciously or not, modelled our daydreams and our play in a way that is impossible to the devotee of Sexton Blake'.

> The book heroes of our generation were boys; we imagined ourselves faring bravely forth into tight corners in school or jungle as boys, and while we were boys we looked on life through boyish eyes, and did not dream ourselves men until the responsibilities of manhood began to force themselves on us. The boys of to-day, with their Buffalo Bill and Frank Darrell models, read the adventures of men, and so forget their boyhood and try to view life through adult spectacles inadequately adjusted to the short sight, soft muscles and inexperience of a boy body.[51]

Many inter-war boys' magazines attempted to adapt to these changing interests by introducing tough working-class characters and schoolteacher heroes who acted as 'companions' rather than rulers, playing games with their young charges and encouraging their independence, although the increasing segmentation of the inter-war magazine market meant that boys tended to move on to different reading matter once they reached their mid teens.[52] These rather more equable relationships and the stress on showing not only authority but guidance reflected similar psychological emphases on the importance of giving appropriate direction through adolescence, and suggest how such stories could become a vehicle for promoting progressive educational methods. Boyd suggests there was little 'open discourse on the topic of manliness' in this litera-ture, which largely ignored the growing visibility of women in post-war society. Indeed, D. C. Thompson 'virtually banished' women from its boys' story papers.[53]

The adolescent development of girls was seen as something very different. What for boys was a period of curiosity and adventure was for girls a time of protection to encourage their refined, civilising devel-opment as 'helpers' and 'guides' to their men-folk and families. It was believed particularly important to curb the 'selfishness' of adolescent girls, which was opposed to the nurturing, supportive expectations of being a wife and mother. Not for them the 'self-centredness' and manly fantasies of adventure thought so important to the boy's development that they could excuse even criminal energies as affirmation of the male drive for 'power, control and domination'.[54]

Clinicians tended to be less concerned with the unruly behaviour that frequently worried parents and more preoccupied with the shy, solitary boy, whose diffidence and nervousness were assumed to be trou-bling portents of a compromised adult masculinity. Boys who expressed fear, anxiety and timidity may have appeared particularly worrying in the 1920s, when shell-shocked soldiers seemed an alarming reminder of the consequences of psychological 'weakness' during war time. Indeed, the magnitude of war-time losses reinforced the significance of boyish energy after the First World War, as is suggested by several books pub-lished by leading boys' club workers in the early 1930s whose sympathies towards and understanding of young working-class males owed much to their war-time experiences.[55] These works were part of a broader reflective moment in the late 1920s and early 1930s as a new genera-tion of memoirs, novels, poetry and plays were published by men trying to understand and come to terms with their involvement in the war.[56] Grounded in personal experiences, these publications demonstrated not only survivors' guilt about the generation of young lives lost during the war, but also a strong sense of the need to pay something back to the next generation.[57]

All the youth books by ex-soldiers cited here expressed in varying degrees a sense of how the young 'hooligans' of the residuum, who had so worried contemporaries during the Victorian and Edwardian years, had rallied to their country during its time of need, often dying in the process.[58] Hubert Secretan's *London below Bridges* and Sidney Hatton's *London's Bad Boys* were both published in 1931.[59] Hatton's subject was 'what our U.S.A. Cousins call the "underprivileged" boy, who is not necessarily a "bad 'un" but has possibilities – sometimes great ones – for good or evil'.[60] Hatton had considerable experience teaching adolescents, in Juvenile Unemployment Centres, Compulsory Day Continuation Schools and Junior Men's Institutes.[61] Drawing on traditional notions of manliness, he called for 'the sportsmen' of the day to work cheerfully in 'slum-land's' clubs and institutes and to fight not only for better conditions for contemporary manhood but also for great clemency and understanding for the 'bad boys': 'If war could breed love of man for man, "passing the love of women," cannot peace do something to create a true fellowship and brotherhood also?'[62] James Butterworth's best-selling *Clubland* was published in 1932 and Basil Henriques's *Club Leadership* in 1933.[63] Given the 'rather sparse' literature on the subject, Henriques's work became a popular handbook for club organisers and was praised for how it had 'moved with the times . . . One feels that it is just because he has always been ready to scrap pre-conceived ideas that he now avoids the fatal error of offering pre-War methods to the present generation.'[64]

These writers have often been cited in histories of inter-war youth culture, but with little explanation of their background. All, in fact, had strong boys' club connections in London, and were aware of the 'scores of managers and thousands of Old Boys' who had died on active service.[65] Several were linked by university settlements such as Toynbee Hall and Oxford House, which had been important sources for boys' club leaders from the public schools since the 1880s and 1890s.[66] The motivations for their pre-war involvement in work with 'rough lads', whose 'aboriginal boyhood' was 'uncorrupted by an emasculated, civilizing process', seems to have owed much to hopes of developing a 'mature', manly comradeship which would transcend class barriers.[67] Henriques and Secretan, both Oxford graduates shaped by the late-Victorian years, shared connections with the Oxford and Bermondsey Boys' Club in south London, founded by John Stansfeld in 1897 as the Oxford Medical Mission.[68] The Mission, inspired by Stansfeld's evangelical links at the University of Oxford, started life in a small house in Bermondsey where free medical advice and treatment were given to the poor.[69] By the early 1900s it had moved to larger premises, with a dispensary on the ground floor and boys' club on the first.[70] Stansfeld was an inspirational figure who, through regular visits to Oxford colleges, significantly influenced many Oxford students, notably Alexander Paterson, the well-known advocate of penal reform and the rehabilitation of young offenders, who became a prison commissioner in the 1920s.[71] Paterson came into contact with Stansfeld and the Mission's work as an undergraduate, and after graduation went to live in Bermondsey as an unpaid teacher in a local elementary school. He became assistant director of the Borstal Association in 1908, and in 1911 published *Across the Bridges*, which highlighted poverty in south London and stressed the importance of religious faith as a means of reforming social conditions.[72] Paterson served in the Bermondsey Battalion during the war with many men who were former members of the Bermondsey club and was awarded the Military Cross after being wounded in action.

Paterson's reforming 'new liberalism' was grounded in boys' clubs and the settlement movement. Influenced by T. H. Green and L. T. Hobhouse, he was part of a pre-war generation of social reformers and government officials who were committed to bringing Christian and humanist values to social policy and practice.[73] Despite hostility and a great deal of 'liberal rhetoric', Paterson succeeded in introducing more compassionate values into the inter-war penal system and his approach inspired many followers. *Across the Bridges*, for example, influenced a new generation of socially aware young intellectuals such as Henriques, who described its effects as 'spellbinding' on reading it as an Oxford undergraduate.[74] Paterson also influenced and wrote the introduction to Secretan's *London below Bridges*, based on working-class life in south London, written when Secretan was warden of Oxford and Bermondsey.[75] Reviewers described it as 'suffused with imaginative sympathy' for the working-class boys who were its subject, although one thought Secretan believed so 'strongly in the virtues and code of the Public School system' that he was 'perhaps a shade over-anxious that they should all be implanted in these victims of our great industrial system', and was rather too sympathetic to their bad behaviour.[76]

James Butterworth's background was very different, although the war left a similarly strong mark on his post-war youth work.[77] He left school at 11, after his father died, to work a ten-hour day in a dye works, besides selling newspapers.[78] Butterworth struggled for an education, which he completed through part-time evening classes.[79] As he later observed: 'I have hardly yet stumbled across a boy who was more unprivileged than I was. I was a newspaper boy and knew both loneliness and privation and the rest of it. I was the eldest of five children, when my father died we were all under 12 and I think I touched the lowest rung of privation.'[80] Butterworth served as a Lancashire Fusilier, and after the war trained for the Methodist ministry in Manchester, subsequently moving to London to take over a chapel in Walworth, which became the focus for his youth work.[81] He set about developing a venue called Clubland for boys and girls, and by the 1930s had raised sufficient funds to construct a purpose-built set of buildings, including a church and a range of rooms for different club activities, which attracted national publicity.[82] Butterworth emphasised the importance of self-government, and the boys of Clubland held their own parliament, to which they could present their own bills, although not all club workers were comfortable with his youth-centred approaches.[83]

Despite differences in class background, all these writers shared a belief in the boyish 'spirit for adventure', 'natural' high spirits and the unharnessed power of masculinity.[84] Their books brim with rowdiness, vandalism, petty theft, the 'terrorising' of elderly women, bad language and riotous behaviour in youth clubs, yet are also full of sympathy for the youthful 'miscreants' they describe. Hatton described cravings for adventure and outbursts of extreme behaviour as 'thoroughly mascu-line', echoing Hall's recapitulation theory, which argued that hooligan-ism merely expressed some of the 'primitive' instincts which were 'so assertive during the period of adolescence'; Hatton attributed 'about eighty per cent' of juvenile crime in London to a spirit of adventure 'rather than to definite criminal instincts or cupidity'.[85]

Beliefs that the apparently aimless energies of young, working-class males could be channelled in the positive direction of 'useful citizenship and service to the State' were shared by others sympathetic to the boys' club movement.[86] F. W. Griffin suggested that although 'outbursts of passion or arrogance' were 'sometimes regarded as loss of control', they ought to be recognised as 'energy wrongly directed'.[87] He, too, believed the boy of 14 to 18 ought to be 'increasingly an explorer', and that the 'play and comradeship' of club life should encourage initiative and the spirit of adventure.[88] Play was 'Nature's way of preparing youngsters for the struggles of adulthood', while boys' 'instinctive sense of comrade-ship or companionship' was the 'germ of citizenship'.[89] These emphases would certainly have been shared by Victorian and Edwardian club lead-ers, but acquired a different significance in the inter-war years, as social and cultural changes and the growing influence of mass leisure activities caused many contemporaries to believe that young people were growing up too quickly. A. E. Morgan thought the 'average lad of sixteen' was happiest when at play with other boys of his own age:

> Their pastimes must give an outlet to bodily energy; they must satisfy the desire for physical expression and competitive accomplishment. The craving for friendship is strong, and the boy will devote himself to a pal, it may be on terms of equality, or according to temperament as a dominant or a subservient partner. Or again it may mingle with the lust for adventure in a gang of kindred spirits.[90]

Morgan suggested that 'among the many forces' that acted upon the growing boy, 'one of the most powerful, and one fraught with the deepest consequences for good or evil' was 'the impulse towards friendship'.[91] The *Principles and Aims* of the NABC, introduced in 1930, placed great emphasis on the 'spirit of comradeship', a 'social instinct' described as 'absolutely natural and almost universal'.[92] The best clubs were said to achieve a 'wonderful degree of sympathy and understanding', amounting to 'an Aristocracy of Comradeship'.[93] Emphases such as these owed much to pre-war public school ideals, expressed in the Bermondsey 'principle' of brothers or fratres, which it was believed was powerful enough to bridge class boundaries. The post-war years, however, gave such ideals fresh impetus, as they were inflected by the idealisation of war-time comradeship and need to 'keep the faith' with those who had fallen.[94] Secretan highlighted how pre-war 'hooligans' had faithfully served their country with a 'crowning demonstration of comradeship', which was 'one of the very few realities left in a period when wanton destruction of life was the unjustifiable price for the settlement of rather vague grievances'.[95] Butterworth described the spiritual bond which connected former boys' club members, left behind on the battle-field, with contemporary members, the 'young brothers' of those who had fallen who 'all unconsciously' forged 'strong links and ties with those who did not return'.[96]

Religious morality, new psychology and social awareness reinforced such sensitivities, combining to produce not inconsiderable sympathy for even the most anti-social of working-class young men, building on traditional sympathies for 'boyish character', which had often been understanding of even violent 'mischief-making'. A female club worker highlighted the negative side of this persisting 'manly' morality when she observed how she, unlike her male colleagues, did 'not think the boy "bright"' if he tried to 'settle his quarrels by fisticuffs'.[97] There were more positive aspects, however, as club workers were urged to empathise with their adolescent charges and appreciate what later generations would describe as their lack of self-esteem. D. S. H. emphasised the young male's strong 'need' to save face:

> Boys are extraordinarily resentful of being 'told off' ... Never give your opinion of one boy in the hearing of others, because lads are even more 'catty' than women. However unpleasant your verdict has been, and perhaps just because it has been derogatory, it will most probably be repeated, with numerous embellishments, to the miscreant himself. From then on, whatever hold you may have had over him will vanish, never to return.[98]

Club workers were very alert to the problems of 'extreme sensitiveness' and unreliability among adolescent boys, and urged that 'emotional instability' between the ages of 14 and 18 should 'be regarded as a perfectly normal phenomenon'. 'Intense jealousy' was described as being part of the street boy's make-up: 'He cares for nobody, for unconsciously he considers nobody cares for him. But he cares tremendously for himself. The slightest suggestion of unfairness brings out his temper and often is the reason he leaves his organization.'[99] Secretan advocated 'understanding and a sense of humour' in order to get the 'best out of boys' because any 'attempt to drive them' would only end up prolonging even worse behaviour.[100]

Such understanding was fed by belief in the power of a shared 'boyishness', which made some men 'naturally' attuned to young boys and their needs. The idealistic Oxbridge undergraduates who first published *The Boy* stressed the importance of 'enlightened and sympathetic teacher-comrades', and the journal's articles continued to stress the working-class boy's unfulfilled potential, the need to communicate with him at his own level.[101] They especially stressed the need not to patronise. Christian workers, for example, reflected on how quickly working-class boys recognised a 'do-gooder', criticising Jesus's gentleness as effeminate and disliking those who appeared too 'pi' (pious).[102]

Recreating comradeship

It is interesting to consider how the meanings of the emotional volatility associated with working-class boys in adolescence were accentuated after the First World War, at a time when depression and anxiety haunted many ex-soldiers, although their feelings were often left unspoken or implied. Henriques admitted that he had experienced 'what can be called a nervous breakdown' after his first battle experience on the Somme, where he was wounded in the first tank attack there in 1916.[103] 'The physical, mental and nervous exhaustion after my first experience of warfare ... still haunts me and fills me with horror.'[104] Henriques had a 'good' war, in the sense that he was 'twice mentioned in dispatches' and was awarded the Italian Silver Medal of Military Valour, acknowledgements of bravery which perhaps made it easier for him to acknowledge the immense strain he had been under. It was, as he put it, something which could not be 'publicly admitted' and would 'take years to heal', yet had helped to forge

> that curious steel-plate armour, which, as the war advanced, seemed to grow round one's heart, so that one scarcely felt the pain of sorrow.

The parting at the death of a loved one has never hurt so much since the war as it did before. The plate has remained round the heart. I think, perhaps, it has made me less sympathetic, but it has also made the sorrows of life more tolerable.[105]

Henriques's description of the war's psychic impact suggests the therapeutic implications which club involvement had for many youth workers. Butterworth referred to his experiences of the war's 'unspeakable suffering' and suggested that those who worked in clubs were 'redeemed again and again by their new found friends'.[106] The responsiveness of such working-class boys to friendliness and trust enabled men such as Butterworth 'to pick up again the thread of life, to regain a hold on reality, to believe once more in ideals and with renewed zest for revived interests, to revel afresh in the sheer joy of living'.[107] Butterworth certainly saw Clubland as a commemoration of those who had fallen, something that might become 'a practical and eternal cenotaph' if it taught that 'the Kingdom of Comradeship, if more idealistic, is more sane, whilst the Realm of Carnage is but a thousand hells let loose.'[108]

Henriques, whose work was with St George's Jewish Settlement, expressed similar sentiments. He, like Paterson, had kept in close touch with his boys' club even when at the front, where he had received such 'a huge mail every day' that there was 'hardly a detail' of club life or its members that he did not know about.[109] He later observed how 'so many of those who had become enthusiastic for club work had fallen in the war' that he felt 'there could be no finer lasting memorial of the Spirit of Service than the settlement'.[110] Secretan similarly saw the development of the boys' club movement as a memorial to members who had lost their lives during the war, a permanent reminder that there still existed in the poorest areas of the nation's cities 'the same splendid natural material' which had volunteered for London's war-time regiments.[111] For club workers such as these, the horrors of military slaughter helped to put street brawling and assault into a very different perspective:

For four weary years we poured out the best of our manhood . . . on the battlefields of half the world. Brains and characters that were meant to give a lifetime's service to the state spent all their treasure in a few short months of intensive service. To-day we suffer as a nation from the gap left by that glorious but prodigal giving. Our primary need is to make it good.[112]

Hatton mused on the symbolic qualities of his war-time experiences in the Holy Land and on the 'bitter disillusionment' which many ex-servicemen subsequently experienced, having believed that they had fought and suffered to build a new Jerusalem, to find that not only had the former comradely spirit quickly dissipated in the post-war world but also their country had let them down 'badly' and betrayed 'all its promises' to them:[113]

> Have all those dear fellows that we knew, those we laughed and played with, those with whom we shared discomfort, privation, suffering and sorrow; those who gave up all in the sweetness of their fresh young lives – have they died in vain? Or can we who were spared do some little service to prove that in us at least 'their spirit liveth for evermore'?
>
> There be memorials of wood and memorials of stone. Let us build a true memorial of the spirit. Let us help the living, for in so doing can we best pay tribute to the sacred memory of those many dear 'bad boys,' who passed over, who died in the spirit of adventure, with a *ça ne fait rien*, a jest, a smile on their lips, that we might live in Freedom.[114]

In the final chapter of *London's Bad Boys* Hatton described how he had experienced something of an epiphany in his post-war youth work, a resolution of despair by recreating the brotherhood of the war years, a masculine fellowship in which women, significantly, could not share.[115]

The desire to recreate the male comradeship of the war years undoubtedly motivated the involvement of many former veterans in the boys' club movement as an older generation of men endeavoured to redefine a manliness which had been badly compromised by war experiences.[116] The Scouts provided a similar comradely environment for many other ex-soldiers who joined the Rovers, the Scout section for older members, and worked with those who had no direct memories of the war 'in an attempt to redefine their masculinity around the campfires of Britain'.[117] The youth culture of working-class males, long characterised by the gang intimacy and bonding of adolescence, held a particular attraction for men defined not only by frequently horrific memories of war but also by intense ties of friendship.[118] Many boys' club workers seem to have invested emotionally in the working-class boys with whom they worked, psychological assumptions about adolescent males as a volatile mix of emotions in need of guidance and support perhaps having a particular resonance for men whose own emotional lives been traumatised by their war-time experiences and who found it personally and socially difficult to articulate their feelings. Michael Roper suggests that studies of the First World War have tended to emphasise the 'social ideals' of manliness at the expense of understanding how the 'emotional effects of trench warfare' were 'assimilated mentally or contained in writing'.[119] The writings of these youth organisers are powerful testimony to these neglected emotional legacies.[120]

The post-war relationships of civilian life were, of course, a pale reflection of bonds forged in the extremities of battle, particularly as far as the relationships between older and younger soldiers were concerned, as was apparent with Sergeant-Major Sam Shapton, who had 'success-fully disciplined the most unruly company of the battalion' yet was seen crying after 'digging his men out and attending the wounded', exhausted and terribly distressed 'at losing so many of his "boys"'.[121] The emotional intensity of Shapton's response and his parental identification with a particularly difficult group of young men suggest how the bravery and collective responsibility of working-class young soldiers, who might in pre-war years have been dismissed as undeserving delinquents, helped inform a re-evaluation of their potential in the 1920s.[122] As B. E. Asbury of the Chester Federation of Boys' Clubs observed:

> The War taught us that boys in their teens could be entrusted not only with authority, but with the lives of their fellow-men. During the third battle of Ypres, a relieving battalion arrived at the front line in charge of a very young officer. The young subaltern in charge of a section of the line apologised for not having everything shipshape, saying 'it's my birthday to-day.' 'How old are you?' asked the officer in charge of relief. 'Twenty-three,' was the reply. 'It must be awfully nice to live to be old like that. I'm nearly nineteen.' 'Nearly nineteen' had set off from Zillebeke Lake as the junior subaltern. They were shelled with shrapnel and gas the whole way, and 'nearly nineteen' arrived at Polygon Wood as second in command of the Battalion. He was killed the same night leading his men to a safer position. The boys of to-day possess the same qualities as 'nearly nineteen'. They have the same courage, the same ambition, the same devotion to high ideals.[123]

The willingness with which working-class battalions in particular had sacrificed themselves for the greater good of the nation was not only an important counter to eugenic concerns about breeding from inadequate 'stock', it was also a reminder not to ignore the potential that resided in even the poorest and most neglected sectors of the population. Pre-war lads' clubs workers such as Charles Russell had, of course, been sympathetic towards such boys and well aware of how channelling the 'natural and healthy' desires of Manchester's scuttling gangs could help produce the 'ideal' soldiers the nation so needed, particularly after only one in ten of the Manchester volunteers to fight in the South African war against the Boers had been passed as 'completely fit'.[124] The experiences of working-class young men as 'actual' soldiers, however, invested belief in their potential with a complex mix of both war-time memories and the 'new liberal' imperative epitomised by Paterson's sympathies, which urged that the 'spiritual and moral energies' of the poor should be recognised and redirected as part of a new model of social interaction between the classes.[125] This approach undoubtedly supported dominant class interests in a period of economic retrenchment, yet the examples discussed here also suggest how gender inflected these class emphases. The war, by intensifying fears of losing self-control, challenged the psychological resilience of many men shaped by pre-war cultural traditions which emphasised male emotions as a sign of weakness and the public expression of profound feeling as deeply unmasculine. Returning to civilian life with much unresolved anger and anxiety, the possibility of channelling the unruly 'spirit' of working-class young males into more productive outlets may have been particularly appealing to an older generation of men who were endeavouring to redefine a Victorian and Edwardian manliness badly compromised by war experiences. Popular contemporary gender stereotypes of 'aggressive' middle-class females and their 'passive' emasculated male counterparts may also have heightened the significance of young working-class masculinity among some youth workers for whom, in a period of growing sexual ambiguity, it represented a less compromised sexuality. The 'natural' physicality of the working-class male had long been an object of fascination and desire among both heterosexual and homosexual writers, as has been observed of the homoerotic appeal of working-class boys to some London social welfare reformers in the 1880s and 1890s.[126] By the 1900s, however, not only had the scandals of Oscar Wilde's sexual encounters made many contemporaries more sensitive to the sexual implications of relationships between middle-class men and working-class boys, but psychological theories of adolescence such as those by Hall were also encouraging greater professional awareness of adolescent sexuality.[127] At the same time, the 'mob violence and disorderly youth behaviour' that attended the relief of the siege of Mafeking in 1900 transformed the adolescent aggression and energy which club workers often idealised as manly vigour in the 1880s and 1890s into signs of a more dangerous masculinity.[128] The working-class boy's emotional 'volatility' and aggression were increasingly perceived as an energising source expressive of virile manliness which needed proper discipline and control to achieve their true potential.[129] The First World War and the horrors of trench warfare subsequently infused this energy and physicality with a complex commemorative significance which allowed ideas of manliness to be redefined in relation both to the quasi-heroic forms of pre-war masculinity and to the emotional sensitivities of the post-war world.[130] Discourses of the interwar boys' club movement, which became well-recognised nationally in the inter-war years, are suggestive of how work with working-class boys and young men helped to mediate these broader social anxieties and invigorate the contested manliness of an older generation of middle-class males. It is to these questions that the next chapter turns.

Notes

1   T. M. Proctor, *On My Honour: Guides and Scouts in Inter-war Britain* (Philadelphia: American Philosophical Society, 2002), pp. 89–90; J. Savage, *Teenage: The Creation of Youth, 1875–1945* (London: Chatto and Windus, 2007), pp. 185–91; J. Davis, *Youth and the Condition of Britain: Images of Adolescent Conflict* (London: Athlone Press, 1990), pp. 77–8, 81. See also S. Levsen, 'Constructing elite identities: university students, military masculinity and the consequences of the Great War in Britain and Germany', *Past and Present*, 198:1 (2008), 147–83.

2   A. Bingham, *Gender, Modernity and the Popular Press in Britain* (Oxford: Oxford University Press, 2004).

3   J. Giles, *Women, Identity and Private Life in Britain, 1900–1950* (London: Macmillan Press Ltd, 1995), p. 52; Bingham, *Gender*, pp. 242, 246, 247.

4   P. Tinkler, *Smoke Signals: Women, Smoking and Visual Culture* (Oxford and New York: Berg, 2006), p. 82.

5   Bingham, *Gender*, p. 49.

6   B. Melman, *Women and the Popular Imagination in the Twenties: Flappers and Nymphs* (New York: St. Martin's, 1988). See also S. Kingsley Kent, 'Gender reconstruction after the First World War', in H. L. Smith (ed.), *British Feminism in the Twentieth Century* (Amherst: University of Massachusetts Press, 1990).

7   Giles, *Women, Identity*, pp. 21, 33.

8   R. Bowley, chap 2, 'Amusements and entertainments', in H. Llewellyn Smith (ed.), *The New Survey of London Life and Labour*, vol. IX, *Life and Leisure*, (London: P.S. King and Son Ltd., 1935), p. 203; G. Braybon and P. Summerfield, *Out of the Cage: Women's Experiences in Two World Wars* (London: Pandora Press, 1987).

9   The Order of Woodcraft Chivalry was founded in 1916, Kibbo Kift Kindred in 1920 and the Woodcraft Folk in 1925: J. Springhall, *Youth, Empire and Society: British Youth Movement, 1883–1940* (London: Croom Helm, 1977), p. 110. See also L. W. Bruce, 'Creating a socialist scout movement: the Woodcraft Folk, 1924–1942', *History of Education*, 13:4 (1984), 299–311; D. Prynn, 'The Woodcraft Folk and the labour movement, 1925–70', *Journal of Contemporary History*, 18:1 (1983), 79–95; P. Wilkinson, 'English youth movements, 1908–30', *Journal of Contemporary History*, 4:2 (1969), 3–23.

10 Giles, *Women, Identity*, p. 21.

11 C. Haste, *Rules of Desire. Sex in Britain: World War I to the Present* (London: Chatto and Windus, 1992), pp. 61–2.

12 *Daily Mirror* (27 October 1927), p. 4.

13 S. K. Kent, *Gender and Power in Britain, 1640–1990* (London: Routledge, 1999), pp. 287–8. See also L. Doan, 'Passing fashions: reading female masculinities in the 1920s', *Feminist Studies*, 24:3 (1998), 663–700.

14 'Healthy young girls are more boyish than boys', *Daily Mail* (18 January 1921). See also *Daily Mail* (19 April 1927), cited in Doan, 'Passing fashions', pp. 672–3; Melman, *Women and the Popular Imagination*, pp. 20, 24.

15 Melman, *Women and the Popular Imagination*, pp. 1, 20, 147. Besides 745,000 dead, there were also 160,000 wounded or gassed ex-soldiers. See also E. Scarry, *The Body in Pain: The Making and Unmaking of the World* (Oxford: Oxford University Press, 1987); K. Canning, 'The body as method? Reflections on the place of the body in gender history', *Gender and History*, 11:3 (1999), 499–513.

16 S. Koven, 'Remembering and dismemberment: crippled children, wounded soldiers and the Great War in Great Britain', *American Historical Review*, 99:4 (1994), 1167–202, at p. 1189.

17 Koven, 'Remembering and dismemberment', pp. 1169–71, 1201.

18 Melman, *Women and the Popular Imagination*, p. 20.

19 C. Crossley, Review of John Neubauer, *The Fin-de-Siècle Culture of Adolescence* (New Haven, CT: Yale University Press, 1992), in *Journal of Modern History*, 67:1 (1995), pp. 115–16; P. Brendon, *Eminent Edwardians: Four Figures who Defined their Age: Northcliffe, Balfour, Pankhurst, Baden-Powell* (London: Secker and Warburg, 1979), pp. 201–2, cited in J. Richards, ' "Passing the love of women": manly love and Victorian society', in J. A. Mangan and J. Walvin (eds.), *Manliness and Morality: Middle-Class Masculinity in Britain and America 1800–1940* (Manchester: Manchester University Press, 1987), pp. 107–8.

20 *The Boy* (December 1932), p. 98.

21 For an exploration of the American boy–man, see W. Register, *The Kid of Coney Island: Fred Thompson and the Rise of American Amusements* (New York: Oxford University Press, 2003).

22 C. Carrington, *Soldier from the Wars Returning* (1965; Barnsley: Pen and Sword Books Limited, 2006), pp. 252–3.

23 Carrington, *Soldier from the Wars*, pp. 219, 259. Carrington describes how badly he wanted to identify himself 'with the lads' under his command. On leave, he escaped 'the world of subalterns and "flappers" into the life of cockney London', where he could associate with his 'true friends': p. 220.

24 *The Boy* (February 1926), pp. 13–15. He first took charge of a club in 1902.

25 Pringle was an expert investigator for the Royal Commission on the Poor Law from 1906 to 1907. Towards the end of the First World War he became chaplain to the Royal Garrison Artillery: Anne Pimlott Baker, 'Pringle, John Christian (1872–1938)', *Oxford Dictionary of National Biography* (Oxford University Press, 2004), www.oxforddnb.com/view/article/69003 (accessed 20 August 2007).

26 R. McKibbin, *Classes and Cultures: England, 1918–1951* (Oxford: Oxford University Press, 1998: 2000), pp. 216, 248. See also G. A. N. Lowndes, *The Silent Revolution: An Account of the Expansion of Public Education in England and Wales, 1896–1965* (Oxford: Oxford University Press, 1969); R. J. Selleck, *English Primary Education and the Progressives, 1914–1939* (London: Routledge and Kegan Paul, 1972).

27 *The Boy* (Autumn 1934), p. 67.

28 *Ibid.* (February 1926), p. 15.

29 J. Tosh, 'Masculinities in an industrializing society: Britain, 1800–1914', *Journal of British Studies*, 44 (2005), p. 337; A. J. Hammerton, 'The English weakness?

Gender, satire and "moral manliness" in the lower middle class, 1870–1920', in A. Kidd and D. Nicholls (eds), *Gender, Civic Culture and Consumerism: Middle-Class Identity in Britain, 1800–1940* (Manchester: Manchester University Press, 1999); A. J. Hammerton, 'Pooterism or partnership? Marriage and masculine identity in the lower middle class, 1870–1920', *Journal of British Studies*, 38 (1999), 291–321.

30 Tosh, 'Masculinities', p. 337. Boys' club leaders often drew attention to the affection in which 'their' boys held them.

31 M. Francis, 'The domestication of the male? Recent research on nineteenth and twentieth-century British masculinity', *Historical Journal*, 45:3 (2002), pp. 641, 643.

32 Tosh, 'Masculinities', p. 337.

33 See J. Springhall, 'Building character in the British boy: the attempt to extend Christian manliness to working-class adolescents, 1880–1914', in J. A. Mangan and J. Walvin (eds), *Manliness and Morality: Middle-Class Masculinity in Britain and America, 1800–1940* (Manchester: Manchester University Press, 1987).

34 J. Bourke, *Working-Class Cultures in Britain, 1890–1960: Gender, Class and Ethnicity* (London: Routledge, 1994), p. 148.

35 B. Beaven, *Leisure, Citizenship and Working-Class Men in Britain, 1850–1945* (Manchester: Manchester University Press, 2005), pp. 92–3.

36 J. Kett, *Rites of Passage: Adolescence in America, 1790 to the Present* (New York: Basic Books Inc., 1977), p. 228.

37 G. Pearson, *Hooligan: A History of Respectable Fears* (London: Macmillan, 1983), pp. 34–5, 43; Davis, *Youth and the Condition of Britain*, p. 71.

38 Pearson, *Hooligan*, pp. 34–5.

39 *The Boy* (October 1926), p. 8.

40 *Ibid.*, p. 11.

41 R. Aldrich, *A Century of Education* (Falmer: Routledge, 2002), p. 16; *The Confederate*, 3:2 (1935), p. 14.

42 J. Grant, 'A "real boy" and not a sissy: gender, childhood and masculinity, 1890–1940', *Journal of Social History*, 37:4 (2004), p. 12.

43 R. E. Muus, *Theories of Adolescence* (1962; New York: Random House, 1982), p. 27.

44 J. Springhall, *Coming of Age: Adolescence in Britain, 1860–1960* (Dublin: Gill and Macmillan, 1986), p. 29; P. Tinkler, 'Cause for concern: young women and leisure, 1930–50', *Women's History Review*, 12:2 (2003), p. 241; C. Griffin, *Representations of Youth: The Study of Youth and Adolescence in Britain and America* (Cambridge: Polity Press, 1993), p. 22; McKibbin, *Classes and Cultures*, p. 207.

45 His romantic definitions of youth also owed much to German idealism and progressive educational ideas: N. Lesko, *Act Your Age! A Cultural Construction of Adolescence* (London: Routledge, 2001), p. 51.

46 C. Dyhouse, *Girls Growing up in Late Victorian and Edwardian England* (London: Routledge and Kegan Paul, 1981), p. 122. The word 'sissy' originated in the 'boy culture' of mid-nineteenth century America. 'Real boys', unlike 'sissy boys' were viewed as naturally combative and physically capable: Grant, 'A "real boy" and not a sissy', pp. 1, 10.

47 Grant, 'A "real boy" and not a sissy', p. 3.

48 *Daily Mail* (18 January 1921) and *Daily Mail* (19 April 1927), cited in Doan, 'Passing fashions', pp. 672–3; Melman, *Women and the Popular Imagination*, pp. 20, 24.

49 Richmal Crompton, author of the *William* books, alluded to Hall's recapitulation premise when explaining the anarchic character of William, who as a boy of 11 was 'at the stage of the savage'. M. Cadogan, *Richmal Crompton: The Woman Behind Just William* (1986; London: Allen and Unwin, 2003), pp. 72–3. Many titles of the *William* books (and the name of William's gang, the Outlaws) suggest the 'bad boy' character of her 11-year-old anti-hero. See, for example R. Crompton, *William the Outlaw* (London: Newness, 1927); *William in Trouble* (London: Newness, 1927); *William the Bad* (London: Newness, 1930); *William the Pirate* (London: Newness, 1932); *William the Rebel* (London: Newness, 1933); *William the Gangster* (London: Newness, 1934). The *William* books portray generational tensions, not just between the Brown parents and their children but notably between William and his older brother Robert and sister Ethel, 'a fatuous and work-shy "flapper"', both of whom were in their late teens. Crompton, born in 1890, published twenty *William* books between 1922 and 1938. She appears to have modelled much of William's character on her outdoor-loving younger brother, Jack. Her books, translated into many different languages, never achieved the same popularity in the United States. Crompton thought this was because American youth avoided 'the William period of boyhood', leaping 'straight from the cradle to the petting party': Cadogan, *Richmal Crompton*, pp. xv, 7, 11, 82.

50 A. J. Jenkinson, *What Do Boys and Girls Read?* (London: Methuen & Co. Ltd., 1940), pp. 25, 140, 141, 159. Les and his brother Lou were *William* fans.

51 *The Boy* (July 1926), p. 2.

52 K. Boyd, *Manliness and the Boys' Story Paper in Britain: A Cultural History, 1855–1940* (Basingstoke: Palgrave Macmillan, 2003), pp. 102, 106.

53 *Ibid.*, p. 102.

54 J. Spence, 'Youth work and gender', in T. Jeffs and M. Smith (eds), *Young People, Inequality and Youth Work* (London: Macmillan, 1990), pp. 72–3.

55 Beaven, *Leisure, Citizenship*, p. 159.

56 Proctor, *On My Honour*, p. 97; I. R. Bet–El, 'Men and soldiers: British conscripts, concepts of masculinity, and the Great War', in B. Melman (ed.), *Borderlines: Genders and Identities in War and Peace, 1870–1930* (New York and London: Routledge, 1998), p. 74.

57 Pearson, *Hooligan*, p. 43.

58 *Ibid.*, pp. 40–1; J. Butterworth, *Clubland* (London: The Epworth Press, 1932), p. 22. See also S. Koven, 'From rough lads to hooligans: boy life, national culture and social reform', in A. Parker, M. Russo, D. Somer and P. Yaeger (eds), *Nationalisms and Sexualities* (New York and London: Routledge, 1992), pp. 365–91.

59 H. Secretan, *London below Bridges* (London: Geoffrey Bles,1931); S. F. Hatton, *London's Bad Boys* (London: Chapman & Hall Ltd., 1931).

60 *The Confederate*, 1:2 (February 1932), p. 14.

61 *The Boy* (December 1931), p. 79.

62 Hatton, *London's Bad Boys*, p. 202.

63 Butterworth, *Clubland*; B. L. Q. Henriques, *Club Leadership* (London: Oxford University Press, 1933).

64 F. Dawes, *A Cry from the Streets: The Boys' Club Movement in Britain from the 1850s to the Present Day* (Hove: Wayland Publishers, 1975), p. 137; *The Boy* (September 1933), p. 88.

65 W. M. Eagar, *Making Men: The History of Boys' Clubs and Related Movements in Great Britain* (London: University of London Press, 1953), p. 410.

66 Dawes, *A Cry from the Streets*, p. 42. Eton, the first public school to establish a boys' club in London, in 1880, was followed by several similarly inspired missions and boys' clubs. Public schools also contributed to the early development of boys' clubs in Birmingham: *The Confederate*, 1:2 (February 1932), p. 9; Tosh, 'Masculinities', p. 335. Some clubs introduced public school forms of organisation, such as the house system, but not all agreed with such models: *The Confederate*, 1:1 (December 1931), p. 11; *The Confederate*, 3:1 (October 1934), p. 8.

67 Koven, 'From rough lads to hooligans', p. 374.

68 Smith (ed.), *The New Survey of London Life and Labour*, vol. IX, p. 22. Henriques was at University College. Secretan was at Balliol, as was Arnold Toynbee.

69 Stansfeld earned his living as a clerk in the civil service while working evenings as a doctor among the poor in Bermondsey, where, with the support of Wycliffe Hall, an evangelical training college at Oxford, he established the Oxford Medical Mission. After working there for more than a decade, he was ordained and took parishes in Bermondsey and later St Ebbe's, Oxford, the city's poorest parish. He went to Africa as a missionary and died in the late 1930s, Rector of Spelsbury parish in Oxfordshire: *The Boy* (Winter 1939–1940), p. 115; B. Baron, *The Doctor. The Story of John Stansfeld of Oxford and Bermondsey* (London: Edward Arnold, 1952); A. Paterson, *The Doctor and the OMM* (London: Oxford Medical Mission, 1910).

70 It subsequently changed its name to the Oxford and Bermondsey Mission before becoming the Oxford and Bermondsey Boys' Club.

71 Eagar, *Making Men*, p. 383. Paterson spent his early life in Lancashire and Cheshire and first became interested in the problems of working-class boys in Manchester, influenced by the work of C. E. B. Russell: C. Smith, 'Paterson, Sir Alexander Henry (1884–1947)', *Oxford Dictionary of National Biography* (Oxford University Press, 2004), www.oxforddnb.com/view/article/35405 (accessed 24 June 2006).

72 Smith, 'Paterson'.

73 M. Nellis, review of W. J. Forsythe, *Penal Discipline, Reformatory Projects and the English Prison Commission, 1895–1939* (Exeter: University of Exeter Press, 1990), in *British Journal of Criminology*, 34:3 (1994), pp. 404–5.

74 B. L. Q. Henriques, *The Indiscretions of a Warden* (London: Methuen & Co. Ltd., 1937), p. 20. *Across the Bridges*, which stressed the importance of the relationship between religious faith and social reform, was 'recommended reading' for Eton boys who were 'preparing for confirmation': Eagar, *Making Men*, pp. 382–3.

75 Secretan was involved with the NABC. He had previously written *Unemployment among Boys* (1925) with Waldo McGillicuddy Eagar, a warden of the Oxford and Bermondsey Mission, who had also known Paterson. Secretan was Warden of the Oxford and Bermondsey Club, 1922–6: *Manchester Guardian* (28 June 1969), p. 4.

76 *The Boy* (September 1931), pp. 27, 49.

77 Butterworth, *Clubland*, p. 22.

78 *The Boy* (December 1932), pp. 98–9.

79 M. K. Smith, 'James Butterworth, Christian youth work and Clubland', *The Encyclopedia of Informal Education* (2002), at www.infed.org/thinkers/butterworth.htm (accessed January 2006).

80 *The Boy* (September 1931), p. 46.

81 Eagar, *Making Men*, pp. 374–7; Dawes, *A Cry from the Streets*, pp. 136–7.

82 Dawes, *A Cry from the Streets*, p. 137; Eagar, *Making Men*, p. 373; *The Boy* (March 1933), p. 135. It was referred to in a House of Lords Debate on the Training of the Unemployed on 28 February 1933.

83 *The Confederate*, 3:1 (1934), p. 6; *The Boy* (December 1932), p. 99.

84 Pearson, *Hooligan*, pp. 39, 41; H. S. Bryan, *The Troublesome Boy* (London: C. Arthur Pearson Ltd., 1936), pp. 30–5.

85 Hatton, *London's Bad Boys*, pp. 23, 29, 41.

86 *Ibid.*, p. 49.

87 F. W. Griffin, 'The Club Boy' (London: National Association of Boys' Clubs, n.d.), p. 9.

88 *Ibid.*, pp. 10–11.

89 *Principles and Aims of the Boys' Club Movement*, As approved by the annual conference of the National Association of Boys' Clubs assembled in July, 1930, *Boys' Club Handbook*, No. 1 (National Association of Boys' Clubs, London, repr. March 1936 and June 1938), p. 7.

90 A. E. Morgan, *Young Citizen* (Harmondsworth: Penguin, 1943), pp. 136–7.

91 Secretan, *London below Bridges*, pp. 72–3.

92 *Principles and Aims of the Boys' Club Movement*.

93 *Fourteen to Eighteen: The Critical Years of Boyhood*, Annual Report, 1930–1931 (London: National Association of Boys' Clubs, n.d.), p. 4.

94 Butterworth, *Clubland*, p. 195; Davis, *Youth and the Condition of Britain*, p. 77; Secretan, *London below Bridges*, pp. 207–8.

95 Butterworth, *Clubland*, p. 22.

96 *Ibid.*

97 *The Boy* (February 1928), p. 6.

98 *Ibid.* (October 1926), pp. 11–12,

99 *Ibid.* (March 1930), p. 77.

100 Secretan, *London below Bridges*, p. 72.

101 *The Boy* (January 1925), p. 8. *The Boy* eventually became the journal of the National Association of Boys' Clubs (NABC). It originated in two short-lived Oxbridge publications of the same name whose financial difficulties led to their absorption into the NABC in 1927. The first *Boy*, 1920–4, was started by a group of Oxford undergraduates. The Cambridge *Boy* started in May 1924, ostensibly to further the work of the League of Help, whose members worked with Homes for Working Boys in London. The editor, R. S. Tunnell, worked at Toynbee Hall. Early articles included a passionate critique of militarism entitled 'Cannon-fodder in the making', highlighting how boys were inculcated with militarism from infancy. It suggests the strong anti-militarism of the 1920s, part of a broader international movement for peace and disarmament.

102 *The Boy* (January 1925), p. 8.

103 S. McCabe, 'Henriques, Sir Basil Lucas Quixano (1890–1961), *Oxford Dictionary of National Biography* (Oxford University Press, 2004), www.oxforddnb.com/view/article/33821 (accessed 1 November 2006). See also L. L. Loewe, *Basil Henriques. A Portrait Based on his Diaries, Letters and Speeches as Collated by his Widow Rose Henriques* (London: Routledge and Kegan Paul, 1976).

104 Henriques, *Indiscretions*, pp. 119, 120.

105 Henriques, *Indiscretions*, p. 123.

106 Butterworth, *Clubland*, p. 22.

107 *Ibid.*, pp. 22–3.

108 *Ibid.*, p. 23. Many clubrooms, schools and reformatories had commemorative plaques and memorials to dead former members.

109 Henriques, *Indiscretions*, p. 125. Tammy Proctor has examined correspondence between former Scoutmasters and leaders and their patrol leaders and Scout troops: Tammy M. Proctor, '"Gone home": Boy Scouting and the writing/re-writing of the war in Britain, 1914–1920s', www.inter-disciplinary.net/ptb/wvw/wvw3/proctor%20 paper.pdf (accessed 12 January 2007).

110 Henriques, *Indiscretions*, p. 130. In 1924, a club building was established as a local war memorial at Nantymoel in the South Wales coalfield: *The Boy* (March 1933), p. 120. In the late 1920s, the Shaftesbury Boys' Club, Birkenhead acquired over six acres of playing fields as the club memorial to members who had fought or died in the war: *The Boy* (January 1929), p. 64.

111 Secretan, *London below Bridges*, p. 202. Proctor has also suggested how 'Scouts and Guides functioned as a living memorial to the fallen and as a public reminder of the resilience of youth': Proctor, *On My Honour*, p. 156.

112 Secretan, *London below Bridges*, p. 206.

113 Hatton, *London's Bad Boys*, pp. 53, 59, 202.

114 *Ibid.*, pp. 202–3.

115 Hatton served in the Middlesex Yeomanry in the First World War, when he was in Gallipoli, Salonika, Egypt, Sinai, Palestine and Syria. He described his service experiences in *The Yarn of a Yeoman* (London: Hutchinson, 1930).

116 For the impact of such memories on inter-war culture see J. Bourke, *Dismembering the Male: Men's Bodies, Britain and the Great War* (London: Reaktion Books, 1996); S. K. Kent, 'Remembering the Great War', *Journal of British Studies*, 37:1 (1998), 105–10; Nicoletta Gullace, 'White feathers and wounded men: female patriotism and the memory of the Great War', *Journal of British Studies*, 36:2 (1997), 178–206, cited in Proctor, *On my Honour*, p. 8.

117 Proctor, *On My Honour*, p. 91. The war remained an important context for many in the organised youth movement. A. P. Braddock of Birmingham University, another pre-war youth worker, introduced his address to the Annual Meeting of the Birmingham Federation of Boys' Clubs by recalling a wartime conversation he had had while on the Somme with Norman Chamberlain, about the club work he had started for newspaper boys of the City: *The Confederate*, 4:1 (June 1936), p. 7.

118 E. Leed, *No Man's Land: Combat and Identity in World War One* (Cambridge: Cambridge University Press, 1979).

119 M. Roper, 'Between manliness and masculinity: the "war generation" and the psychology of fear in Britain, 1914–1950', *Journal of British Studies*, 44:2 (2005), 343–62, at p. 345.

120 E. Jones, 'The psychology of killing: the combat experience of British soldiers during the First World War', *Journal of Contemporary History*, 41:2 (2006), 229–46, at p. 245.

121 Jones, 'The psychology of killing', p. 244, citing E. Shepherd, *A Sergeant-Major's War. From Hill 60 to the Somme* (Marlborough: The Crowood Press, 1987), p. 75.

122 For the homoerotic aspects of life on the front line, see P. Fussell, *The Great War and Modern Memory* (Oxford: Oxford University Press, 1975, 1977), especially ch. 8, 'Soldier boys', pp. 270–309.

123 *The Boy* (June 1930), p. 105.

124 A. Davies, *The Gangs of Manchester: The Story of the Scuttlers, Britain's First Youth Cult* (Preston: Milo Books, 2008), pp. 289, 299.

125 Nellis, Review of Forsythe, *Penal Discipline*, p. 405.

126 M. Houlbrook, 'Soldier heroes and rent boys: homosex, masculinities and Britishness in the Brigade of Guards, circa. 1900–1960', *Journal of British Studies*, 42 (2003), 351–88, at p. 367; Koven, 'From rough lads to hooligans'.

127 Koven, 'From rough lads to hooligans', pp. 374, 378.

128 *Ibid.*, p. 376.

129 G. S. Hall, 'A study of anger', *American Journal of Psychology*, 10 (10 April 1899), pp. 570, 589, cited in P. N. Stearns, 'Girls, boys, and emotions: redefinitions and historical change', *Journal of American History*, 80:1 (1993), 36–74, at pp. 44–5, 72.

130 Roper, 'Between manliness and masculinity', pp. 343–4.

2

Ordinary boys and masculine men

The First World War significantly compromised pre-war expectations of 'being a boy', particularly in relation to militarism and the
jingoistic expectations of youthful masculinity. Youth movements
were forced to adapt to these post-war sentiments, and non-militarised
youth bodies such as boys' clubs benefited from the anti-militaristic sentiments of the early 1920s, just as their non-military associations gave
them an advantage in the distressed areas where many such clubs were
established in the 1930s. The views of those in the inter-war boys' club
movement were nuanced in many different ways, but a strong unifying thread was the desire to reassert a particular form of manliness in a
period of social uncertainty and change. These efforts in some respects
reflected trends which were particularly pronounced in parts of the
teaching profession, where the National Association of Schoolmasters
(NAS) was very sensitive to the growing influence of women teachers,
who were seen as undermining manliness and feminising the male body
as pre-war emphases on drill gave way to less harsh forms of exercise.
Guided by ex-servicemen and physical training instructors, the NAS
urged the need for more 'male teachers to mould a new generation of
boys into "masculine men"', a mission very similar to that asserted by
the inter-war boys' club movement.[1]

The inter-war years were an important moment in the history of
boys' clubs, which, unlike the Scouts and BB, lacked centralised coordination until the mid 1920s.[2] They achieved coherence as a national
movement for the first time in 1925, with the foundation of the NABC,
and the debates and ideological emphases which attended its emergence
and conservative definitions of gender in many respects encapsulated the
shifting sands of inter-war masculinity as leading club workers endeavoured to shape a project clearly distinguished from that of other, larger
youth organisations such as the Scouts and BB, whose mass expansion in

the inter-war years has attracted much scholarly interest.[3] The boys' club movement, which entered a period of 'unprecedented' growth in the late 1920s and 1930s, has received less attention, although its conservative model of non-militarised masculinity had significant implications for the broader development of youth work in the first half of the twentieth century. Boys' clubs claimed to be particularly successful in attracting older youths in difficult working-class districts, 'many of the poorest and roughest boys' aged between 14 and 18 who 'were not amenable to other methods'.[4] They were thought to fill an important gap by working with poorer boys who were little interested in the 'schoolboy' games of the Scouts and BB and were the only large-scale inter-war youth movement whose membership was largely confined to the 'problematic' older age group of working-class young men.[5] A. E. Morgan's *Needs of Youth*, published in the late 1930s, made much of this achievement and devoted more time to boys' clubs than to any other youth organisation, describing their work, for all its 'weaknesses', as a 'vital factor in national life'.[6] Increasing emphasis on citizenship and anxieties about the nation's future, particularly during the 1930s, made ameliorative models of the sort offered by boys' clubs all the more appealing both to those developing government policy and to many business people, and the attention which Morgan (and the national media) paid to them in the 1930s suggests how warmly its model of working with underprivileged boys was received by those in positions of power and authority.

Attempts to develop a national focus and coherent set of aims for boys' clubs in the 1920s were not straightforward. Clubs were diverse and many leaders who held to their independent traditions were indifferent to or sceptical of such moves. The establishment of a national body consequently reflected the determination of a dedicated minority. One of these individuals, Waldo McGillicuddy Eagar, played an important part in the club movement's evolving national identity, becoming a well-known voice through his editorship of its national journal, *The Boy*. Eagar not only stamped his mark on the journal but remained a stalwart upholder of the distinctiveness of boys' clubs, particularly in relation to the feminising influences of the inter-war years, highlighting what he saw as their primary task in the title of his 1950s history of the club movement, *Making Men*.[7] This mission to inculcate the characteristics of normative masculinity placed great emphasis on the promotion of healthy minds and bodies, something particularly resonant in the 1920s, when the national corpus was recovering from the physical and mental ravages of war. This same determination to uphold the values of an older type of manliness acquired more sinister overtones in the 1930s when Eagar, like many other club workers, proved susceptible to the organisational success of fascist youth movements in Germany and Italy. Before examining how the national movement changed over the course of the 1920s and 1930s, however, it is necessary to place boys' clubs within the context of the broader inter-war youth movement.

The inter-war youth movement

The Scouts and Guides, by far the largest and most successful of the voluntary groups working with young people in the 1920s and 1930s, were particularly flexible in responding to the new expectations of the post-war world.[8] Indeed, so changed were their 'ideology and image' that they have been described as in many respects 'defining' inter-war youth.[9] Scouting lost much of its pre-war imperialist colouring in the inter-war period and developed a more 'streamlined, "liberal" programme' of activities which was more successful in attracting working-class members.[10] This popular 'mix of modern activities and nineteenth-century values' perhaps helped to appease many contemporary adult anxieties by mediating the troubling divide between tradition and modernity.[11] Scouts and Guides were often featured in the contemporary press and inspired numerous fictional stories in books and magazines.[12] By the late 1930s, Morgan thought it 'scarcely necessary' to describe 'in detail' the Scout movement's principles and activities 'since they were so well known'.[13]

Membership of the Scouts, and particularly the Guides, grew in the 1920s and into the early 1930s. Guiding was especially successful, not least because girls had far fewer leisure opportunities than boys. This momentum slackened during the course of the 1930s, however, as commercially based leisure activities eroded the popularity of many youth-based voluntary organisations. Retaining membership became increasingly difficult in the face of competition from the cinema and dance halls, problems exacerbated by the difficulty of attracting committed volunteers.[14] Both Scout and Guide membership began to fall back from 1933, levelling at about 200,000 after 1935. BB membership followed a similar pattern, peaking in 1934 at over 96,000.[15] Les's own membership coincided with something of a down-swing from what had been a high point in the Northampton battalion's fortunes as working-class housing in the town centre, where most companies were located, was demolished and families relocated to outlying council estates (Figure 8).[16] Turn-out at Les's club room seems to have fluctuated, and in spring 1936, he recorded going over to the fish shop with the company leader

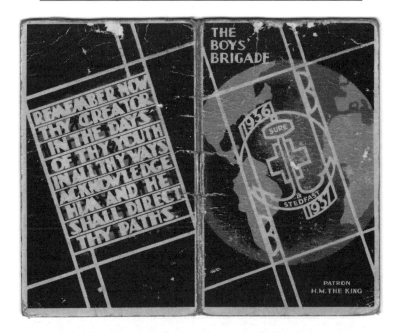

Figure 8 Les's Boys Brigade membership cards, 1936 and 1937

'and a lot more' to 'wagg a boy about leaving'. In the autumn he noted how boys were still trickling away.[17] The following year saw his BB connections loosening, as he developed new leisure interests. References to staying in bed on Sunday mornings and arriving too late to attend the BB's morning service were growing by spring and summer 1937.[18] His attendance over the autumn, until Christmas, continued to be sporadic. 'I was going to B.B. this morning, but I didn't feel like getting up so I stayed in bed all morning reading. I got up at about 2.5 p.m. & did my exercises.' 'I stayed in bed this morning & did some reading until I got up. I then did my exercises & messed about until dinnertime.' 'I stayed in bed again this morning & I did some reading & I had my breakfast in bed. I also had my dinner in bed.'

The leaders of boys' clubs thought adolescents were best left to be 'boyish' until mid-adolescence, and many looking back on their teen years in the 1920s and 1930s recalled their own immaturity at that age.[19] For a reserved boy like Les, the BB played an important part in building up his confidence, as was particularly apparent during the time he spent at the company's annual camp, a major attraction for most boys in the organised youth movement. His descriptions of three camps illustrate a growing sense of autonomy and independence. The first, a few days at Whitsun 1936, took place in the Northamptonshire countryside and comprised more childish pursuits such as a treasure hunt, 'ping pong' and 'looking for birds eggs'. A longer, annual week-long camp in August went further afield, to the seaside resort of Lowestoft.[20] This followed the usual BB pattern of Sunday 'drumhead' services, church parades and prayers, and a week-day a mix of organised and unsupervised leisure activities, which included outings to Lowestoft for trips on a pleasure steamer, speed-boat excursions to the Norfolk Broads, a visit to the pictures, tea in Woolworths, 'messing about' in camp and on the beach, playing football and wandering along the cliffs into Lowestoft with girls from the Northampton Girls' Life Brigade, only to miss the last bus back to camp.

In 1937, the long-anticipated annual camp took place at Mablethorpe, Lincolnshire, where Billy Butlin had established an amusement park in 1928.[21] Les kept the camp's information leaflets, which warned boys to be especially careful about their conduct so as not to disgrace the brigade and to 'come neat and clean and have their hair cut before attending'.[22] Les often noted washing his legs or feet, testament to the difficulties of 'personal washing' which lacked a bath or bathroom and took place in the scullery. The evening before he left, however, he noted not only having gone to the barber's for a haircut but having had 'a wash all over ready for camping' as he prepared to assume a 'new skin' on holiday, free from the usual restraints of work and family.[23]

The following day, after meeting up with friends at the station, they arrived two hours late as a result of missing the connecting train. His account of the day's events scarcely accorded with the kind of discipline which the BB expected, but conveys something of the excitement and self-consciousness of being away from home in a strange place, a sense of watching and of being watched:[24]

> Got up at about 6.15 p.m. I packed my kit bag and I got ready. Mum and Gwen [*his sister*] went to Blackpool at 8 p.m. [*sic*] and I met the boys at Castle Station at 8.10 a.m. and we went. Our train started out at 8.30 a.m. Frank and Snowy [*one of Frank's friends*] saw us off. We were supposed to arrive at Mablethorpe at 12.45 p.m. but we didn't get there until about 2.45 p.m. because we were supposed to change at Firsby but we were carried on to Skegness then we had to catch another train back and Jack Asbrey accidently pulled the communication cord and we had to wait about 10 mins. We had dinner late and we messed about until tea. After all of the boys went into the town to the fair there. Our camp was in the middle of a lot of small tents belonging to other people so we weren't on our own. Everybody could see us. We had to be in by 9.15 p.m. We went to bed tonight at about 10.15 p.m. (Saturday, 31 July 1937)

Camp in 1937 followed the same pattern of a structured Sunday and more informal events during the week, with plenty of time to lie in the sand dunes, play football and games on the beach and visit the cinema, but there was greater boldness than in the previous year, as Les and his friends broke camp rules about evening curfew and wandered further afield in search of girls (Figures 9, 10 and 11). Roll Call and Prayers at 9.30 p.m. were compulsory, with lights out at 10 p.m., but Les noted how he and a friend crept out to go for a walk on the first night and evenings were marked by visits to Butlin's Pleasure Fair. His note about having coffee and biscuits for breakfast, one of the diaries' few references to food, conveys the novelty of a very different kind of meal from that eaten at home, while hints of horse-play and the focus on 'nearly' getting off with some girls again suggest how the well-known 'liminal' delights of being away from home and at the seaside helped to disrupt and subvert the BB's expectations of disciplined behaviour.[25]

> Got up at about 7.40 a.m. After breakfast we had tent inspection and then we got ready at about 11 a.m. and we took our dinner with us to the beach to the north and we laid on the sand dunes and played foot-ball on the beach until about 3 p.m. and then us chaps we walked up to

Figure 9 Boys' Brigade camp, Mablethorpe, Lincolnshire, 1937. Les is standing second from the right.

Figure 10 Boys' Brigaders relaxing in the sands at Mablethorpe, 1937

the town and we went into the Butlin's pleasure fair. At night after tea we went down onto the beach and we played at cricket. Our side won. Went to bed at about 10.5 p.m. (Bank Holiday Monday, 2 August 1937)

Got up at about 6.40 a.m. We had coffee and biscuits and then we went down onto the beach and we played at football. Our side won

Figure 11 Group photo, Boys' Brigade camp, 1937. Diary entry, Sunday, 8 August 1937: 'Got up at about 7.35 a.m. In the morning we had tent inspection then we got ready and we went into town for a service in a Methodist church ... When we got back we had some photos took and we lazed about camp after trying to get sunburnt. In the afternoon we lazed about camp for a while and some of the boys tried to get a date for me with that girl.'

again. I fell over in some mud and dirtied my clothes all over. After tent inspection we had some games on the beach and then we had a bathing parade. In the afternoon we messed about camp. At night I went into town with the boys to the pleasure fair. I was on General Orderly today and last Sun I was on Kitchen Orderly. Bed at about 10.15 p.m. Wetty and I crept out tonight after lights out and we went for a walk. We got back at about 11 p.m. (Tuesday, 3 August 1937)

Got up at about 6.30 a.m. Had coffee and biscuits and then we went down on to the beach for football on the sands. After breakfast we had tent inspection and we then just before dinner went for a bathe. In the afternoon we messed about. At night we all went into town to the fair and there Ron Leason and I got off nearly with some girls. About 9 p.m. we had a thunderstorm and it lasted about an hour. Bed at about 10.5 p.m. (Wednesday 4 August 1937)

We went to bed at about 10.10 p.m. and then about 10.45 p.m. the 8 who stayed yesterday we crept out. The boys were Miller, B. Maris, Coles, Wetty, Leason, Asbey, Flowers and me and we met Arch, Jeff and Sid and we went along the prom for a walk and let off fireworks. We got back at about 12 p.m. (Sunday, 8 August 1937)

Given that surviving accounts usually express the viewpoint of the camp organisers, Les's descriptions offer a valuable alternative view to these more usual ones.[26] They also suggest the barriers facing those boys who did want to stay within the movement. Les's liking for his company's leisure facilities and annual camp were apparent in his attempts to stay on as he neared his 18th birthday. BB rules established that boys could remain members only until the end of the session in which they became 17, and despite his asking if he could have a year's extension, it was not granted.[27]

An unusual comparison of membership figures of the different boys' organisations in mid 1930s London by Llewellyn Smith suggests the extent to which membership was age differentiated.[28] Of the youth groups surveyed, the Scouts gave the most detailed figures, with a membership almost double that of the BB, Church Lads' Brigade and boys' clubs combined. In 1919, Baden Powell, recognising the need to cater for older boys, had established a Rovers section, which by 1928 was 'providing 30 per cent of new Scoutmasters'.[29] What was clear, however, was the extent to which Scouts and Guides catered mainly for school-children up to the age of 14, Llewellyn Smith suggesting that a third of London Scout members were aged between 14 and 18, as compared with about 'half the members of the brigades and three-quarters of the members of boys' clubs.[30] Boys' clubs, as suggested earlier, were the only movement whose membership was largely confined to the 'problematic' older age group and, despite being much smaller, were said to be almost as successful as the Scouts in working with boys aged 14 to 18.[31] Nevertheless, most Scouts were said to drop out when they reached 14 because membership was 'not regarded as being quite in keeping with the sense of grown-upness' which children felt when they left school and started work.[32] For all its flexibility and success in adapting to the new needs and challenges of the inter-war years, poorer and older working-class males had little interest in Scouting's romanticised notions of boyish innocence. *The New Survey of London Life and Labour* pointed out that membership was most popular among those who remained boys for the longest possible period, at secondary school, in apprenticeships 'or even to a certain extent in one of the clerical occupations'.[33] Scouting's 'exceedingly acute appreciation of the characteristics of pre-adolescent boyhood' made it, as Morgan suggested, 'more a schoolboy movement' than other youth organisations such as the BB:

> It appeals to the adolescent who has the imagination to see its application to the larger sphere of life and to the one who grows out of boyhood more slowly, for whom the game of make-believe is carried over into maturity. It will hold the under-developed lad and a Baden-Powell or a Robert Louis Stevenson. But the ordinary boy, caught into

the machinery of examinations if he is still at school or imbued with
an exaggerated sense of his manhood if he is at work, and in any case
a little weary after several years of Scouting, wants a change, and so he
slides out of the movement.[34]

The Scouts, Guides, Brigades and club movement as a whole, of course,
attracted only a minority of young people; perhaps one in six boys aged
between 14 and 18 belonged to any of the three movements in 1930s
London. Bryan Reed, possibly extrapolating from this figure, suggested
that only a sixth of the 14 to 18 age group in England and Wales belonged
to voluntary youth organisations in the 1930s.[35] Scouts averaged 57 per
1,000 of the boy population in London 'with fair consistency' over the
whole area, although membership was 'rather higher in the better-to-
do boroughs'. The BB, like the boys' clubs, averaged 16 per 1,000. Boys'
clubs were less successful in the more prosperous outer ring of London
boroughs, where they averaged 7 per 1,000, and were much stronger
in the poorest boroughs, averaging 33 per 1,000. BB and club members
were more likely than Scouts to be 'engaged in some form of manual
labour'.[36] Boys' clubs, less regimented and requiring neither uniform
nor overt religious affiliation, perhaps appealed most to older, poorer
boys. A north London scoutmaster pointed out that troops 'working in
slum areas of cities', faced with an ever-changing population, had only
a few members active for any lengthy period and suggested that clubs
succeeded where scouting failed, keeping their members for longer and
attracting and holding boys who were 'frightened by scouting'.[37]

One reason for boys' clubs' popularity was the fact that they
were frequently a good deal more chaotic than other organised youth
groups.[38] Club leaders were often reluctant to clamp down on members,
for fear of driving them away, and tended to channel the energies of
large numbers of boys through sports such as football, which required
few helpers, given the difficulty of keeping volunteers. Many clubs had
well-established traditions of 'engaging' with and 'sanctioning' working-
class youth culture, with workers speaking up on their members' behalf
with the police and alert to the practical problems of delinquency, unemployment and poor job prospects.[39] Club workers were, by the inter-war
years, 'increasingly ... from respectable working-class backgrounds',
and had often been members themselves. Shaped by the gender expectations of working-class life, they had little in common with the professional, middle-class young women who were becoming involved in the
girls' club movement.[40] The lofty aspirations of many leading exponents
of national organisation in London, Liverpool, Manchester and Salford

were often undermined by the individualism of club leaders at a grass-roots level whose success owed much to their own personalities. As one correspondent to *The Boy* suggested:

> Many who run clubs seem to have mistaken a desire to do such work as a call from on high rather than a liking for boys, which is frequently coupled with a belief that they are specially suited to and qualified for such work. Unfortunately, this is not necessarily the case, but it does quite often lead to a rather odious form of petty dictatorship.[41]

Such individualistic attitudes and independent traditions were a considerable obstacle to national organisation and contrasted with the history of clubs for girls, whose National Organisation of Girls' Clubs was founded before the First World War, in 1911.[42]

The National Association of Boys' Clubs

Before the NABC was established in 1925, the main connection between boys' clubs was through the federations which existed in large cities like Manchester, Liverpool, London and Birmingham, whose joint activities were largely confined to running inter-club sports and games competitions.[43] The problems which attended early attempts to develop a national focus and coherent set of aims stemmed from the diversity and independence of clubs whose origins were very varied, some having grown from church associations, others from rescue work and local philanthropy.[44] Awareness of the need to develop a collective national voice was reinforced, however, in 1916 when the Home Office established the Juvenile Organisations Committee (JOC) to deal with concerns about rising levels of juvenile delinquency, which made many club workers aware of the need for a more coherent voice when dealing with government departments.[45] Significantly, the JOC involved several individuals who had been key players in the pre-war boys' club movement, notably C. E. B. Russell (who had become Inspector of Reformatories and Industrial Schools in 1913) and C. E. Clift, JOC secretary, both of whom had experience of boys' club in Manchester.[46] Indeed, Russell had been very popular with boys at the Heyrod Street Lads' Club in Ancoats, but had been criticised by fellow workers for tending to befriend 'the more reckless lads, whilst having much less time for the "steady, reliable type"'.[47]

Several regional clubs tried to build on the strength of local federations during the war. In May 1917, for example, the Committee of the London Federation of Boys' Clubs held a 'special meeting' involving representatives from Liverpool and Manchester to discuss how to develop a national voice.[48] A fresh push for national organisation came when the war ended, particularly from enthusiasts such as Frederic George D'Aeth, Secretary of the Liverpool Union of Boys' Clubs, who was particularly keen for the Boys' Club Federations in Liverpool, Manchester, Birmingham and London to 'get together to play their part in the coming era of reconstruction'.[49] In 1920, D'Aeth was joined as secretary of the Liverpool Union by E. Jeffreys Humble, another exponent of national organisation, and in the same year Liverpool approached the National Council of Social Service, calling for a national conference of club leaders to discuss how to expand the boys' club movement. Although nothing came of the suggestion, the Liverpool Union continued to argue the cause of national organisation with individuals such as Clift, then manager of the Salford Boys' Clubs, who, in November 1923, agreed to support the idea of a national conference and the compilation of a national list of boys' clubs.[50]

Signatories to the letter of invitation to the subsequent 'National Conference of Boys' Club Men' reflected the strength of the boys' club movement in particular regions, notably Lancashire and Cheshire (Liverpool, Manchester, Birkenhead, Burnley and Salford), London, Birmingham, Nottingham and Middlesbrough.[51] This conference, at Coleshill near Birmingham in June 1924, formally resolved to establish a National Federation of Boys' Clubs and to set up a provisional committee to prepare a scheme for a national association. The group drew up a draft constitution and Lionel F. Ellis, Secretary of the National Council of Social Service, became the new organisation's honorary secretary, John Heron Eccles, another stalwart of the Liverpool movement, the chair, and C. A. Wrench of the London Federation, honorary treasurer.[52]

Minds in the London Federation at least may well have been focused favourably in the direction of national organisation at this time by what Eagar later described as an 'astonishing' approach to affiliate with the National Organisation of Girls' Clubs, which was rejected, ostensibly on the grounds of the positive progress being made nationally towards greater boys' club coordination.[53] Eagar, ever sensitive to the relationship between boys' clubs and national virility, argued that not only had the war 'emphasised the need to conserve the nation's manly vigour' but it had also left those 'who survived' with a 'tradition of robust common sense to preserve and re-establish'.

> The women had been splendid in the war period. Let them, by all means, run Girls' Clubs. Boys' Clubs were a man's job – if only because,

if anything so obvious need be argued, boys needed manly pursuits and manly ideals to complete their manhood before they thought of mating.[54]

Eagar believed boys' clubs provided training for 'all-round manhood', preparing boys to be 'Practical Idealists and Citizens of To-morrow, the Husbands of the Future and Fathers of Posterity':

> fops, fancies and fanaticisms – this queer feminism which would affiliate Boys' Clubs to Girls' Clubs Federations! It was evidently time that Boys' Clubs got together to stand for robust and wholesome boy-hood![55]

What was 'properly' described as the first NABC conference was held at Toynbee Hall in 1925, attracting an attendance of seventy-nine men and '1 woman boys' club leader, Mrs Tuke of Hereford – let her bravery be remembered!'[56] The new organisation recognised that clubs would continue as independently managed groups, but encouraged them to affiliate either directly or through local federations, aiming to provide advice and information, encourage the establishment of new clubs and raise standards by providing localised help through county associations.[57] Formally constituted on 24 October, the NABC quickly acquired a royal president in the form of Prince Henry, later the Duke of Gloucester. By 1926, it was sufficiently organised to appoint a full-time salaried secretary and to move into a new office in Bloomsbury.[58] In 1927 it acquired its own journal, *The Boy*. The first annual report in 1928 showed a membership of 715 clubs, 644 of which were affiliated through local federations or groups.

The establishment of a national body reflected the determination of a dedicated minority in the face of indifference and scepticism among many who held to the independent traditions of their local clubs. Alec Paterson rejected an invitation to chair the new national body, described in any case as 'a vain hope as he had no belief in a national association of boys' clubs'.[59] Paterson had become 'the dominant influence' in the Oxford and Bermondsey Club after Stanfeld's departure and the club was not represented at any of the NABC's early conferences. He 'strongly disapproved' of Eagar affiliating Oxford and Bermondsey to the London Federation of Boys' Clubs and Eagar, despite being club warden, attended conference as a Federation representative.[60] Nevertheless, despite initial scepticism, the number of affiliated clubs expanded rapidly in the decade after the NABC's foundation.[61] By 1939, when the Association became incorporated by Royal Charter, the number of affiliated clubs had grown to 1,670, with a total membership 'of almost exactly 160,000 boys'.[62] Hubert Llewellyn Smith's address to the national conference in 1938 commended the progress made since 1930:

> the number of affiliated clubs and their membership had doubled, the most rapid rate of increase being in the poorest areas and of boys of 14–18 years of age. The present state of the Movement was 1,545 clubs with a membership of about 143,000 boys. The 14–18 age group was and must remain the special charge of the movement.[63]

The Boy was moved to declare that the boys' club had 'proved itself to be a most successful means of catering for the post-school boy', and as such was increasingly 'recognised by magistrates, educational authorities and everyone concerned with the welfare of adolescents'.[64]

Despite such national success, clear regional differences remained and methods continued to vary so widely that it was 'difficult to reach an agreed common basis', as Eagar found when he tried to write a club handbook.[65] These difficulties convinced him of the need to draw up a set of guiding principles and aims and, despite initial resistance from the national committee, led him to form an 'informal' sub-group to draft some ideas with a fellow sympathiser, Colonel Ronald Campbell, treasurer of the London Federation of Boy's Clubs, who was also linked to the Oxford and Bermondsey Boys' Club.[66] Campbell had left the Army in 1924 to devote himself to club work and, having 'helped many shell-shocked soldiers to re-orientate themselves', was described as now 'trying to find *himself* in almost the same way'.[67] He and Eagar were subsequently joined by Lionel Ellis, Secretary of the Advisory Council for Physical Training and Recreation, and Henriques, another Oxford and Bermondsey Club associate.[68] The larger group seems to have been a less than happy mix and Eagar described the eventual emergence of the *Principles and Aims of the Boys' Club Movement*, laced with ideas of citizenship, manhood and the rational use of leisure, as bearing 'only too plainly' 'the marks of committee compromise' after 'much travail and some disagreement'.[69] Very familiar military metaphors celebrated the adoption of what subsequently became known as the 'NABC bible':[70]

> After years of trench warfare, during which there had been, it is true, amazingly brilliant personal successes too often counterbalanced by aimless and disastrous wanderings in No Man's Land, it seemed that at last the whole line was set in motion and if adequately reinforced would sweep forward to its new objective.[71]

The war played an important part in the NABC's foundation mythology.[72] Eagar, for example, stressed how the movement's 'philosophy' had been 'focused to definition' by the light the war had shed on 'human values and social duty', and took credit for their inception by emphasising how he had first started to work on a set of national aims when serving as a gunner at an observation post behind Bailleul.[73]

Continuities and change: the inter-war boy

By the 1930s, the NABC was becoming increasingly professional, with the introduction of training, the formalisation of aims and procedures and the employment of full-time workers, which did much to raise the movement's profile. As *The Boy* pointed out towards the end of the decade, 'The club-leader nowadays has a good deal of reading to do. His objectives and his technique are being thought about and written up. He has to keep abreast, or at least to know the jargon of what is becoming a craft.'[74] Drives to raise club standards generated extensive and often unpopular paper trails. Many criticised the sheer number of pamphlets being published and there were rumblings about the NABC's centralising tendencies and London focus.[75] In 1933, Jonathan Harlow of the Edgbaston Unity Club, Birmingham, highlighting the difficulties that local voluntary leaders had in attending the national conference, 'pleaded' for greater 'decentralisation' and the appointment of salaried men in the big towns to run local federations. Harlow claimed that local voluntary leaders were not 'in any way' represented on the Executive, which consisted 'almost entirely of paid leaders of large organisations, chiefly in London, who know nothing whatever of the difficulties of leaders of countless clubs up and down the country'.[76] His emphasis on the need for more attention to be paid to small clubs run by volunteers was enthusiastically endorsed by another correspondent, who criticised the NABC's tendency to become 'a meeting place for professional Club workers'.[77]

Trends towards appointing full-time workers were, however, encouraged in part by a lack of volunteers both 'competent and financially able to devote the whole of their time' to club work.[78] Getting the 'right kind of helpers' was often difficult. Many who had been around for years were described as 'well-meaning but exceedingly unhelpful', tending to regard the club 'rather as their own' and distrusting 'younger leaders with new ideas and less experience', whom they often drove to distraction, gross humiliation or 'premature resignation'. D. C. Temple, of the Shrewsbury Mission Boys' Club in Liverpool, suggested that as a 'general rule . . . one might almost lay it down that nobody above the age of forty ought to continue as a Helper in a Boys' Club'. After that age 'he should marry, settle down, pay his annual subscriptions, and leave the Club to the tender mercies of younger men'.[79] Such criticisms of what were coming to be seen as outmoded approaches reflected broader social and cultural changes. The male adolescent was widely regarded as more independent and less deferential than his pre-war equivalent, B. A. Campbell of the Peel Institute, Clerkenwell observing in the late 1920s how those 'who still worked among boys of the present generation' found a 'great contrast between the two'. The pre-war boy had worked longer hours, had smaller wages, less leisure time and fewer opportunities to spend his money. His outlook on life was different:

> He accepted the authority of his foreman, or club leader, without question. He was far less independent and more amenable to discipline. It was true, as Henry Drummond said, 'If you put a cap on his head and belt round his middle you could order him about anywhere'.[80]

The contemporary boy was a 'changed creature'. He had become insurable for both health and unemployment at the age of 16 and was eligible for trade union membership at the same age. His hours were shorter, he had more leisure opportunities and took little or no interest in jobs made more monotonous by 'the growth of repetition work in modern industry . . . He shows little desire to enter a skilled trade.'[81] Campbell believed that a 'fundamental change' had taken place in the boy's psychology and urged the importance of club managers' changing with the times, since 'What constituted a well-run Boys' Club for the pre-war type of boy would not meet the need of the boy of 1928.'[82]

> It is not long since we spoke of him as a man for military purposes at the age of 18 years. These and other causes un-named have produced in him a spirit of independence. The idea of democracy has gripped him. Most Club Managers and Scoutmasters are compelled to take him seriously. He shows a spirit of freedom unknown in the pre-war boy. Like the Pharisee of old, he asks, 'By what authority doest thou these things?' He questions authority, and asks the why and wherefore of things. He has his own views of how things should be done. He no longer blindly accepts the rulings of his club manager as correct. By taking entire charge and running a football team for one season he thinks he knows how to run a country! His critical air is apt to become annoying.[83]

The final sentence suggests the difficulties some club workers experienced dealing with members' more questioning attitudes. Every club was said to have a boy who wanted to know the whys and wherefores for every movement. 'Our natural impulse is to suppress him; he is always telling us more than we know or care to know concerning everything and everyone connected with the Club. We should not lightly suppress him; very often he is a budding investigator, and with patience and training will develop into a first-rate case worker.'[84]

Boys' own opinions of club life are difficult to discern from *The Boy*, although its pages do suggest a certain restlessness as far as the desire to become involved in the running of their own clubs was concerned. In 1932, the NABC attempted to ascertain the views of 'leading boys' by organising its first Boys' Conference in Birmingham, the first time in its history 'that boys had been called into consultation on their own welfare!'[85] A hundred members attended from Scotland, the mining districts of Wales and Durham, the industrial districts of the Midlands and the North of England and seaside resorts on the south coast to discuss topics such as the aims of a Boys' Club, the boy's part in club management and club programmes.[86] Many expressed strong desires for a much greater share in club management, but this new democracy remained very top-down, and although boys' conferences became an annual event, delegates were largely 'hand-picked', with events carefully policed by older workers.[87]

Despite steady expansion during the 1930s, there was growing sensitivity to the difficulties of retaining older members, particularly once they reached 16, a problem said to have scarcely existed before the war and which was encouraged by better education, changing social conditions and 'unlimited counter attractions' in the leisure sphere.[88] Like other youth organisations, the NABC remained very alive to the need to keep up to date to retain its membership. 'As the world changes and takes on a new orientation, so must the character of club work change in order that it may be always a little in advance of the conscious needs of the boys.'[89] This was easier said than done. The extent of 'drift' varied greatly and difficulties in estimating it were reinforced by broad definitions which included not only those who had dropped out but those who attended, yet over whom the club had 'little or no influence'.[90] Poorer districts were said to suffer less from the problem because boys with little money had fewer alternative leisure options.[91] London clubs, whose large membership was concentrated in the poorest, central, most overcrowded areas of the city, were said to be more successful in appealing to working males aged between 14 and 18 precisely because their poor members could not afford other leisure activities.[92] (London clubs tended to have more sophisticated facilities than their regional counterparts.)[93]

Manchester's three leading lads' clubs all experienced 'severe difficulties' in maintaining boys' interest in the 1930s, partly because of a failure to recognise the changing leisure interests of older young men.[94] Younger club members were more easily retained because they had less money and were more amenable to discipline. By the time they reached 17 the tendency to regard club leaders as another breed of schoolmaster had worn off and they more readily complained about club rules and being ordered about.[95] Club workers were urged to remember that a club was not a school, and that if they tried to make it one, they would lose exactly the type of lad they were most keen to help. As Bell observed, 'the working lad' was not interested in academic ways of teaching and disliked 'methods that savour of the elementary school'.[96]

Adolescent upbringing

Such views were also influenced by psychological discourses of freedom and control which represented male adolescence as a 'natural' and 'inevitable' phase characterised by 'volatility', rebellion and risk taking. Young men's malleability during adolescence was thought to make them particularly susceptible to the period's expanding consumption opportunities and expressed long-standing concerns about the feminising influence of consumption, although such fears tended to underestimate the extent to which many 'traditional' values of working-class masculinity flowed into commercialised leisure activities. Fears of feminisation reflected broader educational and psychological trends. It was not unusual, historically, for men to be abused for effeminacy, but such anxieties had taken a fresh turn towards the end of the nineteenth century as worries about encouraging incipient homosexuality reinforced concerns to instil gender identity and masculinity much earlier in childhood than had formerly been the case. By the inter-war period, the early years of childhood were increasingly stressed as an important developmental stage on the road to 'normal' adulthood, and effeminacy in young boys became a significant cause for concern in the clinical practice of American child-guidance practitioners, whose teachings were influencing professionals on both sides of the Atlantic in the 1920s. The 'new psychology' of sexologists such as Havelock Ellis warned against the dangers of the feminine qualities of the male nature becoming over-dominant.[97] The 'excessive emotion' which had acceptably expressed maternal devotion in the nineteenth century acquired 'pathological' overtones in the twentieth as the 'maternal instinct' was subordinated to the expertise of child-guidance and social welfare experts and sentimental, over-protective mothers were blamed for the emotional and sexual 'disturbances' of adult masculinity, particularly in relation to homosexuality.[98] Despite a certain blurring in the 'emotional cultures' of boys and girls in the inter-war years, clinicians emphasised the need to ensure that little boys received an appropriately masculine upbringing, and growing emphasis on companionate marriage enhanced the role of fathers, who were encouraged to become more involved in family life, particularly by harnessing their sons' restless energy.[99] A writer in the *Manchester Evening News* urged fathers to 'look after' their boys, offering six reasons why it was their responsibility to 'know' them and 'fraternise' with them.[100] Working-class families were, however, seen to more frequently fail such models of middle-class behaviour and many psychologists saw working-class boys as vulnerable to sentimental, overly protective mothers, and feckless fathers who had little influence over their adolescent sons, having been largely absent during their childhood.[101] Male youth workers consequently regarded themselves as valuable role models and saw the club as a substitute family and a manly environment in which to nurture the development of 'normal' adult masculinity.[102] Both 'feminism and femininity' threatened these manly aspirations. In 1928, for example, Miss Katharine C. Dewar, one of the few women to write in inter-war editions of *The Boy*, took up what she described as the 'burning question' of exactly what place women had in boys' clubs. Dewar, an experienced worker with girls' and women's clubs, had been the leader of a junior boys' club (ages 14 to 18), of a senior boys' club (ages 18 to 21) and of a men's club (age 21 and over). As she wrote:

> Most men would, I believe, say that a woman has a real place in a boys' club if the members are not over fourteen years of age, but that after that – well, she is usually led to understand that she should absent herself, or begin again with a new lot of little boys, or, if she must 'hang on' to the club, interest herself with the boiling of the kettle for the evening cocoa! It is a curious position to take up, and seems to me to run contrary to life itself.[103]

Dewar, an advocate of mixed clubs, was part of a generation of upper- and middle-class young women who joined voluntary organisations as a route into 'formal political life' in the inter-war years, when their commitment to greater equality with men was expressed in considerable enthusiasm for mixed youth initiatives.[104] Growing numbers of girls' clubs started to accept boys as members, but repeated approaches to the NABC on the matter were received at best lukewarmly and at worst with outright rejection. A 'strong force of conservatism' meant that many boy's club leaders' opposed the idea of mixed activities, and the debate prompted considerable disagreement within the movement, although many clubs started experimenting with occasional joint social activities, while members themselves often asked for more 'joint recreation'.[105] Younger male leaders tended to be more sympathetic to the idea, recognising the inevitability of interest in girls which, if ignored, would only result in boys' going off to find them in more unsatisfactory ways:[106] 'There will come a time when he will be torn between the Club and his girl-friend; what will the Club do for him then?'[107] In 1938, a London inquiry into what club leaders thought about having regular mixed activities with girls showed 'a large consensus of opinion' in favour, 'especially dances and socials, when suitable premises were available' and when there was a 'competent leader of both sexes'.[108] The NABC conference of the same year also gave grudging acceptance to mixed activities of a limited kind, although it remained opposed to 'mixed clubs', reflecting a belief that segregation was vital to ensure appropriate manly character formation during adolescence.[109] Henriques thought mixed clubs were 'almost certain to be a failure' for both sexes, but stressed the importance of cooperation between boys' and girls' clubs and favoured boys and girls meeting up for dances, debates, dramatics and rambles, especially after the age of 16 or 17. He advocated boys' taking their girlfriends to such dances, which he saw as an ideal opportunity for the leader to 'express his views on the loud type of girl who displays all the vulgarities of her sex. He must create a public opinion on the decencies and indecencies of female conduct, so the boys gradually get to perceive the difference.'[110]

Older attitudes continued to undermine initiatives to 'mix the sexes', and even when girls' needs were considered, those of boys continued to be seen as more important. Discussing proposals for boys and girls to share the same gymnasium, *The Boy* pointed out how 'Boys could have physical training, basket ball and boxing on three nights; girls keep-fit classes, folk dancing and net ball on two nights; and one night (Saturday) could be left free for dances, displays, concerts etc.'[111] Girls' organisations tended to be more vocal in arguing for greater mixing, concerned that girls' earlier sexual maturity made them more likely to go off in search of leisure activities involving boys.[112] Some highlighted the growing irrelevance of many girls' clubs based on traditional principles, pointing to how membership was declining in those 'run on old-fashioned lines', which did not take sufficient account of the 'present-day independent spirit'.[113] Most leaders of girls' clubs were said to favour mixed activities, and by the late 1930s the tendency for girls' clubs to make arrangements for 'introducing boys' was growing.[114] Morgan thought that boys needed clubs more than girls because they were more immature. He suggested that club life for a girl was only slightly different from her home life, 'a temporary release' or a 'happier addition' to it 'rather than another life in itself'. For a boy, it was very different, something which made a 'more engrossing claim on his enthusiasm and his time', 'a world different in kind from home life'.[115] Dewar, on the other hand, implicitly endorsed more companionate family forms in stressing the familial possibilities of a mixed environment:

> It seems to me that the only clubs which can be of any real use are those which imitate the ideal family. In the family, thank heaven, there is not this regimentation of fathers with boys only, or mothers with girls only, but a wholesome jolly mixture of both sexes, with both father and mother as leaders.[116]

Dewar's article, published, perhaps, as a sop to women's votes in 1928, fell on deaf ears and *The Boy* failed to develop her theme in subsequent issues. Eagar particularly objected to the 'dilution' of the boys' club spirit by involving girls and young women and, as we have seen, argued that boys' clubs needed to band together to oppose such feminising influences on their separate identity. Nevertheless, Dewar's views were suggestive of broader social changes. Rising living standards meant the homes of the 'deserving' working class were seen more sympathetically in the battle against popular cultural influences. Indeed, nostalgia for the working-class home grew among some club workers 'as facilities for amusement and travel' became 'ever greater and cheaper' and eroded its influence, taking 'young members of a family away from the centre around which their lives once gravitated'.[117] In the early days of the organised youth movement, the street, for all its pitfalls, was where boys were expected to experience their protracted passage to manhood, as Alexander Paterson made clear when he observed that for many boys 'every hour at home' was 'a step back'.[118] Charles Russell had similarly accepted the importance of encouraging boys' involvement in activities outside the home to stimulate manly behaviour. As he put it, the scuttler's 'real desires' were natural and healthy; the problem was that they were neither controlled nor directed 'to proper ends'.[119] In the 1920s, however, Major the Hon. E. Cadogan, MP, supporter of Eton Manor and Hoxton Manor Clubs in London, was suggesting that it 'could be justifiably argued' that a boy's 'leisure time should be dominated by his home life ... always provided his home is a reputable one'.[120] Concessions to more domesticated versions of masculinity were reflected in greater awareness of the need to prepare boys for marital responsibility and companionship rather than homosocial comradeship. Some even suggested that the aim of the boys' club movement should be to prepare boys not just for manhood but for 'parenthood, life as a whole, and death'.[121] There were limits to such new dispensation, however, and those who failed to make the transition from home to a more public sociability during adolescence were still viewed as rather inadequate. As a boys' club worker in 1931 put it, the 'home-limited boy' was 'rather like a drifting jelly-fish, very slow in developing the backbone of resistance and self-determination, the fins with which he ought deliberately to steer a course'.[122]

Health, fitness and manliness

If recognition of more domesticated models of behaviour was apparent among some club workers in the 1920s, by the 1930s growing international tension and fears of national decline led to increasing emphasis on the health and fitness of adolescents and reinforced pre-First World War ideas of manliness in some sectors of the club movement. Debates about the 'quality' of young people were invigorated by the belief that the youth population would peak in 1937. As *The Boy* observed in 1935, 'What people do not realise is that the nation is becoming more and more a middle aged and senile nation.'[123] The birth-rate, youth numbers and death-rate were all declining and an increasingly middle-aged country needed to appreciate more fully the 'value' of its children, who were so important to Britain's democratic future.[124] The juvenile population was projected to have reduced by a fifth in twenty years and by a third in forty: 'In 1968 there may be some 1,170,000 less boys and girls in the stage of matriculating into citizenship than to-day.'[125] Eagar, ever keen to impress a particular notion of manliness upon the club movement, highlighted the racial implications of a declining birth-rate:

> Certain old theories, ideas and principles are clamouring for re-admission to current controversies. Some 'modern' ideas are wearing dangerously thin under the test of indefinite extension. It is perhaps true after all that large families are the best school of character, that safety first is not the most important rule in marriage, that an exportable surplus of population is necessary for the Empire and good for the world at large ... [*sic*]. Birth control, carried beyond a certain point, may outrun its justifiers and be confessed a social and national menace ... We, who care for the growing boy, cannot disconnect ourselves from such discussions. As the number of boys decline, the importance of each boy becomes more manifest. That gives us a special opportunity and a responsibility even greater than before.[126]

Anxieties about the physical condition of British youth were also shaped by the growth of centralised youth programmes in fascist and communist Europe as the internationalist, pacifist tendencies of the previous decade gave way to growing fears of totalitarianism and militarism.[127] Working-class masculinity was once again foregrounded, leading to a renewed interest in disciplining the body, which was apparent in many lads' clubs.[128] By the mid 1930s, for example, physical training had become 'one of the main activities' of clubs in London, where several had well-equipped changing rooms and shower-baths.[129] The physical culture movement was an important 'site' for this 'reconstructed' male body, reinforcing connections between fitness, manliness and national identity.[130] *The Boy* frequently featured articles on physical fitness and many of its correspondents urged the need for greater state support. One, for example, argued that a 'lack of clearly defined purpose and direction' was 'stultifying English manhood' and, recalling Priestley, suggested that 'Modern English youth' knew nothing of the 'real England which grew from experience and was not manufactured for commercial advantage'.[131] His comments suggest the appeal of collectivist fascist and Nazi youth organisations for some workers in the club movement, where long-standing interest in the poor physical condition of many club members drew them to fascist images of strength and discipline, reinforced in press photographs and newsreels of 'monster' rallies and gymnastic displays.[132] As the correspondent continued, where English youth were only familiar with 'the arterial road with its ribbon development . . . cinemas, Woolworth stores, garages, factories, offices and shops of the 20th century', contemporary young Germans saw 'Deutchsland' as:

> a vital blood-and-soil experience retained by indelible memories of action. These young men know their fatherland and its living unity-in-diversity by remembrances of magnificent hiking forays across its length and breadth, of camps on crucial frontiers, of festivals in lovely towns . . . of weeks of toil and gaiety spent in the volunteer labour service together with young peasants and workmen, of summer months aiding dispirited farmers along the austere border territories adjoining Poland, of expeditions with gifts of song and drama to cousin peoples in Scandinavia and the British isles.[133]

Parts of the physical culture movement were similarly responsive to fascist ideology, particularly in the early 1930s, although this weakened towards the end of the decade as the physical culture press backed government initiatives to improve national efficiency, such as the 1937 Physical Training and Recreation Act and the establishment of the National Fitness Council.[134]

Admiration for German youth organisations and their more

advanced physical training methods blinded many club workers to the political implications of their enthusiasms. In 1934, the Birmingham and District Federation of Boys' Clubs described its participation in what was hoped to be the first of a series of Anglo-German labour camps, near Hamburg, where delegates stayed at a 'modern school, used for the training of Hitler Jugend'.[135] 'Discussions . . . in the woods' included National Socialism, the political situation and events in Austria, English opinion of National Socialism and the 'Hitler Jugend'. They were visited by several high-ranking German guests and articles about the camp 'appeared all over Germany'. The group subsequently travelled to Berlin, where they were 'treated as privileged guests', the 'crown' of the visit being an introduction 'to no less a person than Rudolf Hess, the deputy of Hitler'.[136]

Eagar was similarly inspired by the youth movement's expansion in Germany and Italy, with the Hitler Youth and the Italian Balilla (8 to 14) and Avanguardisti (14 to 18): 'Fascist Italy is aiming at producing men of heroic mould by classical military methods . . . Italy means her boys to be strong men, and healthy fathers.'[137] *The Boy* published several articles favourable to the German youth movement and emphasised 'the profound impression which is made on an Englishman's mind by contact with the present day youth in Germany and Italy'.[138] In 1933 a piece by a German student put what Eagar admitted was a point of view that readers would 'only take with great difficulty', by arguing that the Nazi government was 'in effect putting into force the principles of the German Youth Movement'.[139] An anonymous article entitled 'The German Youth and the Nazis' urged readers to 'try to understand the good qualities that fired the movement'.[140] Another was similarly sympathetic:

> Pacific, even pacifist as we may be, we cannot withhold our admiration from a regime which is not allowing its youth to drift, losing, as J. B. Priestley says in the passage in 'English Journey', which we are quoting on the Contents Page of this issue, losing 'the decent boyhood we gave them only to drift towards a shadowy and shiftless manhood'.[141]

Eagar believed that British boys needed similar collective ideals and models of how to demonstrate loyalty and patriotism. 'The Germans and Italians are giving their boys a concrete ideal, a challenge to be fit for their country's sake. The martial values they extol, Englishmen deprecate, hoping that if British boys are not warlike there will be no more war.' He reminded those 'concerned with boys' of their racial responsibilities: 'A boy who does not put his country before himself is in danger of putting himself before everything which has a right to his loyalty.'[142]

Eagar's views did not go unchallenged. J. J. Mallon pointed out the distortions of fascist and Nazi propagandists.[143] Secretan pointed to the dangers of mass propaganda. Others drew attention to the false premises of 'jingo patriotism':

> The spectacle of millions of youths, aflame with high ideals of service and self-sacrifice is, I admit, a dazzling one, and it tempts us too. We are apt to get weary at times of trying to instil high ideals into the minds of boys, who have been deceived from childhood with the false gods of the cinema, and the cheap press; and we long to find some easy way of obtaining our object. But I fear that the way will always be difficult and that the ideal of patriotism is as yet a short cut, which will either lead us to the wrong end, or just nowhere, according to the way we teach it.[144]

Although Eagar rejected the 'repulsive excesses' of the 'intensified nationalism abroad', he continued to laud its 'ennobling calls for service', just as others in the club movement and more generally continued to express admiration for 'the tremendous energy and direction of the Hitler Youth', much to the disgust of writers on the left, such as Harold Stovin, who in a letter published in *The Boy* lambasted the top-down approach of boys' clubs, which 'in no sense' were democratic as they claimed to be in the 'Principles and Aims'.[145] 'What is to me important', he wrote, 'is the appalling disregard of logic and reason, which pervades most philanthropic youth movements in England today, and it seems to me significant that they are largely conceived by an older generation.'[146] Boys aged 14 to 18 needed 'not *Fitness* and *Good Manners*, but more wealth, the chance of a decent education' lasting until well past adolescence and 'the freedom to follow [their] natural bent, which is only possible in a school, which has no bias except the development of its pupils.'[147] (Stovin was a schoolteacher.)[148] He condemned English youth movements generally as 'an expression of senility, of narrowness of vision and outlook, an excessively poor (and perhaps dangerous) substitute for a radical improvement in our education system'.[149] Rising to such criticism, Eagar did eventually publish an article on Soviet youth organisations by Henry Trease.[150]

Eagar was politically naïve, a fence-sitter who claimed that the boys' club movement was 'no more anti-Communist than it is anti-Fascist, or anti-Conservative. It has no politics.'[151] At the time that Eagar was printing articles in praise of fascist youth movements, Henriques was writing in *The Times* of the persecution of Jews in the East End of London and attracted a letter of support from the Durham County Association of

Boys' Clubs.[152] Rather than addressing the problem of anti-Semitism, however, Eagar used the letter to draw attention to the continuing needs of boys' clubs in the Special Areas, although he did publish a letter from the Stamford Hill Jewish Boys' Club urging fellow club leaders to 'counteract and combat this cruel and vicious propaganda . . . imported into this country from abroad, against its Jewish citizens.'[153]

The Boy continued to publish articles which held up Nazi youth work as a model for the British, failing to criticise the racist implications of its eugenicist approach and emphasis on 'racial biology'.[154] The leaders' conference in 1938 highlighted the divergence of views in the NABC as some speakers lauded the Nazi Youth movement's 'superior technique' while others pleaded 'for pacifist methods in cultivating the ideals of youth'.[155] Even with war looming, Eagar continued to promote works on German youth, noting approvingly in spring 1939 how a friend had translated Baldur von Schirach's *Manual of the Hitler Youth* into English after several requests at the previous year's conference.[156]

As Stovin inferred, boys' clubs were controlled by 'largely middle-class, middle-aged adults' whose thinking had been formed in the pre-war period when public school ideals of manliness had resonated across the organised youth movement and elementary-school system. Their model of youth behaviour, which remained in many respects grounded in largely pre-war conceptions, is a reminder of Warren's point that 'manliness was only partially destroyed' by the First World War.[157] Despite the continuing influence of older traditions, however, the boys' club movement certainly did move with the times in its methods, recognising the need to adapt and to introduce more structured, mixed programmes of activities to cater to the different interests of the 'modern' adolescent. There was also greater awareness than in the past of the need to prepare young men for their future roles in the 'private' sphere as husbands and fathers, as well as for their public responsibilities as workers and citizens.

Many involved in the movement at a national level had broader interests in boy labour, youth unemployment and the health and educational experiences of young people, and the fact that club workers often had a professional background in social and welfare work made many very sympathetic to the practical problems their young members faced. They understood the effects of poverty and chaotic everyday lives and recognised that bravado and anti-social behaviour often masked anxiety and lack of confidence. They realised the boys' need for respect, the importance of being non-judgemental, the need for structure and boundaries in young lives otherwise marked by insecurity and neglect, positive attitudes which provided an important 'counterbalance' to negative views of delinquent youth.[158]

The social welfare legislation aimed at children and young people in the 1900s had been significantly shaped by men deeply concerned with the question of how to stop 'rough lads' becoming hooligans, their views honed by extensive experience of 'rough lads' through work in the settlements and boys' clubs of south London and the East End.[159] This social agenda, inspired by 'the bonds of manly camaraderie' and ideals of masculinity, did not disappear in the inter-war years, but rather acquired a higher 'public profile' and considerable 'national recognition', particularly in the 1930s, when contemporary emphases on the 'healthy development of body, mind and spirit' reinforced connections between adolescent masculinity and national character.[160] Attempts by the boys' club movement to develop more understanding models of male adolescence were, however, strongly coloured by concerns about feminising trends and constrained by masculine assumptions about male citizenship and wage earning. The NABC continued to affirm a strongly separatist stance, and where feminists in the girls' club movement attempted to develop joint initiatives, many male workers continued to see such efforts as undermining their members' essential 'boy nature' and masculinity. Despite various grassroots initiatives to introduce mixed activities, opposition to mixed clubs remained an important characteristic of the boys' club movement. The work developed with older, poorer boys, and the value placed on informal methods and the moral, educational and physical well-being of boys nevertheless seemed particularly apposite at a time when the erosion of patriarchal, paternalistic relationships aroused considerable concern, although this vision of boyhood was already being overtaken by developments in the world of popular commercial culture. Most notable was how social interaction between the sexes was changing, with many more opportunities than before the First World War for young people to mix in leisure and in some work-places. Mixed bathing, a notable symbol of these more relaxed attitudes, was a sign of sexualising trends which were becoming increasingly visible by the late 1930s.[161]

The inter-war years saw the 'categories of "manliness" and a "proper femininity"' becoming more diluted, and liberal educational beliefs encouraging greater coalescence between girls and boys. Young people were themselves seeking greater freedom in their social relationships, and those who decided to join youth groups voted with their feet, which increasingly took them in the direction of mixed clubs of the sort pioneered by girls' club workers.[162] These were more of a model for future youth work than that offered by the boys' club movement, whose continuing emphasis on segregation destined it to be outmoded and marginalised after the Second World War.

Boys' club members had always had more pragmatic reasons for joining boys' clubs than the lofty ideals of their founders, and moves towards greater mixing were an extension of well-established patterns. As Roker and Crawford Scott observed of 'slum' boys in West Ham, the minority who did join clubs did so 'with some hope of quick material gain'.[163] Larger clubs often experienced a rush of new members at particular times of the year, with gangs 'invariably' finding their way to the club just before the start of the football season.[164] When one club leader asked members what activities they would most like to do, 'some shouted out, "Fifteen hours football."'[165] The growing popularity of mixed clubs among many boys was, not surprisingly, based on the opportunities they offered to meet girls, although the outcome of such mixing in the postwar years was not the gender equality envisaged by the female pioneers of such provision. Boys quickly came to form a majority in such postwar clubs, where, rather than encouraging greater equality, traditional gender relationships were reinforced by young men's dominance of public space, a reminder of an important distinction between the principle of mixing and actual behaviour in such clubs.[166] As the female pioneers of mixed youth work retired, their places were taken by a new generation of 'mostly salaried youth workers'. Their assumptions and models of working reinforced a masculine model of adolescence which helped to ensure that the post-war period's generic youth work would be monopolised by long-established 'male' issues such as delinquency and anti-social behaviour. These approaches marginalised not only the needs of young women but also those of quieter young men, and were not to be substantially challenged until the feminist youth initiatives of the 1970s.[167]

Notes

1 J. Bourke, *Dismembering the Male: Men's Bodies, Britain and the Great War* (London: Reaktion Books, 1996), pp. 23, 193–7.

2 The National Federation of Young Farmers' Clubs (NFYFC) was also established in the 1920s: B. Davies, *A History of the Youth Service in England*, vol. 1, *1939–1979* (Leicester: Youth Work Press, 1999), p. 17.

3 The Guides and minority youth groups which offered radical alternatives to Scouting, such as the Kibbo Kift Kindred and Woodcraft Folk, have also received much attention. See, for example, T. M. Proctor, *On My Honour: Guides and Scouts in Inter-war Britain* (Philadelphia: American Philosophical Society, 2002); T. M. Proctor, '(Uni) forming youth: girl guides and boy scouts in Britain, 1908–39', *History Workshop*

Journal, 45 (1998), 103–34, at p. 106; J. Springhall, *Sure and Stedfast: A History of the Boys' Brigade, 1883–1983* (London: Collins, 1983), p. 129; P. Wilkinson, 'English youth movements, 1908–1930', *Journal of Contemporary History*, 4:2 (1969), 3–23, at p. 7.

4   S. G. Jones, *Workers at Play: A Social and Economic History of Leisure, 1918–39* (London: Routledge and Kegan Paul, 1986), p. 68.

5   R. Bowley, 'Amusements and entertainments', in H. L. Smith (ed.), *The New Survey of London Life and Labour*, vol. IX, *Life and Leisure* (London: P.S. King and Son Ltd., 1935), pp. 144, 159.

6   A. E. Morgan, *The Needs of Youth. A Report Made to King George's Jubilee Trust Fund* (Oxford: Oxford University Press, 1939), p. 279. The NABC's annual report, 'Building for Citizenship', received extended coverage in *The Times* in 1934: *The Times* (27 August 1934).

7   The standard history of the movement is W. M. Eagar, *Making Men: The History of Boys' Clubs and Related Movements in Great Britain* (London: University of London Press, 1953). Eagar's history was subsequently extended by F. Dawes, *A Cry from the Streets. The Boys' Club Movement in Britain from the 1850s to the Present Day* (Hove: Wayland Publishers, 1975).

8   Proctor, *On My Honour*, pp. 3, 156. For youth movements in the 1920s see Wilkinson, 'English youth movements, 1908–1930'.

9   Proctor, *On My Honour*, p. 2.

10   J. Springhall, *Youth, Empire and Society: British Youth Movements, 1883–1940* (Beckenham: Croom Helm, 1977), p. 118; Proctor, '(Uni)forming youth', p. 118.

11   Proctor, *On My Honour*, pp. 3, 156.

12   Girl Guide stories were a popular feature of the *Schoolgirls' Own*: K. Drotner, 'Schoolgirls, madcaps, and air aces: English girls and their magazine reading between the wars', *Feminist Studies*, 9:1 (1983) 33–52, at p. 41.

13   Morgan, *Needs of Youth*, p. 304.

14   National Association of Boys' Clubs, *Annual Report*, 1938 (London: National Association of Boys' Clubs, 1938), p. 4.

15   Springhall, *Sure and Stedfast*, p. 129.

16   A. V. Eason, *'Remember now Thy Creator': A History of the Boys' Brigade in and around Northampton, Being a Record of its Activities in the Promotion of Christian Manliness* (Northampton: Boys' Brigade, Northampton Battalion, 1982), p. 54.

17   'Diary' (16, 23 October 1936).

18   'Diary' (31 January 1937); *ibid.* (14 March 1937); *ibid.* (4 April 1937); *ibid.* (4 April 1937); *ibid.* (30 May 1937).

19   M. Collins, *Modern Love: An Intimate History of Men and Women in Twentieth-Century Britain* (London: Atlantic Books, 2003), p. 66; The Cinema Culture in 1930s Britain Archive, T94–12, C60, 2 of 3, Transcript, p. 2.

20   Springhall, *Youth, Empire and Society*, p. 101. For a 'typical' pre-war Boys' Brigade camp, see p. 103.

21   C. Ward and D. Hardy, *Goodnight Campers! The History of the British Holiday Camp* (London and New York: Mansell Publishing Limited, 1986), pp. 60–1. Butlin opened his first holiday camp at Skegness at Easter 1936.

22   'Eighth Annual Camp, Mablethorpe, Lincolnshire, 31 July to 9 August 1937', information sheet.

23 Mass-Observation described similar preparations among working-class holiday-mak-
ers getting ready to go to Blackpool: G. Cross (ed.), *Worktowners at Blackpool: Mass-
Observation and Popular Leisure in the 1930s* (London: Routledge, 1990), pp. 56–7.

24 For the complexities of the tourist gaze, see J. Urry, *The Tourist Gaze: Leisure and
Travel in Contemporary Societies* (London: Sage Publications, 1990).

25 Liz Stanley's analysis of Mass-Observation diaries compiled during the same period
observes how rarely men referred to meals or eating: L. Stanley, 'Women have
servants, men never eat'; Walton, *The British Seaside: Holidays and Resorts in the
Twentieth Century* (Manchester: Manchester University Press, 2000), pp. 3, 5, 96–7;
R. Shields, *Places on the Margin: Alternative Geographies of Modernity* (London:
Routledge, 1991).

26 Springhall, *Youth, Empire and Society*, p. 98.

27 'Diary' (22 August 1937).

28 *The Boy* (Winter 1935–36), p. 313.

29 A. Warren, 'Popular manliness: Baden-Powell, scouting and the development of manly
character', in J. A. Mangan and James Walvin, *Manliness and Morality: Middle-Class
Masculinity in Britain and America, 1800–1940* (Manchester: Manchester University
Press, 1987), pp. 199–219, at p. 200; R. W. Connell, *Masculinities* (Cambridge: Polity
Press, 1996; 1999), p. 195; Springhall, *Youth, Empire and Society*, p. 63.

30 H.L. Smith (ed.), *The New Survey of London Life and Labour*, Vol. IX, *Life and Leisure*
(London: P. S. King & Son Ltd., Westminster, 1935), pp. 23–4. Hubert Llewellyn
Smith became chair of the Executive Council of the NABC in July 1935. His son
Harold was, with Philip (P. G.) Nash, responsible for the chapter on London clubs
and other youth organisations which was 'well vetted by several hands before it went
to the printer': *The Boy* (Winter 1935–36), p. 312. Harold was manager of the Crown
Club, Hoxton: *The Boy* (September 1932), p. 30; *ibid.* (Summer 1935), p. 200. In 1936,
1,134 Boys' Clubs with 116,815 members were affiliated to the National Association.
Of these, 82,714 were over 14, of whom 21,388 were over, 18: National Association of
Boys' Clubs, *Youth and the Future*, Annual Report, 1934–1935, pp. 4–5. In 1937, 1,400
clubs were affiliated, comprising 135,000 boys: *The Club or the Street? Training Boys
for Citizenship* (London: National Association of Boys' Clubs, 1937), p. 3. In 1938
there were 1,545 clubs with 143,000 members. Most of this increase in membership
over the previous year was in the 14–18 age group: *Annual Report* (London: National
Association of Boys' Clubs, 1938), p. 7.

31 In 1939, 76,000 boys aged 14 to 18 were in clubs affiliated to the NABC, compared with
85,900 Scouts of the same age range: Morgan, *Needs of Youth*, pp. 280–1, 304.

32 B. S. Rowntree, *Poverty and Progress: A Second Social Survey of York* (London:
Longmans, Green and Co., 1941), p. 394. By the late 1940s the Scouts 'even more than
the Brigades' were said to 'lose their members at school-leaving age': B. H. Reed,
*Eighty Thousand Adolescents: A Study of Young People in the City of Birmingham by
the Staff and Students of Westhill Training College for the Edward Cadbury Charitable
Trust* (London: George Allen & Unwin Ltd., 1950), p. 93. Those who worked with
young people often stressed the importance of getting boys to join youth organisations before they left school and before 'they reached the "high collar, short shirt and
no ambition . . ." stage of fourteen or thereabouts': *The Confederate*, 1:1 (December
1931), p. 11.

33 Smith, *New Survey*, vol. IX, p. 163. There were considerable regional variations in the class composition of membership: Proctor, '(Uni)forming youth', p. 110.

34 Morgan, *Needs of Youth*, pp. 312–13. Very little was known about young adults in the older age groups 18 to 25, whose unemployment caused 'special concern'. C. Cameron, A. Lush and G. Meara, *Disinherited Youth* (Edinburgh: Carnegie United Kingdom Trust, 1943), p. 1.

35 Reed, *Eighty Thousand Adolescents*, p. 1.

36 *The Boy* (Winter 1935–36), pp. 313–14.

37 *Ibid.* (December 1929), p. 78.

38 *Ibid.* (Summer 1937), p. 505.

39 B. Beaven, *Leisure, Citizenship and Working-Class Men in Britain, 1850–1945* (Manchester: Manchester University Press, 2005), p. 93.

40 J. Spence, 'Youth work and gender', in T. Jeffs and M. Smith (eds), *Young People, Inequality and Youth Work* (London: Macmillan, 1990), p. 72.

41 *The Boy* (June 1934), p. 35.

42 www.infed.org/archives/nayc/index.htm (accessed May 2008).

43 B. L. Q. Henriques, *The Indiscretions of a Warden* (London: Methuen & Co. Ltd., 1937), p. 277.

44 National Association of Boys' Clubs, *The Club or the Street? Training Boys for Citizenship* (London: National Association of Boys' Clubs, 1937), p. 4.

45 Similar committees were established throughout the country in 1918 and the original JOC was transferred from the Home Office to the Board of Education. These were the 'official link' between government, local education authorities and youth organisations, the only organisation to cover all juveniles, regardless of gender or religion: *The Boy* (July 1926), p. 5.

46 *The Boy* (Autumn 1938), p. 81.

47 A. Davies, *The Gangs of Manchester: The Story of the Scuttlers, Britain's First Youth Cult* (Preston: Milo Books, 2008), pp. 294–5.

48 *The Boy* (Autumn 1938), p. 81; *ibid.* (July 1929), p. 18.

49 *Ibid.* (Autumn 1938), p. 81; *ibid.* (Winter 1938–39), p. 128. The Birmingham and District Federation of Boys' Clubs was inaugurated in 1928. In 1935–36, 91 clubs were affiliated to it, with c. 9,000 members out a total Birmingham population of approximately 75,000 boys aged between 14 and, 21: Birmingham and District Federation of Boys' Clubs, Eighth Annual Report, 1935–6, for year ending 30 September 1936.

50 *The Boy* (Autumn 1938), p. 83.

51 *The Boy* (Winter 1938–39), p. 123.

52 Eccles, a well-known Liverpool business man and philanthropist, died in 1931. He had been heavily involved in the welfare of 'Liverpool working lads'. His obituary gave its highest accolade: 'He had the heart of a child and the spirit of a boy', *The Boy* (December 1931), p. 56.

53 London clubs, 'shocked by such a challenge to the essential masculinity of the Boys' Club idea', had already turned down earlier overtures to become affiliated to the London Union of Girls' Clubs. Girls' clubs developed national structures earlier than the boys' club movement, reflecting, perhaps, the influence of feminism as well as women's growing participation in voluntary activities. In the United States, the first American boys' clubs were started by women in Hartford, Connecticut, in 1860.

Women's involvement in boys' clubs deserves far greater attention: Eagar, *Making Men*, pp. 409–10; Dawes, *A Cry from the Streets*, p. 113.

54 Eagar, *Making Men*, p. 410.

55 *Ibid.*

56 *The Boy* (Winter 1938–39), p. 123.

57 A. E. Morgan, *The Young Citizen* (Harmondsworth: Penguin, 1943), p. 280.

58 By 1926 NABC membership had risen to 297 clubs, 253 affiliated through local federations.

59 *The Boy* (Winter 1938–39), p. 124.

60 Eagar, *Making Men*, p. 236.

61 Morgan, *Needs of Youth*, p. 282. In 1937 the number of clubs in Special Areas such as Durham had risen from 4 to 36 in the space of five years: *The Boy* (Autumn 1937), p. 565.

62 *The Boy* (Summer 1939), p. 9.

63 *Ibid.* (Summer 1938), p. 11.

64 *Ibid.* (Winter 1937–38), p. 616.

65 *Ibid.* (Autumn 1934), p. 64; *ibid.* (Winter 1938–39), p. 126.

66 It is difficult to tell whether their lack of sympathy reflected Eagar's own opinionated personality or the fierce independence of many club workers. *The Boy* (Winter 1938–39), p. 127; Henriques, *Indiscretions*, p. 278.

67 *The Boy* (Winter 1938–39), p. 127.

68 National Association of Boys Clubs, *Principles and Aims of the Boys' Club Movement* (London: National Association of Boys' Clubs, 1930). Available in the informal education archives: www.infed.org/archives/nabc/nabc_principles_and_aims.htm (accessed 15 October 2006).

69 The Rev. J. H. Parsons, who founded a Boys' Club in Rugby, observed that most of the committee members were ex-servicemen: *The Confederate*, 1:1 (December 1931), p. 12; *The Boy* (Winter 1938–39), p. 127.

70 Eagar, *Making Men*, p. 414.

71 *The Boy* (October 1930), p. 118.

72 National Association of Boys' Clubs, *Annual Report and Balance Sheet, 1928–9* (London: National Association of Boys' Clubs), p. 12.

73 Dawson, *A Cry from the Streets*, p. 111; Eagar, *Making Men*, pp. 415–16.

74 *The Boy* (Winter 1937–38), p. 609.

75 *Ibid.* (October 1936), p. 418.

76 *Ibid.* (June 1933), pp. 33–35, at p. 35.

77 *Ibid.* (September 1933), p. 87.

78 National Association of Boys' Clubs, *Annual Report 1938* (London: National Association of Boys' Clubs), p. 4.

79 *The Boy* (July 1929), pp. 15–16.

80 *Ibid.* (April 1928), pp. 10–12.

81 *Ibid.*, p. 11.

82 *The Boy* published several articles on psychology in the 1930s, such as 'Psychology and the club leader', *The Boy* (March 1934), pp. 163–7; *ibid.* (June 1934), pp. 7–11.

83 *Ibid.* (April 1928), p. 11.

84 *Ibid.* (February 1928), p. 15.

85 *The Confederate*, 1:3 (December 1932), p. 10.

86 National Association of Boys' Clubs, *Years of Experiment*, Annual Report, 1933–4, p. 304; *The Confederate*, 1:3 (December 1932), p. 10.

87 There are occasional glimpses of youthful dissatisfaction; a 19-year-old criticised the frequent lack of time for discussion, which was 'brought to a climax when group reports were shelved in the middle of lively debate': *The Boy* (October 1936), p. 418.

88 *The Boy* (July 1929), p.4.

89 National Association of Boys' Clubs, *Years of Experiment*.

90 *The Boy* (July 1929), p.4.

91 *Ibid.*

92 Smith, *New Survey*, vol. IX, pp. 23–4. In 1933–34, 24 per cent of the club membership in Lancashire was unemployed: National Association of Boys' Clubs, *Youth and the Future*, Annual Report 1934–1935 (London: National Association of Boys' Clubs) p. 4.

93 The scale of some London clubs seemed to be in another league. Some in the East End and south of the Thames 'would make Birmingham boys open their eyes in wonder by reason of their size, scope and management': *The Confederate*, 3:1 (October 1934), p. 6.

94 D. Fowler, *The First Teenagers. The Lifestyle of Young Wage Earners in Inter-war Britain* (London: Woburn Press, 1995), p. 142.

95 *The Boy* (July 1929), pp. 5–6.

96 *Ibid.* (September 1931), p. 42.

97 Bourke, *Dismembering*, p. 198.

98 T. Fisher, 'Fatherhood and the British fathercraft movement, 1919–39', *Gender and History*, 17:2 (2005), 441–62, at p. 452; 'To an expectant father', *National Health*, 225 (1928), p. 453, cited in Fisher, 'Fatherhood', pp. 453–4; J. Grant, 'A "real boy" and not a sissy': gender childhood and masculinity, 1890–1940', *Journal of Social History*, 37:4 (2004), p. 9.

99 A. Bingham, *Gender, Modernity and the Popular Press in Britain* (Oxford: Oxford University Press, 2004), p. 242.

100 'Fathers – look after your boys', *Manchester Evening News* (7 January 1929).

101 See L. Abrams, ' "There was nobody like my daddy": fathers, the family and the marginalisation of men in modern Scotland', *Scottish Historical Review*, 78 (1999), 218–42, at p. 228.

102 Grant, 'A "real boy" and not a sissy', p. 4.

103 *The Boy* (February 1928), p. 5.

104 Spence, 'Youth work and gender', pp. 73, 79–80.

105 *The Confederate*, 1:2 (February 1932), p. 7; Morgan, *Young Citizen*, pp. 137, 139; S. Humphries, *A Secret World of Sex: Forbidden Fruit: The British Experience, 1900–1950* (London: Sidgwick and Jackson, 1988), pp. 51–2.

106 Morgan, *Needs of Youth*, pp. 334, 339. By the mid 1930s, the NABC's Council had appointed representatives to serve with members from the National Council of Girls' Clubs on a Joint Committee to advise clubs on mixed activities for boys and girls: National Association of Boys' Clubs, *Youth and the Future*, p. 11.

107 *The Confederate*, 3:2 (June 1935), p. 14.

108 *The Boy* (Spring 1938), p. 681.

109 *Ibid.* (Summer 1938), p. 31.

110 B. L. Q. Henriques, *Club Leadership* (London: Oxford University Press, 1933, 1943), pp. 186–7.

111 *The Boy* (Winter 1937–38), p. 616.

112 Morgan, *Needs of Youth*, p. 334.

113 I. Jacobs, 'Social organisations for adolescent girls', in H. L. Smith (ed.), *The New Survey of London Life and Labour*, Vol. IX, *Life and Leisure* (London: P. S. King & Son Ltd., Westminster, 1935), pp. 200–1.

114 Morgan, *Young Citizen*, p. 139.

115 *Ibid.*, p. 138.

116 *The Boy* (February 1928), p. 6.

117 *Ibid.* (Summer 1937), p. 517.

118 Paterson, *Across the Bridges*, cited in E. Ross, *Love and Toil: Motherhood in Outcast London, 1870–1918* (New York and Oxford: Oxford University Press, 1993), pp. 153–4.

119 G. Pearson, *Hooligan: A History of Respectable Fears* (London: Macmillan, 1983), p. 57.

120 *The Boy* (August 1927), p. 4.

121 *Ibid.* (Summer 1935), p. 212.

122 F. W. Griffin, 'The Club Boy' (London: National Association of Boys' Clubs, n.d.), p. 10.

123 *The Boy* (Spring 1935), p. 151.

124 Morgan, *Needs of Youth*, p. 28.

125 *Ibid.*, pp. 1–2.

126 *The Boy* (Spring 1935), p. 151.

127 Morgan, *Needs of Youth*, pp. 1–2; J. Davis, *Youth and the Condition of Britain. Images of Adolescent Conflict* (London: Athlone Press, 1990), pp. 75–6.

128 J. Bourke, *Working-Class Cultures in Britain, 1890–1960: Gender, Class and Ethnicity* (London and New York: Routledge, 1994), pp. 42, 44.

129 P. Tinkler, *Constructing Girlhood: Popular Magazines for Girls Growing Up In England, 1920–1950* (London: Taylor and Francis, 1995), pp. 19–20; *The Confederate*, 3:2 (June 1935), p. 15.

130 I. Zweiniger-Bargielowska, 'Building a British superman: physical culture in inter-war Britain', *Journal of Contemporary History*, 41:4 (2006) 596.

131 *The Boy* (Autumn 1934), p. 61.

132 *Ibid.* (Spring 1935), pp. 150–1. The British Universities Newsreel Database (BUND) contains many such examples: *Mussolini calls to youth* (1930); *Drill for Il Duce. Italy's rising generation* (1932); *The new Germany. Hundreds of thousands of boys and girls in great demonstration of youth* (1933); *How Mussolini catches 'em young* (1935); *Russian youth keeps fit. Thousands take part in spectacular mass drill* (1935); *Mussolini reviews fascist youth* (1935); *Balilla review by King of Italy* (1936); *Hitler Youth in Italy* (1936); *Soviet youth stages parade in Red Square* (1936); *Young Italy learns art of war* (1937); *Youth rally. Huge gymnastic display in Nuremberg arena* (1938); *Hitler Jugend in Japan* (1938); *Fascist youth on parade* (1939).

133 *The Boy* (Autumn 1934), pp. 62–3.

134 Zweiniger-Bargielowska, 'Building a British superman', pp. 596, 607–8.

135 *The Confederate*, 3:1 (October 1934), pp. 13–15.

136 *Ibid.*

137 *The Boy* (June 1934), p. 11.

138 *Ibid.*

139 *Ibid.* (December 1933), pp. 105, 125–7.

140 *Ibid.* (March 1934), pp. 145, 149.

141 *Ibid.* (June 1934), pp. 2, 11–13. Priestley wrote: 'We should have bred men, thousands and thousands of strong, capable, self-respecting men, instead of a crowd of bewildered, resentful and indifferent idlers who have lost the decent boyhood we gave them only to drift towards a shadowy and shiftless manhood.'

142 *Ibid.* (June 1934), p. 5.

143 *Ibid.* (Autumn 1934), pp. 56–7.

144 *Ibid.* (Winter 1935), p. 126.

145 *Ibid.* (Summer 1935), pp. 208, 237. *The Boy* reproduced an article from *The Times* (12 February 1937), which commented favourably on 'national fitness' developments in other countries, including Germany and Italy: *The Boy* (Summer 1937), pp. 523–7.

146 H. Stovin, *Totem: The Exploitation of Youth* (London: Methuen, 1935), cited in *The Boy* (June 1936), p. 395.

147 *The Boy* (June 1936), p. 397.

148 *Ibid.* (Winter 1935–36), p. 329. Eagar encouraged club leaders to regard themselves as very different from teachers: 'The strength of the Club leader in relation to his boys is that, more than any teacher who is accustomed to deal with childhood, he knows how to "let go" ': *ibid.* (Winter 1937–38), p. 648.

149 *Ibid.* (June 1936), p. 397.

150 H. Trease, 'Boys' organisations in Soviet Russia', *The Boy* (Winter 1937–38) pp. 627–630.

151 *The Boy* (June 1934), p. 6.

152 *Ibid.* (October 1936), p. 412.

153 *Ibid.*, p. 448.

154 *Ibid.* (Autumn 1937), pp. 593–4; *ibid.* (Winter 1937–38), p. 646.

155 *Ibid.* (Summer 1938), p. 8.

156 *Ibid.* (Spring 1939), p. 163.

157 A. Warren, 'Sport, youth and gender in Britain, 1880–1940', in J. C. Binfield and J. Stevenson (eds), *Sport, Culture and Politics* (Sheffield: Sheffield Academic Press, 1993), p. 63.

158 Beaven, *Leisure, Citizenship*, p. 157.

159 S. Koven, 'From rough lads to hooligans: boy life, national culture and social reform', in A. Parker, M. Russo, D. Somer and P. Yaeger (eds), *Nationalisms and Sexualities* (New York and London, Routledge, 1992), pp. 376–7.

160 Koven, 'From rough lads to hooligans', pp. 380–3; M. Collins, *Modern Love: An Intimate History of Men and Women in Twentieth-Century Britain* (London: Atlantic Books, 2003), p. 63; Spence, 'Youth work and gender', pp. 72, 77.

161 A. Bingham, *Family Newspapers? Sex, Private Life and the British Popular Press, 1918–1978* (Oxford: Oxford University Press, 2009), p. 101.

162 Springhall, *Youth, Empire and Society*, p. 125; R. H. MacDonald, 'Reproducing the middle-class boy: from purity to patriotism in the boys' magazines, 1892–1914', *Journal of Contemporary History*, 24:3 (1989), 519–39.

163 P. Roker and H. Crawford Scott, 'Juvenile unemployment in West Ham', *Economica* (16 March 1926), 58–77, at p. 73.
164 *The Boy* (November 1927), p. 10.
165 *Ibid.* (September 1931), p. 43; Warren, 'Sport and gender in Britain', p. 61.
166 Collins, *Modern Love*, p. 84.
167 P. C. L. Heaven, *The Social Psychology of Adolescence* (London: Palgrave, 1994, 2001), p. 3. For the persistence of conservative ideas of gender in the youth club movement, and the NABC's post-war determination to maintain the masculine character boys' clubs, see E. Latham, 'The Liverpool Boys' Association and the Liverpool Union of Youth Clubs: youth organisations and gender, 1940–70', *Journal of Contemporary History*, 35:3 (2000), 423–37. Abigail Wills has highlighted the influence that a background in scouting or boys' clubs had upon many post-war youth workers: A. Wills, 'Delinquency, masculinity and citizenship in England, 1950–1970', *Past and Present*, 187 (2005), 157–85, at pp. 166–7.

3

Bodies and appearance

Battered bodies and broken spirits lived on in the memories of many who grew up in the 1920s, for the war's legacy was not only death and bereavement but also the physical debilitation of many who returned. Seventy per cent of war amputees were under 30, and the shocking visual testimony of their bodies remained a vivid recollection for many who grew up in the 1920s.[1] Oral history testimonies and autobiographical accounts of working-class childhoods from this period often dwell on the visibility of such disabled veterans, 'one-armed and one-legged old sweats', begging or selling trinkets on the streets. For some, they were an accepted part of the landscape, something which 'every boy of that day saw, but took for granted'.[2] Gorbals-raised Ralph Glasser recalled the 'young men, or rather young in years', who dragged themselves about the local tenements and streets, 'some on crutches with an empty trouser leg, or a sleeve crudely sewn up and swinging in the wind'; 'seeing them we felt guilty that our bodies were still whole'.[3] The frequently theatrical quality of such descriptions hints at their broader cultural power.[4] One of Harry Chadwick's earliest memories was of 'groups of men dressed in tattered scraps of army uniform, walking slowly down the middle of the street and singing for pennies given by sympathetic onlookers'. Again, many were on crutches, having lost a leg, or 'had an arm missing and their empty sleeve pinned up'.[5] Bernard Scott was born in Stockport in 1920. During his childhood it

> was a town of broken men; some were limbless, blind and often grotesque. All were shattered remnants of the 1914–18 trenches. These 'lads', as I shall call them, were still young, but so badly injured they couldn't do normal work. These heroes who had often volunteered to defend our shores were selling shoe laces and papers, carrying sandwich boards, or even pushing rag and bone carts. Not one or two, but scores of them ... One poor man was called 'Noddy', but not

in an unkind way. We kids did not know his real name. He was so badly shell-shocked that his whole nervous system was very seriously affected. 'Noddy' shook from head to toe; his head lolling hither and yon, hither and yon, on his shoulders. I can see him now in my memory, sitting on a cart hauled by a donkey.[6]

For children of the 1920s, like Scott, the sense of betrayal such 'broken men' embodied combined with more personal anger, in his case, 'bitterness' at how badly treated his father and brother were during the Depression years, when both found it impossible to find work.[7] To Joe Loftus, born in 1914, the war's 'slaughter' and its 'brutalizing and crippling' after-effects, 'sanctified on all sides', were 'not lost on lads like me'.[8] Neither were they on Ralph Glasser, who described one Armistice Day morning when the signal sounded for the eleven o'clock silence and 'a group of youths at the Broo' violated it by 'stamping back and forth along the pavement, filling the air with the ugly staccato of tackety boots slamming down, saying nothing. People in the street all round them, held fast in the silence, glared in shock and fury.' When the siren terminated the two minutes' silence, 'The stilled figures exploded in roars of indignation and abuse', yet for Glasser, the incident vividly recalled years later represented not disrespect but emotions unusually forced into the open by 'revulsion' at the waste and senselessness of the war.[9]

Throughout the 1920s, the male body, whose fragility had been so cruelly exposed in the war, was invested with immense symbolic significance which expressed deep cultural anxieties about the erosion of traditional masculinity.[10] Disabled bodies contested the military manliness of the pre-war world and helped to shape the broader anti-militaristic sentiments of the early 1920s, just as fears of working-class militancy informed how commemorative art publicly memorialised the fallen. The authorities were reluctant to condone public imagery which presented the working-class soldier as powerful and commanding. The sentimentalised figure of the soldier-martyr consequently embodied an unthreatening notion of pacified masculinity which both contained and denied the horrific consequences of war; simplified dichotomies of the soldier as pitiable victim and as idealised hero which also had implications for how the masculine 'authenticity' and potential of working-class boys and young men were perceived.[11] By the 1930s, this was increasingly focused on the future of the nation and the physical fitness of contemporary youth, whose collective potential when controlled and disciplined was powerfully represented in newsreel footage of youth movements in Britain and in Germany, Italy and Russia. For some in the boys' club movement, images such as these only served to highlight the perceived inadequacies of working-class boys and young men, who were enfeebled by the effects of mass commercial leisure culture. Hatton professed himself:

> a little ashamed of some of the youths of to-day who are more given to the softer delights of the cinema and the dance hall, than the more vigorous and manly sporting instincts of boxing, football and such-like pastimes. There is a definite tendency for the young man of to-day to be soft; and for effeminizing I blame the young girls to a certain extent. Woman sets the fashion and the pace for man and she unconsciously creates the type of man she desires. Does she want a knight in armour, we have the age of chivalry; does she require her man to be manly, courteous, musical, with a full-blooded taste for beauty in all things, we have the typical Elizabethan. Yes, and if all she requires is a soft-faced, mealy-mouthed, dolled-up pomaded puppet as a dancing partner and cinema attendant – we get that: and many of us itch to use the toe of our boot, but forbear, it being sheer cruelty. In some quarters a revival of good healthy, lusty masculinity is long overdue.[12]

The 'healthy lusty masculinity' of the young male body became a significant focus for notions of national identity and virile fitness throughout Europe in the inter-war years, as desires to construct an uplifting vision of youth (and national) potential reinvigorated support for the regenerative capacities of body culture. The League of Health and Strength, for example, targeted boys and young men over 14 with a model of physical exercise, temperance and chastity which had brotherhood, national strength and unity at its heart.[13] Its model of muscularity and self-control, a leitmotif of contemporary boys' clubs, was paralleled in sex education publications, where boys were urged to overcome their sexual urges through exercise and self-discipline.[14] Founded in 1906, the League was relaunched in 1919 and by the end of the 1930s had a membership of about 125,000 lower middle-class and working-class young men, who were drawn together by a weekly magazine called *Health and Strength*.[15] The League's discourse of male physicality exploited a frequently strong sense of physical inferiority among working-class boys, although its high ideals of national fitness were far removed from the pragmatic motivations of many who took up its activities, who were less concerned with its national mission and more interested in building up a body with which to show off to their peers and impress the girls. Commercial firms were well aware of the underlying sexual impulses to body-building, and young people who replied to advertisements from 'certain physical culture experts' often also received 'batches of contraceptive literature'.[16] Body-building and fitness procedures which promised self-discipline and mastery over the body revealed much about the vulnerabilities to which working-class boys and young men were often prey. 'Muscles' may have 'meant masculinity', but were difficult to achieve in nutritionally poor working-class households.[17] Many young people were certainly more healthy than they had been before the war. In the 1930s, 16-year-old boys examined for employment in the Post Office weighed on an average sixteen pounds more and were one and a half inches taller than those from a similar background twenty-five years previously; 16-year-old girls weighed on average ten pounds more and were an inch taller. Nevertheless, of every 1,000 school children examined in England and Wales in 1932, 267 had some kind of physical 'defect' that required treatment, while 115 had something which needed 'observation'. Two-thirds had dental problems. Another 1930s survey of 2,676 children in the county of Durham found that 83 per cent showed signs of rickets, as was also the case with 87 per cent of 1,638 children examined in London. In 1934, 26 per cent of children in routine school examinations were said to need 'more and better food', and the proportion returned as under-nourished would have been much higher, had conditions such as 'round shoulders, protruding bellies, easy susceptibility to fatigue, and poor muscular development' been taken into account.[18] Boys' clubs were well aware of such deficiencies. Medical inspections of members of the Oxford and St George's Boys' Club in Whitechapel revealed only 47 of 313 boys (15 per cent) to be 'free from defect'. A similar examination at the Shrewsbury House Club in Liverpool found that most (80 out of 86 boys) had health problems, ranging from the 'comparatively trivial' to serious ones likely to lead to 'grave impairment of health and possibly permanent invalidity in adult life'.[19] The health of children and young people in the distressed areas was particularly bad. Surveys of nutritional deficiencies in South Wales in the mid 1930s found many signs of the 'strain which depression and unemployment imposed', particularly during adolescence.[20]

Growing emphasis on physical perfection only accentuated individual awareness of the 'defects' which frequently humiliating medical inspections highlighted, so the embarrassment working-class boys and young men often had about their under-developed bodies is hardly surprising. Bernard Scott's brother, for example, came home on leave from the army with 'a mate, a Welsh man so self-conscious about his slimness that, to disguise his very thin legs, he wore two pairs of puttees'.[21] Self-consciousness meant that many preferred more private forms of training, and a substantial publishing field of self-help manuals and correspondence courses not only encouraged beliefs that environmental and nutritional deficiencies could be remedied by will-power, but also articulated the physical insecurities of adolescence and unwillingness to attract attention by exercising in public.[22]

The government's fitness campaigns in the 1930s to improve the health of the nation's youth were supported by many national newspapers. In 1936, for example, the *Sunday Dispatch* published a series of physical exercises and nutritional suggestions intended 'to start a campaign to make Britons the fittest people in the world'. Every young man 'with a sense of duty to himself and to his country should carry out the course'.[23] The author was a reporter training under Harold Lawrence, 'the Northamptonshire lad who became Britain's strongest youth' and whose exercises had 'transformed him from a puny lad into a record-breaking weight-lifting champion'.[24] The local connection was an additional incentive for Les, who regularly recorded in his diary the times he had done his exercises at home, and he cut out and saved details of the first work-out in the newspaper series, just as he often wrote off for fitness information. He sent postcards 'to [*Charles*] Atlas in London and another bloke in Hull' for particulars of their 'health and strength' courses, much like Max Bygraves and his friends, who 'scraped and saved to raise the half-a-crown' to send for a Charles Atlas course 'that could make us take on a Tommy Farr or Joe Lewis [*sic*], if we wanted'.[25] Les's interest owed much to his hopes of joining the police force, which had particular regulations for height and chest measurements.[26] He signed with a correspondence college in Sheffield, which had a 'specially designed' course to prepare candidates for entrance to the Metropolitan Police College, and started it in spring 1937, paying for it in monthly instalments, with his father as guarantor.[27] The tutorial system was accompanied by an advert for the 'Stebbing System', which promised a money-back guarantee if the purchaser was not taller in fourteen days.[28] Studying was difficult in a cramped household where the dining table served as desk, as Les noted on his second evening of lessons:

> Got up at about 7.25 a.m. Work. As there was no drill I got ready and went to the Savoy but when I got there the second house had gone in and people were waiting outside for odd seats so I came back home and got my lessons out and did some more work. When dad came in he started shouting at me so I packed up and went upstairs to bed without any supper at just before 11 o'clock.[29]

Nevertheless, he persevered, paying four shillings a month until at least November 1938, although the promise of the Stebbing System and his own police ambitions came to nothing, since he failed the Metropolitan

Police height regulation by half an inch, an abiding disappointment. (His National Service card recorded his height as 5 feet 7½ inches.)

Physical development through exercise also offered agency and self-help defence against the 'hard' masculinity of street life in poor neighbourhoods. Bill Naughton's enthusiasm for 'physical culture' in early adolescence came about because he thought it would help him to scare 'off opponents', because 'not a day passed without some challenge or other', and he did half an hour of press-ups and leg and abdominal exercises most evenings, based on reading *Health and Strength*.[30] In London, the Lucas-Tooth Institute, a well-endowed gymnasium, criticised how many groups of 'youngsters' who were keen on physical culture had to club together by themselves, 'often in grossly inadequate premises' and under leadership which was 'incompetent or worse'.[31] Naughton recalled how groups of boys in Bolton would rent a cellar for sixpence a week and similarly pool their resources to buy weight-lifting equipment and boxing gloves.[32] Jack Preston initiated just such a group in Salford. He had joined the League shortly after leaving school, quickly becoming a district officer with responsibility for promoting the organisation locally, and brought fellow enthusiasts together by fitting up his own small cellar at home as a gymnasium and boxing ring, for which he scrounged odd pieces of equipment and bought second-hand boxing gloves. He organised training nights and even an exhibition boxing match to which spectators were invited at twopence a time and which was so successful that he wrote to the editor of *Health and Strength*, who asked him to contribute an article about it.[33]

In the 1920s, the male body was a subject of rehabilitation, idealised and endowed with a 'hyper-masculinity' which encapsulated many male anxieties about women's growing social visibility. The sexuality of such images was contained by classical references and allusions, but by the 1930s, the growth of mass consumer culture was manipulating physical uncertainties more suggestively by marketing the perfect, muscular and invulnerable male body as a route to sexual success.[34] Adverts for Irvona, a 'nerve and body builder' (exploiting the dual spectres of mental and physical debilitation), were typically illustrated by pictures of healthy-looking women, stretching to reveal their increased bust size, juxtaposed against much smaller photos of thin, under-developed men. Headlines proclaimed, 'Men! Put on 1lb. a day as I did. Men! Don't be skinny and weak. IRVONA has given me attractive curves and a lovely rounded figure. For YOU it spells a healthy, robust body – he-man muscles and an iron constitution.'

> If you are a Skinny Man with Sunken Chest . . . Matchstick Limbs . . .
> Pale Cheeks and Weak Appearance prove NOW how 'Irvona' Brand
> Nerve and body Builder will give you A strong healthy figure, Firm,
> well-moulded limbs, A dominating presence and appearance, Great
> stamina and strength, the figure of an Apollo![35]

New words such as sunbathing, tanning, dieting and slimming reflected
the commodification of the uncovered body, as Hollywood films and
middle-class holidays to Mediterranean resorts such as the Riviera made
tanned skin a signifier of glamour and affluence as well as good health
for many young people.[36] Les, for example, recorded his efforts to get
'sunburnt' (a rather older way of describing a suntan) at his BB camp
in the mid 1930s. Health and efficiency helped to erode restrictions on
'bodily exposure', and bathing costumes for men and women became
more revealing over the course of the 1920s.[37] By the mid 1930s, open-
air pools or lidos, which helped to popularise mixed bathing among
young people, had encouraged many men to adopt the fashion of rolling
'their costumes down to their waists'.[38] It was, however, the female body
which was most conspicuously displayed and commercially exploited in
such locations, where the many opportunities for a 'sexualised masculine gaze' often resulted in a preponderance of men.[39] Lidos, like dance
halls, became a recognised space for sizing up dating possibilities, by
young men and women, although its conventions could require cautious
negotiation.[40] Many local authorities vigilantly policed the boundaries of
respectability at swimming pools, and young men particularly had to be
careful where they chose to show off fashionable swimming attire. Harry
Watkin, for example, recalled a humiliating occasion when he and a
friend wore new 'continental' style swimming costumes at the local baths
and were forced to leave by the attendant who 'hadn't seen anything like
them before' and felt sure that such 'outrageous swimwear' should be
banned, 'particularly when ladies were present'.[41] Reactions of this sort
were not unusual. In 1938, Chorley Town Council passed a resolution
condemning trunks as 'unsuitable for men' in the local swimming baths,
leading a female councillor to speak out against their 'display of prudish-
ness' which was not 'mid-Victorian' but 'prehistoric': 'Girls are allowed
to wear brassieres and trunks in our swimming bath, but men will not be.
Why? Do the Town Council think a man's body is more seductive than a
woman's?'[42] Her comments suggest the ambivalence which surrounded
the sexualised male body and sensitive distinctions between idealised
images of physical masculinity and the real male bodies of public space.
Where the sexualised female body on display in lidos and beauty contests
was acceptable because of its iconic and untouchable glamour, the barely

clothed male body in the same context was morally undesirable, quite unlike the narcissistic 'muscular' unclothed and 'heroic body', whose sexuality was neutralised by classical allusions.[43]

The spectre of broken male physicality made young male bodies a target for both national initiatives and commercial interests in the inter-war years, on the one hand for repair and improvement, on the other in ways which exploited the many physical insecurities to which working-class young men were prey. The national mission to secure the physical future of youth was reinforced by the enervating implications of commercial leisure culture, which privileged appearance and personality over the strength and 'character' associated with pre-war masculinity. Commercial advertising increasingly emphasised the importance of demonstrating physical confidence and sexual allure, and by the 1930s young people were becoming sensitised not only to how they looked physically but also to how they dressed. While these preoccupations seem to have been stronger among working-class girls and young women they also had, as we shall see, considerable resonance in the lives of their male counterparts.

Clothed bodies

The commercial leisure world of the post-war years was characterised by visceral popular music and a kinetic energy which flaunted the pleasure and vitality of healthy young limbs. The physical counterpoint to images of 'broken' young men was the free-wheeling 'anarchy' of dances like the Charleston or Black Bottom, so popular with those in their teens and twenties, whose jerking movements some saw as parodying the paroxysms of shellshock. Boys like Bernard Scott, born towards the end of the war or in the early 1920, were not of this generation. By the time they left school in the 1930s, social dancing had become much more restrained and the idea of personality, particularly as expressed through clothing and style, was becoming much more important.

Post-war marketing and leisure initiatives offered sensual gratification and salve to the senses as the fashion and cosmetics industries encouraged self-consciousness about appearance and smell.[44] By the 1920s, for example, Listerine, originally marketed as an antiseptic, was being promoted as a mouth-wash. Sensitivity to the 'problem' of body odour (and body hair) was reinforced by the greater exposure of the female body, the expansion of energetic leisure pastimes like dancing and the use of synthetic fabrics, which were easily 'ruined' by perspiration. Young women in particular were afraid of sweating, and some in the Chicago dance halls in the 1920s tried to avoid the problem of soiled dresses by wearing black.[45] 'Dinkie, 'The Dainty Deodorant' and Decoletene 'The Liquid Hair Remover' were targeted particularly at dancers, as was Ban-O-Dor, the 'Oxygen Deodorant', 'sweet as a rose', which removed 'offensive body odours' 'often unnoticeable except to others'.[46] Odo-ro-no urged young women to ask their brothers the 'truth' about perspiration odour. 'He'll probably remember many girls he'd be only too glad to take out but for this fault.' Arrid headlined its advertisements, 'Girls that Men avoid', asking readers if they realised how men talked about girls who 'offended' with 'underarm perspiration odour'.[47]

The new leisure sites and work-places which expanded opportunities for private intimacy and public display were uncharted waters for many working-class young people more used to the social codes and expectations of close family and neighbourhood, and marketing strategies did much to exploit these uncertainties. Leisure 'ailments' were 'medicalised', and residual war-time anxieties and common inhibitions about bad teeth and constipation were slyly manipulated with references to 'nameless fears', and suggestions that others could detect unpleasant body odours even when the subject did not realise there was a problem.[48] New social intimacies were said to be stalked by 'invisible enemies' such as 'halitosis', which supposedly afflicted hundreds of thousands of both sexes, the 'insidious destroyer' of social and business success, remarkable for the fact that not one in a hundred people who were 'victims' of it were aware of their 'affliction'. Adverts for breath-freshener such as 'Junifloris' targeted those with bad or false teeth, smokers ('Ladies or Gentlemen') and 'All who enter the ballroom', whose hot and sweaty environment and 'anti-social' odours so easily compromised expectations of glamour and beauty.[49]

Women were the main focus for such campaigns, but the implications of poor hygiene for young people's romantic opportunities also produced adverts targeted at boys and men. In the 1920s, Lifebuoy adverts called on mothers to introduce their sons to the Lifebuoy 'habit'. Lifebuoy was a 'manly' soap, good for character, which 'small boys' who had 'a horror of being coddled' and 'girlish nonsense' liked because 'Dad' always washed with it, and it made them 'puff out their chests with a glowing sensation of fitness, which is joy to their sturdy natures'.[50] By the 1930s Lifebuoy was appealing more directly to the body-odour predicaments of both young women and young men in adverts which encapsulated many contemporary assumptions about male and female friendship. Nora, who stayed at home and never went out to dances, suddenly became a siren after a close friend told her 'about the importance of personal freshness', three hours later cuddling up to a young man with film-star looks. Tom, unable to ever get a 'date', was transformed by his friends' sending him an anonymous letter with an advert for Lifebuoy. Six weeks later, he was pictured 'with that girl again – doesn't he look bucked with life? Yes, I'm jolly glad I put him on to Lifebuoy Toilet Soap.'[51]

These 1930s adverts often focused on the lifestyle of young office workers of both sexes. Rose's lack of promotion to become a secretary soon changed once she started to use Lifebuoy. Young men with 'pleasant manners', constantly passed over for promotion and dates, were similarly transformed:

> It's no use disguising the fact, Ralph isn't popular. At the office he doesn't make any headway. He lunches alone. Each night he sits alone reading, when actually he'd much rather be out with the other fellows. But they make it pretty plain they don't want him.
>
> So what can he do about it? Everything, if only he knew what was wrong with him – Body-Odour.
>
> A friendly hint to this young man would make all the difference – he'd thank you for telling him![52]

Where 'frumpish' young women were transformed into 'stars', once they recognised their 'problem', old-fashioned, staid males were transformed into confident office workers or deodorised young men about town, dressed in an under-stated yet stylish way, and often smoking a pipe.[53] These young men were neither sweaty not perfumed, their odourless, well-groomed image proclaiming bourgeois ideas of 'social equality' and domesticity.[54] Such 'bourgeois' good taste, contrasting with body culture's 'hyper-masculinity', owed much to 'democratised' fashion trends which, by the 1930s, were encouraging the uniformity of the lounge suit.[55] Customers of clothing multiples like Burton's and the Fifty Shilling Tailors were mainly from the 'lower middle and respectable working classes', such as 'poorer clerks and industrial labourers'.[56] Montague Burton approvingly noted in the early 1930s how 'the young miner' had abandoned the 'bell-bottomed trousers, vest with clerical opening' and blue check jacket of former years to dress 'exactly like the bank clerk', in the 'same refined designs and styles'.[57] In the Clyde shipyards, the 'roughnecks' of earlier years had been replaced by young workers whose appearance and leisure interests more closely approximated what was once associated with clerical workers, dressing well in their free time and devotees of dancing and the pictures.[58]

Male fashion sense discouraged assertions of individuality, and 'showing-off' did not have the acceptability of the unclothed body in physical culture. Male fashions, more stylised and sober than those of their female counterparts, were largely limited to hues of black, brown, navy blue and grey.[59] Convention held back even those who might have liked to be rather more adventurous, a respondent to J. P. Mayer's cinema survey suggesting that he had not been 'swayed by any star' as far as clothing was concerned, because 'men' were far more restricted in what they wore than 'girls'.[60] George Turner, on the other hand, found it difficult to say whether his fashion interests had been modelled on any particular star, but he did like Clark Gable, and was keen on borrowing fashion tips from what he saw at the cinema to try to make himself look smart, because otherwise there was no-one else to learn from.[61]

Young men who flouted 'conventional' dress codes too obviously ran the danger of being a 'dandy', although some were willing to take the risk. At Morris Radiators in Oxford, in the 1930s, being modish was wearing 'leisure' clothing to work. Arthur Exell described one of his fellow workers, a Sunday-school teacher who 'thought he was a gentle-man', 'a proper show-off', 'quite a good-looking' man with a 'little black moustache', who attended club 'dos' dressed in spats. Exell liked him, despite describing him as 'a right dandy', which suggests how hostil-ity might be diluted if individuals expressed suitably 'masculine' atti-tudes towards work as well as, perhaps, underlying admiration for young man's nerve.[62]

For most, fashion which confirmed peer-group identity was easier than individual conspicuousness.[63] Members of John Binns's local street gang in Finsbury, north London in the early 1930s sported 'special hair-cuts', the most popular of which was the 'DA' or 'duck's arse'. This 'had a little bit at the back of the hair that seemed to waggle', which was kept in trim by going regularly to the barber's every couple of weeks or so, from the age of about 16 upwards.[64] They also wore 'quite cheap' flan-nel Oxford Bags, about twenty inches across, and pointed shoes called winkle pickers. 'Fortunately I didn't wear them very often, but they're the ones that crippled you, they went right to a point.' Given that both the duck-arse haircut and winkle pickers are iconic styles associated with the Teddy Boys, whose earliest appearance would have been the mid 1950s, this particular interviewee may well have been confusing his styles. It is an example of the care with which such sources must be treated in establishing past style preferences from memory, although Richard Hoggart recalled being sent a rather 'unusual' although 'very good qual-ity' pair of 'black, glossy and very pointed shoes' from a distant relative who attended a minor Yorkshire public school. He thought they might have been for dances. 'They were hateful and if I had known the word "poncy" by then would have instantly used it. Not only did they pinch the toes, they rightly attracted vilification in the playground.'[65]

Trilbies were a favoured male fashion accessory in the 1920s, and especially in the 1930s, particularly among 'flash boys' who thought it made them look like gangsters. Dance halls were an important focus for such stylish expressions.[66] Members of Manchester's Napoo gang were distinguished by their navy blue suits, trilbies and pink neckerchiefs as they congregated at a dance hall in Belle Vue, Manchester, although such styles also enhanced the self-confidence of individuals like George Turner, who recalled feeling 'really posh' wearing his 'very smart trilby'.[67] American crime, gangster and horror movies, especially 'Hollywood's juvenile gang cycle', were much criticised in the late 1930s, when their popularity was associated with a growth in juvenile delinquency.[68] More significant, however, was the challenge such copy-cat gangland styles presented to the class-based deference of the 1930s, which allowed the wearer to assert rebelliousness, even if only 'in imagination'.[69] Gangster 'anti-heroes like James Cagney or Edward G. Robinson' appealed to the tough, competitive, individualistic traditions of boys in some working-class communities, although gangster-inspired styles could just as easily serve as camouflage for those who were not quite as tough as they thought they should be. For others who liked the pleasure of standing out from the crowd, hyper-masculine fashions with a hint of glamour were the safest option. 'Aping the gangsters' was what prompted Jim Godbold and his friends to get measured for suits out of the same light material, with dark shirts and white ties. Thus attired, they travelled to a dance in Ipswich. Returning at half time after going to the toilets, they found themselves in the spotlight, with everyone clapping and cheering because they assumed from what they were wearing that they must be members of the band. It was a swaggering moment which made a powerful impression.[70]

Sartorial exhibitionism was usually frowned on in working-class communities, however, and menswear manufacturers, and 'improper dress' signified dangerous nonconformism across society. Formal, possibly 'best' clothing dominated even on holiday. Of 100 young men whom Mass Observation counted on Blackpool promenade in the middle of the afternoon, only 18 had open necks, while 82 were wearing a collar and tie.[71] Montague Burton's sales code included proscriptions against loud colours, sporting or semi-negligée attire and soft collars.[72] Those most likely to pushing the boundaries by standing outside conventional masculinity were gay young men, particularly in large metropolitan areas such as London, where police officers often kept a close eye on what men wore, since 'smartish suits' were known to be worn by 'nancy boys'.[73] The growth of the mass market 'beauty industry' in the 1920s opened up opportunities for new forms of self-presentation to both working-class young women and gay men, enabling a blurring of social identities which was more difficult for heterosexual working-class young men, who remained very conscious of what was acceptably 'masculine'.[74] Dress 'rules' had to be negotiated very cautiously, and the desire to avoid 'ridicule and censure' curtailed the sartorial interests of many who lacked the assurance individually to transgress established male dress codes.[75] Just as the work-place traditions of heavy manufacturing and mining were intended to 'harden' boys and rein in signs of emotional weakness by bullying, mockery and fears of public humiliation, so the policing of sartorial conformity was based on similar strategies.[76] Bill Naughton recalled how approaching the Bolton street corner where he gathered with friends on summer evenings had to be done

> warily since the least sign of anything unusual would be made fun of. A haircut always invited 'pow slaps', which could be unpleasant when a few hard hands began to slap one's newly cropped head. To anyone not handy with repartee the badinage could be something of a trial, and the slow-witted had to cultivate a bellicose manner: 'Shut up afore I bloody shut thee up!'[77]

The most powerful compulsions to conformist behaviour in male fashion were usually peer groups, but older siblings could also be influential in giving young brothers the confidence to try out new styles. The most significant vector of wider cultural trends into Les's family was his middle, most fashion-conscious brother, Frank, who accompanied him to buy the trilby, gloves and tie which his parents and oldest brother bought him for Christmas 1936. Les's peers were less sympathetic to the arrival of the new trilby – as we have seen, a fashion trend popularised by American film stars – and he was greeted with laughter by some of his fellow Boys' Brigaders when he wore it to BB Bible class in the new year.[78] Nevertheless, he persevered and it became an important part of his attire when, later in the autumn, he joined the 'bunny run', also known elsewhere as the money parade or monkey-run.[79] (A transition which is explored in more detail in Chapter 5.) These names, suggestive of mischief making and sexual licence, were applied to the main streets in most towns and cities, which at weekends became sites of adolescent display and performance as groups of boys and girls strolled up and down, eyeing each other up as 'dating' possibilities. (Sunday evening was

Figure 12 Studio portrait of Les, in his new overcoat, bought for 50 shillings from the Co-op

a popular time because cinemas and dance halls were closed.) Les started to note when he had worn his fashionable head-gear, as when: 'We met Edgar & Ron & then it rained fast so I fetched my trilby & top-coat. Then Edgar & Ron & I went with two girls in the rain. They tried to get rid of me so I left them.'[80] It was not long after joining the bunny run that he acquired a new overcoat, 'a tweed colour', which cost fifty shillings on a club cheque from the Co-op (Figure 12).[81] As Les's BB mishap suggests, individuals could find following new fashion trends a perilous business if tried out in the wrong place, and tensions between the desire to fit in and the temptation to be fashionable could result in mistakes which still coloured memory many years later.[82] Where Les, lulled into a false sense of security by his older brother's self-assurance, recorded the humiliation in his diary, autobiographers looking back on their youth also recalled similar mortification, as with Harry Watkin's embarrassing ban from his local swimming baths.[83]

Since sartorial distinctiveness was still expressed very much in relation to adult models, the move from school into full-time work had particular significance for many boys. Personal reminiscences often focus on the shifts in clothing and personal appearance which attended the transitions of adolescence, both starting work and courtship.[84] Joseph Armitage, who started work in a Leeds foundry in the early 1920s, recalled feeling 'at least a year older and a foot taller' when he first started work. The most important thing was that he was 'now a worker', wearing his 'first ever pair of long trousers and heavy working boots', his schoolboy knee breeches 'discarded for ever'.[85] Joe Kay from north Manchester, who left school in the late 1920s, remembered the pleasures of leaving clogs behind once he started work: 'they were slowly going out of fashion', and few other children had worn them.[86] Charles Hansford 'waited on' bricklayers who were building a workshop in Southampton docks. It was tough work, but he was 'gratified' to go home with a 'dirty face', because returning 'clean-faced from a day's labour made one seem something less than a real man'.[87]

Acquiring the 'long trousers of manhood' was a symbolic change which often marked the beginning of a growing interest in personal appearance. Eli Hague, from the northern cotton town of Stalybridge, caught something of the pride and uncertainties of this transitional stage of adolescence. To accompany his first pair of long trousers, he combed his hair almost every time he went out and spent 'an inordinately long time in front of the mirror, gazing despondently on the rash of pimples and blackheads' which had suddenly 'afflicted' him.[88] His narrative, shaped by growing self-consciousness and interest in how he looked, suggests the tensions between private anxieties and public performance, the ages spent gazing miserably at his reflection set against memories of collective self-confidence on regular Sunday walks through the park with 'lads of his own age', looking out for girls.[89]

Poverty ensured that others remained stuck in their solitary uncertainties. Harry Watkin, who started work in the early 1920s, described how 'lonely and miserable' he was because a lack of 'reasonable' clothes prevented him from going out to enjoy himself with his pals. Everything he had was 'old, shabby and ill-fitting', but he could not ask his mother to get him something better: 'I was seventeen and longed for sociable company, for girls, for romance; yet too ashamed of my appearance to do anything about it.' When Watkin started work, his poor family expected him wear a bib-and-brace overalls over his short trousers, which 'were kept on from getting up until going to bed'. He did not acquire his first pair of trousers until he was 17, and recalled the liberating effects of obtaining new clothing, 'elated' when a workmate made him a gift of a 'collar and shirt front in white material with blue stripes'. He felt 'transformed', 'outwardly and inwardly', and when someone else gave him 'an almost new gaberdine raincoat', took full performance advantage of his new status by strolling 'up and down Stretford Road, feeling so pleased and proud'.[90]

New or 'almost new' was of immense significance for boys who had always had second-hand, or who had to put up with hand-me-downs from older brothers, and male autobiographers often dwell on the pleasure and novelty of their first 'adult' clothes in adolescence, whether their purchases were small or rather larger.[91] George Turner of Ipswich never had a 'decent suit' until he left school, and fondly recalled his first one, which his mother bought on the 'never-never' when he was about 14. She shared her son's satisfaction, feeling a 'little bit of swank' because other people could not afford one.[92] Stanley Rice described his 'joy and pride' in buying his first pair of socks and other small items of clothing, while Wallace Brereton recalled 'a pair of grey flannel trousers and a brown windjammer with one of those new zip fasteners'.[93] Ted Furniss bought his first suit when he was 17, out of the hairdressing tips he had saved.

> I'll always remember that suit, it was green and well padded to make me look a bit fatter, as I was always so slim. It was made by a friend of mine called Lawrence Yarwood, who had an upstairs room in Change Alley. He always had a good clientele but I nearly died when the suit was finished and he told me it would cost five pounds. Blimey, five pounds was a small fortune in those days and I finished up paying him three pounds down and the rest at five shillings a week. . . . I bought this suit myself, on the understanding that she would never take it to the pawnshop like all the other clothes. Mum kept her word and the green suit was always exempt from the sign of the three brass balls.[94]

Furniss's determination to maintain the boundaries between his mother and his expensive purchase suggests clothing's significance in the power negotiations of domestic life, to which boys from poorer families were particularly vulnerable. When Ralph Glasser's gambling-addicted father went behind his back to pawn his first new suit, the incident seemed symptomatic of much larger disruptions in Glasser's life.[95] He, too, was 17 and earning about thirty shillings a week, 'nearly a man's wage', when he decided 'to realise an ambition, to own a decent suit', 'skimping' and saving for nearly a year to afford the necessary 'four pounds or so'. He worked in the garment trade and was able to purchase a made-to-measure suit through a system common in many smaller garment workshops, whereby workers often collaborated to make an item of clothing for someone they knew. He consequently ended up with a 'high class suit' of the best worsted, 'charcoal grey with a delicate white stripe the width of a thread, hand stitched edges, four-button cuffs with real buttonholes. Every penny of it earned with my own hands. I was in glory.' (George Turner was another adolescent who took an obvious interest in the quality of his suit's material.[96]) The detail was significant. While ostentatious dress might have been problematic, etiquette manuals pointed out how it was in the 'small trifles' that the well-dressed man could most 'easily' be detected.[97] On the first occasion Glasser went to wear his suit, however, he opened the clothes cupboard where it was stored, only to find that it had gone. The suit's pawning seemed to symbolise the depths to which his family had sunk since his mother's death several years earlier, a betrayal 'so traumatic, so unbelievable' that the 'shock' remained with him for years. The pawn ticket his father gave him 'was a kind of farewell, a renunciation, a seal on the past and the future, for me the end of that infinite optimism of childhood and youth when all things were malleable, all mistakes could be put right.'[98] When Watkin 'irretrievably' lost his new suit to the pawnshop in 1920s Manchester, the results were less shocking, but just as seared in the memory. In his case it meant a return to 'shabby, ill-fitting clothes' which excluded him from the leisure activities of his contemporaries and proclaimed to the world his poverty and failure.[99] He was so embarrassed by his appearance that he left his course at 'Tech' because it was impossible to remain 'inconspicuous' among throngs of 'smartly-dressed young people with their leather cases and rolled drawings'. The final straw came when one of the lecturers laughed at him for wearing his grandfather's 'cut-down' trousers.[100]

'A new suit and smart clothes' belonged to success, as was apparent among migrant workers returning to their home localities, who announced their achievements by what they wore on their arrival.[101] Clothing's significance as a sign of 'status and wage-earning capacity' grew rather than diminished as working-class young men entered their late teens and early twenties; there was said to be perhaps no other period in life 'in which consciousness of the need for good personal appearance was so marked as between the ages of 18 and 25'.[102] If status distinctions in clothing were in some respects becoming more blurred for working-class young men in employment during the 1930s, the glamorous emphases of contemporary leisure culture helped to make divides between work, play and unemployment much starker. By the 1930s, many smarter leisure venues were becoming less easy going than in the past, when mill workers, warehousemen and engineers were used to visiting their local cinemas in their overalls. Bernard Scott worked in a tool-making workshop and was used to attending the local Plaza in his work clothes, so was surprised one night to see to a sign in its foyer requesting 'no overalls'. The humiliation of being refused admission was recalled years later, and he got his 'revenge' by replacing the soap in the cinema washroom with replicas made out of white tallow, which gave out a horrible stink when rubbed in. Inverting notions of cleanliness and appearance, it was a creative way of asserting a defiant, 'anti-social' and 'dirty' identity.[103]

Emphases on dressing up for evening and weekend leisure activities excluded many poorer working-class young people from glamorous venues such as the cinema and palais. The cinema experience changed dramatically during the 1930s, as national cinema chains such as Associated British Cinemas (A.B.C.) and Gaumont-British embarked on an ambitious building programme of 'super-cinemas', which encouraged greater expectations of having to 'dress-up'.[104] Commercial dance halls were very aware of the need to establish a stylish and respectable reputation and often expected doormen to police what dancers wore so as to ensure the requisite 'smartness'.[105] Boys needed a 'best suit' to make them feel comfortable among the well-dressed patrons of the palais, where girls wore 'smart dance frocks in the latest fashion' and the men were usually dressed in lounge suits.[106] Most of the young men Nora James recalled from her dancing days in the 1920s also wore 'patent leather shoes' and their best 'navy blue serge suit'.[107] Shabby clothes were daytime wear, with the good suit kept 'not for Sundays, but for the dancing!'[108] Les Sutton remembered Manchester dance halls where the 'girls' were in their 'silver shoes and long dresses', while most of the young men wore 'fashionable long tight-fitting black overcoats, white scarves, dark spanish-style [sic] hats and black suede or patent shoes'.[109]

Poverty meant that those who liked to go dancing were very careful over the few clothes they had. The youth worker Valentine Bell had first become aware of much-disliked dance-hall enthusiasts among his 'unemployed lads' because they objected to working in the Gym, 'as the exercise bagged the knees of their trousers'.[110] The 'composite character' 'Thomas Tiddler', whom James Butterworth described in Clubland, had his trouser creases down to a fine art, 'for the trousers have been well pressed under the mattress by night and scrupulously folded in brown paper by day'.[111] Poorer boys in Oldham could be recognised by 'the regulation blue serge' whose worn and shiny seat and elbows were often scraped with fine sandpaper or a new safety razor to rough up 'the shame-making shine'.[112] The constraints and ingenuities of poverty similarly coloured Eli Hague's recollections of his teen years, when lack of work and money made it impossible to buy new clothes and 'sartorial presentation' was consequently 'largely top show'. A 'certain naïve ingenuity' helped considerably. Detachable shirt collars and shirt fronts made it easy to look reasonably well kempt because clipping on a clean collar could hide a dirty shirt if a pullover concealed what was worn beneath. Only a few men could afford a proper 'Sunday shirt'.[113] Ernest Martin did not possess one until his 21st birthday, when his mates clubbed together to buy him a shirt, tie, cuff links and arm bands.[114] Such shirts were sold with two loose collars, fixed to the shirt by a back stud and front stud, which meant they could be worn a for much longer before they had to be washed, because once one collar was dirty, it could be replaced by the other one. Far more common were cover-ups such as the 'front', a rectangle of cloth which covered the chest and was secured at the back by two ties, allowing the wearer to go out without a shirt, so long as it was covered by a waistcoat or jacket:

> Thus attired, with trousers creased by the simple expedient of rubbing the inside of the crease with a piece of soap and laying them under the mattress the night before; with any marks on the jacket assiduously sponged off and with a generous application of Lavender Brilliantine (3d a large tin from Woolworth's) applied to the hair, I would set out to meet my mates for our night's adventure.[115]

Such subterfuges allowed impoverished young men such as Hague to maintain their self-respects when they joined the cheap leisure activities which were still open to them, such as the park or monkey run. As he grew older, the 'gang of youths' with whom he associated grew bolder, and took to wearing stiff wing collars and dicky bows, their discomfort a reminder that it was not only young women who suffered for the sake of fashion:

> It was given the name of the "Come to Jesus" collar because it was the favourite neckwear of the dour church and chapel faithfulls. Classy they might have looked, but they very nigh cut your head off; I know my neck was red raw after a night out so attired. What one will do for the sake of appearances![116]

Where some turned to cheque clubs or other forms of credit to buy clothing, others profited from better-off friends who wanted to capitalise on clothes they no longer wanted. Watkin, so aware of his shabby appearance and unable to afford anything new, eventually bought from a friend a second-hand pair of 'shales' or Oxford bags with enormously wide turn-ups and a very stylish 'jazzy-coloured, sleeveless slipover' to go with them. Having got a new haircut, he 'vividly' recalled his first stroll thus dressed, walking for miles along the main roads of Manchester, 'my slip-over dazzling, my bags flapping, my eyes straight ahead as I basked in the warm satisfaction of being "in the fashion"'.[117] Hague, who was willing to put up with his 'Come on Jesus' collar in the name of fashion, was also 'caught up in the craze of wearing Oxford bags', although the trouser bottoms measuring 'some 24 or 25 inches' posed considerable problems when cycling, because it was almost impossible to find cycle clips which would adequately contain them, and they had the 'distressing habit of catching on the cycle chain and becoming irretrievably greased and damaged'.[118]

Haircuts also helped young people to distinguish themselves from the older generation. Kay recalled the up-to-date styles which swept the country in his teens and differentiated him from his father, whose hair was a very 'old fashioned style' brushed downwards with 'a small quiff of hair curled over his forehead'.[119] Young women, often regarded a conduit for 'modern' trends, were urged by the hairdressing industry to discourage their boyfriends from allowing their hair 'to be hacked off as though they were cattle', and to move them towards the newer styles associated with celebrity culture. Godfrey Winn, for example, commended a new style of men's hairdressing from a recent exhibition at Olympia, which he called on his young female readers to make their boy-friend 'copy' if they wanted him to 'look like a film star'.[120] By 1939, Morgan was suggesting that 'one of the most remarkable changes' in young people's appearance over the previous twenty years was 'in heads'. 'To-day a girl or boy of sixteen or seventeen with unkempt hair is a rarity. For every girl her wave and her hair-washing night: for every boy his comb. Whatever else he lacks even a boy vagrant on the roads will generally have a comb in his pocket.'[121] Male traditionalists despised these trends, a former Inspector of Army Physical Training expressing the hope that contemporary youth would soon sicken 'of the "soft goods" of "crooning" and the eternal tenor of the dance band'. 'The constant combing of well-oiled locks of long hair, tidy clothes, and well-kept hands and nails are indicative of a refinement borrowed from a less masculine atmosphere than there used to be.'[122] (By the late 1940s, the 'effeminate' connotations of such hair 'obsession' would be much stronger and associated with delinquency.[123])

Although working-class boys remained careful of what they copied from the cinema, many, even before the advent of the 'talkies', had emulated stars such as Rudolph Valentino and Ramon Navarro, smoothing their hair 'to a patent-leather, glossy blackness' using brilliantine, Yardley's hair cream 'or, if you were less affluent, Vaseline'.[124] A hairbrush and comb were already 'essential at sixteen', as Harry Dorell recalled of the period just after First World War, when he remembered being very conscious of his 'over-brilliantined hair'.[125] Eyebrow pencils were borrowed from sisters to pencil in an 'inadequate' moustache. Some youths even Marcel-waved their hair, 'using their sisters' curling tongs'.[126] Ted Furniss, who was a barber in Sheffield in the early 1930s, observed how 'the dancing boys used to like you to spend a little extra time on them, doing the old Rudolf Valentino styles'.[127] Such small acts of stylish self-assertion helped considerably in reinforcing a sense of independence and identity, as the impoverished Watkin found, describing how haircuts were one of the cheaper ways for boys to keep up to date.[128]

> I did achieve a little fashion and style which was not costly, but gave me an immense uplift, confidence and pride and even led to my purposely going out for a stroll to display my new image. And it was simply a new haircut style. Called the 'Boston', and coming from that city in the USA, it gave the impression of the wearing of a skull-cap, for the hair was cropped as short as possible up to a line just above the ears, above which it was trimmed to normal length. That is all; but it did look rather peculiar, it was new and it appeared that relatively few had the courage to adopt it, awaiting its becoming more popular and widespread. But I had chanced it and felt rather proud as passers-by gave it a sly glance and children made remarks about the man's 'funny haircut'. It helped to compensate for my permanent overalls attire.[129]

Young people's consumption patterns in the inter-war years still had much in common with those of the pre-war period, but their interest in and capacity to achieve a fashionable appearance was growing, which reinforced the sensitivity of poor and unemployed young men to judgements made about them on the basis of their clothes. Despite some superficial blurring of boundaries, the status group to which one belonged remained clearly defined by both style and poverty.[130] Glasser's sense of separation from the world he had left behind on going to Oxford was reinforced on a return visit to Glasgow not only by his changing accent and ideas but by his clothes – 'sports jacket and shirt and flannels and tie – poor by Oxford standards', yet 'conspicuously middle-class in the Gorbals of shoddy cloth, mufflers and cloth caps'.[131]

Working-class young women and young men often went to great lengths to dress as well as they could with little money, well aware that how they looked was becoming an increasingly important statement of 'personality and character'. Some, like George Turner, took considerable pride in dressing up to go to the pictures, the attention he paid to what he wore expressing both social aspirations and sense of performance: 'I always liked to see how I could dress to appeal to people. Specially if you were goin' out.'[132] The marketing industry did much to promote such self-consciousness, as was apparent in advertisements for the new season's styles from the early 1930s, which urged 'men, youths and boys' to buy 'Summer suits with personality'.[133] (Winn's page in the *Daily Mirror* was called 'My Personality Parade'.) Peer pressure remained extremely powerful in how working-class boys and young men decided to dress.[134] Nevertheless, growing emphasis on personality, together with greater social mixing between boys and girls in their teens, was accentuating sensitivity to personal appearance in ways which, if some enjoyed, others found far more confusing.[135]

Cinemas and cigarettes

The cinema was an important influence among young people in this changing social and cultural climate, its emphasis on human relationships, distinctive dialogue and intimate focus on facial expression and the body influencing not only fashion styles but how young people carried themselves, spoke and interacted with each other.[136]

The cinema was the most popular form of commercial entertainment in inter-war Britain, which by 1939 had almost 5,000 cinemas and 990 million annual admissions.[137] Working-class adolescents were keen cinema-goers, and by the late 1930s their regular attendance was 'almost universal'.[138] Most went at least once or twice a week, and some even three and four times; young wage earners in Hulme, Manchester spent a third of their weekday leisure at the cinema.[139] Boys in their teens attended as much as girls, although this changed as they entered their twenties, when women went far more frequently than men, and many had a very active engagement with what they saw.[140] Girls were noted for self-consciously adopting Hollywood accents, which they thought gave them 'extra smartness and tone', but boys, too, deployed Americanisms to give themselves extra confidence. Hague, for example, recalled how song phrases helped the more 'timorous' lads in their courtship negotiations on the monkey run, once the girls had passed by.[141]

Somehow it seemed easier from distance. How clever we imagined ourselves to be, using the first lines of popular songs as tentative gambits: 'Who's taking you out tonight?' 'Pardon me, pretty baby, is it yes, or is it no, is it maybe?' 'I don't know why I love you like I do.'[142]

Watkin's description of the imitative possibilities of the cinema not only caught the novelty of hearing an American accent for the first time, but also conveyed an image of his youthful self as rather a connoisseur of this 'exotic' new sound:

A grey-haired man spoke. His voice was clear and loud, filling the cinema with a strange, and to me exciting, American-English language. But how peculiarly nasal. And the letter 'r' which, to me, seemed to dominate and affect his speech, as though his tongue were perpetually ready to curl up and cuddle every possible 'r' and in fact any others which could be influenced by it. I noticed the continual use of the expression 'OK' which soon caught on here and became part of our everyday speech. Another was 'right now' where we would say 'now' or 'right away'.[143]

American catch phrases, accents and mannerisms had first become popular at the end of the First World War, and a newspaper survey of the six most expressive slang phrases at the end of the 1920s found that American ones clearly predominated, 'culled for the most part, one suspects, from a close study of film captions'.[144] Hearing an American accent spoken on the 'talkies' from the end of the 1920s was, however, a very different experience, which contributed a new dimension to imitation. The showing of the musical *Broadway Melody* at Barrow Coliseum in 1929, for example, was said to have encouraged young people to learn a 'whole new language . . . "O.K. baby", "Gosh oh gee", . . . and "Hi ya babe"'.[145]

The cinema also influenced the changing choreography of leisure performance. The anthropologist Marcel Mauss commented in 1934, for example, on how 'American walking fashions' had arrived in Paris, 'thanks to the cinema', while in Britain, American films were said to have influenced deportment and posture, 'even the way of entering a room, shaking hands and sitting in a chair'.[146] By the end of the 1930s a 'marked improvement' was being observed, not only in the 'dress' but in the 'bearing of the average lad and girl'.[147]

Girls were commonly regarded as particularly keen admirers and emulators of female film stars, and their engagement with the cinema appears to have been deeper and more complex than among their male counterparts.[148] It was not only female film stars who set fashions trends, however, and their male equivalents were also responsible for them, as with the American 'doughboy' caps which became popular in the early 1930s.[149] Boys too were drawn into the narcissistic and 'personality' aspects of 'celebrity' culture, and copied their favourite stars.[150] Kay, for example, recalled rushing off to see a film starring Eddie Cantor, which his friend was keen to see because people had been telling him that he was 'the dead-spit' of the film star.[151] Clifford Gentle was asked whether it was true that girls always stood on their toes when they kissed because of what they had seen at the cinema. His reply focused on his sister-in-law's experiences, but it also suggests how his own self-awareness was affected by this visual culture.

> Yes, and sometimes they said they heard music. My sister-in-law who's younger than my wife, she said with one American she kissed during the War, she definitely heard music. But I'm sure that was the influence of the movies. And you did it half conscious to the camera.[152]

Dennis Norden suggested that boys of his generation had learned to be 'human beings' from the cinema, modelling themselves on what they saw, and shaping new, imaginary identities: 'you learned how to smoke for example from films, you learned how to hold a cigarette, you learned that only characters that played untrustworthy, very low class, smoked like that, to be suave, to be William Powell, to be Franchot Tone'.[153]

Cigarettes played an important part in these adolescent imitations of adulthood. Young people's relationship with smoking had pre-war origins, having been a significant sign of precocious masculinity since the 1880s, when cigarettes' cheapness and the availability of popular machine-made ones like Woodbines helped them to spread rapidly among working-class boys and young men.[154] Smoking soon became part of the initiation into manhood, a potent symbol of male adulthood. Those who could not afford to buy them improvised. One of Joseph Armitage's school friends, 'a notorious rebel', made his out of 'a bit of soft paper and a discarded fag end'.[155] Others experimented with blotting paper.[156] The furtive rebellion of smoking while still at school assumed a different significance on starting work: 'Hitherto the smoking of cigarettes was a prank, only delightful because forbidden; now it becomes a public exhibition, denoting manhood, independence and wealth.'[157]

Most male smokers probably began experimenting with cigarettes in their early teens.[158] Henriques thought younger boys often tried it for 'mere swank', wanting something 'forbidden' in order to look older or to feel part of a group.[159] Norman Kenyon, born in 1917, recalled how he and his friends, acquired their liking for nicotine when they were aged between 10 and 13, when, 'if you did not do the swallows, you were not really smoking properly'.[160] George Clifton Hughes's 'first real initiation into smoking' was, unlike the 'hurried puff or two' previously sampled, 'a consolidated session where one associated infusion with swallowing like a man'.[161] The cinema taught many different lessons. Where Norden looked for status and sophistication, others preferred signs of hard masculinity, taking their tips on how to hold their cigarettes from gangster films. In one long smoking session, Hughes and his friends worked through several packets of cigarettes as they tried to perfect their technique. Modelling themselves on the most practised among them, they noticed how, 'whilst there was a tendency for us to hold the cigarette tightly between the lips and in the centre of the mouth, Enoch's style was to let it dangle nonchalantly from one or other corner of the mouth'.[162]

Practised smokers were much admired. John Edryd Parry's 'forte' was to be 'like a skilled veteran', able to light a cigarette in a force ten gale, out in the elements and without shelter, with a single match. None of his friends were willing to reveal the extent of their own 'clumsiness', yet never complimented Parry on his skill. 'There was a sort of acceptance that would have been out of place with a chorus of "well dones" or "bravissimos".'[163] Youth workers attributed some of smoking's popularity to changing relationships between boys and girls, and suggested that many took it up at the prompting of a girl because it made them look older.[164] Club workers were urged to encourage pipe smoking rather than cigarettes among those who had 'already become addicts', because it offered a more 'middlebrow, common sense masculine identity'.[165] The suggestion was one which the socially aspiring were keen to follow. Thomas Waddicor, unlike his father and brothers, who worked as makers-up and packers in the cotton trade, had entered an office on leaving school and described reaching the 'last of his teen years' and moving on to the next stage of maturity, when he followed his 'Dad's example' and took up a pipe.[166]

Girls did not take up smoking to any great extent before the First World War, when it was identified with the 'deviant', transgressive behaviour of prostitutes, actresses, lesbians and the 'new woman'.[167] Tobacco marketing outstripped all other advertising in the 1920s, however, and the rates of smoking among women rose over the inter-war years as a whole, and by the 1930s, eight out of ten men and four out of ten women were said to be smokers.[168] Inter-war leisure developments gave new meanings to youthful smoking, and it became an important 'signifier' of 'feminine sophistication', commonly associated with factory, shop and office workers.[169] Particular leisure venues, such as urban bars and dance halls, the cinema and seaside holiday resorts, all helped to make smoking a socially accepted and eroticised part of courtship which gave rise to its own gendered tensions, as we shall see in Chapter 5.[170]

The 1930s witnessed the increasing commodification of the female body and growing opportunities to gaze upon it in leisure venues, popular newspapers and magazines. These sexualised notions of physical appearance were not confined to young women, however, but also had implications for the clothed and unclothed bodies of young men in their teens and twenties.[171] Body-building and keep fit gave working-class boys and young men a certain agency over their own bodies that was harder to achieve through clothing because of the expense, although, as we have seen, the clothed body also had complex meanings which many shaped in their own ways as working-class boys and young men drew on familiar creative strategies to ensure a semblance of belonging to modish adult culture, with subtly nuanced styles, which testified as much to creative agency as to passive consumption.[172] By the 1930s, both boys and girls were experiencing a range of leisure locations where sensitivity to physicality was heightened. These were part of a broader and 'carefully constructed commercial strategy of glamour' whose implications were particularly marked during the transitions of adolescence, when not only were there anxieties about the body but also, as we shall see, there were many uncertainties about personal and social relations.[173]

Notes

1 J. Bourke, *Dismembering the Male: Men's Bodies, Britain and the Great War* (London: Reaktion Books, 1996), pp. 37–8, 163; R. M. Vanderbeck, 'Masculinities and fieldwork: widening the discussion', *Gender, Place and Culture*, 12:4 (2005), pp. 391, 398.

2 C. L. Hansford, *Memoirs of a Bricklayer*, Burnett Archive of Working Class Autobiographies, University of Brunel (hereafter Burnett Archive), p. 42.

3 R. Glasser, 'Growing up in the Gorbals', in *The Ralph Glasser Omnibus* (1986; Edinburgh: Black and White Publishing, 2006), p. 54. Glasser was born in 1916.

4 J. Bourke, *Working-Class Cultures in Britain, 1890–1960: Gender, Class and Ethnicity* (London and New York: Routledge, 1994) p. 102; C. Royle, *Boyhood Recollections of Flixton 1922–1938* (Manchester: Neil Richardson, 1994), pp. 56–7; J. H. Armitage, *The Twenty Three Years, Or the Late Way of Life – And of Living. By The Exile*, Burnett Archive, p. 174; E. Martin, *The Best Street in Rochdale*, Burnett Archive, p. 33.

5 H. Chadwick, *Childhood Memories of Gorton in the Nineteen Twenties* (Manchester: Neil Richardson, 1994), p. 18. Chadwick was born in 1916.

6 B. Scott, *Heaton Norris Boy* (Stockport: Metropolitan Borough of Stockport, Leisure Services Division, 1987), pp. 12–13.

7 Scott, *Heaton Norris*, p. 12.

8 Loftus, *Lee Side*, Burnett Archive, p. 79. Loftus was born in Lancashire.

9 Glasser, 'Growing up', pp. 54–5.

10 Bourke, *Working-Class Cultures*, pp. 41–4; I. Zweiniger-Bargielowska, 'Building a British superman: physical culture in inter-war Britain', *Journal of Contemporary History*, 41:4 (2006), p. 598.

11 J. A. Black, '"Who dies if England live?" Masculinity, the problematics of "Englishness" and the image of the ordinary soldier in British war art, c. 1915–28', in S. Caunce, E. Mazierska, S. Sydney-Smith and J. K. Walton (eds), *Relocating Britishness* (Manchester: Manchester University Press, 2004), pp. 148–66.

12 S. F. Hatton, *London's Bad Boys* (London: Chapman & Hall Ltd., 1931), p. 23.

13 Bourke, *Working-Class Cultures*, p. 43. For the appeal of physical fitness to women, see J. J. Matthews, 'They had such a lot of fun: the Women's League of Health and Beauty between the Wars', *History Workshop Journal*, 30 (1990), 22–54.

14 K. Fisher, *Birth Control, Sex and Marriage in Britain, 1918–1960* (Oxford: Oxford University Press, 2006), p. 174.

15 S. Humphries and P. Gordon, *A Man's World. From Boyhood to Manhood, 1890–1960* (London: BBC Books, 1996), p, 43; Bourke, *Working-Class Cultures*, p. 42; A. E. Morgan, *The Needs of Youth. A Report Made to King George's Jubilee Trust Fund* (Oxford: Oxford University Press, 1939), p. 213.

16 *Hansard House of Commons Debates*, 16 December 1938, Vol. 342, cc. 2420–38, at 2435.

17 A. Carden-Coyne, *Reconstructing the Body: Classicism, Modernism, and the First World War* (Oxford: Oxford University Press, 2009), p. 208.

18 The Save the Children Fund found significant regional differences in the number of children suffering from 'subnormal malnutrition': 9.2 per cent in Leeds; 13 per cent in Merthyr; 17.2 per cent in Newcastle; 21 per cent in Pontypridd: *British Medical Journal* (18 July 1936), p. 158; *Hansard House of Commons Debates*, 8 July 1936, vol. 314, cc 1229–349.

19 *The Times* (30 January 1934), p. 15; *ibid.* (9 February 1934), p. 10; *The Boy* (January 1934). Gaps in national health insurance meant young people were not covered by state support between the ages of 14 and 16.

20 *British Medical Journal* (18 July 1936), p. 158.

21 Scott, *Heaton Norris*, p. 32.

22 State concern about national fitness in the 1930s encouraged the introduction of playing fields and recreation grounds.

23 *Daily Dispatch* (15 November 1936).

24 Howard French, 'Health Given Away', *Sunday Dispatch* (8 November 1936). The reporter, who measured the progress of his trunk-bending exercises by drawing a chalk line on the carpet, pointed out that he had only done so under special dispensation from his mother. British Pathé also publicised Lawrence in 1936.

25 The cutting was kept with Les's diaries and his other papers. M. Bygraves, *I Wanna Tell You a Story* (London: W. H. Allen, 1976), p. 39. Bygraves was born in 1922 in Rotherhithe, London. See also J. Bourke, 'Fragmentation, fetishization and men's bodies in Britain, 1890–1939', *Women: A Cultural Review*, 7:3 (1996), 240–9.

26 Height regulations varied according to different police forces. A 1908 Police Instruction manual for the Manchester police established that police officers should be at least 5 feet 10 inches, and have a 36 inch chest measurement. My

thanks to the Greater Manchester Police Museum and Archives. The height
regulation for the Metropolitan Police in the 1930s appears to have been 5
feet 10 inches. My thanks to Neil Paterson, the Metropolitan Police Historical
Collection.

27 *The Bennett College (Ltd), Sheffield: History of the Bennett College* (n.d.) p. 2; letter
    from The Bennett College Limited, to Les, undated.
28 *Opportunities in the Police Force* (London: British Tutorial Institutes Ltd., 1936), p. 12;
    L. Stebbing, *The Stebbing System of Height Increase* (n.p., 1930).
29 'Diary' (5 March 1937).
30 B. Naughton, *Saintly Billy: A Catholic Boyhood* (Oxford: Oxford University Press,
    1989), p. 1834.
31 *The Times* (30 January 1934), p. 15. The Lucas-Tooth Institute, South East London,
    was a gymnasium started by the MP Sir Hugh Lucas-Tooth for 'unemployed men
    from the northern coalfields and unemployed areas'. Its fitness classes drew boys
    and young men from all around London: *Hansard House of Commons Debates*, 4
    December 1935, vol. 307, cc. 261–2. For a physical fitness demonstration by young
    men at the Institute, see the following film from the British Pathé online film col-
    lection: 'Fit – Fitter –Fittest', 28 March 1938, Film ID: 1166.20, Sort number: PT 418,
    Tape: *PM1166*: www.britishpathe.com/record.php?id=8858.
32 B. Naughton, *Neither Use nor Ornament: A Memoir of Bolton, 1920s* (Newcastle upon
    Tyne: Bloodaxe Books, 1995), p. 91.
33 J. Preston, *Memoirs of a Salford Lad* (Manchester: Neil Richardson, undated), pp.
    11–12. Preston was born in 1910.
34 Carden-Coyne, *Reconstructing*, pp. 2, 10, 172–3, 211.
35 *Daily Mirror* (9 June 1939), p. 26; *ibid* (9 April 1938), p. 16.
36 Zweiniger-Bargielowska, 'Building a British superman', p. 601; J. Giles, *Women,
    Identity and Private Life in Britain, 1900–1950* (London: Macmillan Press Ltd, 1995),
    p. 53.
37 V. Steele, *Fashion and Eroticism: Ideals of Feminine Beauty from the Victorian Era
    to the Jazz Age* (New York and Oxford: Oxford University Press, 1985), p. 239. Many
    local authority bathing facilities still insisted on segregated bathing.
38 C. Horwood, '"Girls who arouse dangerous passions": women and bathing, 1900–
    1939', *Women's History Review*, 9:4 (2000), pp. 661, 664. About 180 lidos were built
    during the 1930s.
39 For fuller development of these themes at the seaside and lido, see J. K. Walton,
    'Beaches, bathing and beauty: health and bodily exposure at the British seaside from
    the eighteenth century to the twentieth', *Revue Française de Civilisation Britannique*,
    14:2 (2007), 119–36. See also, F. Gray, *Designing the Seaside: Architecture, Society and
    Nature* (London: Reaktion, 2006), pp. 182–4.
40 Horwood, '"Girls who arouse"', p. 663.
41 H. Watkin, *From Hulme All Blessings Flow: A Collection of Manchester Memories*
    (Manchester: Neil Richardson, 1985), pp. 88–9.
42 *Daily Mirror* (28 May 1938), p. 2.
43 Walton, 'Beaches, bathing and beauty'; Carden-Coyne, *Reconstructing*, p. 206.
    'Beefcake' images, influenced by American models, did not become common until
    the 1940s and 1950s.

44 C. Classen, D. Howes and A. Synnott, *Aroma: The Cultural History of Smell* (London: Routledge, 1994), p. 182.

45 R. D. McBee, *Dance Hall Days: Intimacy and Leisure among Working-Class Immigrants in the United States* (New York: New York University Press, 2000), p. 122.

46 *Daily Mirror* (17 September 1923), p. 17; *ibid.* (20 March 1923), p. 15; 25 March 1925, p. 17.

47 *Ibid.* (23 May 1938), p. 6; *ibid.* (19 May 1938), p. 24; *ibid.* (7 July 1939), p. 12.

48 Classen, Howes and Synnott, *Aroma*, pp. 183–4; P. Tinkler, *Constructing Girlhood: Popular Magazines for Girls Growing Up in England, 1920–1950* (London: Taylor and Francis, 1995), p. 178. For an excellent analysis of the relationship between masculinity and clothing see L. Ugolini, *Men and Menswear: Sartorial Consumption in Britain, 1880–1939* (Aldershot: Ashgate, 2007).

49 *Daily Mirror* (13 April 1926), p. 6; *ibid.* (13 October 1926), p. 18; *ibid.* (14 May 1931), p. 8.

50 *Ibid.* (31 March 1925), p. 16.

51 *Ibid.* (4 October 1938), p. 8; *ibid.* (21 June, 1939), p. 8.

52 *Ibid.* (10 November 1936), p. 22; *ibid.* (3 March 1939), p. 30; *ibid.* (9 December 1938), p. 26; *ibid.* (2 August 1939), p. 13.

53 *Ibid.* (12 April 1939), p. 8.

54 Classen, Howes and Synnott, *Aroma*, p. 185.

55 Carden-Coyne, *Reconstructing*, p. 31.

56 Ugolini, *Men and Menswear*, p. 183. Montague Burton Ltd was the largest of these firms. Its main competitors were Henry Price's Fifty Shilling Tailors and Hepworths: Honeyman, K., 'Following suit: men, masculinity and gendered practices in the clothing trade in Leeds, England, 1890–1940', *Gender and History*, 14:3 (2002), 426–46, at p. 428.

57 Montague Burton's address to shareholders at the 1932 AGM, reported in *Men's Wear* (30 July 1932), cited in K. Honeyman, 'Following suit', p. 429. Priestley's famous reference to 'factory girls looking like actresses' suggested a misleading 'homogeneity', since 'the cost, value and quality of clothes remained visible and important indicators of social status': J. B. Priestley, *English Journey* (London: Heinemann/Gollancz, 1934), p. 401; L. Ugolini, 'Clothes and the modern man in 1930s Oxford', *Fashion Theory*, 4:4 (2000), 427–46, at pp. 437–8; S. Norris, 'Mass-Observation at the dance hall: a democracy of fashion?', in R. Snape and H. Pussard (eds), *Recording Leisure Lives: Histories, Archives and Memories of Leisure in Twentieth-Century Britain* (Eastbourne: Leisure Studies Association, University of Brighton, 2009).

58 *Manchester Guardian* (2 January 1936), p. 9.

59 E. Hague, *Streets away from Paradise: Reminiscences of a Stalybridge Lad* (Manchester: Neil Richardson, 1987), p. 75.

60 J. P. Mayer, *British Cinemas and their Audiences* (London: Dennis Dobson Ltd., 1948).

61 G. Turner, oral history transcript, The Cinema Culture in 1930s Britain Archive, University of Lancaster (hereafter CCINTB).

62 A. Exell, 'Morris Motors in the 1930s', *History Workshop Journal*, 6 (1978), p. 72.

63 D. Fowler, *The First Teenagers. The Lifestyle of Young Wage Earners in Inter-war*

Britain (London: Woburn Press, 1995), p. 104; C. Breward, *The Hidden Consumer: Masculinities, Fashion and City Life in 1860–1914* (Manchester: Manchester University Press, 1999), pp. 212–15.

64 Cited in S. Humphries, *A Secret World of Sex. Forbidden Fruit: The British Experience, 1900–1950* (London: Sidgwick and Jackson, 1988), p. 159.

65 R. Hoggart, *A Local Habitation*, Vol. 1, *Life and Times 1918–40* (Oxford: Oxford University Press, 1989), p. 151. I am grateful to Lou Taylor for pointing out this apparent discrepancy. There is a similar one in J. Blake, *Memories of Old Poplar* (London: Stepney Books Publications, 1977), p. 23.

66 Ugolini, 'Clothes and the modern man', p. 431; Ugolini, *Men and Menswear*, p. 42.

67 Montague Burton promoted 'fancy worsted or blue serge suits' for the 'smart young man' and businessman: K. Honeyman, 'Style monotony and the business of fashion: the marketing of menswear in inter-war England', *Textile History*, 34: 2 (2003), p. 180. Fowler, *The First Teenagers*, p. 104; Breward, *The Hidden Consumer*, pp. 212–15; Humphries, *A Secret World of Sex*, pp. 159–60. Young Communist Party members in the East End of London were also said to be 'fond of dressing in an outlandish way', in khaki, red shirts and sandals: J. Jacobs, *Out of the Ghetto: My Youth in the East End. Communism and Fascism 1913–1939* (London: Janet Simon, 1978), pp. 79–80, cited in Ugolini, *Men and Menswear*, p. 42; Turner, oral history transcript, CCINTB.

68 A. Kuhn, *An Everyday Magic: Cinema and Cultural Memory* (London and New York: I. B. Tauris, 2002), p. 100.

69 J. Springhall, *Youth, Popular Culture and Moral Panics: Penny Gaffs to Gangsta Rap, 1830–1966* (London: Macmillan Press Ltd, 1998), pp. 102, 107; Kuhn, *Everyday Magic*, p. 108.

70 E. J. Godbold, oral history transcript, CCINTB.

71 G. Cross (ed.), *Worktowners at Blackpool: Mass-Observation and Popular Leisure in the 1930s* (London: Routledge, 1990), p. 152.

72 F. Mort and P. Thomson, 'Retailing, commercial culture and masculinity in 1950s Britain: the case of Montague Burton, the Tailor of Taste, *History Workshop Journal*, 38 (1994), p. 121.

73 M. Houlbrook, *Queer London: Perils and Pleasures in the Sexual Metropolis, 1918–1957* (Chicago: University of Chicago Press, 2005), pp. 77, 90. For work on lesbians and dress, see J. Nestle, *A Restricted Country: Essays and Short Stories* (London: Sheba Feminist, 1988); M. D. Davis and E. Lapovsky Kennedy, *Boots of Leather, Slippers of Gold: The History of a Lesbian Community* (New York and London: Routledge, 1993); J. Schuyf, '"Trousers with flies!" The clothing and subculture of lesbians', *Textile History*, 24:1 (1993), 61–73.

74 M. Houlbrook, '"The man with the powder puff" in inter-war London', *Historical Journal*, 50:1 (2007), p. 153, 157; M. Houlbrook, '"Lady Austin's camp boys": constituting the queer subject in 1930s London', *Gender and History*, 14: 1 (2002), p. 41; *idem.*, *Queer London: Perils and Pleasures in the Sexual Metropolis, 1918–1957* (Chicago and London: University of Chicago Press, 2006), p. 148; M. Cook, 'Queer conflicts: love, sex and war, 1914–1967', in M. Cook (ed.), with R. Mills, R. Trumbach and H. G. Cocks, *A Gay History of Britain: Love and Sex Between Men Since the Middle Ages* (Oxford and Westport, CT: Greenworld Publishing, 2007), p. 164; Houlbrook, *Queer London*, p. 148.

75 Ugolini, *Men and Menswear*, p. 19; L. Ugolini, 'Autobiographies and mens-wear consumption in Britain, c. 1880–1939', *Textile History*, 40:2 (2009), p. 208.

76 R. Johnston and A. McIvor, 'Dangerous work, hard men and broken bodies: masculinity in the Clydeside heavy industries, c. 1930–1970s', *Labour History Review*, 69:2 (2004), p. 138; Ugolini, *Men and Menswear*, p. 98.

77 Naughton, *Saintly Billy*, p. 164.

78 'Diary' (24 December 1936, 10 January 1937).

79 It was also known as the chicken-run in some parts of the country.

80 'Diary', 24 October 1937.

81 *Ibid.*, 30 October 1937.

82 D. Summerskill, *Happy Lad: Reminiscences of a Lancashire Childhood* (Skipton: Katharine Cheney, 2009), p. 24.

83 Ugolini makes a similar point about the power of peer ridicule in discouraging young men from adopting more adventurous fashion styles: Ugolini, *Men and Menswear*, pp. 48–51, 116; Ugolini, 'Clothes and the modern man', pp. 437–8.

84 Ugolini, *Men and Menswear*, pp. 35, 63.

85 Armitage, *The Twenty Three Years*, pp. 143, 148.

86 J. Kay, *The Chronicles of a Harpurhey Lad* (Manchester: Neil Richardson, 1990), p. 7.

87 Hansford, *Memoirs of a Bricklayer*, p. 12.

88 Hague, *Streets Away*, pp. 10, 29.

89 *Ibid.*, p. 29.

90 Watkin, *From Hulme*, pp. 79, 85–7.

91 Hague, *Streets Away*, pp. 17–18; T. Waddicor, *Memories of Hightown and Beyond*, Burnett Archive, p. 16. Waddicor was born in Salford in 1906.

92 George Turner, oral history transcript, CCINTB. For those who could afford it, 'initiation into the culture of the suit' was another important sign of entry into 'manhood': Mort and Thomson, 'Retailing, commercial culture and masculinity', p. 119; Ugolini, 'Autobiographies', p. 203.

93 S. Rice, *The Memories of a Rolling Stone: Times and Incidents Remembered*, Burnett Archive, p. 13. Rice was born in London, in 1905; W. Brereton, *Salford Boy. The Illustrated Memories of Wallace Brereton* (1977; Manchester: Neil Richardson, 1985), p. 45. Brereton was born in 1919.

94 T. Furniss, *The Walls of Jericho: Slum Life in Sheffield between the Wars* (Sheffield: Rebel Press, 1979), p. 22. Furniss was born in Sheffield in 1912,

95 This would have been about 1933. R. Glasser, 'Gorbals Boy at Oxford', in *The Ralph Glasser Omnibus* (Edinburgh: Black and White Publishing, 2006, first published by Chatto and Windus, 1988).

96 George Turner, oral history transcript, CCINTB.

97 E. Terry, *Etiquette for All: Man, Woman or Child* (London: Foulsham & Co. Ltd., 1925), p. 77.

98 Glasser, 'Growing up', p. 191–7.

99 Watkin, *From Hulme*, p. 85.

100 *Ibid.*, pp. 85–6.

101 C. Cameron, A. Lush and G. Meara, *Disinherited Youth* (Edinburgh: Carnegie United Kingdom Trust, 1943), pp. 72–3.

102 Cameron, Lush, Meara, *Disinherited Youth*, pp. 72–3.

103 Scott, *Heaton Norris*, p. 45.

104 J. Hill, *Sport, Leisure and Culture in Twentieth-Century Britain* (Basingstoke: Palgrave, 2002), p. 61.

105 Bolton Oral History Project, Interview 47B, cited in E. Oliver, 'Liberation or Limitation? A Study of Women's Leisure in Bolton, c. 1919–1939' (PhD dissertation, University of Lancaster, 1997), p. 243.

106 R. Bowley, ch. 2, 'Amusements and entertainments', in H. L. Smith (ed.), *The New Survey of London Life and Labour*, vol. IX, *Life and Leisure*, (London: P.S. King and Son Ltd., 1935), p. 65.

107 N. James, *A Derbyshire Life. Autobiography of a South Normanton Woman* (South Normanton: Post Mill Press, 1981), p. 37.

108 Cameron, Lush and Meara, *Disinherited Youth*, p. 105.

109 L. Sutton, *Mainly about Ardwick* (Manchester, 1977), p. 113.

110 F. Dawes, *A Cry from the Streets. The Boys' Club Movement in Britain from the 1850s to the Present Day* (Hove, Sussex: Wayland Publishers, 1975), pp. 139–40.

111 J. Butterworth, *Clubland* (London: The Epworth Press, 1932), p. 40.

112 K. Davenport, *Some Oldham Times* (Manchester: Neil Richardson 1985), p. 20.

113 Martin, *The Best Street in Rochdale*, p. 34.

114 He still had the cuff links and arm bands in retirement.

115 Hague, *Streets away*, p. 30.

116 *Ibid.*, p. 76.

117 Watkin, *From Hulme*, p. 89.

118 Hague, *Streets away*, p. 75.

119 Kay, *Chronicles*, pp. 25, 63. Kay was born c. 1914/15.

120 *Daily Mirror* (23 September 1936), p. 9. Winn, one of the highest paid journalists in Fleet Street, unlike most gay journalists, did not hide his homosexuality: A. Bingham, *Family Newspapers? Sex, Private Life and the British Popular Press, 1918–1978* (Oxford: Oxford University Press, 2009), p. 27.

121 Morgan, *Needs of Youth*, p. 108.

122 *Manchester Guardian* (7 June 1934), p. 8.

123 H. D. Willcock described three London 'youths of a "spiv" type', all of whom had 'carefully cared for hair – long with artificial waves, and a heavily greased "Boston slash back" in two cases': H. D. Willcock and Mass-Observation, *Report on Juvenile Delinquency* (London: Falcon Press, 1949), p. 50. Fyvel also highlighted hairstyles as a 'source of particular pride' among Teddy Boys, involving dryers, hairnets and special barbers: T. R. Fyvel, *The Insecure Offenders: Rebellious Youth in the Welfare State* (London: Chatto and Windus, 1961), pp. 48–51. Both cited in C. Breward, 'Style and subversion: post-war poses and the neo-Edwardian suit in mid-twentieth-century Britain', *Gender and History*, 14:3 (2002), pp. 569, 571.

124 Davenport, *Some Oldham Times*, p. 20.

125 H. Dorrell, *Falling Cadence: An Autobiography of Failure*, Burnett Archive, p. 36. Dorrell was born at Plaistow, London in 1903.

126 Davenport, *Some Oldham Times*, p. 20.

127 Furniss, *The Walls of Jericho*, p. 25.

128 Valerie Steele has highlighted the scarcity of research on hair fashions: V. Steele,

'Letter from the editor', *Fashion Theory: The Journal of Dress, Body and Culture*, 1:4 (1997), p. 337.

129 Watkin, *From Hulme*, p. 88. See F. Davis, *Fashion, Culture and Identity* (Chicago and London: University of Chicago Press, 1992).

130 Ugolini, *Men and Menswear*, pp. 69, 121–2.

131 Glasser, 'Gorbals Boy', p. 409.

132 George Turner, oral history transcript, CCINTB.

133 *Manchester Evening News* (16 May 1930), p. 10.

134 Ugolini, *Men and Menswear*, pp. 19, 21–2.

135 A. Bingham, *Gender, Modernity and the Popular Press in Britain* (Oxford: Oxford University Press, 2004), pp. 82, 217.

136 Ugolini, *Men and Menswear*, p. 122; P. Tinkler, *Smoke Signals: Women, Smoking and Visual Culture in Britain* (Oxford and New York: Berg Publishers, 2006), p. 9.

137 J. Richards, *The Age of the Dream Palace: Cinema and Society in Britain 1930–39* (London, Routledge and Kegan Paul, 1984), pp. 13–14. See also, John Sedgwick, *Popular Filmgoing in the 1930s: A Choice of Pleasures* (Exeter: University of Exeter Press, 2000).

138 Morgan, *Needs of Youth*, p. 239.

139 H. E. O. James and F. T. Moore, 'Adolescent leisure in a working class district: Part I', *Occupational Psychology*, 14:3 (1940), 132–45.

140 R. McKibbin, *Classes and Cultures: England, 1918–51* (Oxford: Oxford University Press, 1998), p. 419–21.

141 Harley, J.L., 'Report of an enquiry into the occupations, further education and leisure interests of a number of girl wage-earners from elementary and central schools in the Manchester district, with special reference to the influence of school training on their use of leisure', MEd dissertation, University of Manchester (1937), p. 109.

142 Hague, *Streets Away*, pp. 30–1.

143 Watkin, *From Hulme*, p. 92.

144 C. Langhamer, *Women's Leisure in England, 1920–1960* (Manchester: Manchester University Press, 2000), pp. 53–4; *Manchester Guardian* (23 January 1929), p. 20.

145 T. P. Benson, *As I Return to Yesteryear* (Owen Sound, Ont.: T. P. Benson, 1983), p. 68, cited in L. Murfin, *Popular Leisure in the Lake Counties* (Manchester: Manchester University Press, 1990) p. 216.

146 M. Mauss, 'Techniques of the Body', *Economy and Society*, 2: 1 (1973), pp. 70 88, cited in B. Morris, 'What we talk about when we talk about "walking in the city"', *Cultural Studies*, 18:5 (2004), 675–97, at p. 684; Harley, 'Report of an enquiry', p. 109.

147 Morgan, *Needs of Youth*, pp. 108, 403.

148 R. Bowley, 'Amusements and entertainments', p. 47; Kuhn, *Everyday Magic*, p. 110; R. Ford, *Children in the Cinema* (London: Allen and Unwin, 1939), p. 40. See also J. Stacey, 'Desperately seeking difference', in L. Gamman and M. Marshment (eds), *The Female Gaze: Women as Viewers of Popular Culture* (London: Women's Press, 1988); Kuhn, *Everyday Magic*, pp. 101, 110, 132.

149 B. Osgerby, *Playboys in Paradise: Masculinity, Youth and Leisure: Style in Modern America* (Oxford: Berg, 2001), p. 34.

150 Bingham, *Gender, Modernity*, p. 225.

151 Kay, *Chronicles*, p. 64.

152 M. O'Brien, *Framing Memories: Experiences of Picture Going and Working in Cinemas in South London between the 1920s and the 1950s* (An oral history research project undertaken for the Research and Information Division of the British Film Institute, April 1992). Gentle was born in 1926.

153 O'Brien, *Framing*. Norden was born in 1922.

154 M. Hilton, *Smoking in British Popular Culture, 1800–2000* (Manchester: Manchester University Press, 2000), p. 162; H. Hendrick, *Images of Youth. Age, Class and the Male Youth Problem, 1880–1920* (Oxford: Clarendon Press, 1990), p. 134.

155 Armitage, *The Twenty Three Years*, p. 140.

156 Waddicor, *Memories*, p. 22.

157 A. Paterson, *Across the Bridges* (London: Edward Arnold, 1912), p. 125.

158 Hilton, *Smoking*, p. 171. See also Tinkler, *Smoke Signals*.

159 B. L. Q. Henriques, *Club Leadership* (London: Oxford University Press, 1933: 1943), p. 203.

160 N. Kenyon, *I Belong to Bolton* (Manchester: Neil Richardson, 1989), pp. 9–10.

161 G. C. Hughes, *Shut the Mountain Gate*, Burnett Archive, p. 62. Hughes grew up Rhossllanerchrugog, North Wales, and started grammar school in 1922.

162 Hughes, *Shut the Mountain Gate*, p. 63.

163 *Ibid.*, p. 63.

164 Henriques, *Club Leadership*, p. 171.

165 *Ibid.*, p. 203.

166 Waddicor, *Memories*, p. 22.

167 Hilton, *Smoking*, p. 147.

168 P. Tinkler, '"Red tips for hot lips": advertising cigarettes for young women in Britain, 1920–1970', *Women's History Review*, 10:2 (2001), p. 250; Tinkler, *Smoke Signals*, pp. 44–5, 66–7.

169 *The Advertiser's Annual and Convention Year Book, 1925–6* (London: Business Publications Ltd, 1926), p. 48; *The Advertiser's Annual and Convention Year Book, 1930* (London: Business Publications Ltd, 1930), p. 18; Hilton, *Smoking*, p. 147. For women's smoking see: R. Elliot, '"Everybody did it" – or did they? The use of oral history in researching women's experiences of smoking in Britain, 1930–1970', *Women's History Review*, 15:2 (2006), p. 298; P. Tinkler, 'Rebellion, modernity and romance: smoking as a gendered practice in popular women's magazines, Britain 1918–1939', *Women's Studies International Forum*, 24:1 (2001), 111–22. Tinkler has written widely on the relationship between women's smoking and visual culture. See also, P. Tinkler, 'Refinement and respectable consumption: the acceptable face of women's smoking in Britain, 1918–1970', *Gender and History*, 15:2 (2003), 342–60; P. Tinkler, 'Sexual Politics', in J. Goodman (ed.), *Tobacco in History and Culture: An Encyclopedia* (Farmington Hills, MI: Charles Scribner's Sons, 2004); P. Tinkler, 'Advertising', in Goodman, *Tobacco*; P. Tinkler, 'Sapphic smokers and English modernities', in L. Doan and J. Garrity (eds) *Sapphic Modernities* (London: Palgrave, 2007).

170 Hilton, *Smoking*, pp. 147–8; Morgan, *Needs of Youth*, p. 255.

171 M. Conboy, *The Press and Popular Culture* (London: Sage Publications, 2002), pp. 117, 127. In 1929, Robert Blatchford pondered what Victorian grandmothers would have said about 'shameless' pictures of scantily clad young women, in the *Manchester*

Evening News (5 January 1929). The *Daily Mirror* started its 'Jane' cartoon strip in 1932.

172 For young men and consumption in the second half of the twentieth century, see F. Mort, *Cultures of Consumption: Masculinities and Social Space in Late Twentieth-Century Britain* (London: Routledge, 1996). For consumer patterns among young men in the United States, see M. A. Swiencicki, 'Consuming brotherhood: men's culture, style and recreation as consumer culture, 1880–1930', *Journal of Social History*, 31:4 (1998), 773–809.

173 J. J. Matthews, *Dance Hall and Picture Palace: Sydney's Romance with Modernity* (Sydney: Currency Press, 2005), p. 244.

4

Sex and sentiment

N ew generational narratives emerged in the 1920s – of young men's anger against the old and older people's incomprehension of the wilful, undisciplined youth of all classes.[1] Criticisms of young people's waywardness are a familiar theme of the history of youth, but were a sign in the 1920s of an informalising culture in which sex and sentiment were assuming new cultural meanings. The boundaries of social life were shifting, albeit unevenly across generations and classes. Young people were more relaxed and less inhibited than their pre-war predecessors, and their 'cheekiness' to parents and elders became a 'favourite theme with many novelists and playwrights'.[2] Robert Roberts, in his teens after the war, recalled how his young contemporaries revelled in the freer social conventions which so agitated their elders:

> Clothes grew lighter in colour and weight. The young men in their ever-widening 'bags' and double-breasted jackets, slicked and fresh, a different race from their fathers, 'jazzed' with the shameless females in those dance halls and they became together, almost incidentally, the first 'moderns' of the twentieth century.[3]

Not all families adapted easily to the new freedoms many adolescents sought, particularly as expanding commercial leisure introduced new opportunities; arguments over curfews and coming home became a common source of disagreement across the inter-war years and were often described in letters to popular advice columns, as we shall see in Chapter 5.[4] Despite continuing parental efforts to instil discipline and maintain control, relationships between adults and young people were loosening, becoming less distant as 'the gulf that had stood so long between parent and child began to narrow at last'.[5] Many returning soldiers wanted greater involvement in bringing up their children and became much closer to them; Don Haworth, born in 1924, thought that the war had encouraged a gentler approach to child rearing.[6] Despite its casting 'the shadow of a great bereavement' over his early childhood, the children of his generation were its 'beneficiaries, cherished, protected and spared harshness'.[7] Soldiers' need for physical contact in the trenches was shadowed in the civilian sphere, where memories shaped when the war's emotional impact was most intense often convey a strong sense of the link between touch and emotions.[8] William Woodruff, born in 1916, was too young for clear recollections of the war years but recalled the physical metaphors his mother used when describing the impact that the first casualty lists from the Battle of the Somme had upon the people of Blackburn: 'Everybody felt they'd been kicked in the belly. "You couldn't go out, without having to stop and hold somebody's hand," she said.'[9]

If post-war family life was marked for some by kindness and greater understanding, other legacies were more damaging. A sense of vulner-ability and need for sensory affirmation shaped distinctive microclimates within families. Joseph Armitage lost his brother, two uncles and a cousin during the war, and the shock of his brother's death at Gallipoli in 1915 so affected his mother that Joseph was not allowed out of her sight for the next two years, making him a virtual 'prisoner' at home.[10] Many who entered their teens and early twenties in the early post-war years and the 1920s had become used to a social world in which the older genera-tion's assumed authority had been undermined by the absence of male relatives and neighbours. Joe Loftus's father returned from war to find that his eldest sons had matured and learned to 'manage without him for four years'.[11] 'Frustrated by family duties he had almost forgotten', he tried 'to re-assert himself against the lightest opposition at every turn if only to save his own face'. 'No longer the lynchpin in a home where his sons could now pay their way and wanted their own say', he started to spend little time there, returning only for meals and then off drinking, becoming taciturn, whether drunk or sober.[12] Woodruff's father, gassed and invalided out of the army in 1918, returned a much changed man. Severe hardship and unemployment in the 1920s accentuated his grow-ing 'moodiness and flashes of temper' and created an oppressive atmos-phere which did much to accentuate his son's emotional sensitivities.[13]

The early lives of many who left school and entered work towards the mid 1920s had been spent in the shadow of mental distress whose full significance they often took years to appreciate.[14] Puzzling undertows of sadness were often remembered, as older family members struggled to cope with the after-effects of bereavement or changed family dynam-ics.[15] 'Grief and sorrow' were a 'fact of life' in Frank Pritchard's child-hood.[16] Eli Hague 'vividly' recalled confusing Christmas day celebrations in the early 1920s at his local Gospel Mission Hall, where children raced about in high spirits while 'crowds of grown-ups', many of them crying, gathered around a large picture frame containing 'rows of small photographs'. Hague was 10 and it was only when he was older that he realised that these photographs, of Mission members who had died during the war, were evoking memories which were still 'painfully raw'.[17]

The psychological consequences of early childhood years spent amidst heightened emotional sensitivities from the war are difficult to evaluate, although some contemporaries recognised their implications. By the 1930s, professionals were attributing contemporary delinquency to the 'sequels' of war stress, seen 'not in the men who served in the war but in the next generation'. Children born during the war remained a particular cause for concern, as became apparent on reaching their 21st birthdays in the mid 1930s; the novelist and writer Francis Evans Baily described them as 'unlike any other generation within living memory', with particular problems, having grown up with their own 'peculiar outlook' and 'handicaps'.[18] Boys, especially, had to be treated 'totally' differently from those born before and after the war because they were 'more highly strung', an inference of nerves and instability which Baily contrasted with their female peers' drive and initiative. Such concerns, accentuated by the worsening international political situation, encapsulated many broader fears about social and cultural feminisation, which was frequently attributed to weak or absent male influence within families. Baily's observations suggest the importance of not conflating the experiences of youth generations across the 1920s and 1930s. Half the troops in France were 18 when the armistice was declared in 1918, and what young soldiers experienced in the trenches bore no comparison to the lives of the generations who left school in the 1920s, or of those who entered adolescence in the 1930s. Working-class young people who entered their teens in the 1930s were a very different generation, part of the first to grow up in the shadow of modern mass culture, whose increasingly sexualised associations added new layers of anxiety to the worries about youthful indiscipline and informality which had emerged so strongly in the previous decade.

Sexual landscapes

By the 1930s, the sensual arousal associated with Hollywood glamour, the growth of human-interest stories in newspapers and magazines and greater social mixing in the teens were investing young people's attitudes and behaviour with a misleading veneer of 'knowingness' and sophistication which led to much misunderstanding and pruri-ence. 'Sexual subjects' and the 'ways of modern youth' were popular topics among readers of both sexes, although actual levels of young peo-ple's sexual activity remained a mystery, some arguing that they were extremely low and others that they were increasing.[19] Many applauded how social relationships between boys and girls were changing.[20] *The New Survey of London Life and Labour* commended their healthier, more natural character and greater public openness over 'matters of sex relationships', although it blamed the war for more relaxed 'moral standards', which had increased the proportion of women and girls who engaged in 'sex adventure'.[21] Morgan agreed that 'companion-ship' and contacts between young men and women were franker and much freer than even twenty years previously and suggested that there was more widespread 'factual knowledge of sex matters', although what exactly this comprised was unclear.[22] Commentators could only specu-late about whether these changes had also led to an increase in sexual relations; there was 'probably more sex experience among adolescents' than 'some simple folk' imagined, although the extent to which working-class people engaged in sexual intercourse before marriage is impossible to estimate.[23] Public discussion of sexual issues was largely restricted to what took place within marriage, and continuing emphasis on will-power and self-restraint reinforced traditional moral pressures and expectations of sexual 'conformity'.[24] Those with sexual knowledge and experience were largely confined to artistic, bohemian circles, sectors of the upper classes, sailors and the lower sectors of the working class.[25] Sexual activity does seem to have been rising, however, among those who were engaged or courting.[26] Eustace Chesser suggested that the incidence of petting and premarital sexual intercourse rose between the 1900s and the Second World War. Nineteen per cent of married women born before 1904 and who reached sexual maturity during or immedi-ately after the First World War admitted to having had premarital sex. This rose to 36 per cent among those born between 1904 and 1914, who were children or adolescents during the war and whose sexual maturity in the 1920s coincided with the more relaxed social attitudes described earlier. The figure rose again, to 39 per cent among married women born between 1914 and 1924, who reached sexual maturity in the 1930s, and to 43 per cent among those born between 1924 and 1934.[27] Admissions of premarital sexual behaviour were marked by considerable class and gender differences; the poorest were most likely to have had sex before marriage, men were more likely than women to admit 'to having had sex with their spouse' before marriage. Most young women sought marriage rather than a casual relationship, and only entertained sex if they were courting or in a serious relationship.[28] Mass Observation investigations of contemporary sexual activity in the late 1930s of young women holidaying in Blackpool suggested the pragmatism with which they regarded their holiday freedoms. 'On holiday, when you didn't know who the man was', there was 'all the more reason to be careful'.[29] Mass Observation 'observer units' 'combed the sands of Blackpool' at all hours looking for sexual activity, but the dunes on which they so assiduously preyed yielded less than they had anticipated; having 'expected to see copulation everywhere', they found only 'petting and feeling'. The survey concluded that the amount of extra-marital intercourse taking place was 'negligible, less than on a Saturday night in Worktown'.[30]

The survey notably failed to address the vulnerability of young women on their own, although older female respondents, more sensitive to such vulnerabilities, warned of out-of-the-way places which were unsafe 'for young girls'.[31] The police regarded these young female visitors as 'hard-boiled' and unlikely to come to much harm; quite a few were brought in drunk, there were 'no cases of rape', although such views were disingenuous, given the immense difficulties of prosecuting cases of sexual violence. Much of Mass Observation's own unwitting evidence suggests the sexual pressures young women came under once they were on their own. The survey casually noted how a girl recorded in the dunes was heard 'sobbing' ' "oh Ted, Ted. Oh, what are you doing" ', which suggests darker stories of Blackpool's sexual licence and the extent to which young women's freedom and security in Blackpool lay with their friendships and group identity.[32]

Changing discourses of sexuality perpetuated the more liberal views of sex which so worried contemporaries. Writers of stories in 'twopenny fiction weeklies' were, by the mid 1930s, for example, able to send their hero and heroine away on a weekend together before marriage, which would have been 'unthinkable' thirty years previously.[33] By the late 1930s, concern at apparently rising levels of sexual activity among the young was encouraging new moral 'panics' around the advertising and sale of contraceptives from slot machines in urban areas like London, Birmingham and Manchester.[34] An MP condemned the ease with which they could be obtained from a machine labelled 'Veribest Cigarettes' outside a shop doorway in Manchester used by 'children' aged 14 and 15.[35] A federation of boys' clubs in an industrial district described how a crowd of young people 'not yet in their teens' had been seen playing with contraceptives after 'manipulating' them from a similar machine outside a shop.[36] There was particular criticism of the ease with which 'factory girls' and young 'party girls' could buy them.[37] (Factory girls and party girls, hinting the promiscuous flapper, were familiar emblems of female immorality.) It was boys, however, who usually bought them, obtaining them surreptitiously in a variety of ways. 'Touts' in factories and workshops sold them, as did most chemists, albeit with 'some sort of sly wink or observation'.[38] They could also be bought in barbers' shops, although Ted Furniss recalled in the 1930s 'selling something that bore the mark "Top Secret" and people used to shout you outside the shop if they wanted to purchase any. I've even let the local boys take them and pay me on Friday, when they got their dole money.'[39] Many of the poor found them too expensive. Glasser pointed out that 'French letters were not cheap',[40] while scholarship boy Dennis Houlston recalled how 'you *knew*' about condoms, 'vaguely', but you couldn't obtain them because:

> you had no money, and if you went in a chemist [*laughs*], Aa mean he would look at *you* in your school cap and blazer, and *probably* if he was to sell them, *even* if you'd got the nerve to ask, which you *hadn't*, and the barber always says, 'Anything for the weekend, sir?' you *knew* that from your elder brother, but Aa mean when you had your *hair* cut, you couldn't say 'Could Aa have something for the *weekend*!' So you had no chance of reaching condoms so you *accepted* you couldn't get them so this, again, kept you on the straight and narrow.[41]

Some feared that more harm than good would be caused by publicising their very availability, and the BBC was criticised for broadcasting a 'résumé' of a Bill on this 'which must have been heard by many thousands of children and adolescents, and aroused their 'natural curiosity'.[42] Others thought that time would have been better spent on improving young people's sex education so that they would know how to use them properly.[43] Such suggestions reflected broader trends among medical, educational and welfare professionals, many of whom were increasingly sympathetic to the need for sex education, in part as a result of better understanding of the role that sexual feelings played in child development.[44]

In 1926, the Hadow Report had stressed the importance of teaching hygiene and physiology, and youth organisations were considering the question of 'sex instruction' among young people in the early 1930s, when the issue was discussed in women's magazines and by social critics, who thought it should play an important role in preparing the young for 'mating' and responsible citizenship.[45]

Many feared that improved knowledge would only encourage sexual experimentation, however, and religious and establishment pressure ensured that there was little official guidance about how to approach the subject in schools. A 'discursive stranglehold' of 'secrecy, shame and embarrassment' continued to surround the acquisition of sexual knowledge.[46] Even those parents who believed in the need for sex education were 'bewildered' about how to go about it, held back by a deeply embedded moral puritanism, while many involved in educational work with adolescents were similarly 'petrified' by lack of confidence in broaching such matters.[47] Henriques thought that 'probably few aspects of club life' caused a club leader 'more anxiety than that of sex', and club leaders were urged to read up on it so they could confidently address the questions put to them, and not be 'embarrassed or nonplussed when consulted in confidence'.[48] Henriques saw no reason why club libraries should not contain 'sex books', so long as they were carefully vetted, although these were more likely guides for unconfident teachers and youth workers.[49] Most young people found out about sex subversively, through street talk, sexual teasing and innuendo, work-place gossip, and advice against the dangers of venereal disease (VD) and masturbation.[50] Much of the slang surrounding sex was aggressive and predatory, and sexual boasting, jokes and swearing gave a misleading air of knowingness to many personal and sexual uncertainties, although boys' 'smutty talk' about sex tended to bear little relation to what they actually did.[51] Harry Dorrell and his mates met up in his father's allotment shed to 'talk and joke, snigger at what we understood as dirty stories' – misleading information which did little to overcome the many private anxieties, as P. H. of Barry explained, describing how his friends had given him the idea that there was 'something beastly and degrading about marriage', and his 'wretched' feelings at knowing nothing about sex.[52] Joe Loftus similarly suggested how 'warnings and fears' reinforced his confusion and guilt, and that of his friends, about their 'sexual desires'.[53] By the time they were 12 or 13 boys were monitoring not only girls' bodies but their own.[54] Harold Gill, for example, recalled how:

> As visible proof of the beginnings of manhood, an embryonic black hair, be it chest or pubic, – a sometimes solitary single strand, – was exhibited proudly to the curious, and envious glances of slighter, and less fortunate scholars in the toilets, or at P.T. This display, – irrefutable evidence of maturity was greeted with all the sounds and the manifestations of a mixture of awe, and reverance [sic]. Whatever the length or texture of the strand, the overall requirement demanded that it should be black. Brown simply would not do, and any exhibitor who displayed, prematurely such a strand was 'laughed to scorn'. Thus, a single black strand of hair was hailed as a more significant portent even than voice breaking that it's [sic] proud owner was poised on the brink of manhood.[55]

The rough and tumble of the work-place gave many working-class boys a more thorough grounding in the sexual facts of life than at home or in school, which contrasted with the longer-lasting ignorance of their middle-class counterparts. Robert Ward, a Lancashire scholarship boy with no sisters and whose social life revolved around the chapel, was 'completely ignorant of the details of the female form, or of the whole business of intercourse and reproduction' until he was nearly 20. Even at college he thought he could make a girl pregnant by kissing her, eventually learning the facts of life from reading Marie Stopes's *Married Love*.[56] Joseph Armitage, a year younger than Ward, picked up what he knew by spying on the sexual couplings of a 16-year-old girl and two lads who had sneaked off to have sex, while he and his companion watched.[57] Loftus, who worked in a mill which employed women and girls, recalled its sweltering atmosphere and sexual excitement:

> There was always the odd moment when you might find yourself in the narrow alley between the tall bobbin racks, near a girl scavenger who felt like giving you the 'come on'. Teasing you with her back to you, stroking your crotch while your tiller got instantly air-borne inside your drawers. Maybe tilting her lightly clad buttocks towards you as she bent to her work, rather lower than she needed, winking and smiling at you over her shoulder. Knowing a swift touch-up was all you had time or opportunity to try, with a giggle and a muted shriek as your reward, plus the lingering tactile impression.
>
> We lads and lassies joked and kidded about it, but most of it was talk, wasn't it, just to pass the time? Boasting of swift insertions, with sharp intakes of breath and thrutching [*sic*] movements to illustrate. Though I wouldn't have put it past one or two, I thought enviously. Because most of us lads walked a bit stiff-legged at times, didn't we?[58]

Bill Naughton's interest in improving his physical strength coincided with a growing obsession about 'what had up to then been a word of little significance – *sex*'.[59] Increasingly alert to the sexual antics and rumours which surrounded friends and neighbours, he was easily aroused by a not too carefully dressed woman kneeling to stone her steps and flags, and gives an unusual insight into the sexual frustrations of early adolescence and the guilt to which they gave rise:

> In what I took to be saner moments I began to regard this erotic excitement as something foul and beastly, a visitation of the devil – it had to be the devil as it was so pleasurable – to plague me, and me alone, since so far as I could see no other boy seemed troubled. One never read of lads in books being concerned with sex.[60]

Boys from strict religious backgrounds, segregated from girls and convinced that sex was a sin, were similarly assailed by many 'clashing emotions'. Albert Mitchell, the son of a 'stern' Victorian father, fell in love twice during his late teens, towards the end of the 1930s, but both affairs were 'completely platonic' and caused him 'great anguish' because he was 'completely unable' to release his 'deeper feelings in any way, and transfer them into the warmth of a human relationship'.[61] Joe Loftus similarly recalled how 'Catholic teachings of inborn sinfulness' ensured he grew up with many inhibitions towards girls and women.[62] Naughton, keen to find anything that would assuage his ignorance 'scoured' the library for books on the human body, drawing sexual titillation and a modicum of understanding from a range of popular and more esoteric publications which included 'erotic bloods', medical literature and leaflets warning against the dangers of VD.

Decades later, James Brooke still recalled the potent message of his youth about being very careful about 'which girl you picked up with', after attending a two-hour lecture by the Health and Strength League on the dangers of venereal disease, at the Palace Theatre, Oldham, where the lecturer told them that 'it took just two seconds for the germ of this disease to penetrate through rubber', and advised them to 'steer clear of sex' until they were certain where they 'were going'.[63] Propaganda films by the British Social Hygiene Council often made a powerful impression on young, sexually ignorant audiences.[64] Frank Pritchard's memories of going with some work-mates to see a film called *The Dangers of Ignorance* when he was about 16 convey something of this lack of knowledge, and the bravado to which it gave rise.

> It was a 'horror film', insofar as it illustrated venereal diseases at all stages, and the consequences when risking casual sexual intercourse. There was a grave risk of going blind, deaf, daft or even of dying. It certainly put the wind up me, completely putting me off associating with girls for at least a month.[65]

While the dangers of VD continued to attract much publicity, denunciations of masturbation were less vociferous than before the war, with liberal writers on the subject more likely to stress the dangers of worrying about masturbation than masturbation itself.[66] Medical science emphasised the need to eradicate old myths about a practice which was common among 'over 90 per cent of people', so that youth could be 'liberated' from 'unnecessary shame' and 'psychical burdens'.[67] The National Sunday School Union welcomed the removal of exaggerated stories which had 'unnecessarily frightened' many boys, but still condemned masturbation for its 'psychological' effects, emphasising that boys could only attain 'full manhood' through self-control; 'mastery over themselves' would help make it little different from 'picking the nose or any other nauseating habit'.[68] Scientific 'facts' replaced religious emphases as a way of persuading boys against masturbation. Before adult maturity, it was said that practically all a male's semen was needed for process of 're-absorption' after reaching the testicles, and if any were 'wasted, either by masturbation or by sexual intimacy with a woman', his body would be deprived of those 'reserves of nervous and physical vigour' which had to be drawn on in 'emergencies'.[69]

The psychological implications of fear and ignorance about sex motivated many inter-war campaigners for sex education, such as Dr Christine Murrell, who had been shocked by how many of her patients were 'mentally embarrassed' because of their inability to find any reliable information about sex.[70] The socialist writer and journalist Leonora Eyles promoted her beliefs in sex education through the advice columns of socialist periodicals such as *Lansbury's Labour Weekly,* and *The Miner,* where her beliefs that sex education would take the fear, shame and 'dirtiness' out of sex were fiercely debated after she wrote a feature emphasising its importance, having received several 'upsetting' letters from single women in their teens pleading for advice because they were pregnant. All were ignorant about sex and their bodies, knowing nothing more than 'dirty and disgusting' rumours. Eyles, who stressed the importance of sex education for both girls and boys, was unusual in addressing not only the physical but also the emotional changes which affected both during adolescence.[71] Not only was it important to tell girls about menstruation; parents should also explain to boys about how their bodies were changing, and how these 'new emotions' and physical transformations could cause 'depressions, tempers, passionate feelings':[72]

> If their parents and the rest of the family will only realise that tantrums are as much a symptom as the breaking voice and bad complexion with which so many boys are afflicted, they will find it easier to be patient.[73]

Most mothers were sympathetic to daughters in their teens, 'even if they did not quite understand them', but many failed to realise that boys had 'just as much to go through'. 'A little sympathy and comradeship' from father and men in authority over boys would go 'a very long way towards making a man of a nervous boy'.[74]

Eyles's article stirred up something of a hornet's nest in *The Miner,* initiated by a member of Tyne Dock Women's Section and of Durham Labour Women's Advisory Council who protested at its 'disgusting' content and threatened to send a copy of her letter to all the women's sections in Durham County if it were not published. She called the idea of sex education for 'children' 'monstrous' and declared she would no longer read either *The Miner* or the *Daily Herald* (in which Eyles also wrote).[75] *The Miner* printed a page of letters supporting Eyles, claiming to have received only one other letter of disagreement, which was 'couched in such libellous and abusive terms' that it had been returned. Most focused on girls' sexual vulnerability, several stressing how sexual ignorance aided the exploitation of girls and young women by boys and men inside and outside families.[76] Others, like the 'mother' whose 13-year-old son had read the article and passed it on to his school mates, thanked Eyles and highlighted the reticence which prevented even sympathetic parents from talking to their adolescent children about such matters:

> My son told me how glad he was when I told him to read Mrs Eyles's article, as he heard such a lot of horrid things at school, and he had been hoping I would tell him the truth for quite a long time (I have been asking his father to explain things about twelve months, but he has fought shy of the matter), so thanks to Leonora Eyles I have been able to explain.[77]

Despite a trickle of dissension, most letters were in her favour, including several from men whose memories of the ignorance and confusion they had experienced made them more sensitive to what their adolescent sons were going through.[78] One 'young father', for example, described how the 'mental and physical' suffering he had experienced when young would help him to ensure that his own sons were properly 'forewarned' against the youthful 'temptations' with which he had had to 'contend'.[79]

For all the public preoccupations with young people's sexual activity, and personal anxieties about sexual feelings, however, the many uncertainties to which both boys and girls were prey in adolescence were a complex mix which ranged beyond the sexual, as the Home and School Council suggested in a report on the sorts of queries which frequently came up on visits to schools to speak about the problems of adolescence. Boys 'equally with girls' wanted to know how to deal with babies and small children, and there were questions about how to stop friends telling smutty stories; why ninety-nine out of a hundred parents 'tell us lies about where we come from'; how to overcome self-consciousness; how to increase 'courage' at a certain exercise in the gymnasium; whether friendship with a girl could help a boy; whether it was possible to be in love at 16?[80] Confessions of sexual uncertainty were understandably absent in such a public setting, but the issues which were raised suggest a common intermingling of social uncertainties, personal anxieties and family responsibilities. Adolescent sensitivity to social situations and relationships, intensified by the physiological changes of adolescence, was exacerbated not only by friendships, family and work-place dynamics, but by coming into contact with the bewildering new behavioural etiquettes which accompanied the expansion of modern mass culture. Adults may well have been troubled by increasing sexualising influences upon adolescents, but young people themselves were grappling not only with sexual ignorance but also with their own vacillating emotions. As we shall see, cinema inflected these emotional and sexual landscapes, offering a potent combination of moving images, sound and colour which manipulated 'body senses and feelings' and accentuated personal uncertainties, yet was also a channel for emotional expression and release.[81]

Imagination and emotions

The sexualized emphases of the mass media and visual cultures in the 1930s reinforced post-war concerns about liberalizing social mores, particularly in relation to the emotional and psychological impact of films and film stars on adolescents. Broader adult fears about loss of control over the adolescent imagination combined, in the case of boys, with worries that their emergent adult masculinity might be compromised at a time of particular psychological vulnerability.[82] By the 1930s many young people had been influenced by the cinema since their earliest years, often having accompanied older relatives as toddlers or young children.[83] Those who entered their teens from the mid 1920s and in the 1930s were not only the first generation to have been familiar with the cinema from early childhood, but also the first to experience the powerful visual and auditory combination of the 'talkies'. Their advent in 1927 contributed a significant new sensory dimension to films, and gave young people useful cultural small change in relation to older generations, who were oblivious to the innuendo and wise-cracking which working-class boys and young men particularly liked about American films.[84] Such was the 'vividness' of Hollywood films that it had capacity to 'stir the curiosity, heat the imagination, and work upon the fantasies, of boys and girls of every age'.[85] Nineteen-year-old Walter Wilkinson, who believed film was 'the greatest boon of modern times', remarked that whenever he had 'a few idle hours', his thoughts usually went to the cinema.[86] Moral advice had, since the nineteenth century, cautioned against the 'treacherous effects' of fantasy, but such concerns were intensified by the cinema's capacity to fill the adolescent imagination with unsuitable 'models and material'.[87] Cyril Burt thought that adolescents were particularly susceptible to 'all-engrossing day-dreams', and that 'most delinquents – indeed, nearly all at adolescence' were 'habitual day-dreamers'. Reverie among boys was also considered an especially worrying sign of effeminacy, which, though short-lived among 'ordinary lads', might last for 'days at a time' with girls and 'highly-strung and sensitive youths'.[88] Day-dreaming was also associated with obsessive masturbation and the 'sex impulse', which the cinema's 'visual and visceral' power was said to aggravate, although the erotic charge of films varied over the course of the inter-war years.[89] The Depression, for example, encouraged the film industry to ignore moral sensibilities in efforts to push up their audiences, and gangster, sex and horror films produced between 1930 and 1934 were more daring than after the middle of the decade, when censorship controls were tightened.[90] Dennis Houlston recalled these earlier, more sexually suggestive films. He had passed to grammar school, and frequently referred to himself as 'still a schoolboy' when describing them, a term whose inexperienced connotations allowed him not only to recall but to dwell on his evocative memories of the scanty underwear worn by female stars, 'leg shots', 'decolletage', 'stocking tops', 'bits of those female bodies which, you know, we'd only dreamed about'.[91] Houlston's unusual glimpse into his youthful erotic imagination, sparked by a particular period in film history that was already passing by the mid 1930s, suggests the cinema's tantalising power in a sexually repressive culture, its capacity to enhance the 'unclean mental pictures' which made masturbation 'sinful' when 'consciously and deliberately entertained'.[92] Youth organisers such as Valentine Bell were very alive to the impact certain kinds of film had on young male wage-earners, the humorous response he elicited from an audience of boys' club workers suggesting the casual violence and semi-pornographic images which had titillated an earlier generation:

> His interest in the 'pictures,' especially those with sex appeal, is enormous, and a great deal of nonsense is talked about the harmful effect of them. It is a problem that has to be faced, but after all, at that age, the desire for sex knowledge is perfectly natural. It was the same when we were young, before the cinematograph was invented. If I remember rightly, we went to the local paper shop to gaze at the 'Police Budget' with its picture of a woman hanging halfway out of bed with her throat cut (laughter).[93]

The mass leisure industry made deliberate use of 'film star glamour' in targeting young people's 'sex instincts', as was very apparent in Blackpool, whose reputation as a seaside resort was marketed through the scantily clad female body (male bodies were largely confined to jokes about nudist camps). Images of bathing girls in the latest swimwear, mainly 'brassiere and shorts' rarely seen in Blackpool, targeted a youthful masculinity with the implication that the unmarried man was 'more "male" than his married counterpart'.[94] Hollywood glamour and film-star pin-ups helped to fashion erotic day-dreams and fantasies for young people in many different ways. 'Serious' cinema-goers frequently expressed their annoyance at being 'surrounded by a lot of dreamy youngsters bent on emulating the silly close-ups on the screen'.[95] Mass Observation, eavesdropping on a group of young women who were planning what games to play at a forthcoming Sunday party heard them discussing not only the familiar 'Postman's knock' but another game called 'film stars', which involved all the 'girls' going out while the men chose a film star, 'such as Robert Taylor, Clark Gable, etc.' The girl then returned, and if she said a correct name, went to sit with whoever had chosen it. 'When each film star has a girl, the lights are turned off.'[96]

Many who worked closely with boys and young men, sensitised by the new psychology of adolescence, were mindful of distinctions between inner feelings and outer show, and the educationalist A. J. Jenkinson suggested the insecurity and malleability of adolescent masculinities. He observed how boys in their early teens were beset by growing 'self-consciousness' and often 'intensely aware of themselves in relation to and in comparison with others'. They tried to control their uncertainties and doubts 'by abject heartburning conformity' and aggressiveness. Boys of 12, 13 and 14 suspected 'all expressions of emotion' and tried to hide their feelings in many different ways, including 'a fearful reluctance to let themselves go' and acute embarrassment at any reference to 'love affairs'.[97] Younger boys particularly disliked screen 'sloppiness', often greeted with catcalls and shouting, although the conservative nature of peer-group pressure established not only how they should respond to particular kinds of film, but also that they should keep their real feelings hidden:[98]

> the ooing and aahing when someone kissed a girl for the *boys* anyway that was totally *unmanly!* [laughs] And obviously, they *pretended* to think that it was! [laughs] It was a *convention*.[99]

As they moved, in mid adolescence, from group interaction with girls to 'dating' and courtship, many boys became more receptive to the erotic potential of much-derided love films and much more aware of the cinema's courtship potential. Les's diaries, for example, often referred to girls he had seen there. After watching a film with his brother, for example, he observed how 'Some girl in there kept making eyes at me.'[100] He 'got off with a nice girl' while waiting in the queue at one local cinema, and later coyly noted seeing 'a girl who sat near us who looked at me and who I should like to know and speak to'.[101] On a visit to the newly built 'super-cinema', one of the attendants stood near him, who was 'a very nice girl', and he was on the look-out for her again in the following weeks, noting when he had seen her, and when he had not.[102] Northampton had twelve cinemas by the mid 1930s, and Les attended most of them over the two years of his diaries.[103] With the loss of both of his cinema companions, as described in the Introduction, he started going more often on his own. Boys had greater freedom for such solitary activities, which, as we have seen, were less risky than for girls, and his willingness to range widely around different cinemas and to attend both alone and with friends con-trasted with his sister's practice. Gwen went to the pictures only with friends or family members because, as she put it, 'girls never went on their own, unless they were like, on the look-out'. Many 'girl wage earn-ers' in Manchester expressed similar sentiments, preferring 'see the same film twice rather than go to a less familiar cinema' where they did not know the people who went there.[104]

By their mid teens, George Hughes and his friends were select-ing their films with greater care than in early adolescence, altogether more responsive to 'romances' that were 'adult in concept'.[105] Others also recalled how their film interests had gradually altered. One young man, for example, described how he had gravitated from cowboys, murders and mysteries towards 'stories and romances' at 'about the age of four-teen' as love 'crept' into his heart.[106] Many boys by the age of 15 were said to be much more interested in 'love stories', and demon-strated a 'fresh (adult) interest in poetry'.[107] The adventure stories which boys read (though 'few' written for them) often had a 'love interest', and Dave Russell points to the 'rather unexpected' fact that almost all of the 'sporting adventures' popularised in inter-war sport and adven-ture serials 'involved a serious, and always requited, love between hero and heroine', with moments of sporting triumph 'invariably followed by the hand of the trainer/manager/director's daughter'.[108] Such themes could, of course, reflect authorial awareness of a female readership; many girls were keen readers of boys' magazines, attracted by the assertive role models they found there.[109] Nevertheless, as Russell urges, their 'preva-lence' should encourage some reconsideration of assumptions that boys' literature 'traditionally served to keep the opposite sex at a very safe distance'.[110]

The cinema had an important sensory impact upon young people's developing sense of self, as is evident from autobiographical and oral history testimonies which recreate the intensity of early encounters with film, but the particular influence of glamorous Hollywood films in the 1930s was perhaps heightened by the fact that these young cinema audiences were less cynical than later ones about their 'message' and the 'authority' of their content.[111] J. P. Mayer's 'first in-depth' academic research into cinema audiences, published in the late 1940s, offers a suggestive account of the emotional and psychological implications of film-going for some young audiences.[112] The anonymous, self-selected sample on which he based his findings was the result of a competition in *Picturegoer*, a popular magazine for film fans, which had requested readers to write in with their 'motion picture autobiographies'. Respondents were asked to give their age, sex, occupation, parents' occupation and nationality, and received guidance notes about how to structure their answers by tracing the history of their interest in films, how films had influenced their play and other activities, examples of being frightened by films, how films had affected their emotions and how films might have influenced occupational ambitions or desires to travel. Two hundred film-going 'autobiographies' were submitted, of which sixty were published 'practically unedited . . . as we received them'.[113] These were overwhelmingly from clerks and 'other black-coated' workers, and mostly (forty-two) from girls and women, which supports well-established interpretations of their absorption in cinema culture. What are of particular concern in what follows, however, are the accounts by young men which, while not representative of cinema-goers as a whole, offer suggestive alternative narratives of the role that films played in their lives.

Mayer noted how many respondents 'seemed to welcome the opportunity of expressing themselves', using the competition as something of an 'emotional outlet'.[114] Not surprisingly, most were avid cinema-goers, often very knowledgeable about the films they saw, several young men using their passion for the cinema to highlight their own distinction from the crowd of mainstream film-goers. A 25-year-old clerk in a printing office described his main claim to fame as the longevity of his cinema-going, calling himself a 'veteran' who first entered the cinema (in his mother's arms) 'at the age of one month'. 'Even in this movie-minded era, I fancy that must be a rather unusual record for one of my age.' His parents were working class (his father was an electrician) and he described his life other than that as 'commonplace and dull enough', but his story was of a serious-minded individual with strong literary interests, including 'books, drama and particularly the movies', who felt apart from ordinary cinema-goers and others in his class.[115] Movies were not a 'habit' but a 'hobby', having been his 'one absorbing interest' since about the age of 15. A self-conscious critic, he made the point that he was not duped by what he saw, having since his earliest years been conscious that 'screen actors were merely actors playing a part'. 'Being unemotional and not romantically inclined', he had 'never' felt himself 'in love with leading ladies'.[116] He was a bachelor who had 'every intention of remaining in that happy state' and claimed never to have 'yearned' for the 'company of the opposite sex' or even of his own sex. He was not a good mixer, and had never experienced anything 'in the nature of romance or sexual love'. He went to the cinema 'not for companionship' but to enjoy the films. 'For that reason, when I do not go by myself, I go with my mother – for the simple reason that my mother is the only person I have met whose tastes coincide with mine.'

The social snobbery and elitism of this rather self-obsessed young man contrasts with other writers' accounts which suggest how films became a means of reflecting on themselves and coming to a clearer appreciation of their own individuality and identity, growing familiarity with artificial film conventions making them more aware of the value of 'being oneself' and having their own 'personality'. A 24-year-old joiner described how he had gone through a phase of thinking that films made him 'more receptive to love-making', when he had believed that

> an imitation of Gable or Power would delight the girlfriend. Whether it did or not I cant [sic] say as my imitation probably had no resemblance. I soon realised though that imitations are cheap and naturalness is the only course.[117]

Several writers clearly distinguished their own 'love-making' from what they saw on the screen, a 20-year-old factory hand in a plastics firm typically professing to have more confidence in his own romantic techniques: 'To change the subject to Love, I'm not very keen on seeing those films, I happen to use my own according Love on girls, and no film star imitating.'[118] Another 20-year-old was going out with a girl who saw the same films as he did and knew when he was play-acting:

> Love making to me is, as yet, a subject not broached very freely. Luckily enough, my girl friend is also a keen film fan and she, like myself, has a hearty dislike for most love scenes, especially those of Char. Boyer. So I need no technique but my own and should I try to imitate a star, she'd know at once, and I'd be in the soup.[119]

Films played a different role for those with little or no experience of having a girlfriend, feeding fantasies that they might one day be able to put what they saw into practice. A 23-year-old male shop assistant described how he tried 'to take tips in love affairs and romance pictures' because 'one never knows that one day it may provide me with an ever lasting sweetheart of my own'.[120] A bank clerk a couple of years younger 'freely' admitted that he had 'learned a lot on the technique of love-making from the films. Probably all I know in fact.'[121] A schoolboy claimed that 'flims' had given him 'knowledge and a lot more ideas in love making', while a reserved 'sixteen and a half' year-old short-hand typist thought they had made him 'more receptive to love-making', but was sorry to say it was 'of very little use' to him since he was still 'very shy towards where girls are concerned'.[122]

Films clearly provided a welcome escape from shyness and social anxieties for several respondents, as was very apparent in the case of this 'sixteen and half' year-old. He had been 13 and still at elementary school when he started regularly going to the cinema at the suggestion of a friend who thought it would help 'broaden his outlook on life' because he was 'rather shy'. This implies he was not very sociable, but he had, in fact, been a keen member of the Young Men's Christian Association, attending as often as six times a week and cycling or walking with his 'pals' every Sunday. 'Broadening his outlook on life' could have meant many things, but, given this established pattern of recreation, the encouragement to become a film-goer may have had much to do with the belief that it would broaden his understanding of girls, women, love and romance. The well-meaning advice had had rather unfortunate results, however, since he had become rather obsessive, attending as often as five times a week and becoming so absorbed that his 'ordinary life' had completely changed. All his previous interests had come to 'a terrific Halt', the loss of so much social contact apparently intensifying his personal problems, because since he had so keenly 'taken' to films he had become 'easily irritated and upset' and had very little interest in his work.[123]

Some young men had far more pragmatic views of what they saw, a 21-year-old miner professing never to have been frightened or emotional over any film, and not 'minding' the 'love scenes . . . as long as there's not to [sic] much of it', but others were not quite so sanguine.[124] A younger respondent, the son of a welder, who was about to leave school in 1945, observed:

> I do find it hard to controle my imotions aroused by flims, for instance if I see a good flim I tell everybody to go and see it but if it's a bad flim I tell them it a waste of money to go and see it. I used to have a lot of auguments with my school-pals about this subject and I have lost quite a few pals this way.[125]

A 20-year-old cinema operator admitted to 'tear shedding' at times, although 'in general it is only when watching a film which reminds me of something that happened to me in real life that I find it difficult to control my emotions'.[126] The reserved shorthand typist admitted that he found it hard to conceal his feelings and had 'really cried' when Flicka the horse, who had nearly died earlier in the film, recovered at the end of *My Friend Flicka*.[127] A particularly detailed account by a 25-year-old writer suggests just how powerful film could be in the lives of those whose home lives were disrupted or dysfunctional. This young man was in the army when he replied to Mayer's survey, but much of what he described related to his teen years, when he had been an errand boy in a general food stores in south-west London, where he was born. He was described by friends as a 'film fanatic', his parents had been in a 'bad way financially' during his childhood and he had been boarded with strangers between the ages of 9 and 11, when their marriage broke up. When he later returned to live with his mother and her new husband, their new baby had made him feel 'left out in the cold' and that he was 'an imposition'. '"Packed off" when in the way' to make his own amusements, he had regularly gone to the pictures on his own. He had left school at 14 to become an office boy, and his parents had again sent him away, this time to a boys' home for eighteen months, where he had come to rely on films as his sole form of entertainment, making his own small world around the cinema and friends from the home. Estranged from family affection, he described himself as 'deeply moved' by sentimental films of the sort that Americans specialised in and which 'unfortunately' did not always seem to be appreciated by the 'staid Britisher'. Many films 'of the tragic and sentimental type' seem to have made a great impression on him, including *Boys Town* and *Winterset*.[128] He went into telling detail about *Tough Guy*, released in 1936 (when the writer himself would have been in his early teens). This was the story of an adolescent boy, played by Jackie Cooper, and how he and his beloved dog managed to survive in a hostile world after running away from a dog-hating father and falling in with gangsters, whose leader was played by Joseph Calleia. Both the dog and gang leader died at the film's climax, at which the writer admitted that he 'found Cooper's tearful outburst on finding his dog shot and Calleia dying almost too much for my pent-up emotions, I honestly confess I was in tears . . . Many films from that time have brought tears to my eyes, and still do.'

This young man had eventually left the boys' home when he was 16 to go into lodgings, and from then until he was called up described himself as living a 'secluded lonely life outwardly . . . but my love of films, and the enjoyment they gave me, quite compensated for my more depressing thoughts of the small world I lived in. I was unsociable I know, but I attribute this to a shy and embarrassed nature.' 'As for love-making, with my shy temperament, I have had little experience.' His loneliness, lack of social contact and focus on films had made him 'bitter towards real life'. 'During that four years, I can honestly say that but for the films, and my enjoyment of them as a pastime, and ideals associated with them, I would have found life unbearable.'[129]

Cinema was undoubtedly a sociable experience for many young film-goers, but these accounts offer a less usual perspective on its meanings for young men who were shy or reserved. Their narratives suggest the power of some types of film to expose deep emotions, which respondents more easily described because of the survey's anonymity and because such feelings were to an extent legitimised by contemporary cultural assumptions of the cinema's sensual influence. The cultural power of the American film industry gave film-goers such as the lonely ex-errand boy the confidence to write about how they felt in ways which contested conventional assumptions of masculine restraint, as was apparent in his defiant assertion of finding 'un-British' comfort and consolation in the sentimentality of some American films. These Americanising, 'feminis-ing' films were, of course, very disturbing to many contemporaries, for whom their emphasis on 'romance', 'moral and emotional intensity' and relaxed portrayals of personal feelings unsettled 'traditional' notions of English manliness and character.[130] Such male fears of 'inadequacy and weakness', reinforced by contemporary anxieties about the feminisation of national identity, made many men sympathetic to the idea of a return to the 'traditional' gender order, as was apparent in the anti-feminist discourses of the late 1930s, which attempted to revive a more heroic form of masculinity.[131] The relaxed popular culture of the 1930s not only threatened well-established cultural inhibitions about emotional expres-sion but was perhaps particularly unsettling for an older generation of men whose emotional survival had depended on keeping their feelings under lock and key. The Times complained how people were losing 'the phlegmatic temperament formerly regarded as an English characteristic' and 'becoming more emotional', which reinforced the importance of a healthy, 'virile' future for youth.[132] Hubert Secretan urged the develop-ment of a 'native' film industry to help remove 'a lot of sentiment, which, though mainly innocuous, is foreign to our national temperament'.[133] Marie Stopes similarly complained about how the American film indus-try was degrading 'national character', 'subtly' instilling 'vulgar' sex atti-tudes into the 'minds of the younger generation'.[134]

Others who were interested in encouraging 'modern' social relationships between boys and girls viewed the self-awareness which these new cultural experiences encouraged far more positively. The Youth Advisory Council, for example, applauded how better 'film standards' and 'growing discrimination in the taste of audiences' were increasing the cinema's role in educating young people's 'imagination and emotions'.[135] Emphases on controlling the body, as we saw in the previous chapter, an important aspect of post-war reconstruction, were complemented in the 1930s by broader trends which were heightening awareness of emotional sensitivities, encouraging a shift from 'physical towards psychic ascendancy' which would become more apparent in the decades after the Second World War.[136] Mayer's case studies are consequently a valuable addition to a literature which has tended to focus on the popular significance of romance and glamour among working-class girls and 'macho' action, crime and violent films among boys. 'Love pictures' and 'love scenes' continued to discomfort some young men, who criticised them for making men 'soft instead of tough'.[137] As we shall see in the next chapter, however, despite the shaping power of 'hard' masculinity, boys' views of love were often more idealised than those of girls. Nor were they immune to the more sympathetic, expressive masculinity of films such as musicals, whose popularity among heterosexual young males was apparent in Kuhn's research on adolescent responses to 1930s cinema culture, which suggested that men's memories centred 'on dancing more often than on combat or sport'.[138]

The glamour of Hollywood films was part of a broader and pervasive 'commercial strategy' of glamour which placed increasing emphasis on personality and appearance.[139] As has been suggested, assumptions that such changes had little impact on working-class boys and young men neglect subtle shifts occurring, not only in relation to appearance but also in social and personal relationships.[140] Mayer's case-studies may in many respects have been exceptional, the reflections of self-confessed film fanatics whose competition entries imply desires for affirmation and recognition. The intense feelings and sensitivities they describe, however, suggest the gulf which often existed between individual uncertainties and public expressions of masculinity, between adolescent preoccupations with sex and their frequently tremulous feelings.[141]

Notes

1 M. Roper, *The Secret Battle: Emotional Survival in the Great War* (Manchester: Manchester University Press, 2009), p. 285; *The Times* (6 July 1925), p. 11; *Ibid.* (10 January 1930), p. 7.

2   *The Times* (7 April 1926), p. 13; *ibid.* (13 April 1926), p. 15; A. M. Royden, *Sex and Common-Sense* (London: Hurst and Blackett, [1922]), pp. 15–16; *Picture Post* (4 January 1941), p. 41. Similar comments were made of children and young people in the 1890s: J. Bourke, *Working-Class Cultures in Britain, 1890–1960: Gender, Class and Ethnicity* (London: Routledge, 1994), p. 28.

3   R. Roberts, *The Classic Slum: Salford Life in the First Quarter of the Century* (London: Penguin Books, 1971, 1990), p. 224.

4   *Ibid.*, p. 235.

5   *Ibid.*, pp. 215, 228.

6   Roper, *The Secret Battle*, pp. 284–5; 293–4.

7   D. Haworth, *Figures in a Bygone Landscape* (London: Methuen, 1986), p. 216. Haworth was born in Bacup, Lancashire. The development of child psychology also encouraged maternal anxieties: M. Macdonald, *Representing Women: Myths of Femininity in the Popular Media* (London: Edward Arnold, 1995), p. 77, p. 80.

8   S. Das, *Touch and Intimacy in First World War Literature* (Cambridge: Cambridge University Press, 2005).

9   W. Woodruff, *Billy Boy: The Story of a Lancashire Weaver's Son* (Halifax: Ryburn Publishing, 1993), p. 87.

10 J. H. Armitage, *The Twenty Three Years, Or the Late Way of Life – And of Living. By The Exile*, Burnett Archive of Working-Class Autobiographies, University of Brunel (hereafter, Burnett Archive), pp. 27, 60–2. Armitage was born in 1908, in Leeds.

11 J. Loftus, *Lee Side*, Burnett Archive, p. 29. Loftus was born in 1914.

12 *Ibid.*

13 Roper, *The Secret Battle*, p. 294; Woodruff, *Billy Boy*, pp. 17–18, 26, 42–3, 87.

14 Roper makes a similar point about ex-soldiers taking many years to psychologically process the implications of their front-line experiences: Roper, *The Secret Battle*.

15 G. Winter, *Sites of Memory, Sites of Mourning: The European War in European Cultural History* (Cambridge: Cambridge University Press, 1995); G. Mosse, *Fallen Soldiers: Reshaping the Memory of the World Wars* (Oxford: Oxford University Press, 1990); S. Hynes, *A War Imagined: The First World War and English Culture* (New York: Athenaeum, 1990).

16 F. Pritchard, *My Manchester* (Manchester: Neil Richardson, 1986), p. 3.

17 E. Hague, *Streets away from Paradise: Reminiscences of a Stalybridge Lad* (Manchester: Neil Richardson, 1987), p. 40.

18 *British Medical Journal* (11 July 1936), p. 91; *Daily Mail* (3 February 1936), p. 10.

19 See S. Alexander, 'The mysteries and secrets of women's bodies: sexual knowledge in the first half of the twentieth century', in M. Nava and A. O'Shea (eds), *Modern Times: Reflections on a Century of English Modernity* (London: Routledge, 1996). Oral history interviews highlight the lack of sexual knowledge among young males and females: S. Humphries, *Hooligans or Rebels? An Oral History of Working-Class Childhood and Youth, 1889–1939* (Oxford: Basil Blackwell Ltd., 1981), pp. 138–9; E. Roberts, *A Woman's Place: An Oral History of Working-Class Women, 1890–1940* (Oxford: Basil Blackwell, 1984); S. Humphries, *A Secret World of Sex: Forbidden Fruit: The British Experience, 1900–1950* (London: Sidgwick and Jackson, 1988), pp. 16–17; *British Medical Journal* (22 April 1933), p. 709. A survey of 300 letters from the Stopes-Roe collection for 1918–29 revealed that although women predominated, many men

also corresponded (56 per cent women and 44 per cent men). Twice as many men as women asked for advice on 'sexual technique' and about sex on their wedding night: R. Hall (ed.), *Dear Dr Stopes: Sex in the 1920s* (Harmondsworth: Penguin Books, 1978), p. 219, 222–3.

20 A. Bingham, *Family Newspapers: Sex, Private Life and the British Popular Press, 1918–1978* (Oxford: Oxford University Press, 2009), pp. 98, 100.

21 H. L. Smith (ed.), *The New Survey of London Life and Labour*, vol. IX, *Life and Leisure*, (London: P.S. King and Son Ltd., 1935), pp. 33, 339.

22 A. E. Morgan, *The Needs of Youth. A Report Made to King George's Jubilee Trust Fund* (Oxford: Oxford University Press, 1939), pp. 272, 334.

23 A. E. Morgan, *Young Citizen* (Harmondsworth: Penguin, 1943), p. 163; Bourke, *Working-Class Cultures in Britain*, p. 29. The first large-scale British sex surveys were not published until the late 1940s and early 1950s. See Humphries, *Secret World of Sex*, pp. 31–2.

24 L. D. H. Sauerteig and R. Davidson, 'Shaping the sexual knowledge of the young', in L. D. H. Sauerteig and R. Davidson, *Shaping Sexual Knowledge: A Cultural History of Sex Education in Twentieth Century Europe* (London and New York: Routledge, 2009), pp. 2–3.

25 H. Cook, *The Long Sexual Revolution: English Women, Sex, and Contraception* (Oxford: Oxford University Press, 2005), p. 178; Bingham, *Family Newspapers*, p. 45; L. Hall, *Sex, Gender and Social Change Since 1880* (London: Palgrave Macmillan, 2000), pp. 99, 132. See also R. Porter and L. Hall, *The Facts of Life. The Creation of Sexual Knowledge in Britain, 1650–1950* (New Haven, CT: Yale University Press, 1995); C. Haste, *Rules of Desire: Sex in Britain; World War One to the Present* (London: Chatto and Windus, 1992); J. Giles, '"Playing hard to get": working class women, sexuality and respectability in Britain, 1918–40', *Women's History Review*, 1:2 (1992), 239–55; Humphries, *Secret World of Sex*, p. 42.

26 Hall, *Sex, Gender and Social Change*, p. 99.

27 E. Chesser, *The Sexual, Marital and Family Relationships of the English Woman* (London: Hutchinson's Medical Publications, 1956), pp. 311–16.

28 Humphries, *Secret World of Sex*, pp. 26, 32.

29 G. Cross (ed.), *Worktowners at Blackpool: Mass-Observation and Popular Leisure in the 1930s* (London: Routledge, 1990), p. 190.

30 *Ibid.*, p. 189.

31 *Ibid.*, pp. 138, 166.

32 *Ibid.*, p. 186.

33 I. Clephane, *Towards Sex Freedom* (London: John Lane, 1935), p. vii.

34 *Hansard House of Commons Debates* (16 December 1938), vol. 342, cc. 2420–38, at 2435. Attempts to ban sales were criticised as a back-door measure to undermine the general availability of contraception.

35 *Hansard House of Commons Debates* (3 November 1938), Vol. 340, p. 367.

36 *Ibid.*, (16 December 1938), Vol. 342, cc. 2420–38, at 2435.

37 *Ibid.*, cc. 2420–38, at 2426; S. J. Smith, *Children, Cinema and Censorship: From Dracula to the Dead End Kids* (London and New York: I. B. Tauris, 2005), p. 55.

38 *Hansard House of Commons Debates* (30 March 1938), Vol. 333, cc. 2007–11, at 2008.

39 T. Furniss, *The Walls of Jericho: Slum Life in Sheffield Between the Wars* (Sheffield: Rebel Press, 1979), p. 26.

40 R. Glasser, 'Growing up in the Gorbals', in *The Ralph Glasser Omnibus* (Edinburgh: Black and White Publishing, 2006, first published in 1986), p. 122.

41 Dennis Houlston, oral history transcript, The Cinema Culture in 1930s Britain Archive, University of Lancaster (hereafter CCINTB).

42 *British Medical Journal* (3 March 1934), p. 413.

43 *Hansard House of Commons Debates* (16 December 1938), Vol. 342, cc. 2420–38, at 2428. The Bill aimed to limit contraceptive adverts.

44 See, for example, W. M. Gallichan, *The Poison of Prudery: An Historical Survey* (London: T. Werner Laurie Ltd., 1929), pp. 10, 72–3, 77. Gallichan, a secularist and freethinker, was raised among Plymouth Brethren. O. Dekkers, 'Walter Matthew Gallichan: fiction and freethought in the 1890s', *English Studies*, 83:5 (2002), pp. 407–8. He published several books on sex education during and after the First World War: W. M. Gallichan, *How to Love. The Art of Courtship and Marriage* (London: C. Arthur Pearson, 1915); *Letters to a Young Man on Love and Health* (London: T. Werner Laurie, 1919); *A Text-Book of Sex Education for Parents and Teachers* (London: T. Werner Laurie, 1919); *Youth and Maidenhood, or Sex Knowledge for Young People* (London: Health Promotion, 1920).

45 Hall, *Sex, Gender and Social Change*, p. 125; Morgan, *Young Citizen*, p. 139.

46 Bourke, *Working-Class Cultures*, p. 37; J. Pilcher, 'Sex in health education: Official guidance for schools in England, 1928–1977', *Journal of Historical Sociology*, 17:2/3 (2004), p. 190; B. Crowther, 'The partial picture: framing the discourse of sex in British educative films of the early 1930s', in L. D. H. Sauerteig and R. Davidson, *Shaping Sexual Knowledge: A Cultural History of Sex Education in Twentieth Century Europe* (London and New York: Routledge, 2009), pp. 176, 179–80; *British Medical Journal* (1 August 1931), p. 216. Various books on the subject were published for parents and teachers, e.g. T. F. Tucker and M. Pout, *Awkward Questions of Childhood. A Practical Handbook on Sex Education for Parents and Teachers* (London: Gerald Howe Ltd., 1934).

47 The Rev. T. Wentworth Pym, 'The need of education in questions of sex', *British Medical Journal* (1 August 1931), p. 188; M. Atkinson, 'Sex education of the young', in W. A. Lane (ed.), *The Golden Health Library: A Complete Guide to Golden Health for Men and Women of all Ages* (London: Collins, [1929]), pp. 287–8.

48 B. L. Q. Henriques, *Club Leadership* (London: Oxford University Press, 1933: 1943), pp. 174, 183; C. E. B. Russell and L. M. Russell, *Lads' Clubs: Their History, Organisation and Management* (London: A. & C. Black Ltd., 1932), p. 211.

49 Henriques, *Club Leadership*, p. 184. He recommended Weatherhead's *The Mastery of Sex*, which stressed that adults should educate themselves about sex if they were to teach children about it: L. D. Weatherhead (assisted by Dr Marion Greaves), *The Mastery of Sex through Psychology and Religion* (London: Student Christian Movement Press, 1931), p. xiv. Contemporary books on sex education stressed the importance of fathers understanding 'the scientific side of sex', so they could strike the right 'impersonal' note when discussing such matters with their adolescent sons: E. D. Hutchinson, *Creative Sex* (London: Allen & Unwin, 1936), pp. 45–6; Humphries, *Secret World of Sex*, p. 62; E. Bold, *The Long and Short of it. Being the Recollections and*

Reminiscences of Edna Bold, Burnett Archive, pp. 20–1; Armitage, *The Twenty Three Years*, pp. 171, 187–8.

50 Humphries, *Secret World of Sex*, p. 62; E. Bold, *The Long and Short of it*, pp. 20–1; Armitage, *The Twenty Three Years*, pp. 171, 187–8.

51 Humphries, *Secret World of Sex*, p. 40.

52 Dorrell, *Falling Cadence*, Burnett Archive, pp. 22–3; *The Miner* (8 October 1927), p. 9. VD or venereal diseases were sexually transmitted diseases.

53 Loftus, *Lee Side*, p. 151.

54 *The Miner* (8 October 1927), p. 9; G. M. Cox, *Youth, Sex, and Life* (London: George Newnes Limited, 1935), p. 153; Cook, *The Long Sexual Revolution*, p. 180.

55 H. Gill, [Untitled], Burnett Archive. No page numbers.

56 R. Ward, *A Lancashire Childhood*, Burnett Archive, p. 4. Ward was born in 1907.

57 Armitage, *The Twenty Three Years*, pp. 187–8. Armitage was born in 1908.

58 Loftus, *Lee Side*, p. 121

59 B. Naughton, *Saintly Billy: A Catholic Boyhood* (Oxford: Oxford University Press, 1989), pp. 185–6, 187–9.

60 *Ibid.*, ch. 25, 'The Captain of my soul', pp. 190–8, at p. 191.

61 Humphries, *Secret World of Sex*, pp. 46–8, 53. He was born in Manchester, in 1921.

62 Loftus, *Lee Side*, pp. 89–90.

63 J. Brooke, *The Dukinfield I Knew, 1906–1930* (Manchester: Neil Richardson, 1987), pp. 44–5.

64 Hall, *Sex, Gender and Social Change*, pp. 104, 120. See also A. Kuhn, *Cinema, Censorship and Sexuality, 1909–1925* (London: Routledge, 1988); R. McKibbin, *Classes and Cultures: England, 1918–51* (Oxford: Oxford University Press, 1998), p. 318.

65 F. Pritchard, *My Manchester*, p. 45.

66 C. S. Read, 'The adolescent boy', in W. A. Lane (ed.), *The Golden Health Library: A Complete Guide to Golden Health for Men and Women of all Ages* (London: Collins, [1929]), p. 65; Weatherhead, *The Mastery of Sex*, pp. 124–7.

67 N. Haire with A. Costler, A. Willy et al (eds), *Encyclopaedia of Sexual Knowledge* (London: Francis Aldor, 1934), pp. 103, 111–13, 117, 152.

68 Weatherhead, *The Mastery of Sex*, pp. 128–30.

69 A. H. Gray, *Sex Teaching* (London: National Sunday School Union, [1929]), pp. 48, 50–4.

70 *British Medical Journal* (18 March 1939), p. 115. Murrell was a pioneer in infant welfare and better health-care for women. She also lectured on adolescence: see J. Youngran, 'Murrell, Christine Mary (1874–1933)', Oxford Dictionary of National Biography (Oxford: Oxford University Press, 2004), www.oxforddnb.com/view/article/54293 (accessed 20 October 2009).

71 *The Miner* (18 January 1930), p. 10.

72 *Ibid.*, p. 10.

73 *Ibid.* (17 December 1927), p. 9.

74 *Ibid.*, p. 9.

75 *Ibid.* (18 January 1930), p. 10.

76 *Ibid.* (15 February 1930), p. 10; *ibid.* (18 February 1930), p. 9.

77 *Ibid.* (15 February 1930), p. 10.

78 *Ibid.* (22 February 1930), p. 10.

79   *Ibid.* (18 February 1930), p. 9.

80   *The Boy* (Winter 1937–38), pp. 652–3.

81   A. Kuhn, *An Everyday Magic: Cinema and Cultural Memory* (London and New York: I. B. Tauris, 2002), p. 147.

82   C. Wouters, *Informalization: Manners and Emotions since 1890* (London: Sage Publications, 2007), p. 181.

83   Kuhn, *An Everyday Magic*, p. 38; R. McKibbin, *Classes and Cultures*, p. 420. Some argued that those who 'reached early adolescence *before* seeing any films' were less likely to be influenced by the cinema because they were already involved in other forms of recreation: J. P. Mayer, *British Cinemas and their Audiences* (London: Dennis Dobson Ltd., 1948), p. 119.

84   S. J. Smith, *Children, Cinema and Censorship*, p. 47; J. Richards and D. Sheridan (eds), *Mass-Observation at the Movies* (London and New York: Routledge and Kegan Paul, 1987), p. 59.

85   A. Calder-Marshall, *The Changing Scene* (London: Chapman and Hall, 1937), pp. 78–9.

86   Richards and Sheridan, *Mass-Observation at the Movies*, p. 82.

87   C. Burt, *The Young Delinquent* (London: University of London Press, 1925, 1931), pp. 144–5.

88   Burt, *The Young Delinquent*, pp. 149, 371; S. F. Hatton, *London's Bad Boys* (London: Chapman & Hall Ltd., 1931), p. 45; Cox, *Youth, Sex, and Life*, pp. 149, 158; Read, 'The adolescent boy', p. 65.

89   J. Springhall, *Youth, Popular Culture and Moral Panics: Penny Gaffs to Gangsta Rap, 1830–1966* (London: Macmillan Press Ltd, 1998), p. 119.

90   Smith, *Children, Cinema and Censorship*, pp. 47–8, 52; Kuhn, *An Everyday Magic*, pp. 154, 157. The Hays Code was introduced in 1930.

91   D. Houlston, oral history transcript, CCINTB.

92   Kuhn, *An Everyday Magic*, p. 163; Weatherhead, *The Mastery of Sex*, pp. 128–30.

93   *The Boy* (September 1931), pp. 41–2.

94   G. Cross, *Worktowners*, pp. 9, 180–1, 183, 209.

95   N. Hiley, ' "Let's go to the pictures": The British cinema audience in the 1920s and 1930s', *Journal of Popular British Cinema*, 2 (1999), p. 48; *Manchester Evening News* (15 April 1930, 16 April 1930).

96   Cross, *Worktowners*, p. 31.

97   A. J. Jenkinson, *What Do Boys and Girls Read?* (London: Methuen & Co. Ltd, 1940), pp. 4–5, 27–8.

98   J. Mackie (ed.), *The Edinburgh Cinema Enquiry: Being an Investigation Conducted in to the Influence of the Film on Schoolchildren and Adolescents in the City* (Edinburgh: Edinburgh City Library, 1933), pp. 14–18, cited in J. Richards, *The Age of the Dream Palace: Cinema and Society in Britain, 1930–39* (London: Routledge and Kegan Paul, 1984), p. 69; Kuhn, *An Everyday Magic*, pp. 147–8.

99   Norman MacDonald, 'The Cinema Culture in 1930s Britain', CCINTB.

100 'Diary' (15 February 1936).

101 *Ibid.* (13 May 1936).

102 *Ibid.* (3 November 1936; 19 November 1936).

103 M. Eavis, 'The picture palaces of Northampton, with particular reference to the

Exchange and the Savoy', *Cinema Theatre Association Bulletin*, 9:4 (July–August 1975), 27.

104 J. Harley, 'Report of an enquiry into the occupations, further education and leisure interests of a number of girl wage-earners from elementary and central schools in the Manchester district, with special reference to the influence of school training on the use of leisure' (MEd dissertation, University of Manchester 1937), p. 108, n.3; 'Diary' (15 February 1936). More boys than girls went to the pictures regularly each week on Merseyside, reflecting girls' greater domestic responsibilities. D. C. Jones, *The Social Survey of Merseyside*, 3 vols (Liverpool: Liverpool University Press, 1934), vol. III, pp. 219–20.

105 G. C. Hughes, *Shut the Mountain Gate*, Burnett Archive, p. 16.

106 Mayer, *British Cinemas*, pp. 33–4.

107 Jenkinson, *What Do Boys and Girls Read?* pp. 28, 140.

108 D. Russell, *Football and the English* (Lancaster: Carnegie Publishing Ltd, 1997), pp. 110–11.

109 J. Holt, *Public School Literature, Civic Education and the Politics of Male Adolescence* (Aldershot: Ashgate, 2008), p. 4; J. Rose, *The Intellectual Life of the British Working Classes* (New Haven, CT and London: Yale Nota Bene, 2002), pp. 379–81, 390.

110 D. Russell, *Football and the English* pp. 110–11.

111 Crowther, 'The partial picture', p. 181.

112 *Ibid.*; Kuhn, *An Everyday Magic*, p. 216; Mayer, *British Cinemas*, p. 145.

113 Mayer, *British Cinemas*, p. 15.

114 *Ibid.*, p. 15.

115 *Ibid.*, p. 16.

116 *Ibid.*, pp. 16–17.

117 *Ibid.*, p. 117.

118 *Ibid.*, p. 76.

119 *Ibid.*, p. 96.

120 *Ibid.*, pp. 33–4.

121 *Ibid.*, p. 94.

122 *Ibid.*, pp. 33, 117.

123 *Ibid.*, p. 119.

124 *Ibid.*, p. 125.

125 *Ibid.*, p. 32. The spelling is as in the original extract.

126 *Ibid.*, p. 105.

127 *Ibid.*, p. 118. *My Friend Flicka* was released in 1943. It was the story of a boy's love for a wild horse and his attempts to tame it.

128 *Winterset* was released in 1936. The plot involved a son who set out to prove the innocence of his immigrant, radical, outsider father, falsely accused and executed for a crime he had never committed: Review, *New York Times* (4 December 1936). *Boys Town*, released in 1938, was based on the real-life story of Father Edward J. Flanagan (played by Spencer Tracy), who believed there was no such thing as a 'bad boy', and founded a 'sanctuary' for delinquents called Boys Town.

129 Mayer, *British Cinemas*, pp. 132–43.

130 Calder-Marshall, *The Changing Scene*, pp. 72, 77.

131 Such attitudes were very apparent in the middle-class 'life-style' magazine *Men Only*,

first published in the late 1930s: J. Greenfield, S. O'Connell and C. Reid, 'Fashioning masculinity: *Men Only*, consumption and the development of marketing in the 1930s', *Twentieth Century British History*, 10:4 (1999), pp. 462–3.

132   *The Times* (6 February 1936), p. 11.

133   H. Secretan, *London below Bridges* (London: Geoffrey Bles, 1931), pp. 86–7. Jazz's 'black American associations' and the 'Jewish American origins of many popular songs' similarly focused preoccupations with declining national culture: J. J. Nott, *Music for the People: Popular Music and Dance in Inter-war Britain* (Oxford: Oxford University Press, 2002), pp. 211–13, 231–2.

134   M. C. Stopes, *Sex and the Young* (London: G. P. Putnam and Sons, 1926), pp. 100–3.

135   Board of Education, *The Youth Service After the War: A Report of the Youth Advisory Council appointed by the President of the Board of Education in 1942 to advise him on questions relating to the Youth Service in England* (London: His Majesty's Stationery Office, 1943), p. 13.

136   C. Wouters, *Informalization*, pp. 90–1

137   Smith, *Children, Cinema and Censorship*, p. 137; Richards and Sheridan, *Mass-Observation at the Movies*, pp. 43, 45, 77, 82, 90.

138   Richards and Sheridan, *Mass-Observation at the Movies*, pp. 32–3, 38–9, 41, 47–8, 53, 65; Kuhn, *An Everyday Magic*, pp. 109–10.

139   McKibbin, *Classes and Cultures*, p. 431.

140   J. J. Matthews, *Dance Hall and Picture Palace: Sydney's Romance with Modernity* (Sydney: Currency Press, 2005), p. 244; B. Beaven, *Leisure, Citizenship and Working-Class Men in Britain* (Manchester: Manchester University Press, 2005).

141   Smith, *Children, Cinema and Censorship*, p. 137; Richards and Sheridan, *Mass-Observation at the Movies*, pp. 43, 45, 77, 82, 90.

5

Seeking advice

As we have seen, by the inter-war years, new cultures of consumption and leisure were drawing young people away from the scrutiny of families and neighbourhoods, allowing them much greater freedom in their social relationships. This was apparent, particularly in the 1930s, as 'romance', leisure, commodities and youth became 'increasingly entwined'.[1] These changes, part of broader shifts from formal social relations to more informal ones, occurred unevenly across the social classes and had regional, urban and rural variations.[2] This expansion of 'emotional and behavioural alternatives' created confusion and uncertainties as young people learned new ways of relating to each other.[3] Young women were particularly adept at responding to the novel opportunities for agency and self-fashioning offered by new consumption and leisure developments.[4] Their involvement in these cultural changes was highly visible, and together with assumptions of working-class young men's embeddedness in work and local masculine leisure cultures, has helped to mask how young men responded to this climate of 'emancipating' emotions.[5] Yet the impact of these cultural shifts raises many questions. How did young men respond to more informal expectations of behaviour? To what extent did sexualising pressures merely reinforce well-established prejudices against women? What impact did these changes have emotionally and in terms of behaviour? The difficulty in answering them is accentuated by the familiar historical problems of articulating young people's own voices and the cultural reticence obstructing male revelation of personal feelings. This chapter offers a starting-point for what deserves deeper and more extended examination, by addressing such questions through letters from young men in their teens and twenties that were published in the advice pages of popular newspapers and magazines. Both the letters and the advice subtly shaped the 'acceptability' of particular discourses of male behaviour, yet should not be judged purely in these terms.[6] Not only was there a degree of interaction between the advice page and its correspondents, but the thousands of letters columnists received each year are a window onto uncertainties and dilemmas which young people usually kept to themselves. The presence of young men's letters in these feminised sections of the press testifies to elements of male sensitivity which often receive little professional attention even now, when, despite a substantial literature on sexual characteristics and sexual differences, the question of boys' 'vulnerability' to physical and mental pressures has attracted little curiosity from most scientific writers (until recently overwhelmingly male), who have 'implicitly' assumed 'that "boys will be boys." '[7]

Considerable problems attend historical investigations of sexual behaviour, yet, as Langhamer points out, 'we seem to know far more about English sexual lives than about how men and women constructed, negotiated and maintained emotional intimacies' not only within marriage but before it.[8] A social climate in which 'emotions and moods' were beginning to be discussed more openly presented considerable challenges to traditional masculinities, and the correspondence on which this chapter is based provides a suggestive if not unproblematic counterpoint to many more familiar assumptions about young men's emotional lives between leaving school and getting married.[9] They evoke struggles over girlfriends who failed to behave as they expected, how unemployment and low wages subverted traditional power dynamics based on assumptions of the male breadwinner's dominance. Some letters intimate the discomfort at girlfriends who seemed to be more interested in treats and entertainment than in a mutually sustaining relationship. Others imply how changing social and leisure cultures were feeding male self-consciousness and anxieties about appearance in new ways, particularly among those without a traditionally masculine work-place identity.

'Emancipation' of the emotions placed far greater emphasis upon the need for 'internal regulation' than 'external constraints', and many young men, culturally patterned to expect social and emotional dominance, struggled with such changes. Advice columns, for all their limitations, intimate the effects of these changing social and emotional expectations. They offered liberating prospects of obtaining advice discreetly, without the knowledge of parents or peers, and of eavesdropping on other people's everyday conundrums, the solutions to which often led to debate or disagreement in subsequent correspondence. Adolescents were particularly drawn to such pages (much as today they are to the internet) and male interviewees often recall turning, if surreptitiously, to the advice sections of their mothers' magazines for intriguing if often opaque insights into personal and vaguely alluded-to sexual problems and to improve their understanding of girls and young women.

Most of the original correspondence on which these answers were based (and the immense number of letters which were never published) has perished, but occasionally there are lucky survivals. It was amongst the memorabilia that I found after Les's death that I discovered the letter he received from Ruth English of *Everybody's Weekly* after he had written to her asking for advice about a girlfriend (or rather, a girl he hoped would become his girlfriend). The letter started my own particular journey into these columns and, complemented by his diaries, offers an unusual opportunity to track the route whereby he came to write to her. This chapter explores both the circumstances that led to this letter, and letters from other boys and young men published in a number of contemporary advice columns. Some of these columns were the work of many writers, as appears to have been the case with Mary Marryat of *Woman's Weekly*, and possibly Ruth English of *Everybody's Weekly*. Others were the pseudonym of a single adviser, such as 'Dorothy Dix' (Elizabeth Meriwether Gilmer) in the *Daily Mirror*, 'Ann Temple' (Vyrnwy Hughes) in the *Daily Mail*, 'Evelyn Home' (Peggy Makins) in *Woman* magazine, 'Jane Dawson' (Dorothy Critchlow) in the *Manchester Evening News*, and Leonora Eyles, who wrote under the pen-name 'Martha' in *Lansbury's Labour Weekly* and *The Miner*, and took on the letters pages of *Woman's Own* in the early 1930s.[10] Before we examine the story of Les's letter, we need first to consider the background and context of these columns.

Advice columnists and letters pages

The 1930s was an era in which advice columns of all sorts proliferated in the popular press. Like the 'human interest' stories which helped to boost contemporary newspaper sales, they were a significant expression of a more informal cultural climate. Just as a familiar narrative of female absorption in cinema culture has tended to overshadow the role that film played in the lives of young men, it is easy to see personal advice pages in the popular press as feminised spaces into which young males rarely ventured. The well-established letters pages of women's magazines often published queries from men of all ages, however, while men had been involved with advice columns 'as readers, writers and editors' since the late seventeenth century.[11] The expansion of personal advice columns into the mass readership of the mainstream popular press in the mid 1930s, as a strategy to draw in more female readers, extended a distant and anonymous means of communication to many more men, including those in their teens and twenties, and encouraged them to broach questions they would have found difficult to raise with peers, relatives, teachers or work-mates.

The *Daily Mirror* was at the forefront of these popularising initiatives to draw in a broader readership and dramatically revamped its style and content from the mid 1930s, 're-inventing' itself as a 'working-class tabloid' with a sensationalist, campaigning mix much influenced by American newspapers and advertising agencies such as J. Walter Thompson.[12] Working young women were specifically targeted with features and specialist advisers, while young men were drawn in with pictures of scantily clad young women, cartoon strips like 'Jane's Journal' and sports reporting. American influence was apparent in a syndicated column by the internationally known American columnist, Dorothy Dix, perhaps the best-known inter-war advice columnist.[13] By the time the *Daily Mirror* introduced her to its readers in 1935, her columns were syndicated in 300 newspapers across the world, including Canada, the Philippines, Japan, China, South Africa and Australia.[14] When she died in 1951, she was described as the 'most widely read columnist in the world', with a readership of sixty million.[15]

The *Daily Mirror* introduced Dix in December 1935.[16] The *Daily Mail* followed suit not long after, with Ann Temple's 'Human Casebook',[17] which in turn appears to have prompted a weekly 'personal problems' section in the *Manchester Evening News*.[18] Such columns deliberately pitched themselves at a broad readership. Dix's correspondents fell into three main categories: those in their teens, young adults and the middle aged.[19] About half the letters she received were from men. This was not unusual. Peggy Makins, who became *Woman's* Evelyn Home in 1937, thought that even in such a specifically female publication men sent about 'one in six' of the letters she received.[20] There was a popular belief that the content of such letters pages was bogus, but advisers received so much correspondence that there was usually little reason for fabrication.[21] Most letters were 'intended to be private' and were usually 'accompanied by the required stamped, self-addressed envelope for a reply'.[22] Well-established popular correspondents had 'correspondence assistants' who dealt with most of these letters.[23] Critchlow had a standard format for certain recurring problems, although she often added a personal note.[24] Columnists were well aware of the social and cultural conventions within which their replies had to be framed. Dix, the most commercially successful, was particularly attuned to the importance of maintaining her popularity by not placing herself 'too far in front of' contemporary 'social norms'.[25] The tone of her column was more sensationalised than other letters pages and she was a clear draw for readers of the *Daily Mirror*, where it was highlighted on its front page.

The selection of letters published in other advice columns depended on a number of factors, and it is difficult to generalise. Dix focused on what she considered were particularly interesting or difficult ones, although she had limited editorial control over her syndicated columns, and what was published tended to be geared towards topics that 'male editors favoured'.[26] Makins observed how, knowing 'so many eyes, were going to see the page', it was 'of little use to choose very extraordinary situations' even if they were 'perfectly true'. She preferred to publish 'average cases' rather than 'exceptions, not in the general run of worries and conflicts'.[27] Eyles's columns in *Lansbury's Labour Weekly* and *The Miner* frequently exposed the distressing work and home conditions afflicting the personal lives of her many working-class readers. Critchlow chose 'the most striking' letters for publication.[28] As was the case with post-war columnists such as Marje Proops, 'darker', more complex problems were more likely to be answered privately, and personally.[29]

Telling young men's tales

Given that these letters were selected, what can they tell us about the interior lives and anxieties which beset young men in their teens and twenties? There are obvious limitations. These are, of course, mediated narratives, a handful of published letters drawn from the much greater volume of correspondence that writers of advice columns regularly received. Writers to advice pages, like autobiographers, were characterised by their literacy. They were not from the poorest sectors of the working class and probably reflected a mix of lower middle-class and upper working-class newspaper readers. Nevertheless, like autobiographies, they suggest the sense of isolation which not only quieter, more bookish boys and young men experienced but also more socially assured ones did if their interests and worries fell outside conventional expectations of masculinity. That the published queries were snapshots of social, sexual and personal uncertainties may also be inferred from autobiographies, which suggest why some writers might find the anonymity of an advice page appealing. John Edmonds, for example, described the lack of peers with whom he could discuss 'many of the deeper problems' which concerned him, and how his 'armour of reserve' made discussing them with teachers impossible.

> Experience had taught that attempts at serious discussion invariably invited ridicule from my acquaintances. Though well able to hold my

own in oral and physical battle, I learned the uselessness of remarking upon the beauties of plant and animal form, of sunset and cloud formation, the mysteries of religion, animal reproduction and the examples of art, music and literature which gave me pleasure.[30]

The adolescent Joe Loftus, 'gawky', 'shy and lacking in cheek' and increasingly questioning his Catholic faith, with 'wicked thoughts' and 'guilty fears', was plagued by oppressive dreams: 'It wasn't easy to find someone to discuss these things with, and my mates managed to turn every subject into a joke.'[31] The youngest of five brothers and two sisters, he could not talk over the 'problems of adolescence' with them, either, since he found it so difficult to get through to them. 'They didn't understand me. Wasn't I the youngest, so what could I know "about owt" in spite of my book-learning.'[32] As a child, Syd Metcalfe was isolated from other children on the street by his mother's disreputable, quarrelsome and 'foul' mouthed behaviour. He described the desperate poverty and loneliness of his teens, when he lost the companionship of his 18-year-old older brother, who became a 'lad about town', spending every evening with his mate 'trying to pick up girls'.[33] Metcalfe described how these experiences had made him 'withdrawn', 'lacking in confidence' and 'out of tune with the rest of the world'. 'This feeling, nurtured in childhood, persisted right throughout life and is very much a part of me yet.'[34]

Masculine assumptions of 'strength in silence', which reinforced the unacceptability of discussing personal anxieties with peers, meant that young men who were poorer and less literate than these writers were more likely to find aggressive ways of expressing their emotional frustrations.[35] Similarly, the advice queries which this chapter examines may seem innocuous by present-day standards. Nevertheless, they suggest not only the extent to which contemporary conventions stymied the discussion of even innocent personal (and sexual) matters, but the levels of embarrassment and worry to which changing social relations and behaviours were giving rise, while their very publication helped to shape new discussions about how relationships between young people were changing. The letter which Les wrote to Ruth English emerged out of a particular moment of adolescent transition, the increasingly tightly packed pages of his diaries perhaps signifying a particular notion of time and its passing, a desire for secrecy, a need to hold on to the assurance of daily routines as he moved towards the uncertainties of adulthood, as his leisure activities broadened to include girls. The diaries, the letter and the correspondence between him and a putative girlfriend (all of which he kept) provide a glimpse into this critical time. They suggest something of an adolescent infatuation which started when Les attended BB camp in 1937 and noted the arrival one evening of a 'caravan with a nice girl'. Les observed how she watched him and his friends arrive back late, on their late pass, after a 'grand' night out in the town, having had a fish and chip supper and gone to Butlin's Pleasure Fair, where they had 'nearly' got off with some girls. He spent much of the subsequent week 'lazing about' endeavouring to get 'sunburnt' while some of the boys tried to get a date for him 'with that girl', although even amidst these pleasant preoccupations family sentiment intervened as he went to buy presents.

> Got up at about 7.30 p.m. In the morning we had tent inspection and then we went down on the beach and had cricket on the sand. Gardner who played on our side left us about 12 p.m. to see his sister off on the train back home. Our side lost. In the afternoon us boys went into the town to buy presents to take back home. It took us all afternoon. After tea at camp we went back into town after 8 of us chaps had asked if we could have a late pass he gave us one till 10.10 p.m. We had a grand time in town and then we had a fish and chip supper and went back into the fair where we met Cleaver and Burdy who told us Gardner was waiting for us when we got back at 10.40 p.m. The girl from caravan watched us come in tonight. (Saturday, 7 August 1937)

> Got up at about 7.35 a.m. In the morning we had tent inspection then we got ready and we went into town for a service in a Methodist church. There was another company from Chester there who were just starting there [sic] week. When we got back we had some photos took and we lazed about camp after trying to get sunburnt. In the afternoon we lazed about camp for a while and some of the boys tried to get a date for me with that girl. We then went for a bathe. At night we had a service in the mess tent. After I and the boys we followed the two girls from the caravan and I took one of them for a walk along the sand dunes. (Sunday, 8 August 1937)

Joan, the girl in the caravan, stayed on Les's mind after he got back home. A couple of days after his return he wrote how he had stopped out, talking to a friend 'for a time about the girl at Nottingham', before 'messing about' with the gang and some local girls until 10 in the evening. The following day he posted a letter to the Mablethorpe campsite, 'to that girl at Nottingham', who was staying on for another week. The reply suggested that he had not had much time to get acquainted with her while they were away: 'I received an answer to the letter I sent in Friday. It came from Nottingham. The girl's name is Joan Burton. I received the letter by first post this morning.'

Dear Leslie,

Thank you very much for letter. I never thought I should hear anything about you after you left camp. I wondered how I could find out your address, and then I thought perhaps you wouldn't like it.

I enjoyed Sunday night very much, and when you went back on Monday I was simply longing to go home. I watched your train go passed [sic], did you see me? I felt terrible on Wednesday morning, how did work go down with you?

My father and I went down on Saturday night and it simply poured with rain all the time until after dinner, and then we went for a bathe it was so warm.

How did you get the letter to the farmhouse?

Well I must close now so Good-bye.

Yours Truly,

Joan Burton

P.S. Remember me to the other boys.

Encouraged by her response, Les wrote again, this time requesting a photo, and then again a few days later, when he still had not heard from her, asking her why she had not replied. Another letter arrived, this time addressed to 'Les', apologising for the lack of response because she had been busy at work.

I was sorry to hear you had had a cold, and I hope it is quite better now. I thought it was very nice of you to ask for my photograph. I have enclosed one, but it is not awfully good, I am going to have it taken again, so I will send you another. I should be very pleased if you would send me your photograph to remember you by.

It seems ages since my holiday, and I am beginning to feel like another one. I wish we had gone to Mablethorpe at the beginning of the week, and then perhaps I should have got to know you better.

Did you enjoy the picture you went to see? I haven't been since a fortnight before my holidays. I am very sorry I spelt your name wrong, but I never looked to see if I had left anything out or not.

Well I must say Good-bye for now.

Yours Truly

Joan

P.S. my sister's name is Dorothy

They arranged to meet, and on the first Sunday in September, Les set out to cycle to Nottingham, nearly sixty miles away:

Got up at about 7 p.m. I washed my feet and then I got ready and I got out my bike and I borrowed Lou's touring bag. I then packed ready and I started out for Nottingham at 9.35 a.m. I meant to start at 8 a.m. It was a nice sunny day. I had my dinner at just outside Loughboro at about 1 p.m. I got to Nottingham at about 3.5 p.m. Joan wasn't there so I waited for a time and then I went down a side road and I met Joan outside her house. We went for a walk then I stayed with her until 6 p.m. I then had to hurry back and I had my tea at about 7 p.m. at the same place as I had my dinner. From Loughboro to Leicester I was paced by a lorry. I then got lost in Leicester for about 45 mins. I left there at 9 p.m. and I arrived home at just as it was striking 12 p.m. Mum and Dad were waiting up for me. Bed at about 12.30 a.m.[36]

On his return, he posted off another letter, but recorded no replies over the following few weeks, although life seemed to be passing as usual, with plenty of reference to wandering the neighbourhood with his pals and 'messing' with girls. A month after his first visit to Nottingham, he described being 'subbed' by his mother to go Nottingham Goose Fair with one of his friends, the entry ending with rather a sad little admission.

9 October – Saturday
Got up at about 7.15 a.m. Work. In the afternoon after dinner I messed about for a time and then I got ready did my exercises and went down to All Saints at 3.45 p.m. to meet Edgar. We then went for a walk around Woolworths. Then we went down to Castle Station. Our train started at 4.15 p.m. We got to Nottingham at about 6.55 p.m. We then went in a store and then walked along the main streets to where the Goose Fair is held at about 8 p.m. We nearly got off with two girls. Left there at about 10 p.m. and went in a fish shop but it was 1/- a plate so we came out and went in another and had our chips in the street. We then walked about the streets until 11/30 p.m. then we went in the station. Our train was supposed to start back at 11.50 p.m. but it was late coming in and we started back at about 12.25 a.m. I slept a good way home. We had 7 or 8 stops and we then got in the Castle Station at 3.35 a.m. I walked with Edgar to top of Bridge St. I got home at 3.45 a.m. and went to bed at about 4 a.m. We didn't see Joan at all today.

He wrote a Christmas card to 'Joan Burton at Nottingham' and diary entries suggest that he was still holding a shine for her in the spring of the following year, when uncertainty as to how to proceed with his long-distance courtship finally led him to write to 'Ruth English', 'agony aunt' on *Everybody's Weekly*.[37] He kept her reply, which offered the pragmatic advice that he was not likely to get very far with his one-sided correspondence:

Dear Mr. Tebbutt,
In reply to your letter. As you do not live so very far from this girl, why not go along and see her one weekend? There may be some reason why

she has given up writing to you, and it is far better for you to go and see her, and have it out.

I am afraid you are not likely to get any satisfaction by just continuing writing to her.

With best wishes.

Yours sincerely,

Ruth English[38]

By the end of 1937 Les was moving into new recreational pursuits which involved the 'bunny run'. Gaining confidence on the bunny run was an important rite on the path to more intensive patterns of courtship, although its banter and larking about also gave it a rather uneasy reputation.[39] His entrance to it came in autumn 1937, not long after his return from the annual camp where he had met Joan. He was introduced to it by his friends, who walked with him for his first outing after they had told him that a girl named Peggy 'wanted to know him'. Such indirect recommendations were not unusual. Harold Gill recalled the monkey run in Southport, where he first became acquainted with

> the 'putting a good word in' practised by the local girls to help each other in their attempts to become the girl-friend of the boy they fancied . . . For the boy, if he fancied the same girl who fancied him, the opening gambit in the game was less painful if he had fore knowledge of her liking for him, and with the chance of a rebuff removed, could proceed with confidence and without fear of loss of face, among his circle of friends. In those days a boy had to make, or appear to make, the first moves. That the rules were being bent a little was conveniently overlooked – by both sexes.[40]

Les and Peggy do not seem to have 'clicked', but a Sunday stroll up the bunny run was soon a regular activity, although not without risks, as Les observed towards the end of November when 'some copper in plain clothes' 'clipped' his ear 'for standing about tonight'.[41] Joining the bunny run signified movement into a new phase of adolescence which involved greater concentration on girls. References to going after them with his friends became more frequent, followed as often as not by the postscript that they had not been 'lucky', although he did note one occasion when he had 'cuddled' a girl and kissed her on the lips. By the end of 1937, diary entries were altogether more confident as he chirpily recorded, 'We called after a girl who goes to the chapel to arrange a date for Bob. We got one for him on Sunday.'[42]

Girlfriends and courtship

Les's diaries suggest the kinds of anxieties which social encounters with girls caused boys from the mid teens onwards, and which were frequently expressed in letters to advice columnists, in queries about how to make the first approach, reticence over revealing feelings and sensitivities about being rebuffed. Courtship, a 'career' path into marriage for young women, dominated their lives to a much greater extent than was the case with young men, who were often more uncertain about its social 'rules', and advisers across a range of columns fielded many similar questions, from diffident suitors and young men 'very much in love', from those who were engaged and from those unable to see a way forward after unsuccessful courtship.[43] Ann Temple described 'love' as 'by far the most popular theme' among the problems she received and suggested how such correspondence was gendered; while most of the marriage problems with which she dealt were from women, 'love problems' were 'as often as not from men', which perhaps suggests how women were taken for granted, once they lost their independence on marriage.[44] Young men frequently wrote of their uncertainties about courtship and of being single; 'shyness, perplexity about feminine nature and behaviour, fear of qualities in a girl which might make her a possessive or a boring wife, fear of the responsibility of marriage'.[45] Not all older readers sympathised with such correspondence. One of Temple's readers declared he could not understand why the 'vapid outpourings of a moonstruck, callow youth should constitute a problem of interest', and criticised such 'nonsense' as unworthy of her 'valuable time'.[46]

Most advisers assumed a sympathetic, practical approach to the romantic faltering of male courtship. Dix advised 'Downhearted' that he was 'very young' and should try to 'forget' the young woman for whom he had fallen. 'I think if she is a nice girl she would hardly act this way to punish you. It would be cutting off her nose to spite her face, if she loves you.'[47] She admonished a so-called 'chump', telling him there was nothing wrong with telling his 'young lady' that he loved her. 'As it bores her to hear it, are you sure she loves you in return? Most girls cannot hear it too often.'[48] A bashful would-be suitor was urged to be brave to tell his 'dream girl' what was in his 'heart and mind'.[49] Unlike their female counterparts, who were frequently warned against being too forward in their relations with young men, shy male suitors were often urged to take a bolder approach. In another letter to Ann Temple, 'Dejected 16' wrote that he wanted to get to know an attractive girl he had met the previous week. As his friend had failed to introduce them, she did not know his name and he was worried that he would feel rather a 'fool' if he spoke to her again in the street and she failed to recognise him. Temple suggested this was unlikely and advised him to smile and take off his hat when they next met, since she was, after all, 'just an ordinary human being'.[50] In another letter, 'No courage', who was unsure about asking a girl to go to the pictures with him, was told that 'of course' he should invite her. 'Nothing very dreadful could happen if she refused you! You will not get very far if you do not make the effort yourself.'[51]

Many queries suggest confusion over understanding and expressing feelings, difficulty with rejection or accepting that relationships had finished (or were unlikely to start), self-consciousness, jealousy, guilt and impatience over quarrels and disagreements. Columnists did not always have much sympathy for what they heard. Eyles, for example, described her frustration with the 'cave-man' idea in the 'Movement':

> Why on earth young men should seriously think of breaking an engagement because a girl dances with another young man, beats me altogether. What possible harm could dancing do? It is splendid for the nerves, it promotes comradeship and freedom. Of course some dances are horrid, but then, you need not go, nor take your girl to such places. But if you young men are so jealous that you cannot be happy if another man does a foxtrot with your girl, all I can say is that you should take yourselves in hand firmly. The girl who has nothing to do with men makes a dull and uncomprehending wife. Do not forget that![52]

Among the most frequent questions Temple dealt with from men 'young and old' was lack of confidence about women. These often 'very confidential letters' suggest much about the effects of segregated education and upbringing, as well as Temple's own irritation with the writers' self-absorption.

> They are usually men who have been brought up with men and have not had girl companions in childhood. They think of women as a different species to themselves. They believe there is a 'technique' for attracting them. Really it is the certainty of their wholly mistaken technique or the uncertainty of their stumbling, blundering approach that bores women.[53]

The letters Temple received from young men 'were not wildly romantic', and such functional emphases were particularly marked in correspondence from a 21-year-old called 'Wonderer', in the *Manchester Evening News*, sardonically headlined 'He's got a little list', the refrain from Gilbert and Sullivan's *Mikado*. This young man explained that his parents wanted him to marry, but despite having enough money 'to keep a house going', he could not decide which of the two girls with whom he was 'friendly' he should choose. (A familiar dilemma on advice pages.)

> No. 1 is beautiful, doesn't go to the pictures or amusements, only with her mother. I love her, but I don't think she cares much about me. She will not go out with me, except for walks. Good worker. Knows everything a girl should know.

> No. 2 is not beautiful, goes to the pictures, and loves me; but I don't love her because she goes out with other men. She will give me everything she has. Please give me your advice.[54]

Such extreme dispassion was unusual, and it could have been a hoax letter of the sort for which advisers were always on the alert. What comes over strongly in many letters from such young men are expectations of loyalty and expressions of love, which support oral history evidence about the importance men placed on 'falling in love' and love at first sight, which contrasted with the more pragmatic views young women frequently had of potential suitors.[55] This was very apparent in another letter to the *Manchester Evening News*, from a young man in his late twenties whose exaggerated prose explained how he had met his 'absolutely ideal girl' and fallen 'desperately in love'.

> She is simply marvellous and I would marry her tomorrow for I am 28 and in quite a good position. But the snag is that she goes out a lot with another man. I don't think they are engaged. Would it be caddish to try to win her away from him? I know we are suited in every way and would be wildly happy.[56]

Makins described the emotional power of letters from male correspondents, who often expressed a strong sense of personal belittlement, very apparent in complaints about girlfriends' attitudes and requests for advice about how to change them.[57] B. P., for example, described his great attraction to a girl who was 'flippant', and his frustration at her apparent inability to take things seriously. How, he asked, could he make her more 'serious minded'?[58] Many correspondents disliked the instrumental, off-hand treatment they received at the hands of some girls, again supporting research on women's pragmatic choices during courtship, which was often as much a 'state of being' as being 'tied to an individual'.[59] There were frequent complaints about their girlfriends' apparent reluctance to settle down in ways thought appropriate to a fiancée. A 'Young man' described how his work meant he could see his girlfriend only two nights a week, yet she was never 'quite satisfied with the outings' he gave her,

> but must let other boys take her out. I've never objected as long as it did not happen too often. Lately she has been out with a different man friend each night, and I objected very strongly to this. Now I'm afraid she will tell me lies if she has been out with other men friends.
>
> The only pleasure I have had has been with her. I've worked hard, denied myself, and made a secure position by keeping to the grindstone and saving the money. I believe that a girl should think of the future. She never stays at home, not even one night in the week. She must go to shows and dances which I pay for, though I don't dance myself. I've warned her that if she insists on behaving like this I must break the engagement off. Am I justified in taking such a serious step? I care an awful lot for her and giving her up will hurt. She is twenty.[60]

'Fed Up, Salford', regularly treated his girlfriend to 'dances, pictures and motor runs', but she showed little gratitude, curtly replying 'Yes, thanks', when asked if she had enjoyed herself. He did not feel much like a couple, since 'rather than siding with me, as I do with her, in any argument with friends she opposes me'. His greatest difficulty, however, was how she never addressed him by name. 'She might be talking to a stranger the way she says, "Have a sweet". These things seem trifling, but are maddening and discouraging. Should I give her up?'[61] Even those not as affluent as 'Fed Up' were disconcerted by such cavalier treatment. 'Baffled, Levenshulme', while 'not in a position' to give his girlfriend treats, was unhappy at the lack of reciprocity in their relationship. He had been 'friendly' with his girlfriend for two years, yet she was 'always' telling him of the 'wonderful times' she had had before meeting him. 'When I ask her if she is happy with me she puts me off with a flippant "Oh, I'm all right," and sometimes she says it so curtly that it hurts my feelings. I do my best to give her an enjoyable time, but what a difference a little appreciation would make. Can you advise me how to make her realise this?'[62]

Anxieties such as these were possibly exacerbated by the expectations which surrounded 'first love', especially as men 'tended to marry the first woman' to whom they were seriously attracted.[63] Underlying many queries, however, were the difficulties both sides had in discussing their feelings and male unease at young women's independence and reluctance to settle down. Twenty-four-year-old 'Very Anxious', who had been 'company' with a girl of his own age for three years, had asked her to marry him several times but she always saying that she wanted to be 'free' and did not want 'to settle down'. He loved her 'dearly' and would do anything for her, but she seemed to prefer her friend's company to his. Was it worth him 'wasting' his time, in the hope that she might change? 'Or would it be best to give her up?'[64]

Despite professions of love and loyalty, many letters suggest a pragmatic desire to cut one's losses before losing yet more time and opportunity for a traditional relationship. 'Jimmy', for example, was in love with a 'northern' girl who worked in the same firm. He saw her home most nights and went out with her two or three evenings a week but she only wished to be friends, because she was already going out with a boy in her home town. Jimmy, rather hopefully, pointed out that she did not hear from the boyfriend very often and, despite professing friendship, seemed quite fond of him. Like 'Very Anxious', he wanted certainty. 'Do you think she will ever be serious with me and should I go on with this affair. It's difficult for me not to see her as we work together, and yet if she is never likely to marry me I do not want to go on with it.'[65]

Engagement was, in fact, a serious step at which many others faltered, due to family and financial worries. 'Baffled' (a not uncommon *nom de plume*), described his 'fondness' for a girl he had known for several months. Despite being 'greatly sought after', she seemed to prefer his company to any other man's but as she was 'of the type' that did 'not show her feelings', he had received no encouragement. 'Financial reasons' meant he was unable to offer her 'any concrete proposal' and he knew she was against long engagements. What should he do? 'Carry on as just friends', admit his feelings, or finish it all?[66] Where some found it difficult to start and develop relationships, others sought painless ways of breaking them off. Nineteen-year-old John R. of Bournemouth told Dix of his affair with a girl who loved him 'dearly' but in whom he had lost interest. He wanted to know how to leave without hurting her. 'She would feel terrible if I stopped going out with her. Can you tell me a painless way of separation?'[67] Dix placed his dilemma within the wider context of adolescent growing pains. There was no painless solution and he should let her down gradually: 'there is this consolation for you, that in the teens hearts heal almost overnight, and probably the girl can forget you as easily as you will forget her. Few people marry their first loves.'[68]

The stresses and strains of long engagements, common in the inter-war years, were another frequent topic of such correspondence. Twenty-six-year-old James of Timperley precisely defined the 'two years and two months' during which he and his girl had been 'madly in love with each other'. James had saved up £100 towards their marriage, which he hoped would happen when she was 21. He 'hadn't slept for nights', however, because she had broken off her relationship with him after meeting another boy at a party where they had played 'kissing games'. Mary Marryat sympathised and offered the familiar advice that absence often made the heart grow fonder: 'try to avoid her for a time – and let her miss you'. She implicitly underlined distinctions between commitments such as engagement and less formalised relationships: 'I think that probably this girl is not quite in love with you, or she would not have gone off with the other boy. At the same time, unless you were actually engaged, you had no real right to object to her going out with other young men.'[69] L. S., on the other hand, had been engaged for six years, with marriage postponed several times for financial and other reasons. He had now reached the point where he was 'bored stiff' by his fiancée and hated the very thought of matrimony because they quarrelled every time they met. He did not want to disappoint her, but knew that if they married, he could not treat her as a wife should be treated. 'What on earth am I to do about it?'[70]

Sometimes it was not so much personal misgivings as the pressures of family and friends that writers felt caught between. In the case presented by 'Jack', love for his girl seemed to be taking second place to the influence he felt under from his young friends, who were all 'married and always saying sarcastic things about courting couples'. Jack had been 'very friendly' with his girl for three years and was wondering whether he should propose to her, but was held back by the fact that, since he was the last of his family to be left at home, his mother took all his salary, leaving him only spending money and unable to 'save a penny'.[71] Eyles pointed out how this was not uncommon and that 'a good many parents' were 'very unkind' when their children started courting, 'particularly in the case of boys', telling the girl who had 'won the boy's fancy' that she was 'taking the bread-winner away'.[72]

Unemployment took its own toll of romantic relationships. The *Manchester Evening News* published several letters from young men perturbed at their girlfriends' loss of interest in them under the stress of no work or low wages. A twenty-four-year-old described his history of many different jobs and negligible prospects. He had been with his girlfriend for two years, but she had suddenly grown 'most cold', despite previously sticking by him when he was unemployed. Critchlow suggested that she was disheartened, because any ambitious girl hated to feel that her man so lacked 'push and ability' that she was likely to be poor all her life. He should pull his socks up. 'What is the matter with you? Why so many jobs? Surely one was worthwhile. Try to develop concentration by writing out tasks for each day and doing them. What sort of job are you in now? If you jump to it, are smartly turned out, willing and obliging, your employer won't let you go.'[73] Such views were not unusual and reflected the importance which women placed on finding 'financial security' in a future husband, a theme repeated in many articles about how girls could help their boyfriends 'get on' and 'spur' their ambitions to do the difficult things they did not have the 'courage' to do themselves.[74]

The emotional costs of job loss and unemployment were also very apparent in correspondence. A young unemployed man in his twenties typically worried about whether his girlfriend was losing 'her respect' and love for him, describing how, when he was with her, his 'pride' would not even let him mention his plans for the future, 'as we used to do when I had a good job'.[75] Anxious girlfriends also wrote in, troubled by their boyfriends' loss of confidence. 'Blue Eyes' of Ardwick, Manchester had been friendly with a boy for seven months, but he had recently become unemployed and she was upset by how he had changed towards her. 'How can I make him realise that it makes me wish to be with him ten times more? He often speaks about girls he knows, and if I say anything he says: "Can't you stand a joke?" Please help me.'[76]

Advice pages were feminised spaces where personal problems could expect, on the whole, to find understanding and sympathy. More conventional attitudes towards such anxieties were often found in other sections of newspapers, as in the *Daily Mirror's* 'Live-Letter Box', which parodied such correspondence, particularly romantic queries from young men. A purported query from an unemployed young man with the rather effeminate sounding *nom de plume* of 'Patience' asked how he could attract a 'pretty girl' he knew, now that he was out of work. The answer was that he had 'better wake up to some hard facts', since he would be better finding a job first and thinking of romance later. It might not be easy 'but for Heaven's sake, man, what have you to offer any girl now? You'd only make yourself miserable because you hadn't enough money to take her around. No, better take your eye off that pretty girl and get it glued on any possible jobs.'[77]

Boys seeking advice

Belief in boys being boys dominated the inter-war years, and asking for help fitted uneasily with contemporary definitions of masculinity. For those who conquered such reservations, there were still the expectations of the advisers themselves. Even on advice pages, approaches to male diffidence were nuanced in different ways, with hints of unease at what were perceived as 'un-masculine' admissions or lack of manly character. A 'desperately shy' 18-year-old, in love with a girl of 20 but afraid that she would 'scoff' if he asked her out, was told to be more assertive, since it was 'good for a man to put an issue to the test'. If it did not go the way he wanted, he would just have to learn to 'take it on the chin smiling'.[78] Two young men in their twenties, complaining about the tight hold their widowed mother had over them, yet unwilling to hurt her, were told that a 'straight manly talk' might do wonders.[79] Another young man, courting for a year, had lost a good job and been forced to take an inferior one. When he told his girl that they would have to economise, she had left him to spend all her time with a girlfriend. He was bereft, and would 'do anything to get her back'. Hadn't he 'any self-respect?' was the reply:

> The girl who would leave you just as you needed her love and sympathy to combat adverse circumstances, looks to me as though she would be a poor support in times of trouble. And what good to a man is a fair-weather wife. Don't go hanging about, asking her to take you back. Be a man. If she prefers the girl friend to you, let it go at that. Find a man pal to go about with. You will find his companionship manly and stimulating after being so much with a girl.[80]

Advisers on women's magazines expressed similar impatience with male prevarication and uncertainty. 'Unhappy Howard' described a 'worrying' problem to do with his journey to work, when he regularly passed a 'charming' girl whom he liked 'very much'. One morning he had done exactly what Critchlow had advised the 'desperately shy' 18-year-old to do, stopping and asking her if she would go to the cinema with him that evening, but she had 'just smiled' and told him not to be 'a silly cuckoo!' He was flummoxed about what to do next, although he remained hopeful, as she still smiled at him. Marryat replied with some exasperation: 'I think you must be a little more subtle than this, Howard!' He should stop every now and then to chat with the girl about everyday things, gradually leading up to whether she was courting anyone else. 'If she isn't, you can ask her to go out with you.'[81]

This was not a period when sexual frustrations could be overtly discussed, yet there are glimpses of what may have been more openly expressed in unpublished correspondence. Eyles was more alert than some to the sexual uncertainties behind some dissatisfactions and requests for help, as was apparent in her response to a 20-year-old boy. He was in a job where he had no contact with girls, and described how 'envious' and 'shy' he felt when he saw other boys go out with them. Eyles urged him to get out more and become involved in social activities at his church. She indicated her awareness of the reasons behind his uncertainties, however, by suggesting that if he wrote to her privately she 'might be

able to explain just why' he felt 'so shy and awkward'.[82] Eyles had cut her
teeth with advice work in *Lansbury's Labour Weekly* and *The Miner*, and
while the queries she responded to there overlapped with those in the
mainstream press, there were also significant differences.[83] These letters
more obviously reflected the experiences of working-class writers, and
in 1926 she underlined the impact of contemporary economic conditions by observing 'how few love problems' she had received, because the
'lock-out' seemed 'to be taking people's minds off love!'[84]

Letters published in *Lansbury's Labour Weekly* and *The Miner*
tended to be more candid about the reasons for young men's unsettled
feelings. Another 20-year-old told how he had 'never made friends with
a girl' because he was 'too frightened', but sometimes felt so 'terrible'
that he could not 'work or think or do anything'. 'Ought I try to get rid of
sex by the will-power methods advocated by Coué?' he asked. And was
it true that work would take away the desire for sex? The young man's
rather desperate reference was to Emile Coué's book *Self-Mastery by
Conscious Auto-Suggestion*, which Eyles often recommended to unconfident correspondents and those 'afflicted with nerves, stammering and so
on'.[85] This early self-help book, first published in Britain in 1920, which
was a best-seller on both sides of the Atlantic, stressed the importance of
positive thinking to boost motivation and self-confidence and emphasised how self-hypnosis could help to manage negative and unsettling
thoughts. Eyles suggested that in this case relying on 'autosuggestion' to
remove such a 'natural' desire was rather 'silly', and advised the conventional solution of sexual satisfaction through marriage, while reminding
him that sex was no substitute for a properly rounded marital relationship: 'What you want, comrade, is to marry; but don't just go about looking for a girl who will meet your physical needs, because there is much
more in marriage than that. Find one whom you can respect, and who
will be a pal to you. The rest will follow.'[86]

Eyles received many letters in the 1920s from young women strug-
gling with the consequences of having an illegitimate child or worrying
about whether to reveal the details of their sexual past to a new boyfriend
or husband, problems which were, in part, a legacy of more relaxed war-
time relationships. Less usual was a letter from a young man finding it
difficult to make up his mind whether to take on 'an important position
in the movement', because he and a 'young girl' had had a baby when
he was 17. His mother was looking after the child and the girl had since
married someone else, but he was afraid that the story might leak out.[87]
Eyles reassured him that that was very unlikely to happen, but thought
it 'wise' that he should seek advice from a political ally about whether

he could 'possibly injure the movement by taking on the job in these circumstances'.[88]

The economic, health, sexual, social and moral problems coursing through these letters suggest ambitions and sensitivities which at times challenge assumptions about young men's lives and responsibilities. John O'C. in the *Manchester Evening News* told a tale of early love, secrecy and misunderstanding about a girl with whom he had once been 'friendly' but who had suddenly grown 'sad', insisting they could not meet again because 'she was not good enough' for him. They parted, and he 'missed her greatly', but subsequently found that the probable reason for her breaking up the relationship was that she had had a child before she met him. He was prepared to marry her, if she would have him, but was unsure how to go about it. 'Can you help me? ... I am suffering from no boyish delusions when I tell you I am in love' with the girl.[89] He was advised, 'without further preamble' to go ahead but to be 'certain', before he took this important step, that whatever happened in the future, he would never bring this up, nor ever reproach her with her past. 'Your love and need of her now is great; you want the girl to complete your happiness. Don't forget this; many men unfortunately do.'[90]

Advisers were rather ambivalent about some of the concerns which young men raised and their personal problems were not on the whole subject to the same extended consideration as those of their female counterparts, which more frequently received headline attention and were discussed in feature-length articles; a common disparity in the present day, when many more publications on emotions and relationships are aimed at teenage girls than at boys.[91]

Confidence and self-consciousness

Lack of confidence, shyness and uncertainties about how to behave were frequent themes in letters from young men between their mid teens and mid twenties. Worries about the physiological changes of adolescence are apparent in replies such as to 'Sixteen', who was advised there was not the 'slightest need to seek medical advice', because voices were 'a trouble' at his age and 'it' would 'soon right itself'.[92] Eyles often dealt with queries from young men about how to cure themselves of blushing.[93] Letter writers in their early teens were rare, although there were occasional indications of discomfiture, as in the case of a 14-year-old who was unhappy because he had 'spots and pimples all over his face' and was called names by his schoolfellows.[94] There are also hints of insecurities in trying to measure up to celebrity models of masculinity, which placed great emphasis on particular types of appearance. A 'boyfriend' was concerned about his hair problems.[95] 'Adrian's sight was failing and he had been advised to wear glasses, but had not done so because he was 'definitely not handsome', had never had a girlfriend and with glasses 'would have to give up all hope', since it seemed to him that women only went in 'for the good-looking fellows'.[96] J. A. V. described the suicidal 'self-consciousness' he felt as a result of his 'queer shaped nose'. The comments it attracted 'hurt' him 'to the quick . . . I am only a youth, but sometimes I feel I cannot go on.'[97] Some correspondents had already tried the solutions frequently advised for low self-esteem. One young man, who described how lack of self-confidence was draining him of all his 'zest' for life, had 'tried dancing, physical training, all to no effect. Other people have confidence in me, but I cannot help myself alone.' He was advised to return to his dancing class, 'find one of the shy wallflowers' and forget himself in putting her at her ease.[98] 'A Trier' was similarly told to stop thinking about himself and what the girl might be thinking of him. 'Keep your thoughts on her and her entertainment and you will forget to be shy.'[99]

Letters seeking job and careers advice hinted at the pressures associated with work-place expectations. 'Alan' was so 'nervous and afraid of failure' that even his best efforts made him 'restless and depressed'.[100] Desires for self-improvement mixed with frustration and anxiety.[101] A 'lad' working as an under-gardener on a ducal estate had good prospects but hated his job, was unable to concentrate and felt 'terribly lonely'. It was an example of what Eyles suggested came with every post, 'youngsters trying to get out of the morass' they were in.[102] A 'pit lad', 'very fond of music', who was learning to play the piano, sought affirmation that it was all 'worthwhile', because he had so much trouble 'with cut and stiff hands' and so 'little time'.[103] Jim, who was trying to study at night after working in the pits, worried because his eyes were aching so badly that reading was 'almost impossible', a sign, perhaps, both of academic worries and awareness of the prevalence of nystagmus (involuntary oscillatory eye movements) among miners.[104] *Lansbury's Labour Weekly* and *The Miner* often published queries from young men who were nervous about public speaking. J. R. of Glasgow was typical in wanting to know how to train his memory because each time he started to make a speech, he forgot 'every point'.[105]

The language which letter writers and advisers used in relation to lack of confidence suggests how psychological theories were seeping into popular culture in the 1930s, albeit in often very raw form.[106] Parents and teachers were warned against setting up 'inferiority complexes' in the minds of the young because boys who felt the constant disapproval of adults were apt to grow up lacking 'self-confidence and independence', and advisers received many letters from both men and women who thought they might be suffering from just such a complex.[107] By the 1940s, Temple observed how 'most people' had now adopted the term, although it was used 'with little or no understanding of its meaning'.[108] Emerging cultures of consumption, personality and celebrity were helping to transform the self-mastery which underpinned Victorian ideas of character building into an aspect of self-development. Early twentieth-century 'personality manuals' were full of warnings 'against feeling inferior' and being held back by lack of confidence.[109] Like self-help advisers, they urged that confidence was based on 'being yourself', on being willing to make an impression by standing out from the crowd or the 'herd'.[110] These 'new languages of self' and the 'external' performance of personality were apparent in the popular press's focus on 'likeability' as a quality which could be learned.[111]

Growing awareness of self-presentation was apparent in many queries about the etiquette of new social and consumption habits, as in a letter from three 'rather self-conscious and retiring boys' who felt it difficult to be natural with people and were concerned about how they might acquire 'attractive manners'.[112] A feature by Dix on hints to girls about how they could be 'charming' was followed by one aimed at 'boy readers', ostensibly prompted by their asking 'What about us?'[113] New social habits, such as the growth of smoking among young women as a sign of stylish modernity, encouraged new resentments and uncertainties, and young men's letters suggest some of the confusion which attended women's social and economic visibility. B. of Southampton asked Dix what she thought of girls who 'cadged' cigarettes:

> Why don't they use their own and maybe offer a boy one occasionally? The minute you meet a girl she will say: 'Got a cigarette?' And the chances are she won't stop smoking until she has used the last one you have, although you can see in her bag she has plenty of her own. Now these girls all have well-to-do fathers or they work and get just as big salaries as the boys do, and they are just as able to pay for cigarettes as the boys are. Most of us boys are getting a mighty thin envelope in these days, and by the time we have paid for half a dozen girls' cigarettes for the evening it almost means no lunches for the next week.[114]

Dix thought it 'absurd and unfair for the boy to have to pay for a girl's amusement' when they went out together, and advised that a girl should contribute her share.[115] Not all correspondents agreed, one young woman suggesting how she had 'always understood that it was

the height of discourtesy to pay for oneself when invited out by a boy'.[116]
The question of whether girls should pay their own way remained a
common source of grievance on both sides in 1930s advice columns.
Assumptions that young men should pay when taking out their girlfriends was grounded in expectations of their higher wages, although
boys were often 'mean' in what they paid for in the early days of going
out with a girl. Cultural sexualisation and young women's greater opportunities for financial independence gradually accentuated awareness of
the sexual obligations they might be placed under if they agreed to their
boyfriends treating them.[117] Such sensitivities grew after the Second
World War. Traditional ideas of social reputation remained strong in
the 1930s, however, and could leave young women feeling humiliated if
their boyfriends did not seem to value them sufficiently to pay when they
went out. Jessie T. of Edinburgh was angry at her boyfriend's reluctance
to pay because it looked 'so bad', particularly when they were out with
other people. He never thought of paying, wherever they went, 'he just
gives the bus conductor his own fare and leaves me to pay mine, and
the same in a teashop'.[118] 'Bess' of Sunderland felt she was 'always being
made to feel small' because her boy never paid for anything when they
were out. He had a good job, and although she did not mind paying her
fares and cinema entrance when they were alone, disliked how her girlfriends 'sneered' about his meanness. Eyles, ever alert to signs of poverty,
suggested that she should avoid jumping to conclusions and find out
why he was so careful before condemning him. Perhaps he was saving up
to be married; maybe he had to help out some poor relatives?[119] Not all
young women were insensitive to the constraints of being hard up or in
poorly paid jobs, however, and some developed subtle ways of negotiating male self-respect, James Brooke recalling his appreciation of being
helped out financially, which he took as a sign of the girl's being 'the right
sort'. Taking a girl to the pictures with a

> quarter pound of chocolates and two seats in the ninepennies would
> set you back 2s – a week's pocket money for the average boy. Any
> decent girl would realise that, and when you got comfortably settled
> in your seat, she would slip her hand in yours and there would be a
> shilling in it for you as her half share of the expenses – 'playing Dutch',
> we called it.[120]

As the popular press discovered the commercial advantages of 'human
interest' features on personal relationships and domestic life, male
behaviour started to be questioned in new ways, as did expectations
of adolescent masculinity and relationships between adolescents and

their parents.[121] Parental expectations of financial entitlement over their children's lives still produced strong feelings of both duty and guilt. Most working-class young people lived at home until they were married, and such family responsibilities encouraged disagreements that were, not surprisingly, exacerbated by unemployment.[122] Anxiety and resentment at having to support dependent parents were very apparent in Eyles's columns, where she warned the sons and daughters of her mining readers to remember the feelings of their unemployed fathers and not 'keep harping on the fact' that they were keeping the home going.[123] W. worried that, with his unemployment benefit coming to an end, he would be left 'more or less dependent' on his elderly mother because his father, a coal porter, 'was getting poor pay at the best of times.' He thought he might be better off in Australia but had always given his mother 'a good proportion of his wages' and wondered if he was justified in depriving her of an extra income when he started earning good money again.[124] Bert S. was similarly torn. Having been educated at 'great sacrifice' on his parents' part, he now had a teaching post and was living at home, where he was handing over most of his income. His loyalties were split, however, because he had fallen in love with a typist. His parents liked her but were against him 'taking on the expenses of married life' when he could have been helping them. He felt he could not let them down, after they had been so good, but this girl meant 'everything' to him. 'What ought he to do?' Eyles suggested that the answer might be for his girl to carry on working after they married, a solution which this young man, rather tellingly, does not seem to have considered.[125]

Nineteen-year-old X. Y. Z. faced a rather different problem. He was living in rooms with his unemployed father and resented the fact that he was 'practically keeping' him. He and his girlfriend could never afford to go to the cinema, yet his father went three or four times a week, took the 'boy's money as a right' and 'dictated' to him. Matters had come to a head when the young man returned late from a party at his girlfriend's house, to be greeted with a 'terrific row' when his father 'ordered' him to give the girl up. 'I have done all I could for him and never said a word at having to keep him. But don't you think this is a bit too steep? I am thinking he won't work now he has me to keep him.'[126]

In better-off working-class and lower middle-class households, smaller families and more domesticated expectations of family life not only allowed some young men to develop quieter, home-based leisure interests but may also have accentuated awareness of tensions around parental control, discipline and behaviour which would become 'central to the notion of adolescence' after the Second World War.[127] Disagreements with parents and the shifting power relationships of adolescence were well reflected in letters to advice pages, where mothers usually, but also fathers, asked how to deal with 'unruly' sons, 'coming in at all hours', never saying where they were going or whom they were seeing.[128] The first letters published in Ann Temple's column focused on the particular difficulties that had developed between the younger generation and their parents since the early 1920s, concerns also expressed in sex-education and advice literature.[129] A father typically lamented the disappearance of a formerly close friendship with his son, who had 'thrown off his companionship and developed a dance-band mentality'. The boy was obsessed with 'dancing, cinema and girls', and became irritable and impatient, 'slamming' out of the house if his father remonstrated with him.[130] Fathers not only complained but were complained about, particularly as young men moved from their mid to late teens.[131] Dix's columns encapsulated growing American beliefs about the mid teens as an age that kept 'parents jittery with fear and anger'.[132] There was no other period in his whole life when a boy was so 'cocksure' of himself as when he was 17 or 18, nor was there any other time when he was 'so jealous of his independence', 'so determined to come and go as he pleases'.[133] Dix warned parents of adolescent children not to go into a 'blind panic' as a result of hearing so many 'hair-raising tales about the goings on of modern youth'.[134] Dix contributed a significant American discourse of teen experiences and dating to Britain and a wide international audience, which would become more familiar after the Second World War.[135] Much of her advice was grounded in the liberal assumptions of the American dating system, which had emerged in the 1920s and had no counterpart in Britain. Her sympathies with teen predicaments and youthful romance owed much to this different social climate, which was based on 'getting to know' the opposite sex by dating many different girls or boys.[136] Her reflections on the teen years and youth were peppered with references to consumer goods and activities rare among British youth, such as cars, telephones, sodas and shows. Names like 'Chuck', 'Mamie' and 'Sadie' slipped in, while her writing introduced readers to a rich vocabulary of American phrases and terminology, such as 'gold-diggers', feeling 'lonesome', wise-crackers, feeling 'cut-up', 'going crazy', feeling 'blue', 'dating', 'necking' and 'petting'.[137] Such emphases on the distinctiveness of particular types of behaviour in the 'teens' helped to pave the way for the emergence of the distinctive 'teenage' personality of the post-war years, much as the dissemination of domestic ideals in the popular press helped to 'prepare the way for the more domesticated working-class masculinity' which Willmott and Young observed in the 1950s.[138]

The 1920s saw many former social taboos relaxing, and social relations becoming more informal than had been the case before the war. The 1930s were in many respects a period of retrenchment and adjustment to these changes, years when the previous decade's legacy of more fluid emotional and social attachments became more self-conscious. Les's diaries illustrate the importance of friends in negotiating different transitions through adolescence, but also highlight some of the limitations of these friendships, as was apparent on his hitting a brick wall in his relations with Joan, when Les was also willing to try a more 'up-to-date' alternative by turning to Ruth English's reassuringly distant advice.[139] Les's references to friends, girls and 'dating', his uncertainties about how best to proceed with Joan or how to join the bunny run evoke the fragilities which attended commonplace rites of passage during adolescence. His letter and the broader queries examined here suggest the effects of greater opportunities for more mixed, closer and less regulated socialising as informal contacts with girls and young women became not only more frequent than in the past but were informed by the challenge of their economic independence and the glamorous standards of commercial leisure cultures which also accentuated adult worries by drawing young people away from the scrutiny of family and neighbourhoods. These trends were very apparent in the development of social dancing over the inter-war years as the 'individualised', improvised styles of the 1920s were reined in to become more regulated in the decade which followed. Like the well-established assumptions about advice pages, the dance hall was another 'woman's space'; strongly associated with women's agency, its performance expectations had complex implications for many men. Inhibition was particularly apparent in young men's transitions to dancing, and it is to how gendered expectations were both subverted and reinforced on the dance floor that the next chapter turns.[140]

Notes

1   C. Langhamer, 'Love and courtship in mid twentieth-century England', *Historical Journal*, 50:1 (2007), p. 182.

2   Cas Wouters's comparative analysis of prescriptive literature such as etiquette and manners books has illustrated how these changes complemented broader trends across the western world, towards greater 'social and psychic intimacy': C. Wouters, *Sex and Manners: Female Emancipation in the West, 1890–2000* (London: Sage Publications, 2004); C. Wouters, *Informalization: Manners and Emotions since 1890* (London: Sage Publications, 2007).

3   Wouters, *Sex and Manners*, p. 159.

4   J. White, *The Worst Street in North London: Campbell Bunk, Islington, between the Wars* (London: Routledge and Kegan Paul, 1986); C. Langhamer, *Women's Leisure in England, 1920–1960* (Manchester: Manchester University Press, 2000); S. Todd, 'Poverty and aspiration: young women's entry to employment in inter-war England', *Twentieth Century British History*, 15:2 (2004), 119–42; S. Todd, *Young Women, Work and Family in England, 1918–1950* (Oxford: Oxford University Press, 2005), pp. 195–224.

5   C. Heron, 'Boys will be boys: working class masculinities in the age of mass production', *International Labor and Working-Class History*, 69:1 (2006), p. 26.

6   D. Gudelunas, *Confidential to America: Newspaper Advice Columns and Sexual Education* (New Brunswick and London: Transaction Publishers, 2008), p. 212.

7   S. Kramer, 'The fragile male', *British Medical Journal*, December 2000, 1609–12.

8   C. Langhamer, 'Love and courtship', p. 174.

9   P. N. Stearns, Review essay, 'Informalization and contemporary manners: the Wouters studies', *Theory and Society*, 36:4 (2007), p. 375.

10 *Woman's Own* (6 October 1934), p. 816. She had also worked on the problems page of *Modern Woman* and on the woman's page of the *Daily Herald*, and had an advice column in *Tribune* in the early years of the Second World War. For an autobiographical account of her difficult childhood and adolescence before the First World War, see L. Eyles, *The Ram Escapes: The Story of a Victorian Childhood* (London: Peter Nevill, 1953). Eyles also wrote novels, thrillers, social commentaries and several popular books on family relationships and sex, including *Common Sense about Sex* (London: Victor Gollancz, 1936). See also M. Joannou, *'Ladies, Please Don't Smash These Windows: Women's Writing, Feminist Consciousness and Social Change, 1918–38* (Oxford: Berg, 1995), particularly ch. 2, 'The Woman in the Little House: Leonora Eyles and Socialist-Feminism'.

11 M. Beetham, *A Magazine of Her Own? Domesticity and Desire in the Woman' Magazine, 1800–1914* (London and New York: Routledge, 1996), p. 3.

12 A. Bingham, *Family Newspapers? Sex, Private Life and the British Popular Press, 1918–1978* (Oxford: Oxford University Press, 2009), p. 19; B. Hagerty, *Read All About It! 100 Sensational Years of the Daily Mirror* (Lydney, Gloucestershire: First Stone Publishing, 2003), p. 40.

13 Rather unusually in the world of pre-war advice columnists, the pen-name was never used by anyone other than herself. The famous study of small-town America, *Middletown* [Muncie, IN], suggested that Dix was 'the most potent' external 'agency of diffusion' of ideas about marriage: R. S. Lynd and H. M. Lynd, *Middletown, A Study in Contemporary American Culture* (New York: Harcourt, Brace and Company, 1929), p. 116. P. L. Abramson, *Sob Sister Journalism* (Westport, CT: Greenwood Press, 1990), p. 14.

14 *Daily Mirror* (30 November 1935), p. 12. Dix's papers are held in the Woodward Library, Austin Peay State University. Answered letters were said to have been burned by her chauffeur, 'to protect correspondents against blackmail' in case her files were stolen: B. Belford, *Brilliant Bylines: A Biographical Anthology of Notable Newspaperwomen in America* (New York: Columbia University Press, 1986) p. 75. Her column was the 'longest running continuously authored newspaper column in

the first half of the twentieth century': Gudelunas, *Confidential to America*, p. 67. She was published in major newspapers in the United States, including the *Chicago Tribune*, *New York Journal* and *New Orleans Times*.

15 M. G. Schilpp and S. M. Murphy, *Great Women of the Press* (Carbondale, IL: Southern Illinois Press, 1983), p. 113.

16 Emily Post, who also wrote in the *Daily Mirror*, was responsible for 'America's most famous twentieth-century etiquette book', first published in 1922: Wouters, p. 11. Unfortunately none of letters sent to the *Daily Mirror* has survived, other than in the published columns; 'Mounds of letters' found stored in her basement after she died were subsequently sent to the tip. E-mail correspondence with Inga Filippo, 6 November 2008.

17 *Daily Mail* (6 February 1936).

18 D. Critchlow, *'Dear Jane Dawson . . .'* (London: Robert Hale Limited, 1977), p. 12).

19 Gudelunas, *Confidential America*, p. 212. Gudelunas suggests the number of male readers of such columns was increasing by the 1940s, no doubt encouraged by war-time anxieties; E. Kanervo, T. Jones and J. White, 'One hundred years of advice: an analysis of the style and content of Dear Abby and Dorothy Dix', paper presented at the Dorothy Dix Symposium, Woodstock Mansion, Todd County, Kentucky, 27 September 1991 [hereafter Dorothy Dix Symposium], http://library.apsu.edu/Dix/kanervo.htm (accessed 7 February 2007). Dix's mother had died as she was entering adolescence.

20 P. Makins, *The Evelyn Home Story* (London: Collins, 1975), p. 204.

21 A. Phillips, 'Advice Columnists', in B. Franklin (ed.), *Pulling Newspapers Apart: Analysing Print Journalism* (London: Routledge, 2008), p. 98; Makins, *The Evelyn Home Story*, p. 54.

22 Makins, *The Evelyn Home Story*, p. 53.

23 Phillips, 'Advice Columnists', p. 98; Makins, *The Evelyn Home Story*, p. 54.

24 Critchlow, *'Dear Jane Dawson . . .'*, p. 13.

25 Gudelunas, *Confidential to America*, p. 71.

26 *Ibid.*, p. 69.

27 Makins, *The Evelyn Home Story*, p. 159.

28 Critchlow, *'Dear Jane Dawson . . .'*, p. 9.

29 P. Vincenzi, 'Obituary: Marjorie Proops', *Independent* (12 November 1996).

30 J. Edmonds, *The Lean Years*, Burnett Archive of Working-Class Autobiographies, University of Brunel (hereafter, Burnett Archive), p. 81. Edmonds was born in Croydon, London in 1911.

31 J. Loftus, *Lee Side*, Burnett Archive, p. 81. Loftus was born 1914, in Leigh, Lancashire.

32 Loftus, *Lee Side*, p. 151.

33 S. Metcalfe, *One Speck of Humanity*, Burnett Archive, p. 14. Metcalfe was born in London in 1910: p. 85.

34 *Ibid.*, p. 14.

35 S. Kramer, 'The fragile male'.

36 'Diary' (5 September 1937).

37 *Ibid.* (21 December 1937).

38 Letter to Les from Ruth English, *Everybody's Weekly* (21 April 1938). The title paper to the letter was *Everybody's Weekly*, although the magazine changed its title to

Everybody's in 1930. It was a weekly 'tabloid magazine'. Anthony Burgess described a rather differently sided correspondence after a sexual encounter in Blackpool in his late teens, with a girl called Amy. She sent him a love letter on his return home. 'On the back of her envelope she had lettered the conventional acronyms of passion: SWALK for "sealed with a loving kiss"; ITALY for "I trust and love you"; HOLLAND for "hope our love lives and never dies". Under her signature was a cross for a kiss, also BOLTOP: "better on lips than on paper".' Her stepmother warned him against writing back, 'But if I wrote back what could I say? I fearfully awaited other letters': A. Burgess, *Little Wilson and Big God* (New York: Grove Weidenfeld, 1986), pp. 131–3. My thanks to John Walton for this reference.

39 For attempts to regulate disorderly street space in the late nineteenth century see A. Croll, 'Street disorder, surveillance and shame: regulating behaviour in the public spaces of the late Victorian British town', *Social History*, 24:3 (1999), 250–68; S. Humphries, *Hooligans or Rebels? An Oral History of Working-Class Childhood and Youth, 1889–1939* (Oxford: Basil Blackwell Ltd., 1981), p. 137.

40 H. Gill, [Untitled], Burnett Archive (no page numbers). Gill was born in 1919.

41 J. Springhall, *Coming of Age: Adolescence in Britain, 1860–1960* (Dublin: Gill and Macmillan, 1986), p. 139; A. Davies, *Leisure, Gender and Poverty* (Buckingham and Philadelphia: Open University Press, 1992), p. 106; 'Diary' (28 November 1937).

42 'Diary' (3 December 1937).

43 Langhamer has suggested that the fluidity of terms surrounding 'courtship' in the mid twentieth century indicates how the 'intimate personal relations of youth' were being re-worked. This became more apparent after the war, but it is possible to see similar shifts in the 1930s when 'going out' with a girl could also be described as dating, although not in the same sense as in an American context: Langhamer, 'Love and courtship', pp. 179, 181.

44 A. Temple, *Good or Bad – It's Life* (London: Nicholson & Watson, 1944), p. 100.

45 *Ibid.*, p. 105.

46 *Daily Mail* (6 January1938), p. 6.

47 *Daily Mirror* (11 January 1939), p. 22.

48 *Ibid.* (19 August 1938), p. 22.

49 *Ibid.* (5 July 1937), p. 24.

50 *Daily Mail* (1 January 1938), p. 6.

51 *Daily Mirror* (9 December 1936), p. 22.

52 *Lansbury's Labour Weekly* (13 March 1926), p. 14.

53 Temple, *Good or Bad*, p. 112.

54 *Manchester Evening News* (21 December 1936), p. 3.

55 N. Higgins, 'The changing expectations and realities of marriage in the English working class, 1920–1960' (PhD thesis, Cambridge, 2002), pp. 86–121.

56 *Manchester Evening News* (12 November 1936), p. 4.

57 P. Makins, *The Evelyn Home Story* (London: Collins, 1975), p. 204.

58 *Daily Mail* (7 January1938), p. 18.

59 Langhamer, 'Love and courtship', p. 181; J. Giles, ' "Playing hard to get": working-class women, sexuality and respectability in Britain, 1918–1940', *Women's History Review*, 1 (1992), 239–55; J. Giles, ' "You meet 'em and that's it": working-class women's refusal

of romance between the wars in Britain', in L. Pearce and J. Stacey (eds), *Romance Revisited* (London: Lawrence and Wishart, 1995).

60 *Manchester Evening News* (31 December 1936), p. 3.

61 *Ibid.* (14 November 1936), p. 4.

62 *Ibid.* (28 November 1936), p. 4.

63 J. R. Gillis, *For Better, For Worse. British Marriages, 1600 to the Present* (New York and Oxford: Oxford University Press, 1985), p. 287.

64 *Woman's Weekly* (1 November 1930), p. 784.

65 *Ibid.* (27 April 1940), p. 840.

66 *Daily Mail* (6 January1938), p. 6.

67 *Daily Mirror* (6 February 1936), p. 22.

68 *Ibid.*

69 *Woman's Weekly* (13 April 1935), p. 699.

70 *Lansbury's Labour Weekly* (16 October 1926), p. 14.

71 *Woman's Weekly* (1 July 1939), p. 51.

72 *The Miner* (11 January 1930), p. 10.

73 *Manchester Evening News* (26 December 1936), p. 4.

74 Langhamer, 'Love and courtship', p. 188; *The Miner* (27 September 1930), p. 11.

75 *Daily Mirror* (20 October 1936), p. 24.

76 *Manchester Evening News* (26 November 1936), p. 3.

77 *Daily Mirror* (9 August 1937), p. 13.

78 *Manchester Evening News* (21 December 1936), p. 3.

79 *Ibid.* (7 December 1936), p. 2.

80 *Ibid.* (5 December 1936), p. 2.

81 *Woman's Weekly* (24 June 1939), p. 1348.

82 *Woman's Own* (15 October 1938), p. 70.

83 She also had a column in *Modern Woman*.

84 *Lansbury's Labour Weekly* (17 July 1926), p. 15. I am grateful to Sheila Rowbotham for drawing my attention to this source. In the same year, Eyles also suggested she was receiving many letters from 'comrades' who were showing 'every symptom of neurasthenia . . . depressed, suffering from indigestion and other ills, mental and physical': *Lansbury's Labour Weekly* (24 April 1926), p. 15. (Neurasthenia was also associated with shellshock.)

85 E. Coué, *Self-Mastery by Conscious Auto-Suggestion* (New York: Kessinger Publishing, 1922). Coué was a French pharmacist and psychotherapist. *The Miner* (29 October 1927), p. 9.

86 *Lansbury's Labour Weekly* (25 December 1926), p. 15.

87 *Ibid.* (4 December 1926), p. 15.

88 *Ibid.*

89 *Manchester Evening News* (26 December 1936), p. 4.

90 *Ibid.*

91 I. Banks, 'Education and debate. No man's land: men, illness and the NHS', *British Medical Journal* (3 November 2003), 1058–60.

92 *Daily Mirror* (15 January 1937), p. 26.

93 *Lansbury's Labour Weekly* (5 December 1925), p. 15.

94 *Daily Mirror* (10 December 1937), p. 22. Both blushing and facial pimples had in

the past been attributed to masturbation, myths which may have lingered in popular culture: N. Haire, with A. Costler, A. Willy et al. (eds), *Encyclopaedia of Sexual Knowledge* (London: Francis Aldor, 1934), p. 111.

95 *Daily Mirror* (5 July 1937), p. 24.

96 *Manchester Evening News* (3 December 1936), p. 3.

97 *Ibid.* (5 November 1936), p. 10.

98 *Ibid.* (14 November 1936), p. 4.

99 *Daily Mirror* (9 December 1937), p. 7.

100 *Daily Mail* (6 January1938), p. 6.

101 *Men Only*, targeted at middle-aged, middle-class men, contained many adverts for enhancing the memory and improving self-confidence and 'assertiveness': J. Greenfield, S. O'Connell and C. Reid, 'Fashioning masculinity: *Men Only*, consumption and the development of marketing in the 1930s, *Twentieth-Century British History*, 10:4 (1999), p. 473.

102 *Lansbury's Labour Weekly* (10 October 1925), p. 2.

103 *The Miner* (19 November 1927), p. 9.

104 *Ibid.* (26 November 1927), p. 11.

105 *Ibid.* (29 October 1929), p. 9.

106 *Daily Mirror* (5 July 1937), p. 24; *Manchester Evening News* (5 December 1936), p. 2; G. Richards, 'Britain on the couch: the popularization of psychoanalysis in Britain, 1918–1940', *Science in Context*, 13:2 (2000), 183–230.

107 A. H. Gray, *Sex Teaching* (London: National Sunday School Union, [1929]), pp. 47–8.

108 *Manchester Evening News* (4 November 1936), p. 4; *Woman's Weekly* (18 February 1939), p. 33; Temple, *Good or Bad*, p. 149.

109 W. Susman, 'Personality and the making of twentieth-century culture', in W. Susman, *Culture as History: The Transformation of American Society in the Twentieth Century* (New York: Pantheon Books, 1984), essay available on www.h-net.org/~hst203/readings/susman2.html (accessed November 2009); S. Currie, *How to Make Friends Easily* (London: W. Foulsham & Co., Ltd., [1939]), p. 112.

110 Susman, 'Personality and the making of twentieth-century culture'; G. M. Cox, *Youth, Sex and Life* (London: George Newnes Limited, 1935), pp. 58, 60–1.

111 G. C. Bunn, G. Richards and A. D. Lovie (eds), *Psychology in Britain: Historical Essays and Personal Reflections* (Leicester: BPS Books, 2001), p. 119.

112 *Daily Mirror* (5 July 1937), p. 24.

113 *Ibid.* (19 March 1936), p. 25.

114 *Ibid.* (6 April 1936), p. 22.

115 This perhaps owes something to Dix's personal experience of having to make an independent living as a journalist. The American dating system did, in fact, place a great deal of emphasis on men paying for women: Wouters, *Sex and Manners*, pp. 30–1.

116 *Daily Mirror* (4 September 1939), p. 16. The issue was also discussed in the *Manchester Evening News*.

117 Langhamer, 'Love and courtship', pp. 187–8.

118 *Lansbury's Labour Weekly* (25 December 1926), p. 15.

119 *The Miner* (10 September 1927), p. 9.

120 J. Brooke, *The Dukinfield I Knew, 1906–1930* (Manchester: Neil Richardson, 1987), p. 45.

121 A. Bingham, A., *Gender, Modernity and the Popular Press in Britain* (Oxford: Oxford University Press, 2004), p. 236; C. S. Read, 'The adolescent boy', in W. A. Lane (ed.), *The Golden Health Library: A Complete Guide to Golden Health for Men and Women of All Ages* (London: Collins, [1929]), p. 62.

122 The introduction of the Household Means Test in 1931 split many families and forced many employed children to leave home because their income reduced their unemployed father's benefit: M. Pugh, *We Danced All Night: A Social History of Britain between the Wars* (London: Vintage Books, 2009), p. 81.

123 *The Miner* (11 January 1930), p. 10.

124 *Lansbury's Labour Weekly* (18 September 1926), p. 15.

125 *Ibid.* (20 October 1926), p. 15; *Ibid.* (20 November 1926), p. 16.

126 *Ibid.* (27 November 1926), p. 16.

127 D. Christie and R. Viner, 'Clinical review: ABC of adolescence. Adolescent development', *British Medical Journal* (5 February 2005), 301–4.

128 *Daily Mirror* (28 July 1937), p. 23.

129 See, for example, Cox, *Youth, Sex and Life*, pp. 224–8; Haire et al., *Encyclopaedia of Sexual Knowledge*, p. 127.

130 *Daily Mail* (7 February 1936), p. 8.

131 *Manchester Evening News* (28 June 1937), p. 3; *Daily Mirror* (17 December 1935), p. 7.

132 *Daily Mirror* (7 July 1936), p. 21.

133 *Ibid.* (17 December 1935), p. 7.

134 *Ibid.* (16 January 1934), p. 5.

135 Schilpp and Murphy, *Great Women of the Press*, p. 113; Kanervo, Jones and White, 'One hundred years of advice'.

136 Colleges and campuses were important focal points for the emergence of dating practices and American youth culture. Wouters's argument about the 'informalization' of manners and emotional styles over the course of the twentieth century is based on etiquette and manners books from the United States, England, Germany and the Netherlands, many of which sold in their millions. This neglects how advice was disseminated in the popular press. His argument also assumes that these advisers were largely confined within their national boundaries, when they often wrote in newspapers overseas. Emily Post, for example, who wrote America's 'most famous etiquette book', first published in 1922, was, like Dix, also published in the *Daily Mirror*: Wouters, *Female Emancipation*, pp. 6–7, 11, 35, 86.

137 *Daily Mirror* (13 December 1935), p. 7; *ibid.* (14 December 1935), p. 7; *ibid.* (20 December 1935), p. 7; *ibid.* (31 December 1935), p. 7.

138 Bingham, *Gender, Modernity and the Popular Press*, p. 242.

139 'Diary' (4 February 1936).

140 For the opportunities that dancing opened up for queer sociability in inter-war London, see M. Houlbrook, M., *Queer London: Perils and Pleasures of the Sexual Metropolis, 1918–1957* (Chicago: University of Chicago Press, 2005) pp. 72–3.

6

Dancing and gender

'Anarchic' dance styles assailed the popular imagination in the 1920s, subverting middle-class expectations of discipline and order and contesting the emotional equilibrium which many of the older generation sought to re-establish after the war. Such uninhibited, transgressive dancing seemed symptomatic of dissolving gender boundaries and embodied much broader fears about the alienation of modern life.

Social dancing was largely acknowledged as a feminised form of physical expression, and the dance profession's attempts to dispel these associations by restraining and controlling what were seen as unacceptable forms of display consequently placed great emphasis on manly forms of physicality, by reinforcing appropriately masculine forms of movement and posture. The expressive physicality of 1920s dancing, which needed little professional tuition, also threatened the authority of dance professionals, whose promotion of a more moderate physicality not only aimed to tame dancing's youthful energy but also championed a different, curative message about its value as an antidote to the nervous tensions of modern life and as a leisure activity with cross-generational appeal.

By the 1930s, dancing was popular among people of all ages, but its considerable significance among young people made it second in popularity to the cinema, and often more popular by the time they entered their late teens.[1] This was especially the case among girls and young women, who tended to become involved earlier than boys, when they were 13 or 14, and who enthused about its fashions and dance bands in much the same way that boys did about sport.[2] Young women's relationship with dancing has consequently attracted attention as an important expression of female youth culture and agency in leisure. The involvement of working-class young men, on the other hand, has been largely overlooked, often subordinated to assumptions that they were uneasy dancers, unsettled by the challenge which dancing's 'soft' physicality presented to the homosocial masculinities of school, work-place and the street.[3] The palais's mix of sophistication, narcissistic exhibitionism and emphases on physical poise and stylish appearance similarly disrupted 'traditional' notions of working-class masculinity, although the growing sexualisation of inter-war popular culture helped to accommodate many young men to its glamour and seductive potential. Inter-war social dancing embodied many contradictions: sexual tension and sociability, exhibitionism and self-consciousness, individuality and collectivity, which in many respects exemplified the shifting social relations between young people. Efforts to stifle their bodily freedoms on the dance floor were largely successful, yet signs of the 'expressive individualism and sexual intimacy' associated with post-Second World War youth culture were also apparent as dancing in commercialised dance halls acquired increasingly sexualised associations during the 1930s.[4] Youth, race, class and sexuality coalesced in disturbing new ways in cosmopolitan cities such as London and Liverpool, where social dancing often expressed a disconcerting 'spectacle of difference' by transgressing racial and sexual conventions.[5]

What they observed of working-class dance-hall culture in Blackpool in the late 1930s shocked and beguiled the middle-class sensitivities of Mass Observation observers, whose voyeuristic emphases on the sexual opportunities of dancing continued into the post-war years, when sociologists continued to perpetuate a functional view of dancing as a rather mechanistic activity among young men who were only really interested in its sexual opportunities.[6] As we shall see in this chapter, such failure to understand the expressive pleasures of social dancing suggests how gendered assumptions about it as a female form of movement have helped to simplify and conceal the diversity and complexity of young men's relationships with it in the 1920s and 1930s.[7]

Jazz fever: wickedness, sensuality and parental suspicion

The individualised dancing of the 1920s, which blurred who was taking the lead, was emblematic of the period's social and sexual ambivalences.[8] It was also widely seen as signifying the restless uncertainties of the post-war world. Where some regarded the movements of many dances as a grotesque parody of shell shock, others promoted dancing's physical benefits as an invigorating antidote to a prevalent modern condition, nerves.[9] The dance-band conductor Jack Payne identified the 'jazz cacophony' of the 1920s with social dysfunction, 'worry and depression', as people sought to lose themselves in whirling dance steps and an unmusical 'rhythmic noise'.[10] Others were more sanguine about jazz's role among the young as a 'tonic for the jaded spirit', and dance promoters in the early 1920s frequently employed medical and psychological discourses when appealing to men, suggesting dancing as a sedative for 'everyday worries and troubles'.[11] Hammersmith Palais emphasised the release of emotional and physical tension which dancing provided as the 'nation's tonic', a cure for 'more fits of depression than the combined hospitals of London'.[12] The psychological benefits of dancing continued to be advanced in the 1930s, when over-stressed businessmen who filled the waiting-rooms of nerve specialists were urged to take up dancing and forget their worries by concentrating on how they moved.[13]

Popular dance halls had signified immorality and sexual licence since the nineteenth century, and the female dancing body remained an object of control and restraint throughout the inter-war years. Perceptions of social dancing were related in particular ways to the dancers' age and gender, and girls' obsession with dancing in the 1920s was described as a 'dangerous, drugging craze'.[14] Social dancing had played an important part in popular culture since the middle of the nineteenth century but there was an immense 'gulf' between these dances and the 'jazz dancing' of the 1920s.[15] The new dances popularised after 1910 were no longer a question of 'how you moved your feet' but of how you moved your body, which gave young women, in particular, novel opportunities to defy the passive physical injunctions traditionally applied to them.[16] Their greater intimacy and spontaneity helped to erode the Victorian era's restrained physical boundaries and challenged respectable notions of dignified physicality with their indecent closeness, particularly in the case of the Tango.[17] During the war, dances such as the easy-going Foxtrot and 'rag' attracted many young men who had joined up from 'school or college' without ever having had a dancing lesson but, whose need for physical contact and the social exhilaration of the dance floor overrode their inhibitions.[18] The arrival of American soldiers in 1917 not only spread the passion for jazz but also helped to fuel the dance explosion of the immediate post-war years when 16- to 25-year-olds crowded into the dance halls.[19] Tours by American bands continued this enthusiasm, as did the rapid development of large, purpose-built commercial dance halls or *palais de dance*, of which about eleven thousand were opened between 1918 and the mid 1920s.[20] Nearly six thousand people tried to storm the doors of the first and most famous of these, the Hammersmith Palais, when it opened in 1919.[21]

The spontaneity and energy which jazz brought to dance in the 1920s was paralleled by the growing sexualisation of women's fashion, daring 'flapper dresses', which challenged traditional notions of female respectability.[22] Even before the war, flamboyant dance styles such as the Tango were encouraging a greater sensitivity to the body, as many young women abandoned 'orthodox' corsetry in favour of looser, less constricting underwear. (A simple, all-elastic corset slipped on over the head was called the 'tango'.[23]) Artificial silk brought flimsier, better-fitting lingerie within the reach of many working-class young women and allowed women's clothing in the 1920s not only to be more physically revealing, particularly with regard to the limbs, but to suggest the 'unconstrained body' beneath it.[24] Looking back in 1935, Irene Clephane observed how the war had helped to break down 'old taboos' about sex and the naked body. Not only were 'women no longer afraid to show their bodies', but they 'deliberately adapted their clothes for this very purpose – consciously or unconsciously advertising their urgent readiness to secure sexual experience'.[25]

Women's fashions in the 1920s had a tactile quality which reinforced 'jazzing's' scandalous and 'wicked' reputation among older people, which it retained throughout the inter-war years.[26] 'Stewardesses' who demonstrated dances in Robert Roberts's local dance hall in the early 1920s sat in an area nicknamed the 'whores' parlour', and their 'dubious' moral reputation continued in the 1930s, when women who ran their own dance studios in London reported 'unpleasant telephone calls' from men who believed that 'all dancers, and particularly professional ones must be immoral'.[27] Such associations helped to make the dance hall a potent source of inter-generational clashes and 'squabbles'. Fathers often vetoed their daughters' dancing activities, although some mothers also objected, manifesting, perhaps, not only fear of sexual misbehaviour but some resentment at exclusion from the liberty their daughters now enjoyed.[28] Dorothy Dix, who received 'thousands of pathetic letters' from girls whose parents forbade them go to dances or go on a date, was very sympathetic to their frustrations, well aware that they would soon be expected to marry and abandon such fun.[29] Burt highlighted the dance hall as a potent source of clashes with parents, usually over returning home too late, which in the case of girls often led 'to an open rupture'.[30] Dix agreed that the quickest way to drive girls away was for parents to impose 'too tight a rein', while Burt suggested that most cases of 'anti-social behaviour' among the girls in his care dated from disputes over the time they returned from dancing.[31] Being called a 'flighty piece' did little to deter dance enthusiasts, however, and tales of 'dancing-mad' young women sneaking out without permission are common in auto-biographies and oral testimony from the period.[32] Jo Kay's 15-year-old sister, who her father thought was too young to go dancing, crept out secretly to attend the fox-trot and waltz dancing competitions fashionable at popular dance halls.[33]

Dancing was not, of course, confined to commercial outlets, but took place in many different venues, with their own ambience, which helped to spread its popularity.[34] 'Hops' occurred in club rooms, swimming baths, hotels, restaurants, assembly rooms and many local halls. 'Och up the road, everywhere, it was like the cinemas, there was a wee dance hall everywhere.'[35] In rural Cumbria, most villages had a hall or institute where dances were held, often run by local churches. Distance from large urban centres was no reason to be cut off from dance fashions; one of Murfin's respondents recalled a travelling theatre company which organised Charleston competitions in Penrith.[36] While dancing appealed to all age ranges, many commercial dance halls deliberately targeted the youth market and there was an undoubted hierarchy in most towns and cities, where locals were well aware of their different status, ranging from 'seedy' local venues to 'sophisticated' city-centre ones.[37] 'Diggers', a windowless local ballroom in Salford, was 'built, to judge from its colour, in breeze blocks', and looked like 'a vast spoil heap'. Very popular among the 'teenage offspring of labouring men', it had a rather less popular reputation among the neighbourhood's 'matrons'.[38] Many such haunts were unlicensed, such as the 'dance hall' in a loft run by the widowed Elizabeth Sullivan, who charged twopence admission for 'ladies' and fourpence for 'gents'. Access was via a 'rickety staircase' and the local priest, concerned at the lack of supervision, gate-crashed late one Saturday night, causing 'one young fellow' to escape by jumping through a doorway to the ground and several 'young girls' to dash down the narrow staircase to get out of his way.[39] Such opportunities for unchaperoned encounters led to much adult emphasis on the need for close supervision, whether in commercial halls or in private institutions, and MCs played an important part in regulating dance-hall behaviour in order to appease worries about dancing's respectability.[40] So popular was dancing among young people, however, that many religious and youth-based organisations realised that it was better to organise their own dances rather than to let the young run the risk of attending more dubious commercial premises, whose sexual associations were more openly acknowledged by the 1930s.[41] Members of church congregations were not always happy about such initiatives, but as the Reverend George Braithwaite, vicar of a church in Oldham, put it, 'Surely a hall full of dancers is better than shop doorways and dark lanes full of petting couples – YOUR children among them, perhaps!'[42] By the end of the decade, a Catholic church in Bolton had even obtained 'a special dispensation from the Bishop', to run dances during Lent to help pay off its debts.[43]

Clubs, societies, churches and chapels increasingly put on their own dances, which were often serviced by small local bands with their own following, and youth workers were also urged to put on their own dances as an alternative to the less salubrious commercial dance hall.[44] 'Just as the provision of good billiards at a cheap rate keeps boys from low billiard saloons, so do well-conducted dances at boys' and girls' clubs arouse distaste for the vulgarity and excesses of the public dancing-room.'[45] Leaders of boys' and young men's clubs in East London overcame their dislike of mixing and organised dances to which members could bring 'their girls', while other clubs provided dancing classes, although some clubs preferred to encourage Morris dancing as a more appropriate expression of 'traditional' English values.[46] The Manchester and Salford Trades Council proposed holding dances as a way of getting young workers into trade unions, with refreshments, leaflets and an address of no more than fifteen minutes, although not all were convinced by the suggestion, one sceptic observing that the 'sort of people who went to dances were not the sort who could be captured easily for the trade unions, and they would not like a speech to be inflicted upon them'.[47]

The suspicion which surrounded dance halls, fox-trotting and 'jazzing' was particularly focused upon young women, but there were also fears that the wrong kind of dancing might lead young men off the rails.[48] Lillian Russell's update of *Lads' Clubs* stressed the importance of making boys aware of the great difference between the dancing of a family or friendly gathering and that which took place 'in a public hall in doubtful company and with continual alcoholic refreshment'.[49] The dancing itself might be pursued with 'innocence and decorum', and dance halls also allowed young people 'to "pick" each other "up" with frequently disastrous results', particularly if they were located near a public house or if the dancers had developed the unfortunate habit of 'taking a cocktail or a little wine for refreshment' before going there.[50] By the late 1930s, Morgan was distinguishing between 'well-conducted dances' and public dance halls which had become a real problem in city life by tempting the young 'to over-spend and to drink'. Dance hall proprietors were fearful of compromising their entertainment licences and only too aware of the trouble likely to surround the easy accessibility of alcohol, and so they carefully policed its use on their premises. Young men, however, often evaded such prohibitions by taking drink with them to consume outside, or slipping out to visit the pub between dances.[51] In Blackpool, where drinking was an 'essential' part of the evening's dancing, all the public dance halls had bars 'conveniently near to the ballroom floor'. Unacceptable behaviour was monitored by MCs who 'ruled' the dance floor and uniformed attendants who kept watch at its edge, although many girls 'were more or less drunk by closing time' and there was much male and female drunkenness in the resort.[52]

Nevertheless, although the palais retained a doubtful reputation among many social commentators and working-class parents, the rapid development of the commercial dance-hall circuit in the 1930s transformed dancing into a mass leisure pursuit and helped it to move into the realm of a necessary evil.[53] By 1938, two million people were said to go dancing each week, of whom three-quarters of a million frequented public dance halls.[54] The cinema and dance had transformed the courtship experience.[55] The constant changing of dance partners offered 'boundless possibilities'.[56] The search for a mate and dancing went 'hand in hand; dancing leads to courting and courting to marriage'.[57]

Professional suspicions

The dance hall's growing function in courtship intensified attempts to manage what went on there, although young people evaded its prescriptions in many different ways. As dancing became 'the great seaside craze of the 1920s and 1930s', coastal resorts became 'laboratories of informalization', offering 'latitude' and escape from normal expectations of behaviour and the prying eyes of parents and neighbours, Blackpool's Tower Ballroom, for example, becoming a magnet for dance enthusiasts from all over the North West.[58] By the 1930s a 'reformalization' of social manners and relationships was apparent after the dance profession and municipal and commercial interests had made great efforts to rein in the exuberant dance patterns and 'informalizing' trends of the previous decade.[59]

When the Charleston 'swept' Britain in 1925–6, dance halls had presented 'a wonderful sight' as couples leaped up to dance and lashed out so recklessly that dresses were torn and dancers left 'battered' and bruised.[60] Young men were particularly drawn to its physical energy, one writer suggesting how they had not hesitated 'to put a touch of the Rugger scrum' into it.[61] So boisterous were 'rough', 'eccentric' dances like the Charleston, Black Bottom, 'shimmy-shake' and 'varsity drag' that some ballrooms banned them. The youthful, 'modern' exuberance which gave such scope for free expression was seen as undermining traditional English 'character' and propriety, and badly taught dance styles were blamed for promoting the 'gait of a hooligan or a vulgar woman'.[62] In 1922 the British Association of Teachers of Dancing criticised the 'fast degenerating' tone of the ballroom where the rules which should 'govern all good dancing were burlesqued or ignored',[63] and the dance profession subsequently made a determined effort to eliminate 'anarchic' dance practices and make social dancing a more ordered and respectable means of regulating young people's physicality. Indeed, some fitness experts described disciplined forms of dancing as an acceptable alternative to more outmoded forms of rhythmic movement such as drill.[64] Mollie Bagot-Stack, who founded the Women's League of Health and Beauty, emphasised the fox-trot's health benefits and lauded the contribution that ballroom dancing made to carriage and posture, suggesting that the ballroom teacher was the modern equivalent of the drill sergeant.[65] Attempts to discipline disordered dance practices by imposing bourgeois models of manliness expressed desires to re-masculinise young men and de-modernise young women, typically expressed in a 1930s dance manual which urged that the 'lady' 'must not anticipate, she must not have a mind of her own. She must follow whatever the man does and not attempt to correct him.'[66]

Efforts to impose more standardised dance steps and refine the rougher dance styles asserted a restrained notion of manly 'Englishness' which spoke not only of pre-war class models but also of racial otherness.[67] Many popular dances such as the fox-trot, shimmy, Charleston and Black Bottom had originated in America's black communities or from its red-light districts, and although the sexual potential of such dances tended to be toned down in their translation to white culture, their 'negroid' associations attracted suspicion and hostility throughout the inter-war years. Fears of Bolshevism and a sense that the 'primitive', 'chaotic', sexualised movements of liberalised dance styles presaged some kind of social breakdown also coloured campaigns to protect 'rational' dancing and traditional English values in the 1920s.[68] The *Dancing Times* was so concerned about the wild, 'freakish' movements of contemporary dance styles that it called a special meeting to discuss how best to impose manly discipline and control over their 'primitive', libidinous qualities.[69] In 1924 what subsequently became the Imperial Society of Teachers of Dancing (ISTD) established a section specifically devoted to codifying ballroom dancing techniques and improving standards.[70] The only man to be involved was the former world dance champion and professional dancer, Victor Silvester, whose military history was a very useful counter to dancing's effeminate reputation.[71] (He had joined up as an under-age volunteer, took part in the battle of Arras, was wounded and awarded the Italian Bronze Medal for Military Valour, finishing the war with a commission and a place at Sandhurst.[72])

Silvester, like other dancing professionals, recognised the suspicion with which many men regarded social dancing and was careful to emphasise its sporting and health benefits for the modern man's physical and mental well-being.[73] He played an important part in promoting the so-called English style of ballroom dancing which avoided 'vulgar' movements, standardised how the male held his partner and was 'less rhythmic, creative, and musically responsive than American dancing'.[74] ISTD dance teachers promoted the new style, visiting dance centres outside London to teach 'provincial' dancers so that they 'might be brought up in the true faith, and not learn steps as varying as dialects'.[75] Despite such efforts, many recognised the impossibility of imposing preferred dance forms on young dancers who were quite capable of creating their own styles. 'Scouts' from the board of ballroom dancing were consequently also urged to be on the look-out for anything new in the 'night clubs, West End ballrooms, or palais de danse' and to rush back to headquarters with details so that within a month 'the steps for which we have been unconsciously craving will be taught in every part of the country'.[76]

By the end of the 1920s, many recognised that the standard of dancing in popular dance halls was far higher than that in 'Society' because working-class young people took their dancing so seriously and were quite prepared to put in plenty of training and 'earnest practice'.[77] New steps and the latest dances, once seen first in West End ballrooms or other 'smart' London dancing venues, now appeared in the popular dance halls long before they arrived among debutantes in Mayfair. Young shop girls and typists who went dancing danced every dance and were 'quite determined to get their money's worth', studying dancing papers and priding themselves on 'always knowing the very latest steps'.[78] Those who had observed dancers in the East End of London and in the working-class districts of large Midlands cities considered the standard of their dancing to be far higher than that of the big hotels and expensive dance clubs.[79] Generational preferences were also apparent by the early 1930s, when older groups in Manchester were demanding 'pre-war dances' and 'the smartest of the young ones' were 'horrified at the inclusion of the veleta or the old-fashioned waltz in the programme'.[80] By the mid 1930s, dance standards were said to be much better than those of the previous decade when 'The men had little idea of steps, the girls were not much better, and the dance sometimes turned into a "rough house"', encouraged by the kicking movements of dances like the Charleston.[81]

While working-class young women were strongly identified with social dancing, working-class young men also shaped their own connections to it through their involvement in dance bands, dance competitions and passion for dance music which, although liked by all ages, was most popular among young working-class males aged between 15 and 35.[82] The dance band 'craze' of the 1920s was not confined to the listening and dancing public, and many working-class young men formed small bands to make money in their spare time, often drawing on musical expertise acquired through playing the cornet, drums or bugle in BB, Salvation Army or Scout bands.[83] Gramophone records helped them to copy and practise new musical arrangements, supported by self-help literature and 'do-it-yourself' articles in the music press, notably *Melody Maker*. Such amateur and semi-professional dance bands became an essential part of the inter-war music scene, carrying 'live dance music' to all parts of Britain, despite significant regional differences in their distribution.[84] The highest concentration of dance bands and musicians was in London, but northern England dominated within Britain as a whole, where strong musical traditions were grafted onto modern musical forms.[85] Similar creative processes were apparent with the village band traditions of rural areas such as the Lakeland counties, where drum kits were introduced to accommodate the rhythmic demands of modern dance styles.[86]

Birmingham, Leeds, Liverpool, Glasgow and Edinburgh all had thriving dance scenes, while Manchester, the largest dance-band centre outside London, hosted many of the country's leading bands as well as many small ones. Frank Pritchard recalled how Manchester's local radio station encouraged interest in both professional and 'semi-pro' bands and he often fell asleep listening to them:

> Regular late night broadcasts by the Savoy Orpheans, Havana and Tango bands from the Savoy Hotel, London, together with dance music from the 2ZY Manchester station by splendid semi-pro bands such as the Amazon Six and the Garner Schofield Orchestra, did much to popularize ballroom dancing in the Manchester area . . . Many times I went to sleep still wearing headphones after listening to the 10.30pm to midnight session.[87]

Thomas Waddicor, having succeeded in making own his crystal wireless set work in the 1920s, felt that it seemed 'wrong somehow not to spend every second of the then limited broadcasting time' with the headphones over his head so that even when he went to bed he, too, continued to listen until he fell asleep, 'with the headphones under the pillow'.[88]

Stories of these amateur and semi-professional bands weave through the recollections of many whose teen years were in the 1920s, and their number in Manchester made competition particularly 'keen'.[89] This was not such a problem in the early 1920s, when the market was expanding, but the Depression made competition so strong that by the end of the decade the 'rivalry for gig engagements' was 'terrific'.[90] Fee undercutting was common, leaving less experienced and newly formed bands 'to compete for the likes of church dances, wedding receptions and 21st birthday parties'.[91] Dance-music culture took particular root in Manchester, where the standard of dancing among dancers as a whole was said to be 'higher than even in London'.[92] Many local bands acquired their own following, and adolescents like James Brooke and his friends trailed their favourite ones around the city and surrounding districts, competing in the Saturday-night dance competitions which became popular in the early 1920s and sharing a fish and chip supper on the way home if 'one of the boys managed to secure himself a decent partner and be in the prize money'.[93] The growth of such competitions and the eagerness with which they were contested made the 'pot-hunters' who regularly won the cups and prizes very unpopular because potential contestants were often put off once they knew a local 'champion' was to compete.[94] Nevertheless, they played an important part in helping to make many young men as 'dance-struck' as their female peers, and dance competitions, 'novelty items' and 'special exhibitions by professional dancers' grew even more in the 1930s as strategies to draw in more customers.[95]

Acting out gender: inhibition and exhibitions

Dancing's expansion as a popular pastime was held back in the 1920s by economic recession and unemployment, but by the 1930s the 'modern' palais, with 'up to date dances' and professional dance bands, was encouraging new types of dance standards.[96] The 'craze' for eccentric, 'excited' dancing had peaked by the end of the 1920s as dancers settled down with quieter, simpler styles and dancehall managers made determined efforts to assert the respectability of their premises and meet middle-class standards.[97] In 1930, slow fox-trots, waltzes and quick-steps comprised 90 per cent of dance programmes in Manchester, as elsewhere.[98] More sedate dancing was encouraged by changing fashions for women towards the end of the 1920s, when long ballroom dresses meant that girls looked for partners who had been taught properly and would not spoil what they wore with careless dance steps.[99] Commercial dance-hall facilities became much more sophisticated in the 1930s, with lower prices and extravagant attempts to attract customers.[100] Where the powerful ballroom-dancing establishment had been very successful in bringing greater formality to social dancing in the 1920s, this professional influence weakened as a handful of large dance chains like Mecca increasingly dominated the commercial dance-hall industry in the 1930s.[101]

The dance profession's pursuit of respectability, order and status had done much to discourage the expressive movements of post-war social dancing, but in regularising dance steps and emphasising expertise it also removed much of the grassroots spontaneity which had characterised dancing in the early 1920s, highlighting the divide between competent and less competent and reinforcing the self-consciousness of those who did not dance well.[102] Many found the growing professionalism of dance techniques in the larger dance halls very off-putting and complained that dancing was becoming 'too complicated'.[103] Higher technical standards meant that 'professionals' and 'semi-pros' often took up too much room on the 'average-sized' dance floor, where 'twenty experienced couples' sweeping around took up five times as much space as ordinary social dancers.[104] Good dancers were courted in the early days as a means of pulling in the crowds, but competent enthusiasts were less popular in congested popular ballrooms, where there was greater emphasis on styles which could easily be danced on a tightly packed dance floor.[105] As Tom Harrisson pointed out, it was 'hard work' steering on a small floor among the throng of dancers.[106] While the 'shuffling' which had marked many styles in the 1920s became less common, the broader trend by the late 1930s was for dancing to become much simpler.[107] The complex dance steps which professional dance instructors promoted deterred many potential dancers, particularly men, who felt too awkward to risk embarrassment, and commercial dance-hall proprietors, ever responsive to the need to draw in customers, adapted the dance hall's spatial layout to accommodate such uncertainties, enhancing its appeal to males who might otherwise have felt their masculinity embarrassingly compromised by a lack of dancing expertise. A dance-hall manager at the Hammersmith Palais observed how there were 'quite as many male "wallflowers" as there were female "wallflowers"',[108] and it was perhaps to try to counter such self-consciousness that some larger ballrooms had, by the 1930s, developed 'standing' or 'picking-up' areas at the back of the hall:

> where people could mix freely and the gents could invite unescorted ladies to dance without the embarrassment of being observed if they were refused. The standing area was in my opinion a very important ingredient in the box office success of a ballroom and a natural for

fostering relationships. The slogan 'We make couples out of singles' was prophetic and many a romance began in the secluded zone known as the standing area.[109]

Men were often described as 'too self-conscious to dance', and Oliver suggests that many experienced dancing 'as either an unavoidable prelude to courtship or a duty to be performed for social reasons', and were far happier 'propping up the bar' at the nearest pub than dancing with their girlfriends.[110] Frank Goss's sense of physical embarrassment and 'self-conscious shyness' about dancing were so strong that he never learned to dance properly, rationalising his fear of being shown up with a 'feeling of superiority' which made him feel like 'one of those who had passed through the fire and had come out cleansed of any desire for any such primitive amusement'.[111] Frequently, segregated education and early social lives meant that young men, regardless of class, could find their entry into such a public social activity very difficult. R. L. Cook, from a middle-class Edinburgh family, described the trepidation with which he and his male contemporaries approached the question of 'how and where' to learn when they reached 16 or 17 and became eligible to attend their first school dance:

> We hadn't given this a thought till now, but it assumed, quite suddenly, a devastating importance, an arcane significance. For many of the age group concerned, and to which I then belonged, it involved, I imagine, the first close more or less adult physical contact with the female of the species (other than sisters).[112]

The *Dancing Times* described the self-consciousness which held many men back from learning how to dance properly. 'Persuading an ordinary male to have lessons' so that he could be 'a source of enjoyment and not a hindrance to his partner' was said to be like 'trying to get him to go to the dentist. He does not wish it, although it may do him good.'[113] Younger males could be less inhibited, however, and the most enthusiastic patrons of dancing and dance halls were 16- to 21-year-olds, whose involvement usually started when they were 16 or 17 as the dating opportunities of the dance hall started to override their embarrassment.[114] In the 1920s, James Brooke and his friends decided to 'brighten' up their lives by learning ballroom dancing and went every Saturday to local dancing classes, where they had 'a great time' learning a mix of old and new styles, 'the foxtrot, quickstep, tango, Paul Jones, Lancers and pride of Erin'. This 'opened up a whole new world', and once they became proficient they travelled all over Manchester and neighbouring towns, dancing and following their favourite bands.[115] Brooke's comments are a reminder of the pride which many working-class young men took in mastering a leisure skill whose meanings and excitement were much greater than their everyday occupations. Radio dance bands encouraged the less confident to try out and polish up their steps in their own homes before attempting them in public, and keen dancers increasingly improved their techniques with professional tuition at places like 'Diamond's Dancing Academy' in Glasgow's Gorbals district, where lessons cost sixpence, 'which wis [sic] quite dear!'[116] Glasgow had 'more dance halls per head of population than anywhere else in the country', and young men there pursued dancing 'more intensively' than those in Cardiff and Liverpool – an interesting reflection on local dance cultures.[117] Irish and Scots communities had their own dancing traditions, often well to the fore during family events, festivities and in local clubs, which perhaps also gave some young men greater confidence in their dancing abilities.[118]

The wide spectrum of dance venues described earlier could be very helpful to beginners and less confident dancers. Phil Moss made a faltering start at his local Lads' Club and then progressed to the ballroom nearest to where he lived, a 'small and cosy place, where you could see everybody and everything that was going on', unlike in larger, grander dance halls. He finally graduated to the Manchester Ritz, with its 'visiting "name" bands, the flashing lights, the opulent surroundings, the crowds of people and very attractive girls'. From someone who started out as too 'frightened' to try, Moss eventually became an enthusiast, out dancing 'every night of the week'.[119] Having overcome their initial lack of confidence, other young men became equally keen dancers, and *Disinherited Youth* suggests that many passed 'through a phase' described by their parents, their friends and even themselves as 'dancing mad'.[120] Boys' club workers similarly observed how, among many lads, the 'passion' for dancing easily conquered all others, encouraging them to give up evening classes, billiards 'even football'. The 'huge syndicated dance halls' which developed in the 1930s, full of glamour and exciting courtship possibilities, were a particular draw, and a London boys' club worker reported how this popularity meant the clubs found it difficult to get the same number of football and cricket teams as in the past.[121] The criticism boys' club workers directed against dance halls suggests their popularity among the boys with whom they worked, which reinforced worries about youthful sexuality. Basil Henriques claimed that the 'demoralizing' influence of public dance halls promoted 'a low conception of woman through the cheap vulgarity of the girls; the horse-play and loose flippancy; the sensuousness of the dancing' and encouraged a boy to lose 'all sense of reverence and chivalry towards the other sex'.[122]

Valentine Bell detected a distinctive 'dance-hall' type among some of the young men with whom he worked. 'Flashily dressed', they posed as 'very sophisticated in sex matters', trying to 'impress the other lads' by showing off 'certain contraceptives'. Boys spent far too much time at dances: 'Continual dancing with scantily clothed girls is certainly not good for lads who have just become sex-conscious; especially in these days of "bunny-hugging"'.[123]

Broader changes in popular culture contributed to the increasing sexualisation of the commercialised dance hall, particularly in the 1930s, when the sense of being on show in a glamorous setting was a powerful aphrodisiac, reinforced by the crowded, dimly lit physical proximity of dancing. Censorship controls may have restrained more suggestive displays in the dancing of cinema musicals, yet their sexual energy had an immense impact on young people, providing the imaginative backdrop to both male and female dance fantasies.[124] Musicals were the top box-office attraction of the 1930s and their popularity was important in making dancing more acceptable as a male activity. Films supplied powerful imaginative landscapes for kinetic fantasies. Fred Astaire and Ginger Rogers, in particular, had a significant emotional impact on many contemporary adolescents, female and male. A 'self-conscious sense of performance and display' lived on in the memories of Kuhn's male respondents, several of whom recalled being inspired to try out new dance steps after seeing films featuring stars like Astaire.[125] Written reminiscences contain similar stories of young men doing dance-floor impressions modelled on the star, and younger boys were noted watching admiringly as their slightly older peers went through their paces at local dances.

Some dances, like the quick-tempoed Tango and rumba, were particularly unpopular among them, however.[126] Girls often liked the challenge of these more 'difficult' (and sexual) dances, and the percentage of female couples on Blackpool dance floors varied a great deal according to the type of dance, with the rumba producing the highest and the waltz and valeta the lowest. 'In the waltz and the veleta [sic], with its tender romantic music as a background, the girl prefers to dance with a man. But in the rumba, which is characterised by a more deliberately active step and a purer sex significance, females take the floor in greater numbers.' These more overtly sexual dances encouraged the girls' 'exhibitionism' as they showed off their superior skills, not in the centre of the dance floor but around its edges, 'under the eyes of those standing around'.[127] Boys were much less keen on them, as Pritchard recalled of learner lessons at a dance venue in Manchester.

When the dreaded tango was announced, that was the signal for all the lads to dash to the doorkeeper for a 'pass out'. This cost tuppence, but it was worth it as it provided the means of escape to the happiness of a quick couple of pints in the pub across the road. Our return fifteen minutes later was always greeted with ironical cheers from the girls, and who could blame them? It became known as the 'Tango Exodus'.[128]

Philip Richardson, editor of the *Dancing Times*, considered the difficult, sexually suggestive, 'intimate movements' of 'foreign' dances such as the Tango and rumba to be quite contrary to the spirit of the 'average young Englishman', who hated 'making an exhibition of himself', and his comments suggest the class, racial and gender assumptions which underlay professional desires for quieter ballroom styles more in keeping with middle-class notions of manliness and propriety.[129] Pre-war notions of sexual propriety and physical self-consciousness informed such middle-class reticence, which assumed that women made better dancers than men because their 'emotional' temperament gave them a 'natural instinct for grace of movement' and an 'acuter sense of rhythm'.[130] Young men, not expected to be confident on the dance floor, were often confused or self-conscious about appropriate forms of behaviour there. They dithered about where to place their hands, particularly when backless dresses became popular, and, as we saw in the previous chapter, worried about girlfriends who danced too intimately with other young men. Dancing was very different from the 'hard' activities associated with traditional manliness, and the weight of masculine expectations undoubtedly prevented some from accepting dancing as an appropriate vehicle for male self-expression. Young men, whose pride in their bodies was expressed through sport, body-building, heavy manual work and fighting, faced very different challenges on the dance floor. A well-known teacher of dancing, lamenting a 'crop of bad dancing' in ballrooms, blamed men, because they did not 'want to be bothered with intricate steps . . . They haven't time and they don't want to make a business of their pleasure', preferring 'to dance just to enjoy themselves'.[131]

The 'dancing crowd' was, in fact, differentiated by several types of dancer and comprised 'many factions', including couples who sat at tables and watched, and the 'unattached who roamed at will, predators of both sexes'.[132] There was a great divide between the majority of 'social dancers', who danced to meet up with the opposite sex and were 'happy just to negotiate the floor at their leisure', and a 'minority school' of 'dance crazy people' who darted 'in and out of the available open spaces to demonstrate their skills', experiencing an 'intense satisfaction' of harmony between 'partner, band and floor' which was 'quite lost on social dancers and non-dancers'.[133] Twenty-year-old Douglas Vickers claimed to find his 'Utopia' at the Palais de Danse, where he came into contact with 'the best dancers of the opposite sex'. Nothing gave him 'greater pleasure' than a partner who was 'as good or better' than himself.[134] Good male dancers were, in fact, very popular among young women, although less admired by young men, amongst whom they were often described 'as "gigolos", "lounge lizards" and "bloody pansies"', descriptions which suggest dancing's effeminate connotations, unease at how traditional masculine expectations were transgressed and jealousy at their proficiency.[135]

These gender insecurities influenced the dance industry's business 'goals' and dance halls' tone and spatial layout, where particular conventions and social etiquette could make both young women and young men awkward and anxious.[136] Men and women tended to cluster with others of their own sex, most dancers returning to their original groupings once they had finished dancing with their partner.[137] Many young women experienced an 'agony of embarrassment . . . as they stood around the floor waiting to be invited to dance'.[138] Boys too, however, were discomfited by dance hall conventions, nervous and anxious about how to pick up a partner, and the expectation that male should take the lead in asking his partner to dance encouraged a certain brusqueness. (The exception was 'excuse me' dances, when women could choose their partner.)[139] Roberts recalled how, having made his choice, a young man would cross over and take a girl from among the throng 'with the minimum of ceremony' and 'slide into the rhythm'.[140] Similar behaviour was observed at Blackpool in the late 1930s, where boys and girls were observed coming together as dance partners 'without a word being spoken'.[141] Moss suggested that while women were 'not obliged' by such 'invitations', they were not expected to take up 'another offer during the duration of that dance'.[142] Women often refused to dance with small men and developed strategies, such as rushing off to the toilet, to avoid having to dance with someone they disliked, often leaving their erstwhile partner 'stranded in the middle of the dance floor'.[143] Mass Observation suggested the prevarications of young men trying to make up their minds whether to ask a girl to dance, and the disconcerting effects of receiving a refusal:

> Central Pier. Boy asks girl for dance. 'No thanks.' 'Oh.' Boy stands five seconds near girl deliberating, then walks away.
> Palace. Two men, age 25, standing next to observer. One says, 'Ask her for a sweet.' Pause. 'They'll all be gone soon if you don't buck up.' Man doesn't buck up and observer moves on.[144]

A *Daily Mail* columnist recalled his 'terrific inferiority' about dancing, which stemmed from the time he had attended 'one of those "hops" where the standard of dancing is as high as the price of admission in low. The sort of place where – if you're not good enough – the girl just walks off without a word and leaves you red-faced in the middle of the floor. And I wasn't good enough!'[145] Others echoed his sentiments: 'It's a horrible feeling when you go up to a girl, ask her to dance, and she firmly says, "No, thank you!" I never like risking it.'[146]

While commentators often remarked on the apparently dispassionate way in which the dance-hall etiquette of finding a partner was conducted, feelings below the surface could be very different and the process of linking up with a new partner often involved tension on both sides:

> It was always a tricky moment. She didn't always know whether the gentleman could in fact dance and he may have had the same reservation about her. Or how tall would she be when she stood to her full height? Mistakes were common.[147]

Joe Carley attended many dances 'but attempted to dance only on rare occasions – I was too shy and embarrassed and was terrified of girls . . . I stuttered and blushed whenever they were near me, and so kept well away from them.' It was not until he joined a dramatic society at his old school that he began to overcome his 'tong-tied shyness' and found that girls were 'not so terrifying' as he had thought.[148] Eli Hague described himself as having 'two left feet' and spent most of his time 'sitting close to the band and humming tunes softly to himself'.[149] Phil Moss was another too 'frightened' to dance at first, who preferred to watch. He overcame his fear of public failure by practising the steps at home:

> and eventually one Sunday night I asked a young lady to dance with me. Half way through the dance I stood on her foot and she stamped off the floor, leaving me looking ship-wrecked and red-faced. I left the dance early and went home sulking and disgusted with my performance.[150]

The couple-based social dances of the inter-war years presented a novel challenge to traditional gender relations. The male may well have been expected to take the initiative, but the individuality of his performance and the spatial and physical confidence of many young women undermined the 'collective safety' of the peer group from which he usually derived confidence.[151] Such diffidence (and fear of potential humiliation) is very apparent in Hatton's discussion of the discomfort which adolescent males experienced at mixed-club events where an unaccustomed reversal of normal power relations made them uncharacteristically passive in the presence of young women.

> Listen to their eager talk the evening before of what fun they are going to have, how this and that girl is coming, with specific mention of the ones from whom they are not going to stand any 'hank.' Here is the male, the masculine, the cave-man. Watch them at the dance itself, all the girls one side of the room, waiting and anxious to dance, all the lads huddled together in groups in the corners, looking as sheepish and awkward as can be, much too shy to make a move; absolutely longing to mingle with the lasses but as bashful and blushing as a Dickens heroine. It is a most difficult thing to get the lads and lasses to intermingle freely, and it is usually about three dances from the end of the evening before one can get them all together and happy. One would imagine that at the next dance with the same folk one could start on the same terms of intimacy, but no, the same shyness and bashfulness has again to be overcome.[152]

Bodies and sexualities in the 1920s were in a state of flux, and the apparent blurring of gender boundaries, and between the 'hetero' and the 'homo' aroused much anxiety, encouraging greater efforts to more strictly define what constituted the homosexual.[153] Police surveillance and regular, often high-profile prosecutions in the popular press contested these ambiguities, so that by the 1930s, male 'effeminacy' was increasingly a sign of transgressive sexual desires, associated with homosexuality and sexual crimes.[154] Such changes may be discerned on the dance floor, where in 1920s Salford, Roberts suggested men danced together at all the 'common halls', as did women. He attributed this less to 'homosexual inclination', than to the advantages this gave them in eyeing up and judging 'a female pair's dancing ability and charms'.[155] Having made his selection, one could sail up in mid-foxtrot and 'split' the couple of dancing women. A 'couple of males on the move' could also 'mean that they were still too shy to ask girls', although there were also 'the effeminate few who danced together all evening'. The MC of the particular dance hall Roberts described had no objections to even the 'effeminate few' dancing together, but did take exception to any 'males gyrating as they smoked, or with their hats on', because he felt it lowered the tone.[156] It was a very different situation in the 1930s, when young men increasingly had less scope to challenge established expectations of masculine behaviour.[157] The Salford MC's easy-going attitude to men's dancing together contrasts with what Mass Observation recorded in the late 1930s, when three male couples started dancing together at a ballroom in Bolton. On seeing them, the band leader halted the music and called for the men to stop dancing together, a demand greeted with applause from other dancers as the men left the floor.[158]

The phases of development which characterised social dancing in the inter-war years suggest how social manners between young women and young men were changing as social conventions liberalised. The explosive energy and extravagant dance styles which had emerged with the war challenged the physical manliness of pre-war culture on a number of levels. The palais's aura of exotic otherness was reinforced by the origins of many leading proponents of professional ballroom dancing in continental Europe or Latin America, whose models of masculinity were uncomfortably effeminate in the eyes of some young men.[159] The freewheeling 'uncivilized' gyrations of the Charleston, Black Bottom and 'shimmy-shake' embodied the disturbing otherness of racial difference in the form of black, Jewish and Latin American influences on dance culture and jazz; gender difference, in the fluid, expansive physical confidence of many young women's dancing; and class difference in relation to the growing mass appeal of social dancing. The music and dance styles of the 1920s reinforced defiantly modern perceptions of the body and movement whose sensual, rhythmic, undisciplined enthusiasm overwhelmed rules and technique. Social dancing during the First World War embodied contemporary yearnings for physical contact and touch, sensory qualities enhanced in the twenties by the advent of more revealing fashions and materials. Like the disabled body and the shell-shocked body, the 'anarchic' dancing body of the 1920s reinforced fears of degenerating masculine physicality. Teachers of dance and dance schools endeavoured to discipline and control these dangerous enthusiasms by emphasising the 'proper' way to dance, codifying and commodifying these improvised styles and reasserting embodied gender differences by moulding an idealised version of masculine movement based on 'traditional' masculine values.[160]

Commercial dance halls signified sexualised modernity, and dancers' youthful exuberance and enthusiasm for dancing impelled moral and religious interest groups to assert 'disciplining power' to try to contain its implicit sexual threat within their own supervised settings. Dance hall operators also recognised, however, how respectable social mixing on the dance floor promised significant commercial possibilities, particularly as emphasis on more companionate relationships increased. The professional dance world, local authorities and commercial interests combined to rein in the anarchic, easy-going dance styles of the early 1920s and reassert what were considered more appropriate, formal forms of physical interaction. This competition of moral and commercial interests to regulate and discipline the dance floor meant that by the 1930s, dancing was socially sanctioned as well as commercially exploited. The changes in dance styles which occurred towards the end of the 1920s asserted more traditional standards of male physicality, while commercial imperatives to attract even less competent dancers also encouraged the introduction of much simpler styles, such as the uncomplicated group dances of the mid and late 1930s.

By the time Mass Observation was initiating its voyeuristic investigations of contemporary dance halls towards the end of the 1930s, twenty years had passed since the opening of the Hammersmith Palais. During that period dancing had become increasingly accepted as a popular social activity with cross-generational appeal. Decorum and uncomfortably congested dancing often meant dullness, however, and circular progressions around the crowded dance floors of the 1930s had a monotonous quality which encouraged the introduction, towards the end of the decade, of lively, communal 'party' and 'novelty' dances like the Conga, Chestnut Tree, Hokey-Cokey, Blackpool Walk, Park Parade, Palais Glide, Boomps-daisy, Ballin' the Jack and the immensely popular Lambeth Walk, which swept the nation in 1938.[161] These simpler, accessible styles that 'everyone' could do did not replace the fox-trot and waltzes but brought a more informal, relaxed, sociable atmosphere to the dance floor, asserting an asexual communality which was the antithesis of the eroticised values of Americanised popular culture and the closeness and touching of couples dancing.[162] The deliberate creation of a more communal sense of identity as the threat of war intensified testified to the role that dancing had come to play in the lives of not only the young but people of all ages. Such dances not only appealed to the communal traditions of working-class culture but were self-consciously promoted as a means of alleviating anxieties about the contemporary political climate, as in the raised-arm movements of the Chestnut Tree, which were seen as satirising Hitler's one-armed salute. The English collective values and cross-class unity of such dances contested both the political threat of fascism and the cultural encroachment of American 'Negro rhythms', concerns which may be discerned in the criticisms which attended discussions of the American jitterbugging craze towards the end of the 1930s as the exuberant arrival of swing music and 'hotter jazz' introduced more 'expressive', 'creative' individualistic forms of dancing.[163] These went in a very different direction from that of the group dances, giving more scope for 'wilder', 'freer' movement, and more opportunity of 'making it up' as you went along. This would not really take off until the 1940s, with the arrival of the American forces, but it epitomised the dance-floor tensions of grassroots spontaneity and continuing attempts to control youthful exuberance, and gave rise to familiar criticisms.[164] Tropes familiar from the 1920s were used to characterise its 'alien' qualities. Patricia Pearce, the *Daily Mirror* 'girl' who was 'not afraid' to say what she thought, described jitterbugging as 'a cult – almost a disease' which should never be danced in Britain. She pointed out its origins in the black ghettoes of Harlem, where it was as 'natural for the negroes' to dance in such a way, 'to "shag" as they say', as it was for them to breathe. 'They had rhythm in their blood' and danced 'from instinct', so could cope with the wild excesses of such dancing. For their white counterparts, however, it was dangerously addictive, the rhythm, drum beat, 'wailing' saxophones and clarinet like a drug.[165] Such concerns were symptomatic of anxieties about the individualism and vigour of an emerging youth culture which unsettled the dance profession's hard-fought harmony on the dance floor.

By the 'seedier days' of the 1930s, commercial dance halls were maximising their sexual possibilities, insidiously eroding traditional notions of respectability. As dancing's performative, sexualised functions in the social experiences of youth grew, the palais's significance as a courtship location expanded. In Blackpool, by the late 1930s, it did not matter much whether you could dance or not, because ballrooms sanctioned 'the approach without introduction'. There was none of the 'preliminary manoeuvring' which was seen between boys and girls on the promenade, because 'picking-up' and 'getting-off' on the dance floor were accepted as normal behaviour. The popularity of summer dancing in Blackpool was attributed to exactly this 'lack of formality'.[166]

Women's and men's bodies were positioned differently within dance hall space, where male dancing was bounded by tighter social conventions. Dancing gave young women opportunities 'to define what were acceptable heterosocial relations and to challenge the conventional gender norms' of their everyday lives.[167] Despite their being expected to lead in the dance, the role of young men on the dance floor was more circumscribed than that of their female counterparts, restrained by the expectations of their own physicality. Dancing was an activity in which girls and young women often showed greater confidence, yet one in which the male was expected to be the dominant partner and where incompetence could result in considerable public humiliation. Dancehall space was highly gendered, and male and female groups tended to separate once they had finished dancing. Couples' dancing challenged how working-class young men conventionally constructed and experienced masculinity, contesting and subverting it in complex ways.[168]

Same-sex dancing was acceptable among women, but not among men. The lack of male partners during and after the war had given women opportunities to dance with other women and develop their own social space on the dance floor. They could feel free to dance in more uninhibited ways than when they were with a male partner. They could lead, and enjoy the kinetic and sensual pleasures of dancing with each other, and while they could certainly feel vulnerable and discomforted by the male gaze at dances, they were not passive recipients of these encounters, many readily asserting themselves on receiving overtures to dance. Women found it easier to build up their dancing expertise not only because they started younger but also because it was common and quite acceptable for groups of women to dance together and to take another female as a partner, although this was something men were never expected to do, 'except in fun'.[169] Where it was fine for a woman to take the lead as a man, it was not acceptable for another man to assume the 'passive' part of the female partner, as John Slawson recalled. Uncertain how to dance, he asked a salesman with whom he worked to show him the basic steps. 'The salesman rather fancied himself as a dancer and often took a turn around the floor of the front shop, holding as he did an imaginary partner.' Their employer, coming across them as they were practising one morning, 'just stood and gaped at the scene . . . goggle-eyed and nearly choking on his cigarette, purple-faced, stunned in fact'.[170] 'Displaying the male body as spectacle' transgressed masculine norms based on discipline and order and which were embodied in sport and physical fitness, for sport and dance occupied distinctive, even opposing cultural spaces, epitomised by contemporary representations of the 'dancing women' and the 'athletic man'.[171] Not only were cultural attitudes to the male body important, but the meanings of dancing, for young men, depended a great deal on context, the diverse dance cultures of large cities offering more opportunities for self-expression than those of smaller towns and rural areas. For men, the freedoms which young women experienced on the dance floor were more likely to be found within the dance sub-cultures of large cities, such as the private dance halls and night clubs which greater regulation encouraged.[172] 'Entrepreneurs' in metropolitan districts such as London's West End offered opportunities to contest the social and sexual norms which mainstream dance halls promoted by 'deliberately' cultivating 'a queer clientele'.[173] By contrast, the cultural inhibitions which men in rural areas of Ireland exhibited in relation to social dancing were similar to those highlighted by Bourdieu's work in rural France, where men were equally reluctant to engage with such 'urban techniques of the body'.[174]

Although social dancing challenged many expectations of working-class masculinities, there were also continuities in the social culture which young working-class dancers brought to the dance hall, where expectations of 'public presentation' reinforced fears of humiliation not only in front of women but also before the audience of other men. As a result, many attempted to claim dance-hall space by resorting to their 'traditional' collective behaviour, drawing confidence from their homo-social cultures, attending in groups or gangs or disrupting the periphery of this feminised 'private' locale by bringing with them the rivalries and brawls of their neighbourhood street culture and facing off against each other over girlfriends.[175] Among the less keen, good male dancers were both disdained and envied, a resentment sometimes expressed in the casual attempts of other young men to trip them up as they danced past. Good dancers who were also gang members, however, used their dancing skills to reinforce the masculine esteem of the groups to which they belonged, for whom they became an expression of sexual prowess and popularity.[176] Such examples challenge assumptions of male disinterest in dancing and are supported by Mass Observation in the late 1930s, which suggested that there was 'practically no difference between male and female interest' in it.[177] Sexual emphases, while certainly a key part of the dance hall's popularity, were not the only reasons why young men went there. The dance hall's sexual reputation perpetuates a one-dimensional interpretation of their involvement, which is only one part of a story. A closer look at the inter-war years suggests that their engagement with dancing was, in fact, rather more complex, and that its meanings for them were more varied and fluid than is often supposed.

Notes

1   Board of Education, *The Youth Service After the War. A Report of the Youth Advisory Council appointed by the President of the Board of Education in 1942 to advise him on Questions relating to the Youth Service in England* (London: HMSO, 1943), p. 13; F. M. L. Thompson (ed.), *The Cambridge Social History Of Britain, 1750–1950* (Cambridge: Cambridge University Press, 1993), p. 121.

2   See, for example, Elizabeth Oliver, 'Liberation or limitation? A study of women's Leisure in Bolton, c. 1919–1939' (PhD dissertation, University of Lancaster, 1997); J. J. Nott, *Music for the People: Popular Music and Dance in Inter-war Britain* (Oxford: Oxford University Press, 2002), pp. 180, 181; R. McKibbin, *Classes and Cultures: England, 1918–1951* (Oxford: Oxford University Press, 1998: 2000), p. 395; C. Heron, 'Boys will be boys: working class masculinities in the age of mass production', *International Labor and Working Class History*, 69:1 (2006), p. 24. For young women, fashion and the dance hall, see P. Kirkham, 'Dress, dance, dreams and desire: fashion and fantasy in dance hall', *Journal of Design History*, 8:3 (1995), 195–214; L. Murfin,

Popular Leisure in the Lake Counties (Manchester: Manchester University Press, 1990), pp. 195–6.

3   *The Social Survey of Merseyside* described dancing as 'one of the very few' leisure activities in which women engaged 'more frequently' than men. Some 20 per cent of women but only 7 per cent of men made entries under this heading: D. Caradog Jones, *The Social Survey of Merseyside*, 3 vols (Liverpool: Liverpool University Press, 1934), vol. III, pp. 277–8.

4   B. S. Turner, 'Introduction: bodily performance: on aura and reproducibility', *Body and Society*, 11:4 (2005), p. 11.

5   R. Zimring, '"The dangerous art where one slip means death": dance and the literary imagination in inter-war Britain', *Modernism/Modernity*, 14:4 (2007), pp. 708–9, 714.

6   Heron, 'Boys will be boys', pp. 8, 17.

7   The dance 'crazes' of the post-war years involved many young men such as Teddy Boys, Mods, Skinheads and Punks. Although this was associated with a strong collective identity, it also challenges a view of boys as reluctant dancers.

8   J. Bourke, *Dismembering the Male: Men's Bodies, Britain and the Great War* (London: Reaktion Books, 1996), p. 136.

9   A priest described the Charleston's 'meaningless contortions' as nothing more than a 'nervous disease': *Daily Mirror* (6 May, 1927), p. 7.

10 *Ibid.* (14 June 1933), p. 10.

11 *Daily Mirror* (15 November 1921), p. 9.

12 *Ibid.* (27 April 1927), p. 4.

13 *Ibid.* (24 September 1932), p. 15.

14 E. Terry, *Etiquette for All: Man, Woman or Child* (London: Foulsham & Co. Ltd., 1925), p. 70.

15 Murfin, *Popular Leisure*, p. 195.

16 J. Baxendale, '". . . into another kind of life in which anything might happen . . .": popular music and late modernity, 1910–1930', *Popular Music*, 14: 2 (1995), p. 145.

17 L. A. Erenberg, 'Everybody's doin' it: the pre-World War I dance craze, the Castles, and the modern American girl', *Feminist Studies*, 3:1/2 (1975), 155–70.

18 *Dancing Times* (October 1935), p. 54; M. Hustwitt, '"Caught in a whirlpool of aching sound": the production of dance music in Britain in the 1920s', *Popular Music*, 3 (1983), p. 14.

19 Nott, *Music*, p. 128; R. Roberts, *The Classic Slum: Salford Life in the First Quarter of the Century* (1971; London: Penguin Books, 1990), p. 232.

20 S. G. Jones, *Workers at Play: A Social and Economic History of Leisure, 1918–39* (London: Routledge and Kegan Paul, 1986), pp. 44–5.

21 C. Parsonage, *The Evolution of Jazz in Britain, 1880–1935* (Aldershot: Ashgate, 2005), p. 130; *Manchester Guardian* (1 January 1929), p. 6. Hammersmith's success was followed by the opening of the Birmingham Palais: *Dancing Times* (October 1935), p. 49.

22 M. Jordan, *Hulme Memories* (Manchester: Neil Richardson, 1989), p. 17.

23 V. Steele, *Fashion and Eroticism: Ideals of Feminine Beauty from the Victorian Era to the Jazz Age* (New York and Oxford: Oxford University Press, 1985), p. 239.

24 *Ibid.*, pp. 210–11.

25 I. Clephane, *Towards Sex Freedom* (London: John Lane, 1935), p. 201.

26 Steele, *Fashion*, pp. 210–11; *Dancing Times* (August 1934), p. 475.

27 Roberts, *Classic Slum*, p. 233; H.-M. Teo, 'Women's travel, dance, and British metropolitan anxieties, 1890–1939', *Gender and History*, 12:2 (2000), pp. 371–2; *Daily Mirror* (14 August 1935), p. 10; Nott, *Music*, p. 173.

28 S. Humphries, *Hooligans or Rebels? An Oral History of Working-Class Childhood and Youth, 1889–1939* (Oxford: Basil Blackwell Limited, 1981: 1983), p. 139; M. Hinson, *Mary Ann's Girl. Memories of Newbridge Lane* (Stockport: Metropolitan Borough of Stockport Recreation and Culture Division, 1984), p. 506. Judy Giles suggests how some mothers colluded with their daughters' dance passion. See J. Giles, '"Playing hard to get": working class women, sexuality and respectability in Britain, 1918–40', *Women's History Review*, 1:2 (1992), 239–55.

29 *Daily Mirror* (20 January 1938), p. 22.

30 C. Burt, *The Young Delinquent* (London: University of London Press, 1925: 1931), p. 155.

31 *Ibid*, p. 155.

32 Hinson, *Mary Ann's Girl*, pp. 5–6.

33 J. Kay, *The Chronicles of a Harpurhey Lad* (Manchester: Neil Richardson, 1990), p. 35; Jordan, *Hulme Memories*, p. 35.

34 C. Cameron, A. Lush and G. Meara, *Disinherited Youth* (Edinburgh: Carnegie United Kingdom Trust, 1943), p. 105; B. S. Rowntree, *Poverty and Progress: A Second Social Survey of York* (London: Longmans, Green and Co., 1941), p. 375.

35 Nott, *Music*, pp. 161, 166; R. Bowley, ch. 2, 'Amusements and entertainments', in H. L. Smith (ed.), *The New Survey of London Life and Labour*, vol. IX, *Life and Leisure* (London: P.S. King and Son Ltd., 1935), p. 64; Kuhn Archive, T94–4, Mrs Sheila McWinnie, Glasgow, Transcript, Side A, p. 10. Mrs Mcwinnie was born in 1919.

36 Murfin, *Popular Leisure*, pp. 168, 197–8, 220.

37 J. A. Davies, 'Working-class women, Liverpool 1910–1940: social life, courtship marriage and motherhood. An oral history', in J. E. Hollinshead and F. Pogson (eds), *Studies in Northern History* (Liverpool: Liverpool Hope Press, 1997), p. 84.

38 R. Roberts, *A Ragged Schooling: Growing Up in the Classic Slum* (1976; Glasgow: Fontana/Collins, 1978), pp. 180–1.

39 *Manchester Guardian* (17 December 1928), p. 10.

40 Cameron, Lush and Meara, *Disinherited Youth*, p. 105; *Dancing Times* (August 1934), p. 475.

41 A. H. Gray, *Sex Teaching* (London: National Sunday School Union, [1929]), pp. 78–9; M. Pugh, *We Danced All Night: A Social History of Britain Between the Wars* (London, Vintage, 2009), pp. 205–6.

42 *Daily Mirror* (9 May 1938), p. 14.

43 G. Cross (ed.), *Worktowners at Blackpool: Mass-Observation and Popular Leisure in the 1930s* (London: Routledge, 1990), p. 35.

44 P. Moss, *True Romances at Manchester's Dances* (Manchester: Neil Richardson, 1998), p. 5.

45 C. E. B. Russell and L. M. Russell, *Lads' Clubs: Their History, Organisation and Management* (London: A. & C. Black Ltd., 1932), p. 221.

46 Bowley, 'Amusements and entertainments', p. 65; *Manchester Guardian* (20 February 1928), p. 11.

47 *Manchester Guardian* (19 December 1929), p. 15.

48 Kay, *Chronicles,* p. 35; Jordan, *Hulme Memories,* p. 17.

49 Russell and Russell, *Lads' Clubs,* p. 218.

50 *Ibid.*

51 *Manchester Guardian* (1 December 1942), p. 2. Dances held in York, almost all of which were teetotal, were generally well conducted: Rowntree, *Poverty and Progress,* p. 375. Mecca did not serve alcohol and often excluded males who arrived when the pubs closed: McKibbin, *Classes and Cultures,* p. 394.

52 Cross, *Worktowners,* p. 17, 154, 177, 190.

53 Nott, *Music,* p. 154.

54 P. Holt, *Daily Express* (16 November 1938), p. 16, cited in Nott, *Music,* p. 158.

55 H. L. Smith (ed.), *The New Survey of London Life and Labour,* vol. IX, p. 295.

56 Moss, *True Romances,* p. 4.

57 Cameron, Lush and Meara, *Disinherited Youth,* p. 105.

58 C. Wouters, *Informalization: Manners and Emotions since 1890* (London: Sage Publications, 2007), p. 138; J. K. Walton, *The British Seaside: Holidays and Resorts in the Twentieth Century* (Manchester: Manchester University Press, 2000), pp. 108–9. The special evening dance excursion from Bolton was known as the 'Passion Express', reputedly because its young passengers removed the light bulbs to aid their amorous intentions on the train's return late in the evening: Oliver, 'Liberation or limitation?', p. 267.

59 Wouters, *Informalization,* p. 171.

60 *Dancing Times* (October 1935), pp. 62, 68; Nott, *Music,* p. 152.

61 *Manchester Guardian* (30 June 1927), p. 8; F. Pritchard, *Dance Band Days around Manchester* (Manchester: Neil Richardson, 1988), p. 10.

62 Some dance teachers thought the Charleston unsuitable for the English because it was 'much too difficult' for them: *Daily Mirror* (29 April 1926), p. 2.

63 *Manchester Guardian* (28 June 1922), p. 7; *Dancing Times* (October 1935), p. 62.

64 H. Wulff, 'Memories in motion: The Irish dancing body', *Body and Society,* 11:4 (2005), pp. 50, 53, for dance posture and the regulation of Irish dancing. For morality legislation and attempts to regulate 'foreign contemporary dances in Ireland' see: J. Smyth, 'Dancing, depravity and all that jazz: the public halls dance act of 1935', *History Ireland,* 1:2 (1993), 51–4; V. A. Austin, 'The céilí and the public dance halls act, 1935', *Eire-Ireland,* 28:3 (1993), 7–16.

65 *Dancing Times* (January 1929), p. 555; J. J. Matthews, 'Stack, Mary Meta Bagot (1883–1935)', *Oxford Dictionary of National Biography* (Oxford: Oxford University Press, 2004), www.oxforddnb.com/view/article/45797 (accessed 12 July 2009).

66 A. Moore, *Ballroom Dancing* (London: Pitman, 1936), p. 28.

67 Hustwitt, '"Caught in a whirlpool"', pp. 13–14.

68 See T. Cresswell, '"You cannot shake that shimmie here": producing mobility on the dancefloor', *Cultural Geographies,* 13:1 (2006), 55–77.

69 C. Baade, C. (2006) '"The dancing front": dance music, dancing, and the BBC in World War II', *Popular Music,* 25:3 (2006), p. 357.

70 The society had more than 2,000 members in 1930, and 4,000 by 1938. It was originally The Imperial Society of Dance Teachers, formed in London in 1904, and had about 100 members before the war. It became the Imperial Society of Teachers of Dancing in 1925. See www.istd.org/main.html (accessed 27 April 2007).

71 Silvester (1900–78) and Phyllis Clarke won the first world championships in 1922. He established a chain of London dance studios and in 1935 formed the Victor Silvester Dance Orchestra, which promoted strict-tempo ballroom dancing. By 1937 he had his own dance music programme on the BBC: see V. Silvester, *Modern Ballroom Dancing* (London: Herbert Jenkins, 1928) and *idem*, *Dancing is My Life* (London: Heinemann, 1958). Baade, '"The dancing front"', p. 365, citing Silvester, *Modern Ballroom Dancing* (1974 edn), p. 40.

72 D. B. Scott, 'Silvester, Victor Marlborough (1900–1978)', *Oxford Dictionary of National Biography* (Oxford: Oxford University Press, 2004), www.oxforddnb.com/view/article/31685 (accessed 7 June 2007). Silvester had joined at 14. After he died, it was suggested he had been made to serve on a firing squad which shot deserters. He did not mention this in his autobiography, despite describing some traumatic experiences: *Dancing is My Life*, pp. 20, 27. Silvester's grandson, Christopher, subsequently revealed a 'shocking discovery' from his grandfather's army diary, an erased pencil entry, which indicated that Silvester had found two wounded Germans in a shell-hole and 'dispatched them with a grenade'. Christopher suggested that Victor was 'haunted by the memories of these killings and the other deaths he witnessed as a young teenager'. Silvester's military experience provides an interesting perspective on his passion for both the physical freedom and discipline of dance. C. Silvester, 'Boy executioner', *Daily Mail* (12 November 2005), p. 46.

73 Dance writers, challenging the alleged effeminacy of men who dance, have 'borrowed heavily from discourses of sport and male athleticism': M. L. Adams, '"Death to the prancing prince": effeminacy, sport discourses and the salvation of men's dancing', *Body and Society*, 11:4 (2005), pp. 64, 67, 69.

74 Baade, '"The dancing front"', p. 353.

75 *Manchester Guardian* (17 September 1929), p. 13.

76 *Ibid.* (10 May 1930), p. 8.

77 *Ibid.* (20 May 1927), p. 9.

78 *Manchester Guardian* (3 March 1928), p. 12.

79 *Daily Mirror* (25 October 1929), p. 18.

80 *Manchester Guardian* (15 December 1930), p. 11.

81 Nott, *Music*, p. 174; Bowley, 'Amusements and entertainments', p. 42.

82 Nott, *Music*, pp. 127, 193–4; M. Pegg, *Broadcasting and Society, 1918–1939* (London: Croom Helm, 1983), pp. 138, 195–6.

83 Pritchard, *Dance Band Days*, p. 2.

84 Nott, *Music*, pp. 131, 147.

85 *Ibid.*, pp. 127, 137, 140, 145.

86 The present-day county of Cumbria: Murfin, *Popular Leisure*, pp. 199–200.

87 Pritchard, *Dance Band Days*, p. 4. 2ZY Manchester and 5IT Birmingham were the first BBC stations outside London in 1922. For the development of the inter-war music industry see Jones, *Workers at Play*; D. LeMahieu, *A Culture for Democracy: Mass Communications and the Cultivated Mind in Britain between the Wars* (Oxford: Clarendon Press, 1988). See also Hustwitt, '"Caught in a whirlpool"', pp. 7–31.

88 T. Waddicor, *Memories of Hightown and Beyond*, Burnett Archive of Working-Class Autobiographies, University of Brunel (hereafter, Burnett Archive), p. 20.

89 F. Pritchard, *Dance Band Days around Manchester* (Manchester: Neil Richardson,

1988); Nott, *Music*, pp. 127–35; J. Carley, *Old Friends, Old Times, 1908–1938: Manchester Memories from the Diaries of Joe Carley* (Manchester: Neil Richardson, 1990), p. 12.

90 Pritchard, *Dance Band Days*, p. 2; Nott, *Music*, p. 143.

91 Pritchard, *Dance Band Days*, pp. 5–6.

92 *Manchester Guardian* (17 September 1929), p. 13; Nott, *Music*, pp. 3, 129, 132–3, 135, 180.

93 J. Brooke, *The Dukinfield I Knew, 1906–1930* (Manchester: Neil Richardson, 1987.

94 *Dancing Times* (December 1928), p. 359.

95 Nott, *Music*, p. 129; Brooke, *The Dukinfield I Knew*, p. 42.

96 *Dancing Times* (October 1928), p. 496.

97 *Manchester Guardian* (10 May 1930), p. 10.

98 *Ibid.* (15 December 1930), p. 11; McKibbin, *Classes and Cultures*, p. 404.

99 *Manchester Guardian* (15 November 1930), p. 15.

100 Nott, *Music*, pp. 153, 163, 169; Langhamer, *Women's Leisure*, p. 64.

101 P. Moss, *Manchester's Dancing Years* (Manchester: Neil Richardson, 1996), p. 24.

102 Nott, *Music*, pp. 162–163.

103 *Dancing Times* (June 1934), p. 277; MOA File Report 11A, November 1939 'Jazz and Dancing', p. 4.

104 Moss, *Manchester's Dancing Years*, p. 11.

105 *Manchester Guardian* (5 March 1928), p. 6.

106 T. Harrisson, 'Whistle while you work', in *New Writing* (Winter 1938), p. 47, cited in Nott, *Music*, p. 169.

107 Nott, *Music*, p. 174.

108 *Daily Mirror* (21 January, 1927), p. 19.

109 Moss, *Manchester's Dancing Years*, pp. 24–5.

110 *Daily Mirror* (30 September 1922), p. 7; Oliver, 'Liberation or limitation?', p. 256.

111 F. Goss, *My Boyhood at the Turn of the Century*, Burnett Archive, p. 192.

112 R. L. Cook, 'Dancing in the thirties – short story', *Contemporary Review*, 1 July 1999.

113 *Dancing Times* (February 1931), p. 590.

114 A. P. Jephcott, *Girls Growing Up* (London: Faber and Faber, 1942), p. 121, cited in Nott, *Music*, p. 183.

115 Brooke, *The Dukinfield I Knew*, p. 31.

116 S. McWinnie, The Cinema Culture in 1930s Britain (CCINTB) Archive, University of Lancaster (hereafter CCINTB); Murfin, *Popular Leisure*, p. 201. See, for example, a demonstration dance, the Flirtation Waltz, performed by Walter and Bobby Browing: North West Film Archive, Manchester Metropolitan University, Film No 120, 'Glimpses of a Manchester Popular Rendezvous – The Piccadilly Restaurant and Dance Salon', Gaumont, for Charles Ogden Cinema Circuit, 1924. Also, Film No 541, 'Over and Over!', A dance demonstration by the Apache Speciality Dancer, Miss Constance Evans.

117 Nott *Music*, pp. 129, 154–5, 158, 168.

118 *Manchester Guardian* (18 April 1906), p. 2.

119 Moss, *True Romances*, p. 5.

120 Cameron, Lush and Meara, *Disinherited Youth*, p. 105.

121 Russell and Russell, *Lads' Clubs*, p. 218.

122 B. L. Q. Henriques, *Club Leadership* (London: Oxford University Press, 1933: 1943), pp. 67, 131. Despite Henriques's denunciation, the best amateur dancers in London were said to come from Jewish families in Whitechapel: Bowley, 'Amusements and entertainments', p. 65.

123 V. Bell, *The Boy* (June 1932), cited in F. Dawes, *A Cry from the Streets. The Boys' Club Movement in Britain from the 1850s to the Present Day* (Hove: Wayland Publishers, 1975), pp. 139–40. The term 'bunny-hug' had first appeared before the First World War and applied to a ragtime dance. Its use by Bell suggests his lack of connection with contemporary youth culture.

124 A. Kuhn, *An Everyday Magic: Cinema and Cultural Memory* (London and New York: I. B. Tauris, 2002), p. 181.

125 *Ibid.*, pp. 103, 168–9, 173.

126 *Daily Mirror* (24 September 1932), p. 15; *Dancing Times* (December 1935), p. 363

127 Cross, *Worktowners*, p. 177.

128 Pritchard, *Dance Band Days*, p. 10.

129 *Daily Mirror* (15 November 1921), p. 9; *ibid.* (17 April 1928), p. 8.

130 *Ibid.* (28 September 1927), p. 4.

131 *Ibid.* (25 October 1929), p. 18.

132 Moss, *Manchester's Dancing Years*, p. 10.

133 *Daily Mirror* (23 November 1933), p. 12; Moss, *Manchester's Dancing Years*, p. 10; *Dancing Times* (October 1928), p. 21.

134 *Dancing Times* (October 1932), p. 39.

135 Oliver, 'Liberation or limitation?', p. 256, citing Silvester, *Dancing is My Life*; E. Edynbry, *Real Life Problems and Their Solution* (London: Odhams Press, 1938), p. 143. Gigolos and lounge lizards were particularly associated with the dance culture of French hotels and restaurants in the 1920s, where they were paid to dance with unaccompanied women and had a reputation for living off women's money. The term 'lounge lizard' had American slang origins and was applied to men who hung around fashionable bars and venues looking for wealthy women who could become their 'patrons'. See the Oxford English Dictionary, http://dictionary.oed.com/.

136 K. Honeyman, 'Following suit: men, masculinity and gendered practices in the clothing trade in Leeds, England, 1890–1940', *Gender and History*, 14:3 (2002), p. 442.

137 Roberts, *Classic Slum*, p. 233.

138 Oliver, 'Liberation or limitation?', p. 251.

139 Nott, *Music*, pp. 186–7.

140 Roberts, *Classic Slum*, p. 233.

141 Cross, *Worktowners*, pp. 174–5.

142 Moss, *Manchester's Dancing Years*, pp. 9–10.

143 Oliver, 'Liberation or limitation?', p. 251; Pritchard, *Dance Band Days*, p. 14.

144 Cross, *Worktowners*, p. 174.

145 *Daily Mirror* (8 March 1938), p. 12.

146 *Ibid.* (14 February 1938), p. 9.

147 Moss, *Manchester's Dancing Years*, pp. 9–10.

148 Carley, *Old Friends, Old Times,* pp. 11, 21.

149 E. Hague, *Streets away from Paradise: Reminiscence of a Stalybridge Lad* (Manchester: Neil Richardson, 1983), p. 52.

150 Moss, *True Romances*, p. 5.

151 R. D. McBee, *Dance Hall Days: Intimacy and Leisure among Working-Class Immigrants in the United States* (New York and London: New York University Press, 2000), p. 116.

152 S. F. Hatton, *London's Bad Boys* (London: Chapman and Hall Ltd., 1931), pp. 46–7. 'Hank' or 'hanky panky' was surreptitious sexual activity.

153 A. Carden-Coyne, *Reconstructing the Body: Classicism, Modernism, and the First World War* (Oxford: Oxford University Press, 2009), p. 6.

154 M. Houlbrook, '"The man with the powder puff" in inter-war London', *Historical Journal*, 50:1 (2007), 151–60. See also, A. Oram, 'Feminism, androgyny and love between women in *Urania*, 1916–1940', *Media History*, 7:1 (2001), p. 61.

155 The absence of women meant that men danced together at the Front: Bourke, *Dismembering*, p. 133.

156 Roberts, *Classic Slum*, pp. 233–4.

157 Some dance hall managers continued to ignore male couples dancing together, provided they did not draw attention to themselves. For a critical assessment of Mass-Observation's evidence of same-sex dancing, see J. Taylor, 'Sex, snobs and swing: a case study of Mass-Observation as a source for social history', Mass-Observation Online, British Social History, 1937–1972, University of Sussex (see www.massobs. org.uk/accessing_material_online.htm).

158 Mass Observation File, W42D, cited in Oliver, 'Liberation or limitation?', p. 256.

159 Baade, '"The dancing front"', p. 356. See also S. Cooks, 'Passionless dancing and passionate reform: respectability, modernism, and the social dancing of Irene and Vernon Castle', in W. Washabaugh (ed.), *The Passion of Music and Dance: Body, Gender and Sexuality* (Oxford: Berg 1998).

160 This reasserted 'subordination with heterosexuality' would become clearer in the 1940s and 1950s choreography of Hollywood musicals: R. Dyer, '"I seem to find the happiness I seek": heterosexuality and dance in the musical', in H. Thomas (ed.), *Dance, Gender and Culture* (New York: St. Martin's Press, 1993), p. 63.

161 Nott, *Music*, pp. 165–6, 174–5, 190. See R. Samuel, 'Doing the Lambeth Walk', in *Theatres of Memory: Past and Present in Contemporary Culture* (London, Verso, 1994).

162 Wouters, *Informalization*, p. 183.

163 Zimring, '"The dangerous art"', pp. 714–16.

164 Nott, *Music*, pp. 174–5, 182.

165 *Daily Mirror* (3 December 1938), p. 14; Pritchard, *Dance Band Days*, p. 10; McKibbin *Classes and Cultures*, p. 407; The fox-trot was first danced in Britain in 1914: Erenberg, 'Everybody's doin' it', p. 163; *Dancing Times* (October 1928), p. 20.

166 Cross, *Worktowners*, p. 175.

167 McBee, *Dance Hall Days*, p. 83.

168 For American examples, see McBee, *Dance Hall Days*, particularly ch. 4, pp. 115–56.

169 It had become common for young women to dance together during the First World War: *Daily Mirror* (28 September 1927), p. 4.

170 J. Slawson, *Hopwood, Heywood and Me* (Manchester: Neil Richardson, 1986), p. 40.

171 N. Dyck and E. P. Archetti, *Sport, Dance and Embodied Identities* (Oxford: Berg, 2003), p. 1; R. Power, 'Healthy motion. Images of "natural" and "cultured" movement

in early twentieth-century Britain', *Women's Studies International Forum*, 19:5 (1996), p. 551.

172 A. Ward, 'Dancing in the dark: rationalism and the neglect of social dance', in H. Thomas (ed.), *Dance, Gender and Culture* (London: Macmillan, 1993). Cultural studies in the 1980s and 1990s tended to privilege music over dance, perhaps reflecting the notions of many male writers on youth culture that dance was not an appropriate cultural form.

173 M. Houlbrook, '"Lady Austin's camp boys": constituting the queer subject in 1930s London', *Gender and History*, 14:1 (2002), p. 37.

174 B. O'Connor, 'Sexing the nation: Discourses of the dancing body in Ireland in the 1930s', *Journal of Gender Studies*, 14:2 (2005), 89–105.

175 B. Beaven, *Leisure, Citizenship and Working-Class Men in Britain* (Manchester: Manchester University Press, 2005); *Manchester Guardian* (5 August 1927), p. 9; Roberts, *Classic Slum*, p. 233; A. Davies, *Leisure, Gender and Poverty* (Buckingham and Philadelphia: Open University Press, 1992), p. 94.

176 See, for example, S. Humphries, *A Secret World of Sex: Forbidden Fruit: The British Experience, 1900–1950* (London: Sidgwick and Jackson, 1988), pp. 146–7, 149, 158, 160.

177 MOA File Report 11A, November 1939, 'Jazz and Dancing', p. 2. These figures bear comparison with those from *Young People in the 80s* (London: HMSO, 1989) which suggested that 54 per cent of boys and 59 per cent of girls attended discos: cited in Ward, 'Dancing in the dark', p. 17.

7

Place and mobility

laces play an important part in how people construct the narratives of their personal history and identity, as is often very apparent in written recollections and oral-history testimony of childhood and youth in the 1920s and 1930s, given that many such memoirs and interviews were compiled during or after the destruction of many well-established working-class communities.[1] Between 1955 and 1975, 1.3 million houses were demolished, erasing many of the working-class districts in which such people had grown up, and those writing about their younger years in such districts were often very sensitive to their disappearance, even if they had long moved away from them.[2] The topographical elements apparent in many of these memoirs are more complex than the nostalgia which is often assumed, however, and suggest much about the place-based identities fashioned during the impressionable years of childhood and adolescence.[3] Kuhn's interviews with respondents who had been cinema-goers in the 1930s highlighted the extraordinary insistence of place in their memories of childhood and youth, suggesting that 'virtually all' her respondents 'at some point' organised their accounts topographically as the 'walk along familiar remembered streets of childhood' was 're-enacted again and again implicitly or explicitly in . . . in memory talk'.[4] Negotiating the spaces of neighbourhood and locality played an important part in the upbringing of working-class boys and young men, for whom these local landscapes were integral to their sense of identity and belonging.[5] Many club leaders recognised the importance of understanding the local geographies with which their young members were familiar. Henriques, for example, suggested that a leader should become 'thoroughly acquainted with the topography of the district', because 'streets, pubs, wharves, &c.' all had 'a local significance', and it was 'a great asset to be able to talk with knowledge about them, and to be able to understand the boys when they are doing so'.[6] Walking, 'the default mode of getting around' played an important part in generating and sustaining these vivid mental maps of the streets and districts in which people had grown up.[7] Mobility – walking and cycling – helped place and locality to acquire particular meanings during adolescence. It shaped an attachment reinforced by habit, familiarity and the casual rhythms of daily life, suggesting how a 'knowable' landscape might be fashioned as a *'practiced* place' as movement through local and broader urban and rural landscapes helped to mediate entry into the world of adults.[8]

Working-class boys were expected to have greater geographical freedom than girls, and the sense of territorial belonging to which this gave rise generated more than fierce loyalties, but also offered significant freedoms which contrasted with the hierarchical, deferential expectations of school and most work-places. How boys negotiated these urban spaces was deeply rooted in childhood, when their experiences were centred on particular streets, courts or localities in which they learned the skills of 'appropriate' male behaviour.[9] In contrast to gang use of neighbourhood territory, which has dominated interpretations of youth and street life, these more 'everyday' connections to place also played an important part in the development of identity during this stage of life as their relationships with these places deepened and extended in various complex ways during adolescence.[10] Neighbourhood spaces have attracted far less attention than metropolitan ones among cultural critics concerned with exploring spatial practices.[11] Yet, as historians have highlighted, the streets of working-class neighbourhoods not only played an important part in the urban imagination but also significantly shaped the lives of those who lived there, although, unlike the distancing spaces of city centres, they were more often an extension of the private in crowded working-class districts. 'Very local ties to place' have been described as becoming 'increasingly antiquated at all cultural levels' after 1890, particularly among the upwardly mobile 'property-owning or professional classes'.[12] This was not the case with many working-class people, for whom a place-bound sense of identity remained significant until well into the twentieth century. The leisure activities of working-class young boys during adolescence played an important part in this evolving sense of place, for although leisure is often seen as an escape from familiar patterns and experiences, the structure and repetitive nature of many place-based leisure routines contributed to particular topographical identities originating in childhood and extended and reinforced during the teen years. Just as the territorial identities of gangs have tended to dominate much of this literature, so particular kinds of walking have received a disproportionate amount of attention, in particular, rambling, or hiking as it was redefined in the 1930s. Such recreational walking expanded immensely in the inter-war years to become a significant cultural identity for many working-class young people, especially in northern England.[13] This chapter argues that more localised mobilities in both urban and rural settings deserve greater attention, however, given their important if often neglected part in working-class childhood and adolescence.

The authors of *Disinherited Youth* thought it 'surprising' that 'roughly 20 percent' of the men they interviewed said 'most of their time was spent in walking about the streets', and were disquieted to find that although such walking was more 'pronounced' among the unemployed, it was 'also apparent to a disturbing extent among lads who had fairly regular employment'.[14] Casual walking of this sort was so perturbing because it was identified with aimlessness and demoralisation, although its meanings were actually much more varied. These 'repetitive encounters with familiar features' of the everyday world helped to 'consolidate a sense of spatial belonging' which contributed significantly not only to the evolving adolescent identities of working-class young men but also to how they often later narrated their early lives.[15] It is to the spatial experiences of these 'banal or mundane mobilities' that this chapter turns, starting first with that most contentious of youthful places, the street.

Street performance

The urban street was a significant site of 'relaxation' for working-class young people.[16] It was where they played as children and where they relaxed as they entered adolescence, when its part in their lives tended to be reinforced by lack of privacy at home, the desire for like-minded company and a lack of money.[17] Streets were particularly important for boys during early adolescence, since this was where they learned many important lessons of masculinity. The street was a living-space and a social centre 'crowded' with 'institutions designed for entertainment, sociability and courting'. It was a place for spectacle, observation and overlooking others, where the private was often made disconcertingly public by those described as 'uninhibited' women and 'independent', 'precocious' youth.[18] The street as a rather anarchic 'state of mind' looms large in interpretations of young people and was apparent in the criticisms of many social reformers who, from the end of the nineteenth century, viewed it as a dysfunctional site of bad language, smoking, 'wild' behaviour and horseplay, where young people yelled, bawled and swore each other and larked about often until late in the evening.[19] The visibility of working-class young men in such public spaces focused fears of their disruptive, hooligan potential, not least because their activities there were an important source of social power.[20] Concerns about the delinquency and anti-social behaviour of working-class youth grew in the Victorian and Edwardian periods, leading a great many voluntary organisations and statutory bodies to seek increasingly to expand control over their street activities. From the end of the nineteenth century, not only were working-class boys induced to leave the street to join organised youth movements, but the activities of those who remained there were more severely curtailed with the introduction of the policeman on the beat, 'either with formal prosecutions for gambling, loitering, obstruction, playing football and so on, or more commonly with the informal sanctions of a flick of the cape or gloves across the head'.[21] Despite such efforts, streets remained important social centres, and the adolescent wage-earners whom David Fowler described continued to spend much of their free time during the evenings and at weekends outside the home, larking, boasting, telling 'dirty tales' and laughing with each other.[22] 'The long unlovely street' remained such a cause for concern because, as a writer in *The Boy* observed in 1927, it was a period of 'liberty', when the influences brought to bear upon them were 'probably going to determine his character far more than the influences exercised upon him during his school or working hours'. While over-exaggerating the street's influence for its own purposes, such observations nevertheless reflect the significance of the casual encounters made there.[23] Young people's visibility was particularly apparent on Sundays, when the closure of many parks, cinemas and playing-fields cause them to spill over onto local thoroughfares. Christopher Williamson of Edinburgh, a 19-year-old apprentice plater whose respectability was affirmed by the information that he was attending night school and had been a prize-winner there 'for two years running', 'hated' the Scottish Sunday because everything was closed and all that young people could do was 'loaf about the streets and get into mischief.'[24] His use of an epithet such as loaf was significant, in that its indolent and vaguely criminal connotations were frequently applied to young men's 'vacant hours'.[25] Loafing was regarded as the default state of boys in adolescence, particularly if they could not afford to go anywhere other than their local neighbourhood. 'If a lad has no spare cash he loafs. Lounging at the street corner, parading the length of street where the shops are brightest.'[26] *Disinherited Youth* typically condemned the lack of direction of working-class boys with no money in their pockets: 'It may be by the fireside, or standing at the street corner, or aimlessly walking about the crowded streets looking at shop windows. Whatever forms it takes, it is an effortless existence – the negation of any real use of free time.'[27] Too much free time all too easily became policed time, as Bill Griffiths recalled, describing the police harassment which followed young people in his youth in Manchester, after the General Strike in 1926:

> Young men in their teens who couldn't get jobs had nothing to do, no money and nowhere to go except to roam the streets, and they were hounded by the police. They were not allowed to stand about in a group or walk more than two abreast on the pavement without being dispersed and quickly moved on. My eldest brother Frank was in this category and he was always in trouble because he did not like being pushed about. I remember my mother just did not know what to do because the police would not leave the young men alone, taking names and addresses and going round to houses telling parents that their sons would be put away if they caused more trouble. They weren't causing much trouble, just trying to pass idle hours away, talking or perhaps kicking around a piece of paper tied up into a ball, but since the strike the police would not allow anything like this to happen.[28]

John Stainton's description of the walking he did in his unemployed youth suggests how important he felt it was to identify such activity with self-improvement rather than time wasting: 'You did a hell of a lot of walking in those days to save money' and pass the time, especially if you were unemployed. 'Well, what I and plenty of others have done. We walk down to the museums and into town, Manchester and Whitworth Park and the Art Galleries, all round there. It broadened your mind.'[29] Glimpses of the role that walking performed during periods of particular stress and uncertainty, such as unemployment, occasionally emerges in autobiographies, as in Norman Kenyon's recollections of being out of work in the 1930s during his teens, which suggest how walking out on the moors helped to ease his unnamed depression:

> After I had been looking for work for weeks on end I would despairingly give up the task, and for many days following would ask Mother to put me up some sandwiches, fill me the flask with tea and off I would go to the moors.[30]

The same was true for an 'unemployed Worktowner' interviewed by Mass Observation, who said it was only by 'walking into the country' that he managed to 'get rid' of the feeling of being tied to the boundaries of the house 'and his worry'.[31]

Despite the unfavourable reputation which attached to hanging about the streets, it was not limited to those with 'no spare cash', but remained central to the leisure experiences of many working-class boys, even as commercial entertainment such as the cinema and dance hall encroached on their time and interests.[32] Walking helped to join up the meeting points which swelled around the ice-cream parlours and fish and chip shops, sweet shops and cafés from the end of the nineteenth century.[33] In London, by the inter-war years, 'innumerable' cafés, often Italian or Greek run, in London's poorer districts acted as an informal gathering place for 'gangs of lads', attracted by a 'flourishing trade in "cups" and "slabs"'.[34] In Harpurhey, Manchester, Joe Kay, spent much of his time between the ages of 16 and 20 at Tony Gotelli's ice-cream shop, which sold sweets and chocolate ice-cream and became almost his 'second home' during his spells of unemployment because Tony understood their situation and let lads hang about all day 'and not spend a penny'. The shop was particularly crowded on Sunday afternoons, when so much else was closed, and attracted both boys and girls, although an implicit sense of male and female space was apparent, since girls, unlike boys, 'never went into the large room to be served'.[35]

The relaxed, 'irreverent' independence of street culture had a considerable impact of young people's attitudes towards authority as they were growing up, although outsiders failed to appreciate the street's importance as an informal site of learning.[36] Its atmosphere could at times be homosocial, but was not exclusively so, and the suggestive banter which took place there also made it a site for heterosexual 'sexual play and curiosity' among those who managed to keep out of adults' way.[37] The homosocial character of youthful street relationships was most obvious in the poorest districts, where the 'hard' manliness of more violent gang behaviour was enacted before a public audience and 'powerful discourses' about what were considered appropriate gender roles were enforced. Youthful street spaces were defined by the masculine norms of strength encouraged within families, the work-place, schools and youth groups, although Davies challenges Humphries' emphasis that such gang violence was confined to the poorest working-class districts, emphasising its role in constructing a particular notion of working-class masculinity rooted in the hard manliness and tough expectations of working-class culture.[38] The street was where boys learned to 'ignore or "take" abuse' from their peers as a mark of masculinity and a lesson in controlling emotions, expressed in oppositional gestures against the feminising constraints of home and school, such as fighting, smoking, spitting, swearing and telling obscene jokes.[39] But although this world has been characterised by the need to impress and prove masculinity, it was not necessarily recalled as being so competitively harsh. Bill Naughton, for example, described his street corner as 'a sort of male haven, to which men could escape, and relax and regress, free of female presence'.[40] For another working-class writer, Bill Andrews, it was where 'we made arrangements to go to a cinema or a dance, swapped rather crude stories, discovered who was on short-time that week and had an occasional sing-song on a warm evening'.[41] Naughton suggests hierarchies of age and respectability which could make street corners rather selective spaces. In the 1920s, for example, he eventually 'detached' himself from his local meeting place to 'wangle' himself 'in among the younger lads of the Big Corner'. This was 'ideally suited for a gathering corner, with a flow of pedestrians which added to its character; it had a lively mixture of men and youths, spinning-mill workers mostly, but colliers, foundry workers, ex-soldiers, an out-of-work or two, and younger lads on the fringe'. Summer evenings would often see as many as thirty gathered there.[42] The visibility of such groups gave credence to the comments of youth workers, who often commented on the so-called 'pack' mentality of working-class boys, which was represented as a 'natural' part of adolescence. Secretan typically suggested that the London boys with whom he worked seemed impelled 'to do all things in common', coming together in gangs which changed, broke up and re-formed; which lasted a few months or led to life-time friendships.[43] Groups joined together

> any number from three to a dozen . . . such is a 'gang,' a natural social unit by the riverside, and exercising a powerful influence over the lives of its members. At best it may develop fine qualities of loyalty and usefulness, at worst it may degenerate into a crowd of toughs, looking for trouble.[44]

Most working-class boys probably collected loosely together 'at some stage in their lives, usually drifting into [gangs] between the ages of ten and thirteen'.[45] For Jack Jackson from Salford, such involvement coalesced around the age of 8 or 9, when he started to be 'given a bit more slack in the parental restraining rope, and was accepted into the gang of lads from the streets near where he lived, about a dozen boys in all, but usually five or six 'at most gatherings'.[46] Gang membership was seen as one of the main differences between girls and boys, as Morgan suggested of those in their teens, when both boys and girls were 'brimming with trustfulness and thirsty for friendship'. Where girls hungered for a 'confiding relationship', boys, if left to their own devices, would become 'one of a gang knit together by a fierce loyalty'.[47] Hatton outlined what he described as nine 'chief mental tendencies of Adolescence', of which one of the most pronounced was the 'group or herd sense', a shifting identity which, as Secretan suggested, caused worries because it moved easily from larking about to more serious criminal activities.[48] Middle-class boys were seen as manifesting the same energies as their working-class counterparts, the difference being that in their more privileged environments they were channelled through '"Scout" troops, school-house teams, clubs ... Turn the "gang sense" into the "team spirit" and the future of civilization is assured.'[49] Assumptions such as these, which served to normalise gang identity, constructed those who were thought of as 'lone wolves' as not only 'rare' but something of an aberration, and highlight the problematic nature of otherness in working-class neighbourhoods.[50] They are also a reminder that, despite the emphasis youth organisations themselves placed on channelling a 'natural' gang spirit, boys were also attracted by the sense of belonging which clubs offered to the less confident. Clubs (like local street gangs) helped to protect members from the male insecurities and territorial rivalries of adolescent street life.

The streets of working-class neighbourhoods also played a part in the adventure fantasies which were so important to the imaginative development of young boys and in the subjective composure of their masculinity.[51] Working-class boys generally were said to share with their younger middle-class peers a liking for gangster, war, mystery and cowboys films, scenarios which contributed much to their 'make-believe and play' at street level.[52] Kuhn suggests that where women's memories of the cinema were most strongly identified with adolescence, those of male respondents tended to focus more on childhood.[53] 'Who has not', wrote Burt, 'seen street-urchins mimicking Charlie Chaplin, "holding" each other "up" with toy pistols, or masquerading in the feathers of Red Indians or the wide-awake hats of cowboys, every flaunted detail manifestly picked from the romances of the film?'[54] These childhood 'memories of bodily movement' so strongly associated with the particular 'outdoor spaces' in which this 'play, imitation and make-believe' took place, helped to define these re-enactments by the 'sensations of physical energy and release' also very apparent in the autobiographies of working-class men who grew up in the 1930s.[55] To Salford-born Jack Jackson, local cul-de-sacs were 'blind canyons' within which 'any adventurer, no matter how brave, could easily get trapped'. Jackson's exploration of the streets around his neighbourhood was played out within the frontier world of the Wild West, fantasies which also helped to displace any anxieties he might have had about moving through unfamiliar neighbourhoods.[56] Having learned 'that a moving target' 'was harder to home in on', he raced through the strange streets, pretending to be his cowboy hero, Hoot Gibson, a star of the silent screen and one of

Universal's top paid actors in the 1920s. John Wynne, who went to a different Salford cinema every Saturday, described being 'intoxicated' by the excitement of the story as they 'galloped off home – up Broughton Road, across Broad Street, down Hankinson Street then up Ellor Street, smacking our buttocks as we went, no longer Salford kids of the street. We were the goodies riding our trusty steeds against the baddies.'[57] Such fantasies of motion and adventure were also staples of popular story-papers such as *The Hotspur, The Skipper, The Wizard, The Rover* and *The Champion*, aimed at working-class and lower middle-class boys in early adolescence and whose readership probably peaked between the ages of 12 and 14.[58] Starting work at 14 was assumed, in fact, to mark the abandonment of many childish forms of play, although a range of informal neighbourhood-based activities, largely with peers of the same sex, remained common until around the age of 16.

Davies suggests that 'the survival of a Victorian pattern of street life alongside more glamorous modern entertainments such as the cinema forms' was 'one of the most striking characteristics of working-class leisure during the 1930s', with informal street activities accounting 'for at least half of the leisure time of young workers' in inter-war Manchester and Salford.[59] A detailed Manchester study from the late 1930s, based on the leisure activities of adolescents in Hulme, reverses the stereotypes of loquacious females and reticent males by suggesting that 16- and 17-year-old working boys spent about 47 per cent of their weekday leisure time talking. Their female working equivalents, more constrained by domestic tasks, were said at age 16 to spend only about 15 per cent of their leisure time talking, which rose to 24 per cent at 17.[60] Older leisure patterns were in many respects not so much alongside as interwoven with a range of more formal and commercial activities. For Salford-born John Stainton, commercial entertainment such as the cinema was part of a spectrum which also included 'home made' amusements and lads'-club activities. Cricket, football, rugby, swimming 'were all cheap sports and a lot you made yourself . . . You made your own fun, you took part in your own fun.' Stainton highlighted the 'rational' and 'hedonistic' divisions in his recreational pattern, which was distinguished by 'going out' during the week and 'having fun' at the weekend: 'the only night you'd go out during the week would be Monday and Friday. Now Tuesday Wednesday and Thursday you made your own round about, or you went to Salford Lads' Club, er, the sports, the gym or anywhere like that. But all your fun was at weekend. You could, as I say, you could go dancing, skating, go to the boxing booths.'[61]

Contemporary concerns about the expansion of commercialised

forms of leisure tended to ignore or underestimate this wide range of leisure activities in which most working-class young men engaged, many of
which, such as gambling, playing dice and pitch and toss, were favourite
nineteenth-century pastimes. The gambling, sport and informal street
activities of well-established masculine culture in poor districts continued to draw in young men like Stainton, and James Hooley, who grew up
in an impoverished part of Stockport. His 'liking for the pubs' first came
about in the early 1930s, when he was about 17 or 18, from which time he
always frequented the same one because he liked its familiar feel and the
fact that there always seemed to be something going on there, such as
competitions for 'the biggest tater grown, or the biggest onion'.[62]

> Not for the simple reason of the beer, but for the characters that were
> in the pubs, and the singing. I thought it was wonderful, I still do,
> because the songs they used to sing represented the time that we lived
> in, they were all sentimental songs, you know things like 'When I leave
> the world behind' and things like that.

Accounts such as these highlight the importance of the mid teens in
changing leisure interests. Valentine Bell described the ages of between
12 and 15 as a 'heroic age' when boys 'hated' the effeminate and, whatever they might think of girls in secret, were not seen playing or talking with them.[63] By 16 they were starting to enter another important
transitional phase marked, as Bell suggested, by a broadening of leisure
interests to include girls.[64] This age was sometimes described as the 'real
break between post-childhood and pre-manhood', when many young
male wage-earners started to hold back a larger proportion of their
earnings to spend on entertainment. It was also when they were said
to move on from boys' papers to more explicitly adult reading matter,
which included the 'hectic thrills' and 'clotted romance' of imported
American story magazines distributed through cheap multiple outlets
and small shops.[65] Informal leisure activities continued to play a part in
their lives, although between 16 and 19 many were starting to 'drift away'
from street gangs as they became more involved in finding a girlfriend.[66]
The organisers of boys' clubs, very aware of such changes, were of the
'general opinion' that those over 16 did not 'mix well with the fourteen
to sixteen year old boy'.[67] This older age group of 16- to 18-year-olds was
identified with many different problems, such as greater unemployment,
which highlighted 'one of the most vicious problems of modern civilization', that of 16-year-old 'lads', 'out of work and lounging about street
corners'.[68] They were also more difficult to handle and the minority of
gangs which were delinquent tended to comprise young men from this

age group, their often uncertain masculinities intensified by lack of work, background or temperament, which made them more susceptible to the excitement of petty crime and violent gang activities.[69] These older gang members were more sexually aware and knowing, hanging out in private inside spaces such as 'bars, dance halls and billiard saloons' whose 'dim, hushed' interiors shared the dubious reputation which attached to amusement arcades.[70]

The street's social significance during adolescence did, in fact, express important distinctions between public and private, inside and outside space. The working-class home was a 'back-region', where visitors were carefully screened, where boys could drop the social displays expected outside, and where boyfriends and girlfriends were unlikely to be introduced until the establishment of what seemed to be a serious relationship. Boys, unlike girls, were 'in general' 'more prone to wander out after tea', since 'in the ordinary worker's home', especially if there were younger children, his room 'was preferred to his presence'.[71] The home-based pattern associated with girls started in childhood, as Mass Observation suggested, noting that in late 1930s Bolton, 75 per cent of school-age girls were 'indoors at home in the evening playing games, reading or listening to the radio, compared to only 34 per cent of the boys', most of whom returned to the street.[72] Such home-centredness among girls remained common in their early teens, when parental control was most pronounced amongst more prosperous working-class families who were less dependent on their children's wages.[73] Many girls from poor homes, on the other hand, were 'comparatively free from parental control' long before they left school, and were most likely to be out 'more than three evenings a week', roaming the streets because they could not afford to go elsewhere.[74] 'Small, crowded rooms and lack of privacy most certainly hamper home recreation even when a girl has a strong inclination for it and help to drive her out to walk round.'[75] Boys nevertheless maintained greater street visibility, due to expectations of male dominance and because girls were more likely to try to keep out of the way of prying eyes, given the greater constraints on their behaviour. As Burt put it, where 'The older boy must meet his mates at the corner of the road; the older girl must chatter to her friends in the alleys or the parks.'[76]

Walking and wandering

The male sense of locality owed much to the greater spatial freedoms boys were able to enjoy even before they had left school, often roaming 'long and wide' at weekends and during the summer holidays. John Wynne's Salford gang wandered towards the city's green outskirts 'where we revelled in the wide open spaces . . . out in the country, but not quite'.[77] Those in rural districts also often enjoyed very long regular walks. Cliff Royle, who grew up in rural Flixton, reckoned that 'a usual Sunday morning walk' for him when he was 15 was about fourteen miles and on other occasions his brother and the lad from the farm next door happily walked a round trip of 'about forty miles'.[78] Girls participated in some of this topographical enthusiasm, particularly when accompanying boys, and in towns such as Northampton, where it was easy to get out into the countryside, courting couples often took 'a little country walk' along a local 'lover's lane' as an alternative to the cinema.[79] Girls seem less likely to have walked or cycled as individuals in the haphazard manner that boys often described, although the apparently direction-less nature of such jaunts was not always what it seemed.[80] Researchers attributed a 'subconscious motive' to 'aimless wandering' around local streets which 'for those who did not, or could not for lack of money, fre-quent the dance halls . . . provided the second best way of meeting with girls'.[81] Les's diaries record many such wanderings, often on Sunday eve-nings. On one such evening, after posting a letter, he described how he met up with a friend and went 'with him round the Mayorhold district. We followed some girls round Semilong way but we weren't lucky'.[82] (This was about three-quarters of a mile away from where he lived and in a poorer area.) The following Sunday, the two boys 'went after girls round Abington and Kingsley ways', which was about three-quarters of a mile away, but in better-off districts.[83] When friends were not avail-able, walking the dog had other uses, as was the case another Sunday evening, when he recorded visiting one of his aunts and then taking it for a walk round the town. 'I tried to get off with a girl on the course [*a large recreational space near the town centre*] but she wouldn't speak to me.'[84]

Joe Armitage, in his teens in the 1920s and living in Hunslet, was another boy who spent much of his free time out walking the streets, even in winter preferring to go out rather than stay indoors after working all day. He was 'never interested in hanging around street corners' and kept well away from local gangs because their rivalries only led to 'fights and trouble'. Instead, 'one way of having a cheap night out without stay-ing around home was to walk into Leeds on Friday night'. There was plenty to see and hear as he did his rounds. The shops were open until late, there was the patter of 'barrow lads' and market traders, boxing booths and 'at intervals of a few hundred yards . . . disabled or blind people selling matches, playing an instrument, singing cap-in-hand, or just openly begging'.[85]

As they grew older, boys gradually moved beyond the street landscapes of their childhood adventure fantasies and ventured much further afield, demonstrating 'adventurous' tendencies which were interpreted as a 'natural' developmental phase of adolescence.[86] Hatton referred to the 'run-away tendency' whereby it was not 'an uncommon thing for a lad, for no apparent reasons, suddenly to disappear and be discovered some three or four hundred miles away'. He did not, apparently, consider the possibility of abuse or violence precipitating such flight, but stressed the importance of ancient adolescent urges, 'an innate primitive instinct to leave the herd, to have his run, to hunt by himself', in answer to a masculine 'call' which no amount of chastisement would curb:

> There are many of us affected with this 'wanderlust' throughout the whole of life, and at times it is the 'very devil' to control; it requires all the common sense contemplation of the surrounding ties and responsibilities to combat the devouring urge of this runaway tendency. I do not think it affects girls to the same extent – women seldom seem to understand it in a man.[87]

Girls' street wanderings were more constrained by the family and domestic responsibilities which often kept them inside doing the washing and ironing and other household chores after work.[88] Weekly leisure activities were patterned by gender, with girls staying in to help out on Friday 'jingling' night while their brothers went out with the boys. James and Moore's survey noted that when she was 14, 43 per cent of a working girl's weekday leisure time was spent on domestic 'duties', and that this expectation remained throughout adolescence although it lessened as she reached her mid teens, falling to about 31 per cent at 16 and 15 per cent at 17. A similar examination of working boys tellingly included no similar category, reflecting much stronger male expectations of 'free' time. Coming and going freely was a male rather than a female prerogative, signified by the more frequent possession of a house key for boys, who were not expected to be home as early as girls.[89]

Streets took on different meanings after dark, when they were not places for girls to be seen alone. In 1930s Blackpool, for example, the number of single women on the street reduced in the evening, while the number of mixed pairs and single men increased.[90] Boys elsewhere were expected to escort their partners home if they had been out dancing, and sometimes received a 'nasty shock' when they found themselves having to walk two or three miles there and back for their 'gallantry'.[91]

Boys' greater spatial confidence meant, however, that they could also enjoy the solitary experience of urban walking. Joe Carley, another diary keeper like Les, 'used thoroughly to enjoy night walking if the weather was good. As a matter of fact. My late homecomings were so numerous in the years 1931 to 1935 that my dad nicknamed me "The Owl". I liked the comparative silence and solitude of a walk by night and the sound of my footsteps on the almost deserted pavements.'[92] There were certainly areas in large towns and cities where boys experienced discomfort when on their own, although women's childhood recollections of territorial boundaries during the 1930s were more often conditioned by feelings of sexual or physical vulnerability and awareness of how their bodies were being perceived.[93]

On starting work, however, young people had much greater mobility and freedom from adult supervision than before the war, because in the 1920s, expanded bus routes, cheap fares and railway excursions allowed them to start venturing further into the countryside to claim rural space, individually and collectively, in new ways and larger numbers than ever before.[94] Working-class autobiographies and diaries from the period often manifest a sense of delight and adventure in such rural excursions, and the communality of midnight rambles and walking in large groups, particularly popular in northern England, well expressed this novel sense of youthful freedom and distancing from the older generation.[95] Generational tensions within inter-war rambling were particularly apparent in the Kinder mass trespass movement, where the leaders of the official rambling groups were 'at least forty', in contrast to most of those in the British Workers' Sports Federation, mainly if not exclusively young men in their late teens and early twenties, who took the lead in confrontational, direct-action tactics.[96]

By the time they reached adolescence, boys were likely to have a strong, broad sense of territorial space, consolidated by such activities as walking urban streets; fetching, carrying, doing errands; cycle rides.[97] Bicycle ownership had been hugely extended in the 1930s, with mass-produced, cheap machines being ridden by more than ten million cyclists as improved road surfaces greatly extended their range.[98] There was a also a large female market, although 'parental expectations' of girls' behaviour continued to put them 'at a disadvantage' as far as such possession was concerned.[99] For many working-class boys, however, 'getting a "big bike"' came to be something of a 'rite of passage', helped by its being bought on the weekly instalment plan.[100] Richard Hoggart recalled how 'a sign of arrival at real adolescence' was 'the agreement from one's parents to the buying of a bike on the hire-purchase system, paid for out of weekly wages'.[101] Les's brother Frank made exactly such a purchase in 1935, when he put the money down for a B.S.A. 503A with Trivelox gear, which cost £6 10s, an expensive purchase – the equivalent of at least three or four weeks' wages.[102]

The bicycle greatly influenced Les's wandering, as it did for many of his contemporaries. The *Social Survey of Merseyside* remarked how enthusiasm among boys for cycling and walking became more pronounced once they left school, when the proportion who cited cycling as an interest rose from 5.9 per cent to 14.5 per cent and those who cited walking went up from 0.6 per cent to 6.9 per cent.[103] Although the period saw an expansion in organised cycling, many took to the countryside informally and in non-organised ways, and the number of cyclists vastly exceeded the membership of clubs and cycling groups.[104] As the authors of *Disinherited Youth* observed, 'cycling as a recreation and pastime' was mainly 'carried on by small groups of friends from neighbouring streets', between 15 and 20 per cent of those interviewed recording it as 'one of their leisure-time activities'.[105] A familiar masculine rhetoric of exploration was apparent in how some commentators described such cycling expeditions:

> Depend upon it, when two or three set out on Sunday morning on hired bicycles with their little packets of lunch strapped on the back, to visit new towns and suburbs, it is the unquenchable spirit of adventure that animates the explorer, finding its necessary expression.[106]

In 1931, *The Boy* described the 'extraordinary' and 'positive' change that had occurred 'in the attitude of the town-bred boy to country things'.[107] Far fewer lads were said to be attending camp than in pre-war years, in part because 'the more adventurous spirits were out on their own with their cheap bicycles and cheap tents'.[108] Joe Loftus described just such cycling trips which he and four friends made in the late 1920s, cycling from Lancashire to North Wales, Cheshire, Shropshire and Herefordshire, having bought and shared some camping gear between them. 'Memorable holidays, costing us no more than if we'd been eating at home.'[109] Jack Preston's *Memoirs of a Salford Lad* from the 1920s and 1930s include many similar references to long cycling trips to North Wales and the Wirral. What had started as an adolescent passion continued after marriage and into retirement, a compelling mix of physical and visual exhilaration which still had the power to inform recollections much later in life. In describing his acquisition of a garden for the first time at the age of 66, his pride and satisfaction were strongly linked to the memory of a scene encountered as a result of this youthful mobility, when he had 'stopped to admire the front garden of a thatched cottage' where a 'very old gentleman' was 'tending to his flowers'. He recalled how 'a plaque right in the middle of the flower bed' had attracted him. ' "I'm nearer to God in my garden than anywhere else on earth". Now after being forty years without, I fully realise what that means'.[110] Joe Loftus's account displays a similar long-lasting sense of engagement with the Lancashire landscape which started with these early cycling trips.[111]

Many enjoyed pedalling long distances on their days out, although the authors of *Disinherited Youth* suggested that some of the unemployed young men they interviewed did little more than cycle 'around their own neighbourhood', seemingly 'timid of venturing beyond their own town'.[112] Others, like Les, went on both short-distance and long-distance rides. Some of these were fairly local, to local parks, to watch a 'rugger' or football match, to see the Scouts' camping field in a village outside Northampton or apparently aimless cycling around local side streets. At other times there were longer expeditions into the villages and towns of rural Northamptonshire, usually within a fifteen- to thirty-mile radius of the town. This roaming, sometimes alone, sometimes with friends, helped to further a sense of connection to the broader locality, the associations of these places coloured both by family connections and perhaps by the decade's immense outpouring of literature, guide books and radio recordings on English heritage, rural life and the countryside which encouraged many to embark on weekend explorations of local and more distant 'beauty spots'.[113] As Richard Hoggart observed, the bicycle provided 'access to the look and feel and smell of each street in a way no public transport could. The landscapes of early life are indelibly engraved on the mind; for me with the bicycle as the main graver.'[114]

Cycling played a significant part in encounters between the sexes, as Jephcott's survey observed in the early 1950s.[115] It was far more acceptable for girls to pick up boys when cycling than 'going after them on foot', while the bike's useful mediating function allowed boys a quick getaway if encounters failed to turn out quite as intended. Les recorded several such speculative encounters, some within the town itself, others during rides around rural Northamptonshire. At one road junction, for example, he noted getting into conversation with a girl on a bike, only to find out that she was already courting.[116] Cycling through a local village on a Sunday afternoon, he came across 'a girl named Gladys who lives at Paulerspury. I asked her if I could meet her at night but she couldn't.'[117] Undeterred, the following Sunday he biked over to Paulerspury 'to see if I could see that girl of last Sunday'.[118] On another Sunday afternoon, he biked to Salcey forest with his cousin, Fred, to get some primroses.

Fred had two punctures 'and we dirtied our bikes all up. He borrowed some puncture kit from a house and a girl smiled at me there.'[119] The eyeing up was not all one sided. On yet another Sunday afternoon, cycling around the neighbouring town and village of Wellingborough and Sywell, 'We met some girls who called after us and at night I went round Wellingborough and Irthlingboro to see if I could see them.'[120]

Les shared another boy passion of the 1930s, motor-bikes, whose popularity was fed in part by the expansion of speedway racing, which started to take off in the late 1920s after being imported from Australia.[121] 'Even children, while riding their scooters, imitated motorbike noises, kidding themselves they were Broadside Burton or some other popular rider.'[122] Buying a motor-bike became the hope of many a working-class young man and Les, like many others, aspired to own one, spending the whole of one Sunday evening 'writing eight letters to firms about motor-cycles'.[123] Motor-bikes were within the reach of many skilled workers by the 1930s and autobiographers recalled the pleasure of buying a motor-bike, while Rowntree suggested that 'hundreds' of young men in York were 'saving up' or had 'already bought them' and were 'spending their money in touring the country'.[124] The youth worker Valentine Bell described the club boy's main interests ('other than "birds," "fillies," "peaches," or whatever he likes to call them') as 'sport, motor-bikes, the "pictures"'. Members not only knew 'all the batting averages and names of sportsmen' but 'all the makes of engines, motor-cars, and cycles', and considerable prestige attached to owning one, as George Clifton Hughes recalled.[125] The speed and mobility which such possession promised drew much from the geographical fantasies of freedom and adventure so strongly associated with male adolescence, although other masculine and youthful meanings are suggested by young men's strong preoccupations with the capabilities and behaviour of their motor-bikes. Being able to repair and maintain them was an economic necessity for many working-class owners, whose skills reflected a long-established tradition of active involvement with technical objects long seen as a 'natural' part of working-class masculine culture. The individual satisfaction of repairing and improving bicycles and motor-bikes was very different from the collective sense of excitement and community generated on the football terraces, although, like football, it was also a rich source of talk as 'male conversation increasingly turned on "decarbonizing", "adjusting tappets", "feeler gauges" and gaps for plugs and points along with the ritual moans about punctures'.[126] A Mass Observation observer watched two young men as they stood outside a motor-cycle shop 'looking at the same cycle' for five minutes and described how, when he spoke with them, they got into 'a highly technical conversation on camshafts, capacities and price'.[127] Holt's description of how skilled workers would 'lovingly strip down and reassemble' their motor-bikes 'in garden sheds or at kerb-sides' captures another important aspect of this enthusiasm and emotional engagement, whose creative and imaginative dimension was often hidden by narrow expectations of working-class boys' capabilities, based on assumptions of physical strength and practicality.[128]

If motor-bikes inspired much boyish enthusiasm, they nevertheless remained only an aspiration for most working-class young men, whose geographical horizons were more likely to be expanded through walking or cycling. It was these activities which helped them during adolescence to move out from their street corners into complex 'socio-spatial networks' and 'patterns of sociability' often well away from their local and immediate neighbourhoods.[129] The topographical familiarity to which this gave rise combined with locally based informal leisure opportunities and social relationships to generate a distinctive sense of place and locality subtly differentiated from that of their female peers, although greater opportunities for spatial mobility did not always encourage an outward-looking attitude. In poor areas such as London's Campbell Road, Islington, for example, the very locally based street traditions and older masculine cultures of their fathers made many working-class young men much more reluctant than their female peers to move away from the districts in which they had grown up, ensuring that they remained entrenched in their neighbourhood cultures in much the same way as has been observed of working-class young men in other cultural contexts.[130]

Working-class women have commonly been seen as more confined to their neighbourhoods than men, the 'place-bound', 'home-bound' character of their lives within such districts being set against an idea of neighbourhood as a point of male departure and movement into the social relationships of broader public spaces. This underestimates the extent to which a place-bound sense of belonging significantly shaped the lives of some working-class young men, for whom restricted occupational choices, the cultural expectations of being male and the routines and familiarity of home and neighbourhood reinforced a sense of embeddedness different from that experienced by many of their female counterparts. Adolescence and youth is a time when 'seminal steps are taken and decisions reached' which frequently set an individual upon 'a narrowly banded course for the rest of his or her life'.[131] The patterns and relationships set during these teen years remained significant even for those in more prosperous working-class neighbourhoods, and although the working-class district in which Les grew up was not as poor as the one which White describes, the trajectory which his later life took was, like the lives of Campbell Road's young men, marked by the patterns and relationships set during his youth. He did move in the 1950s, away from the town-centre district where he had grown up to a suburban housing estate, but, like many autobiographers of the same generation, experienced a persisting sense of displacement after his old house was redeveloped and neighbours and friends died or moved away.[132] Adult identities, rooted in the transitional years of adolescence 'when identity itself is in flux', often stimulate memories which, as Alexander suggests, remain so acute 'perhaps because they still carry the weight of possibility – the intense wondering what one might become'.[133] Research suggests how the clichés of telescoped time, which compress sequences of events into single, vivid occurrences, are easier to recall than the details of everyday life.[134] Les's diaries reveal a pattern of movement normally lost in the shorthand narratives of retrospective accounts. Their entries suggest interconnections between family and locality which were reinforced by friendship networks and associational and sporting cultures. The spatial routines, habits and relationships of his childhood and adolescence helped to shape an emotional attachment to place and a psychic landscape made resonant though habit, familiarity and the rhythms of daily life. Les never discarded the mementoes he kept of these teen years, diaries, pamphlets, postcards, letters, BB memorabilia, newspaper cuttings. As was suggested in the Introduction, they were packed up during the Second World War, in a much-loved chest of drawers which remained at his old family home in Northampton town centre until the house's demolition in the 1970s, when he recovered it as part of his self-appointed role as archivist and keeper of the family's material history. Their preservation in this fashion, a holding-on to the artefacts of another time and another place, tells another story very familiar among many ex-residents of old-established working-class districts after the housing clearances of the post-war years destroyed many of the areas in which they had grown up. The strong sense of place that Les retained for the rest of his life was grounded not only in his immediate and extended family but in the social networks and spatial confidence developed during childhood and adolescence, when he spent much time walking and cycling around Northampton and the surrounding villages.[135] As the space he inhabited shrank when he was in his seventies, so the meanings of these early spatial experiences expanded, a reminder of how the stories of youth eventually become transformed into the rather different narratives of later adulthood and old age.[136]

Notes

1 G. J. Andrews, R. A. Kearns, P. Kontos and V. Wilson, '"Their finest hour": older people, oral histories and the historical geography of social life', *Social and Cultural Geography*, 7:2 (2006), p. 154; T. Blokland, 'Bricks, mortar, memories: neighbourhood and networks in collective acts of remembering, *International Journal of Urban and Regional Research*, 25:2 (2001), p. 270; D. Vincent, *Bread, Knowledge and Freedom. A Study of Nineteenth Century Working Class Autobiography* (London and New York: Methuen, 1981), pp. 2, 9.

2 C. Waters, 'Representations of everyday life: L. S. Lowry and the landscape of memory in post-war Britain', *Representations*, 65 (1999), pp. 131, 135. See also, C. Waters, 'Autobiography, nostalgia, and the practices of working-class selfhood', in G. Behlmer and F. Leventhal (eds), *Singular Continuities: Tradition, Nostalgia, and Society in Modern Britain* (Stanford: Stanford University Press, 2000).

3 Vincent, *Bread, Knowledge and Freedom*, pp. 2, 9.

4 A. Kuhn, *An Everyday Magic: Cinema and Cultural Memory* (London and New York: I. B. Tauris, 2002), pp. 17, 33–4.

5 J. Shaw, 'Winning territory: changing place to change pace', in J. May and N. Thrift (eds), *Timespace: Geographies of Temporality* (London: Routledge, 2001), p. 129.

6 B. L. Q. Henriques, *Club Leadership* (London: Oxford University Press, 1933: 1943), p. 46.

7 Kuhn *An Everyday Magic*, pp. 33–4.

8 M. de Certeau, *The Practice of Everyday Life*, trans. S. F. Rendall (Berkeley, 1984), cited in A. Mayne and S. Lawrence, S., 'Ethnographies of place: a new urban research agenda', *Urban History*, 26:3 (1999), p. 331.

9 A. Curtin and D. Linehan, 'Where the boys are – teenagers, masculinity and a sense of place,', *Irish Geography*, 35:1 (2002), pp. 63–5; M. Mitterauer, *A History of Youth* (Oxford: Blackwell, 1992), p. 197; P. Thompson, 'The war with adults', *Oral History*, 3:2 (1975), p. 30. See also J. Butler, 'Performative acts and gender constitution: an essay in phenomenology and feminist theory', in K. Conboy, N. Medina and S. Stanbury (eds), *Writing the Body: Female Embodiment and Feminist Theory* (New York: Columbia University Press, 1997), pp. 410–17.

10 Recent studies have also suggested that contemporary sociology underestimated the 'importance of the physical environment to the way young people experience their lives'. T. Hall et al., *Locality, Biography and Youth in a Transforming Community*, full research report, ESRC end of award report, RES-000-23-0878, www.esrc.ac.uk/my-esrc/grants/RES-000-23-0878/read/reports, p. 1 (accessed January 2009).

11 For historical examinations of working-class neighbourhoods, see E. Ross, 'Women's neighbourhood sharing in London before World War One', *History Workshop*, 15:1 (1983), pp. 4–28; E. Ross, *Love and Toil: Motherhood in Outcast London, 1870–1918* (New York and Oxford, 1993; A. Davies, *Leisure, Gender and Poverty. Working Class Cultures in Salford and Manchester, 1900–1939* (Buckingham, 1992); A. Davies and S. Fielding (eds), *Workers' Worlds: Cultures and Communities in Manchester and Salford 1880–1939* (Manchester: Manchester University Press, 1992); M. Tebbutt, *Women's Talk? A Social History of 'Gossip' in Working Class Neighbourhoods, 1880–1960* (Aldershot: Scolar Press, 1995); Kuhn *An Everyday Magic*, p. 35.

12 K. D. M Snell, 'Gravestones, belonging and local attachment in England, 1700–2000', *Past and Present* 179:1 (2003), 97–179.

13 H. Watkin, *From Hulme All Blessings Flow* (Manchester: Neil Richardson, 1985), pp. 42–4.

14 C. Cameron, A. Lush and G. Meara, *Disinherited Youth* (Edinburgh: Carnegie United Kingdom Trust, 1943), p. 107. The research for *Disinherited Youth*, initiated by the Trustees of the Carnegie United Kingdom Trust, was compiled between 1936 and 1939, after concerns about high rates of unemployment among 18- to 21-year-old young men. It was the first official study of this age group.

15 J. Binnie, T. Edensor, J. Holloway, S. Millington and C. Young, Editorial, 'Mundane mobilities, banal travels', *Social and Cultural Geography*, 8:2 (April 2007), 165–7. See also J. Binnie, J. Holloway, S. Millington and C. Young, 'Mundane geographies: alienation, potentialities and practice', *Environment and Planning A*, 39:3 (2007), 515–20; B. Fincham, 'Bicycle messengers and the road to freedom', *Sociological Review*, 54:1 (2006), 208–222; P. Harrison, 'Making sense: embodiment and the sensibilities of the everyday' *Environment and Planning D: Society and Space*, 18:4 (2000), 497–517; D. McCormack, 'Diagramming practice and performance', *Environment and Planning D: Society and Space*, 23:1 (2005), 119–47; C. Pooley, J. Turnbull and M. Adams, 'The impact of new transport technologies on intra-urban mobility: a view from the past', *Environment and Planning A*, 38:2 (2006), 253–67; N. Thrift and S. French, 'The automatic production of space', *Transactions of the Institute of British Geographers*, 27:3 (2002), 309–35.

16 J. Springhall, *Coming of Age: Adolescence in Britain, 1860–1960* (Dublin: Gill and Macmillan, 1986), p. 139.

17 Thompson, 'The war with adults', p. 30.

18 H. Hendrick, *Images of Youth: Age, Class and the Male Youth Problem, 1880–1920* (Oxford: Oxford University Press, 1990), p. 129; McKibbin, R., *Classes and Cultures: England, 1918–1951* (Oxford: Oxford University Press, 1998: 2000), pp. 185–6.

19 Hendrick *Images of Youth*, p. 129.

20 Hendrick, *Images of Youth*, p. 18.

21 S. Humphries, *Hooligans or Rebels? An Oral History of Working-Class Childhood and Youth, 1889–1939* (Oxford: Basil Blackwell Ltd., 1981), p. 175; Davies, *Leisure, Gender and Poverty*, p. 352; Thompson, 'The war with adults'. p. 30.

22 B. Naughton, *Neither Use nor Ornament: A Memoir of Bolton: 1920s* (Newcastle upon Tyne: Bloodaxe Books, 1995), p. 113.

23 *The Boy* (August 1927), p. 4.

24 C. E. B. Russell and L. M. Russell, *Lads' Clubs: Their History, Organisation and Management* (London, A. & C. Black Ltd., 1932), p. 161; *Daily Mirror* (3 June 1939), p. 11.

25 Loafing had been associated with petty pilfering in the 1830s *Oxford English Dictionary*; J. R. Gillis, *Youth and History: Tradition and Change in European Age Relations, 1700–Present* (New York and London, Academic Press, 1974), p. 157.

26 A. E. Morgan, *The Needs of Youth. A Report Made to King George's Jubilee Trust Fund* (Oxford: Oxford University Press, 1939), pp. 193, 276.

27 Cameron, Lush and Meara (eds), *Disinherited Youth*, p. 107.

28 B. Griffiths, *Growing Up in Manchester* (Manchester: Didsbury Press, 1991), p. 13.

29 Manchester Studies Tapes, Ordsall Project, Tape 488. John Stainton, born 1917, Salford. Transcript, pp. 14, 15.

30 N. Kenyon, *I Belong to Bolton* (Manchester: Neil Richardson, 1989), p. 5.

31 G. Cross (ed.), *Worktowners at Blackpool: Mass-Observation and Popular Lesiure in the 1930s* (London: Routledge, 1990), p. 57.

32 See, for example, chapter 'Youths on the Street', in M. Childs, *Labour's Apprentices: Working Class Lads in Late Victorian and Edwardian England* (London: The Hambledon Press, 1992); Davies *Leisure, Gender and Poverty*, p. 96; Childs, *Labour's Apprentices*, pp. 98–9.

33 A. Paterson, *Across the Bridges* (London: Edward Arnold, 1912), p. 43.

34 S. F. Hatton, *London's Bad Boys* (London: Chapman & Hall Ltd., 1931), p. 40.

35 J. Kay, *The Chronicles of a Harpurhey Lad* (Manchester: Neil Richardson, 1990), pp. 74–77.

36 Humphries, *Hooligans or Rebels?* p. 122.

37 McKibbin, *Classes and Cultures*, p. 315. Humphries suggests many working-class boys and girls between 14 and 16 were 'indulging in sexual play with whoever they were lucky enough to "pick up" at parks, dances or on monkey runs'. S. Humphries, *A Secret World of Sex: Forbidden Fruit: The British Experience, 1900–1950* (London: Sidgwick and Jackson, 1988), p. 38.

38 A. Davies, 'Youth gangs, masculinity and violence in late Victorian Manchester and Salford', *Journal of Social History*, 32:2 (1998), 349–69. For a contemporary study of how young people's use of urban space is gendered, see Curtin and Linehan, 'Where the boys are', pp. 64, 65.

39 Curtin and Linehan, 'Where the boys are', p. 71; C. Heron, C., 'Boys will be boys: working class masculinities in the age of mass production', *International Labor and Working Class History*, 69:1 (2006), p. 22.

40 Naughton, *Neither Use nor Ornament*, p. 161.

41 B. Andrews, *Don't Fret My Lad: An Ashton Boyhood* (Manchester: Neil Richardson, 1987), pp. 64–5.

42 B. Naughton, *Saintly Billy: A Catholic Boyhood* (Oxford: Oxford University Press, 1989), p. 162.

43 The 'gang theme' occupied a central place in the sociology of youth, especially after the publication of Thrasher's study of Chicago youth gangs in 1927. C. Griffin, *Representations of Youth: The Study of Youth and Adolescence in Britain and America* (Cambridge, Polity Press, 1993), p. 22.

44 H. A. Secretan, *London below Bridges* (London: Geoffrey Bles, 1931), p. 73.

45 Humphries, *Hooligans or Rebels*, p. 178.

46 J. Jackson, *Under the Smoke. Salford Memories, 1922–1941* (Manchester: Neil Richardson, 1990), p. 17.

47 Morgan, *The Needs of Youth*, p. 202.

48 Hatton, *London's Bad Boys*, pp. 31, 3–40.

49 Hatton, *London's Bad Boys*, p. 40.

50 Secretan, *London below Bridges*, p. 73.

51 G. Dawson *Soldier Heroes: British Adventure, Empire and the Imagining of Masculinity* (London: Routledge, 1994); S. G., Jones, *Workers at Play: A Social and Economic History of Leisure, 1918–39* (London: Routledge and Kegan Paul, 1986), p. 80. See also,

K. Boyd, *Manliness and the Boys' Story Paper in Britain: A Cultural History, 1855–1940* (Basingstoke: Palgrave Macmillan, 2003).

52 J. Mackie (ed.), *The Edinburgh Cinema Enquiry* (Edinburgh, 1933, pp.14–18, cited in J. Richards, *The Age of the Dream Palace: Cinema and Society in Britain 1930–39* (London, Routledge and Kegan Paul, 1984), p. 69. The tastes of older middle-class boys were said to lean more towards 'mystery, travel and musical films'.

53 Kuhn, *An Everyday Magic*, pp. 100–1.

54 C. Burt, *The Young Delinquent* (London: University of London Press, 1925: 1931), p. 145.

55 Kuhn, *An Everyday Magic*, pp. 101, 103.

56 Jackson, *Under the Smoke*, p. 7.

57 J. Wynne, *Where's Mi Chunks, Mam? The Childhood of a Nobody in Particular. Salford Memories, 1930–38* (Manchester: Neil Richardson, 1997), p. 6.

58 Boyd, *Manliness and the Boys' Story Paper*, p. 23. See also K. Boyd, 'Knowing your place: the tension of manliness in boys' story papers, 1918–39', in M. Roper and J. Tosh (eds), *Manful Assertions: Masculinities in England since 1800* (London: Routledge, 1991); K. Boyd, 'Exemplars and ingrates: imperialism and the boys' story paper, 1880–1930', *Historical Research*, 67:163 (1994), 143–55.

59 Davies, *Leisure, Gender and Poverty*, p. 170.

60 H. E. O. James and F. T. Moore, 'Adolescent leisure in a working class district: Part II', *Occupational Psychology*, 18:1 (1944), 24–34.

61 Manchester Studies Tapes, John Stainton, p. 13.

62 Tameside Local Studies, James Hooley, Tape 604, Transcript, pp. 15–16.

63 *The Boy*, Autumn 1938, p. 12.

64 H. E. O. James, and F. T. Moore, 'Adolescent leisure in a working class district: Part I', *Occupational Psychology*, 14:3 (1940), pp. 143–4.

65 D. Fowler, *The First Teenagers: The Lifestyle of Young Wage-Earners in Inter-war Britain* (London, 1995), pp. 98–9; James and Moore, 'Adolescent leisure in a working class district: Part I', pp. 143–4; Boyd, *Manliness and the Boys' Story Paper*, p. 102. Sales were reaching 'vast proportions' by the late 1930s, when 'one of the largest producers of boys' fiction magazines' estimated weekly sales of five to six million copies 'in this class alone': Morgan, *The Needs of Youth*, pp. 233, 281.

66 Humphries, *Hooligans or Rebels*, p. 179.

67 Morgan, *The Needs of Youth*, p. 281.

68 Hatton, *London's Bad Boys*, pp. 70–2.

69 Humphries, *Hooligans or Rebels*, p. 177.

70 Humphries, *Secret World of Sex*, p. 142; E. Hague, *Streets away from Paradise: Reminiscences of a Stalybridge Lad* (Manchester: Neil Richardson, 1987), p. 52.

71 A. E. Morgan, *Young Citizen* (London: Penguin Books, 1943) p. 138.

72 Cross, *Worktowners*, p. 29.

73 J. Harley 'Report of an enquiry into the occupations, further education and leisure interests of a number of girl wage-earners from elementary and central schools in the Manchester district, with special reference to the influence of school training on their use of leisure (MEd dissertation, University of Manchester, 1937), p. 91.

74 *Ibid.*, p. 15; Morgan *The Needs of Youth*, p. 276.

75 Harley 'Report of an enquiry', p. 101.

76 Burt, *The Young Delinquent*, p. 90.
77 Wynne, *Where's Mi Chunks, Mam?* pp. 13, 16.
78 C. Royle, *This Was My Village: Boyhood Recollections of Flixton 1922–1938* (Manchester: Neil Richardson, 1994), p. 10.
79 Mrs E. Ager, Northampton Borough Council Oral History Project. Tape number T3/51, pp. 15–16; 'Diary' (20 July 1937), pp. 15–16.
80 W. Woodruff, *The Road to Nab End: An Extraordinary Northern Childhood* (London: Abacus Books, 2003), pp. 185–8.
81 Cameron, Lush and Meara (eds), *Disinherited Youth*, p. 108.
82 'Diary' (4 April 1937).
83 'Diary' (11 April 1937).
84 'Diary' (20 December 1936).
85 J. H. Armitage, *The Twenty Three Years, Or the Late Way of Life – And of Living. By The Exile*, Burnett Archive of Working-Class Autobiographies, University of Brunel (hereafter, Burnett Archive), pp. 172–4.
86 K. Woodward (ed.) *Identity and Difference* (London: Sage, 1997), p. 30.
87 Hatton, *London's Bad Boys*, p. 43–4.
88 C. Benninghaus, 'Mothers' toil and daughters' leisure: working-class girls and time in 1920s Germany', *History Workshop Journal* 50 (2000), 45–72.
89 E. Pettigrew, *Time to Remember: Growing up in Liverpool from 1912 onwards* (Liverpool: Toulouse, 1989), p. 34; The Cinema Culture in 1930s Britain (CCINTB) Archive, File 94.20, Townhead Oral Reminiscence.
90 Cross, *Worktowners*, p. 145.
91 J. Brooke, *The Dukinfield I Knew, 1906–1930* (Manchester: Neil Richardson, 1987), p. 42.
92 J. Carley, *Old Friends, Old Times, 1908–1938: Manchester Memories from the Diaries of Joe Carley* (Manchester: Neil Richardson, 1990), p. 38.
93 *Ibid.*, p. 38.
94 H. Taylor, *A Claim on the Countryside: A History of the British Outdoor Movement* (Edinburgh: Keele University Press, 1997), pp. 226–72; R. Holt, *Sport and the British: A Modern History* (Oxford: Clarendon Press, 1990), pp. 199–202. The growth of bus companies in the early 1920s played an important part in opening up travel opportunities for young people in outlying villages and small communities. T. R. Flintoff, *Friday the Thirteenth of May*, Burnett Archive, p. 26. Flintoff was born in Preston in 1904.
95 Watkin, *From Hulme All Blessings Flow*, pp. 42–4.
96 Jones, *Workers at Play*, pp. 189–90; P. W. Rickwood, 'Public enjoyment of the open countryside in England and Wales, 1919–1939', PhD thesis, University of Leicester, 1973, pp. 227–34; J. Burchardt, *Paradise Lost: Rural Idyll and Social Change since 1800* (London, New York: I. B. Tauris, 2002), p. 129.
97 Humphries, *Hooligans or Rebels?* 1988, p. 178.
98 Russell and Russell, *Lads' Clubs*, p. 113; S. B. Rowntree, *Poverty and Progress: A Second Social Survey of York* (London, Longmans, Green and Co., 1941, 1942), p. 398.
99 Murfin gives examples of girls in inter-war Cumbria who were not allowed to have bicycles, although their brothers were. L. Murfin, *Popular Leisure in the Lake Counties* (Manchester: Manchester University Press, 1990), p. 123.

100 Russell and Russell, *Manchester Boys*, p. 113; Taylor, *A Claim on the Countryside*, pp. 231–2; Holt, *Sport and the British*, p. 198.

101 R. Hoggart, *The Uses of Literacy* (London: Chatto and Windus, 1957), p. 329, cited in Holt, *Sport and the British*.

102 Family receipt from cycle agent, 12 July 1935.

103 D. C. Jones, *The Social Survey of Merseyside*, 3 vols (Liverpool: Liverpool University Press, 1934), Vol. III, pp. 218–19.

104 Jones, *Workers at Play*, pp. 65–6.

105 Cameron, Lush and Meara (eds), *Disinherited Youth*, p. 107.

106 Hatton, *London's Bad Boys*, p. 42.

107 *The Boy*, June 1931, p. 3.

108 *Ibid.*, pp. 8–11.

109 J. Loftus, *Lee Side*, Burnett Archive, p. 122.

110 J. Preston, *Memoirs of a Salford Lad* (Manchester: Neil Richardson, n.d.) pp. 14–15, 18, 27.

111 Loftus, *Lee Side*, pp. 123–5.

112 Cameron, Lush and Meara (eds), *Disinherited Youth*, p. 107.

113 M. Bunce, *The Countryside Ideal: Anglo-American Images of Landscape* (London: Routledge, 1994); H. Goodall, 'Telling country: memory, modernity and narratives in rural Australia', *History Workshop Journal*, 47 (1999), p. 165; T. Waddicor, *Memories of Hightown and Beyond*, Burnett Archive, p. 24.

114 R. Hoggart, *A Local Habitation* (Life and Times, Vol. 1: 1918–40) (Oxford: Oxford University Press, 1989), p. 32.

115 P. Jephcott, *Some Young People* (London: George Allen and Unwin, 1954), p. 58, quoted in C. Langhamer, *Women's Leisure in England, 1920–1960* (Manchester: Manchester University Press, 2000), p. 119; 'Diary' (11 October 1936).

116 'Diary' (30 December 1936).

117 'Diary' (30 August 1936).

118 'Diary' (6 September 1936).

119 'Diary' (26 April 1936).

120 'Diary' (11 October 1936).

121 McKibbin, *Classes and Cultures*, p. 364.

122 F. Pritchard, *East Manchester Remembered* (Manchester: Neil Richardson, 1989), p. 18.

123 'Diary' (2 October 1937).

124 H. Dorrell, *Falling Cadence: An Autobiography of Failure*, p. 43; P. Vere, *The Autobiography of a Working Man*, p. 2; Waddicor, *Memories of Hightown*, p. 24, all from the Burnett Archive; Rowntree, *Poverty and Progress*, p. 371.

125 *The Boy*, 8 March 1931, p. 176; September 1931, pp. 40–1; G. C. Hughes, *Shut the Mountain Gate*, Burnett Archive, p. 51.

126 Holt, *Sport and the British*, p. 199.

127 Cross, *Worktowners*, p. 151.

128 Holt, *Sport and the British*, pp. 198–9.

129 J. Bourke, *Working-Class Cultures in Britain, 1890–1960. Gender, Class and Ethnicity* (London and New York: Routledge, 1994), p. 143; Curtin and Linehan, 'Where the boys are', pp. 63, 65.

130 J. White, *The Worst Street in North London: Campbell Bunk, Islington, between the Wars* (London: Routledge and Kegan Paul, 1986), p. 161; K. V. Gough and M. Franch, 'Spaces of the street: socio-spatial mobility and exclusion of youth in Recife', *Childrens' Geographies*, 3:2 (2005), 149–166. Most of the youth interviewed in this contemporary Brazilian study wanted to stay in the neighbourhoods where they had grown up and spent their adolescence; K. Canning, 'Feminist history after the linguistic turn: historicizing discourse and experience', *Signs: Journal of Women in Culture and Society*, 19:2 (1994), 368–404.

131 White, *The Worst Street in North London*.

132 Andrews, Kearns, Kontos and Wilson, '"Their finest hour"', pp. 168, 169.

133 S. Alexander, 'Men's fears and women's work: responses to unemployment in London between the wars', *Gender and History*, 12: 2 (2000), p. 207.

134 J. A. Robinson, 'Autobiographical memory', in M. Gruneberg and P. Morris (eds), *Aspects of Memory* (London and New York, 1978, 1992), p. 224.

135 For a contemporary comparison of young people's relationship with place in Northampton, see H. Matthews and M. Limb, *Exploring the 'fourth environment': young people's use of place and views on their environment: full report on research activities and results*, SN 4076, www.esds.ac.uk/findingData/snDescription.asp?sn=4076 (accessed January 2009).

136 J. Davidson and C. Milligan, 'Embodying emotion sensing space: introducing emotional geographies', *Social & Cultural Geography*, 5:4 (2004), p. 526.

Conclusion

Being boys opened with the regenerative significance that youth assumed after the First World War, and focused on how ex-soldiers sought new meanings in reformulating ideas of manliness and masculinity for the post-war boys' club movement. Valorising the manly potential of working-class boys at a time when women's growing visibility in society seemed to be making masculinity more vulnerable and uncertain represented the desire of an older generation to maintain the values of 'traditional' manliness. These preoccupations with moulding working-class boys and young men into 'appropriate' forms of masculinity were in tension with the relaxed models of masculinity which were assuming increasing prominence in commercial popular culture. All had implications for how working-class boys defined and were expected to define themselves, and this book has attempted to explore the complex connections between representations and experience, moving between adult perceptions and the perspective of an individual boy such as Les, whose mundane chronicling of the everyday not only contrasts with the rhetorical constructions of earlier chapters but also illustrates how the contingent, varied nature of youthful masculinities defies easy generalisations.[1]

The challenge of this study has been to examine the leisure lives of working-class boys and young men from new perspectives and to explore less familiar areas of youthful masculinity, which is why some significant aspects of male leisure, such as sport, have received less attention. This era was one in which working-class young people's engagement with commercial leisure was limited by their broader financial responsibilities in the household economy. Yet, although non-commercial leisure pursuits still dominated their daily leisure lives, new influences were infiltrating these traditional expectations and behaviours. As has been suggested, exposure to more relaxed social and emotional codes and models of personal behaviour through the popular press and commercial entertainment subtly influenced the self-image, sense of self and anxieties of working-class boys and young men, particularly during the 1930s, when the mass media's presence extended significantly. New visual forms not only signified the growing commodification of the female body but also helped to shape male self-consciousness and young men's sensitivity to their own body image and fashion. Sexualised leisure spaces such as the dance floor offered working-class young men novel opportunities to perform, yet also introduced new anxieties and uncertainties, while the geography of working-class localities shaped the formation of male social identity in different ways, particularly through walking and cycling, deepening and extending more traditional attachments to place. Taking leisure as a theme has offered opportunities to examine examples of self-shaping, ingenuity and creativity different from those available in the constricting age hierarchies of many work-places and in more familiar leisure activities associated with working-class boys and young men which have received greater scholarly attention. Leisure activities were not discrete interests experienced in isolation from each other, but a mesh of informal, commercial, individual and collective, private and public experiences, as is very apparent in Les's diaries.

Public certainties, private doubts

Learning to suppress emotion, the value of silence and avoiding being seen as vulnerable were important lessons of boyhood, and potentially effeminising forms of masculinity such as showing excess feeling was expected to be confined to very specific contexts, such as winning or losing in sport.[2] The new leisure settings and social behaviours which developed in the inter-war years consequently brought anxiety and confusion to working-class boys who were unused to mixing with girls socially and who had a strong sense of the otherness of the female; uncertainties which were exacerbated by lack of guidance within families, from peers or older males, including fathers, to whom this new leisure world was largely unfamiliar. The protective support of peers was important during adolescence, although these groups could be both inclusive and exclusive.[3] Boys like Harry Dorrell recalled meeting up with friends in his father's allotment shed to swap 'dirty stories' and talk about other boys in their street who were not their mates and not in their group; 'often enough being nasty about them'.[4] This kind of scrutiny was well expressed in male sensitivity to peer-group perceptions of appearance. Much of the 'strutting and swaggering' display which characterised the 'gangster imitation' of working-class boys seems to have been 'posing' directed at their male peers, and they remained on their guard against ambivalent or hostile responses to any perceptions of over-stylishness.[5] The desire for advice in dealing with uncertainties which could not be shared with friends, however, was apparent in the letters to advice columns, although these queries were very partial and had little effect on behaviour more generally. The tough, unsentimental public face of masculinity that was expected of working-class boys eschewed 'femininity' and 'female traits', as did work-place narratives based on romantic and heroic notions of hard manliness 'earned' through rough talk, aggression and 'physical prowess' which were particularly common in the industrial trades. Male-dominated work-places generally were no setting for sensitivity, since 'any weak spot' was likely to be 'immediately picked up and played upon'.[6] Self-regulation and self-surveillance played an important part in learning to be a man and avoiding vulnerability, since most working-class boys experienced violence, real or implied, at some point. Gorbals-raised Glasser grew 'up with violence' which 'simmered and bubbled and boiled over in street and close, outside the pubs, at the dance halls', and in gang raids from neighbouring areas.[7] Other boys experienced lower levels of discomfort and anxiety, and learned to negotiate their masculinities in many different ways, as in the case of body-building, which could be a useful defensive strategy for those who felt they failed to measure up to the expectations and physical ideals of 'dominant masculinity'.[8] These lessons of survival were learned early in life, as Richard Hoggart found to his cost on transferring to a 'rough' school in Hunslet, where he was immediately labelled an outsider and physically and verbally abused by boys who were much tougher than him. 'Without consciously working it out', he recognised the need to establish himself in some way, and survived by creating 'an invisible ring' around himself, joking and making his opponents laugh.[9] James Ward, from a deprived community in North Shields, gained acceptance in a new neighbourhood by accepting a challenge to fight a boy who had a new set of boxing gloves. Despite his being badly beaten, 'The word got round that I was "A Good Lad", and friendship came easy.'[10]

The resonance of sporting metaphors and narratives for how boys learned to cope with individual frailties was enhanced in this era of mass marketing by the 'human interest' emphases of the press, which, preoccupied with 'individual personalities and performances', helped to transform national sporting heroes into significant new male 'fantasy figures' whose aura of 'male virility' appealed strongly to many working-class boys.[11] Glasser unusually articulates the role which such figures could play in the lives of working-class boys and the tremulous balance of public revelation and unspoken uncertainties:

> most of us were not deeply self-regarding. To formulate one's concerns clearly, let alone decide what would cure them, was beyond us. Instead we dealt in image. In our group under the hot showers someone mentioned a folk hero – Benny Lynch the boxer, Johnny Weissmuller, Olympic swimming champion and screen Tarzan, Ronald Colman. Don't you think he was great when he . . .?' – mentioning an attribute he wanted to copy, hoping for the others' approval so that he would

have the confidence to attempt it. There would follow a discussion in minute detail, on whether the hero's behaviour had been admirable or not, which facets of his personality it expressed, and what we each would have done in his place. At the same time, secretly, we chewed over our private doubts.[12]

The growing popularity of 'masculinised' sports such as boxing and football in the inter-war years made them an increasingly important benchmark by which masculinity was judged. Even men little interested in such activities had to learn how to express some enthusiasm for them, and sport remained a singularly male space in which to vent noise, enthusiasm and feeling.[13] Sportsmen were not, of course, the only 'fantasy heroes' available to young men in the press, and film stars offered them 'a master-class in the arts of sex appeal and charisma' which deserves closer examination, given anxieties about effeminacy and fears of humiliation by peers.[14] Working-class boys and young men took great care in negotiating emerging etiquettes of social relations and 'commercially constructed strategies of glamour', for fear of unsettling the delicate balance between appropriate masculinity and stylish, 'feminised' modernity. How the boundaries between appropriate and inappropriate behaviour were policed by peers and by adults, boys' consciousness of physical differences, their understandings of the clothed and unclothed body and the social codes and norms which governed this self-policing are all important if we are to understand how these were fashioned and embodied in ways which were socially acceptable. Expectations of 'hard' masculinity limited the expression of heterosexual male self-creation, notably in relation to appearance, although, as we saw in Chapter 3, despite their spending less time on their personal appearance than their female counterparts, ingenious attention to style among even the poorest suggests an understated male fashion consciousness which is worth greater consideration, particularly as mass commercialisation and cultural standardisation made appearance an increasingly important signifier of cultural status. Changes in the fashion and cosmetics industry certainly allowed more explicitly self-conscious identities to be shaped outside the cultural mainstream by gay young men, who were used to negotiating space and identity across a continuum of shifting codes from subtle to flamboyant expressions of effeminacy; easiest in London, although also apparent in social scenes around pubs and clubs in towns and cities like Manchester, Liverpool, Brighton and Blackpool.[15] A series of high-profile prosecutions for homosexuality in the 1930s, which made effeminate appearance a popular theme with newspapers, are, however, an indication of their implications for other male identities. The press's emphasis upon these supposed threats to the nation's youth was part of broader trends whereby the fluidity of bodies and sexualities apparent in the 1920s was being replaced by greater orthodoxy. This was apparent in the growing commodification of female sexuality, which, in culturally reinforcing traditional gender stereotypes,[16] helped to make heterosexual boys and young men more self-conscious not only about particular types of clothing but also about the sexually compromising overtones of 'expressive' relationships and personal disclosure between males, reinforcing the taboos which continue to stop teenage boys admitting their fears and frailties.[17]

Generations in transition

Older influences and expectations mediated the novelty of mass culture in many different ways in the 1920s and 1930s, when much of British society comprised people whose outlook, shaped in the late-Victorian and Edwardian periods, cast a particular shadow over the interests and experiences of the young.[18] Working-class young people, sharing much of their parents' cultural outlook, were also sensitive to their history, as was apparent in Bolton cinema replies which expressed concern about the 'sad and unpleasant memories' that war films were likely to bring back to the older generation.[19] It was not unusual for those in their teens, however, to complain about family tensions arising from the unwillingness of older parents to listen to their views.[20] Despite evidence of the greater acceptability of domesticated masculinities, cramped living conditions meant that these were inevitably shaped by a range of factors such as the family dynamics of other siblings, the intrusion of domestic tasks and fathers' expectations of spatial dominance in the home. These factors, together with the greater emotional intensity of smaller families, could, as some adolescents themselves observed, leave them feeling desperate for 'breathing space'.[21] Such 'generational skirmishes' were particularly noted among educated and politicised young people, whose views divided them from their parents and communities, as Hoggart noted when he observed that 'almost every working-class boy' who went to grammar school found himself 'chafing against his environment during adolescence'.[22]

Hoggart's upbringing and own teens in the inter-war years (he was born in 1918) are very suggestive of these generational and emotional pressures and deserve consideration because they provide a rather different perspective to that of his own influential analysis of teenage culture in the 1950s, not least because of the influence of older adults in his upbringing. Both his parents died before he was 8, when he was separated from his siblings and taken in by his grandmother, becoming, in effect, a single child in a household which included two aunts and an uncle, all of whom 'seemed old' when he went to live with them, despite being only in their thirties and forties.[23] His sense of childhood displacement is hinted at in *The Uses of Literacy*, where he suggests how the clever working-class boy, even at elementary school, was, 'from as early as the age of eight', to some extent 'set apart'.[24] These feelings of separation were subsequently reinforced by his scholarship to grammar school, where he took time to develop a 'carapace' and had a 'nervous breakdown' at the end of his second year there.[25] Hoggart was emotionally close to his grandmother, but other aspects of his home life were not so sustaining, especially as the whole family was constantly on edge with the 'thunderously unpleasant' atmosphere to which his aunt Ethel's 'black' moods gave rise. Attracting 'plenty' of his aunt's ire in his early teens, he would withdraw into his homework at the living-room table, 'sick to the pit of his stomach' whenever a row started.[26] *The Uses of Literacy* has been notably criticised for attributing an 'emotional sameness' to working-class people, but its intimations of loss imply an emotional vulnerability, the 'sense of a bruised consciousness', especially in adolescence, which becomes more apparent in his autobiographical work.[27] This was well expressed in reflections on staying with his Aunt Annie after her marriage, which describe a pleasant release of tension, 'the lack of certain types of nervous strain, especially that encouraged by fear of the next outburst, the lack of a sense of old to middle-aged individuals almost filling the place'.[28]

In the 1950s, *The Uses of Literacy* evoked a more authentic pre-war working-class community relatively untouched by commercial culture, which Hoggart believed was becoming debased by the importation of American cultural values and having particular effects on the young. His adolescence was, however, very different from that of boys who left school at 14, and rarely intrudes directly into *The Uses of Literacy*, other than in a generalised sense of the scholarship boy's separation 'from the boys' groups outside the home', 'progressively cut off from the ordinary life of his group', playing 'little in the streets', 'no longer a full member of the gang' which clustered 'round the lamp-posts in the evening', his 'sexual growth' 'perhaps delayed' as childhood gave way to manhood.[29] Hoggart's autobiography is more forthcoming about the personal experiences which clearly shaped these earlier observations, describing how, on starting grammar school at 11, he 'turned inwards' from the streets, staying in each night doing his homework, or occasionally called for, when homework was finished, by a boy from his school 'who lived in an alien area about half a mile away'.[30] Hoggart was 'at great pains to play down the American mass produced origins of the popular music enjoyed by the working class audiences of his childhood', yet the radio, which was the main source for most people's listening, played little part in his own upbringing.[31] He unusually attended an early-evening religious service until 'well into' his teens, and the cinema and dance hall, which loomed so large in the lives of many working-class young people in the 1930s, are hardly mentioned in *The Uses of Literacy*, although his description of teenage girls in the 1950s, with their 'thrice weekly visits to the pictures, the "Palais", "Mecca" and "Locarno"' could just as easily have applied to the decade before the war.

Les, of the same age as Hoggart, would undoubtedly have recognised the texture of working-class neighbourhoods and relationships which Hoggart so brilliantly captures, despite their northern setting. Les's diary of a small-town adolescence suggests similarly closely woven connections, consolidated by family relationships and friendship networks, reinforced by a conservative attachment to place. But if the resilience of older patterns is apparent in Les's diaries, so too are glimpses of modern influences like the cinema, popular music, the use of American words and references to popular newspapers and magazines. Much certainly remained the same. Traditional social and moral expectations of behaviour and appearance continued to restrain the lives of young people, especially those of young women, in working-class districts, where the leisure lifestyles of young men retained many continuities with the late nineteenth century. What Hoggart neglects, however, is the extent to which his adolescent contemporaries were on the cusp of older and newer trends, lingering in the shadows of pre-war conventions yet pulled towards the more conspicuous modern lifestyles which would develop with post-war affluence.[32] The adolescents and young people of the 1930s may in many ways more accurately be seen as a transitional generation in a transitional decade as they negotiated old assumptions, changing attitudes and the growth of mass leisure industries. The intermingling of old and new, informal and commercial in these cultural experiences was a more dynamic and complex process than is sometimes acknowledged, just as the emergence of the Teddy Boys in the 1950s testified as much to the continuing significance of many traditional working-class attitudes as to modernist identities of consumption.[33]

Just as regional variations have been overlooked in the youth culture of the late 1940s and 1950s, many similar gaps remain in our understanding of youth and leisure in the 1920s and 1930s. Not only did the commercial leisure cultures of large cities and areas of heavy unemployment differ significantly, but, as Todd urges, there is a need too for more studies on Wales, and particularly of Scotland, with its distinctive legislative and educational systems.[34] Urban experiences of the kind to which Hoggart refers were very different from those of young people in rural communities, in small towns and on new council housing estates, to which almost a fifth of British workers were rehoused during this period. How young people's experiences of leisure were inflected by ethnic and religious cultures deserves greater consideration, as do distinctions between large cities and the more localised youth styles which were developing around urban dance halls and clubs towards the end of the 1930s. The unemployed youth of the inter-war years also deserve their own study. Many were severely limited in their engagement with commercial leisure consumption until the late 1930s, and for the more isolated, unemployment could have severe psychological consequences. Others actively and creatively coped with the stress of unemployment, through politics and activities such as walking, hill climbing and self-help initiatives. Despite the glamorous leisure developments of the 1930s, boys' leisure cultures remained strongly defined by poverty, and the poor and unemployed, for all their resourcefulness, were largely excluded from them.

Representing youth

There were many contradictions in how youth was represented and experienced in this period, as the scope of adult influence through 'official and unofficial bodies' extended over young people between the 1900s and 1940s. These developments were overwhelmingly preoccupied with boys, although, as we have seen, the shifting meanings of femininity and the 'female' were a significant shaping force.[35] Debates over young men and approaches to their behaviour were marked by significant differences. The growth of professional involvement in and authority over young people produced new, sometimes contradictory, discourses of adolescence which were marked by benevolence and coercion. Government and judicial 'theories of discipline' informed a 'punishment' discourse which was heavily preoccupied with constraining and repressing negative 'male energy', for the good of both the individual and the nation.[36] The emphases of psychology and medicine were more sympathetic. The 'new psychology' recognised not only the significance of adolescent sexuality but also how personal and social frustrations drove anti-social behaviour in otherwise healthy boys; many youth workers' commitment to working-class potential reflected the dominance of such debates in the treatment of juvenile delinquency.[37] Psychological discourse which discouraged corporal punishment and promoted the establishment of child-guidance clinics towards the end of the 1920s signified growing professional acceptance that treating young people's behavioural problems was a question not just of discipline and regulation but of understanding the individual's 'psychological make-up'; an approach also apparent among many advisers on the problems pages of popular newspapers, although there were considerable gaps between theory and what was practised in homes and schools.[38]

Psychology, new leisure patterns, consumption and the media were all giving youth a 'distinctiveness' which would significantly influence how young people of the post-war period were understood, although this was at a time when most working-class young people themselves had little sense of a common social or cultural identity, other than as members of organised youth associations, or within political parties and the outdoor movement. Organisations like the BBC were becoming more attuned to adolescence's separations from childhood. *Children's Hour* had been an important part of the its programme planning since its inception, but by the end of the 1920s programmes for adolescents were being considered, and towards the end of the 1930s, more experimental approaches such as discussion programmes were being developed as fears of totalitarianism emphasised the importance of political education and education for citizenship.[39] Charles Madge thought the very success of organised youth groups among 16- to 20-year-olds in Germany and Italy was making young people in Britain more 'age-group conscious' and aware of the right to express their independent views.[40] Most young people found the BBC's approach to adolescent programming too stuffy and middle-aged, preferring the informal, American delivery of commercial radio stations such as Luxembourg, especially after 1935, when reception improved.[41] The BBC's output of popular music was similarly restrained, particularly on Sundays, given religious sensitivities over the Sabbath. The musical vacuum was filled for many adults and young people by a commercial programming mix of variety shows, dance bands and 'personality showcases'. Similar trends would continue after the war, when the BBC's refusal to recognise rock 'n' roll did much to encourage the popularity of juke boxes, which became an important signifier of post-war delinquency.[42]

Coexistence and divergence

If young people lacked a distinctive sense of cultural identity, by the end of the 1930s separate interests and cultural habits were clearly emerging among working-class young people and diverging to some degree from those of their elders, even if still largely focused on adult role models and lacking a strong sense of shared identity. This coexistence of 'traditional' and 'more modern styles' was very apparent in the popular music so often associated with Americanisation.[43] The standardising effects of expanding commercialised leisure opportunities allowed people in all parts of the country to share 'similar cultural experiences', yet these were shaped in particular ways by local, ethnic and religious cultures.[44] Popular music, whose themes were increasingly youthful and romantic, helped to spread American slang and idioms.[45]

In British popular music, however, comic approaches camouflaged the prevalence of sexual allusions and helped to fashion a cosy, domesticated version of British popular culture which mediated the effects of Americanisation. British dance music was more restrained, less spontaneous than its American counterpart.[46] Most young people preferred the 'more lavish settings', 'technique and polish' of 'slick' American films to the stilted, more slow-moving pace of their British equivalents, yet not all young film-goers liked to hear an American accent.[47]

Secondary education and adult education gave working-class autodidacts in their teens and twenties cultural tastes which became a central part of their class identity. New cultural opportunities in the 1930s, combined with growing emphases on individualism, allowed them to distinguish themselves from their working-class peers by expressing a 'lack of ordinariness' and sense of difference.[48] This was apparent in the strong following that 'hot music' (jazz and swing) had among 'aspiring lower-middle-class intellectuals' in the 1930s, who affirmed a distinctive cultural space and status as discerning listeners rather than dancers, their passion limited to enthusiasts because of a musicians' ban on American artists in Britain.[49] Gramophones, often played in specialist clubs and societies, were more important than the radio in spreading new music from the United States, as the American jazz musician Valaida Snow observed when she visited Britain in the mid 1930s and met 'dozens of English boys' who knew more about jazz than the people who played it, through listening to gramophone records.[50] By the end of the 1930s, many young listeners were increasingly knowledgeable about differences between 'genres and artists' of popular music, their preferences diverging more distinctly from those of older generations. Musical tastes more specifically associated with young people were difficult to develop on a large scale until after the Second World War, however, when higher wages and less pressure to contribute to the household budget allowed more to be spent on records, and better housing conditions provided more comfortable bedrooms in which to listen to them away from parents. For the working-class boys and young men of the inter-war years, musical passions had more scope for development outside the home, and localised pockets of particular musical enthusiasms in different parts of the country deserve greater examination. In Liverpool, for example, seafarers and stewards from the White Star Line, Cunard and the Canadian Pacific Railways brought back not only gramophones from the United States but 'the latest American fashions', together with sheet music, records and musical instruments, evidence of the significance of ports and the role of trans-Atlantic seafaring in channelling popular cultural styles.[51]

Eighteen- to twenty-five-year-olds were probably more significant than younger adolescents in shaping inter-war youth culture; the different age transitions of adolescence were nevertheless all informed by the cultural changes which were generally unsettling 'standards, values and conduct'.[52] The press rarely targeted a specific 'teen' market, but was increasingly sensitive to the distinctiveness of youth interests, particularly by the 1930s, with growing differentiation between story papers aimed at adolescent boys and the 'more adult' reading matter of those in their mid to late teens.[53] Rising living standards and levels of disposable income in better-off working-class households opened up leisure opportunities for boys with quieter inclinations. Naughton, with a rather 'pooterish stereotype', distinguished adolescent acquaintances from better-off streets than his own, who never took part in the 'in the arguments and leg-pulling of the street corner' but were more interested in hobbies such as toy railways and collecting stamps.[54] Many specialist publications were being aimed at such youthful audiences, including magazines about celebrities, the cinema, hobbies and motor-bikes, a potent symbol of independent mobility whose iconic significance would greatly increase after the Second World War.[55]

Being Boys started with the notion that emphasising the problematic nature of working-class young males reinforces perceptions of the insensitive male adolescent and neglects the complexity of transitions to adulthood, which often slipped, in one individual, between inhibition and exhibition, rough and respectable, 'acceptable' and 'unacceptable' behaviour.[56] It has suggested how these ambivalent areas of youthful masculinity, the uncertainties of peer relationships, emotional vulnerabilities and fears of humiliation, shifting anxieties about changing social relations, personal relationships and the body were nuanced in many different ways across the 1920s and 1930s.[57] This fluidity and ambiguity, more discernible in the individual and everyday than in the communal and exceptional, suggests how being a boy and becoming a man encompassed more than collectivity, resistance and challenge and could also involve ambivalence, diffidence and loneliness. The historical difficulties of understanding how identity develops during adolescence are complicated by gender and differing degrees of individual confidence and maturity.[58] Class, sexuality, poverty, religion, ethnicity, temperament, siblings, age position within the family, all inflected experiences of youthful masculinity and influenced the delicate negotiations between its 'public' and 'private' faces. As Chapter 4 suggested, the experiences of different youth cohorts were shaded in different ways across the 1920s and 1930s. The leisure opportunities of working-class boys and young men were more varied than those of their female counterparts, and young men, regardless of class, had more freedoms than young women. There were internal differences within the working class.[59] Adolescent masculinities, like the male identities of working-class communities, were intricately textured by occupational, local and regional differences.[60] Les's leisure story, with which we started, illustrates how intimately family, social and leisure relationships were intertwined, challenging easy assumptions about atomised working-class 'communities', intimating the complex networks of family, siblings and peers which underpinned adolescence. One version of many different adolescent realities, his story illustrates the diversity and contingency of adolescent transition, the importance of addressing individual as well as collective identities if we are to understand the personal sensitivities which also shaped working-class boys and young men. Conformity to peer pressure and collective identities was undoubtedly strong in the lives of working-class boys and young men, yet the 'private', personal masculinities revealed in diaries, autobiographies, memoirs and letters of the sort used in this book provide valuable alternative readings, hints of the quieter, more uncertain areas in which adolescent identities were also made.[61] Experiences of this sort not only need greater integration into histories of youth and leisure but also contribute a less familiar perspective to broader historical narratives of how the masculinities of adolescent boys have been shaped and constructed. In doing so, they have considerable contemporary resonance for how working-class boys and young men should be treated if we are to understand them better, and if they are to learn less damaging ways of relating to each other, and to others.

Notes

1 S. Winlow, *Badfellas: Crime, Tradition and New Masculinities* (Oxford: Berg, 2001).

2 Sporting ability expressed personal power and gave social acceptability to many marginalised by ethnicity or religion. Boxing clubs for Jewish youth were very popular in London's East End.

3 The different educational experiences of boys who went to single-sex schools and those who experienced mixed schooling are worth comparative examination.

4 H. Dorrell, *Falling Cadence: An Autobiography of Failure*, Burnett Archive of Working Class Autobiographies, University of Brunel (hereafter Burnett Archive), pp. 22–3.

5 A. Kuhn, *An Everyday Magic: Cinema and Cultural Memory* (London and New York: I. B. Tauris, 2002), pp. 109–10; W. Martino and M. Pallotta-Chiarolli, *So What's a Boy? Addressing Issues of Masculinity and Schooling* (Maidenhead: Open University Press, 2003), p. 3.

6 H. Fagan, *An Autobiography*, Burnett Archives, p. 50.

7 R. Glasser, 'Growing up in the Gorbals', in *The Ralph Glasser Omnibus* (Edinburgh: Black and White Publishing, 2006, first published by Chatto and Windus, 1986), p. 68.

8 Martino and Pallotta-Chiarolli, *So What's a Boy?* pp. 17, 20, 26.

9 R. Hoggart, *A Local Habitation*, Vol. 1, *Life and Times 1918–40* (Oxford: Oxford University Press, 1989), p. 141.

10 J. R. Ward, *Low Street Boy*, Burnett Archive, p. 22. Ward was born in 1917.

11 A. Bingham, A., *Gender, Modernity and the Popular Press in Britain* (Oxford: Oxford University Press, 2004), pp. 217–18, 222. On the need for more research on 'heroic' icons, see M. Jones, 'What should historians do with heroes? Reflections on nineteenth and twentieth century Britain', *History Compass*, 5:2 (2007), 439–54.

12 Glasser, 'Growing up in the Gorbals', pp. 55–6.

13 Just as not all young men liked sport, so some working-class young women demonstrated a knowledge which surprised contemporary commentators. One of the 'dirty girls' whom Mass Observation described, for example, all the while she was 'muzzling' at the observer 'with her head, and crossing her leg over his thigh', talked about 'football – very technically', so that he had 'to confirm her opinion' about 'chaps' he had 'never heard of'. This could, of course, have been a well-tried courtship ploy, although the young woman also told the observer that she went to the 'Worktown all-in-wrestling', and despite knowing it was all a put up job, still liked it. G. Cross (ed.), *Worktowners at Blackpool: Mass-Observation and Popular Leisure in the 1930s* (London: Routledge, 1990), p. 165.

14 Bingham, *Gender*, pp. 224–5, 228–9.

15 In 1930s Britain, suede shoes were supposedly 'a sure sign of deviancy'. Particular colours also had homosexual connotations. Havelock Ellis believed gay men had a preference for green, recalling, perhaps, the green carnations worn by aesthetes and rent boys in the late nineteenth century: S. Cole, *'Don We Now Our Gay Apparel': Gay Men's Dress in the Twentieth Century* (Oxford: Berg, 2000), pp. 62, 68, 79. In the late 1940s, Mass Observation identified 'pale blue' as a favoured 'trade colour' for socks, ties and pullovers among those in its study group on 'Abnormality' and 'Sexual

Behaviour'. Mass-Observation Sex Survey, Sexual Behaviour, Box 4, File E, Appendix 1, Abnormality. 6.7.49; M. Houlbrook, ' "The man with the powder puff" in inter-war London', *The Historical Journal*, 50:1 (2007), pp. 161–2; M. Cook, 'Queer conflicts: love, sex and war, 1914–1967', in M. Cook (ed.), with R. Mills, R. Trumbach and H. G. Cocks, *A Gay History of Britain: Love and Sex between Men since the Middle Ages* (Oxford and Westport, CT: Greenworld Publishing, 2007), pp. 154–5.

16 P. N. Stearns, Review essay, 'Informalization and contemporary manners: the Wouters studies', *Theory and Society*, 36:4 (2007), p. 379.

17 Contemporary interviews with adolescent boys about their difficulties 'expressing emotions' have highlighted homophobia as a major obstacle in developing 'more nurturing and expressive relationships with each other': Martino and Pallotta-Chiarolli *So What's a Boy?* p. 195.

18 J. Stevenson, *British Society, 1914–45* (London: Penguin Books, 1984: 1990), p. 17.

19 J. Richards and D. Sheridan (eds), *Mass-Observation at the Movies* (London and New York: Routledge and Kegan Paul, 1987), pp. 48, 51, 89.

20 C. Madge, A. W. Coysh, G. Dixon and I. Madge, *To Start You Talking* (London: The Pilot Press, 1945), p. 141.

21 *Ibid.*

22 J. Rose, *The Intellectual Life of the British Working Classes* (New Haven, CT and London: Yale Nota Bene, 2002), pp. 144–5; M. Pittock, 'Richard Hoggart and the Leavises', *Essays in Criticism*, 60:1 (2010), pp. 61, 64.

23 Hoggart, *A Local Habitation*, p. 57.

24 For similar discomfort by a working-class scholarship boy, see L. Halliwell, *Seats in All Parts: Half a Lifetime at the Movies* (London: Granada, 1985), pp. 81–2. See also, G. Creeber, 'Dennis Potter and Richard Hoggart, scholarship boys', in V. W. Gras and J. R. Cook (eds), *The Passion of Dennis Potter: International Collected Essays* (New York: St. Martin's Press, 2000), p. 35.

25 Hoggart, *A Local Habitation*, pp. 171–2.

26 *Ibid.*, pp. 18, 20, 17–28.

27 C. Steedman, *Landscape for a Good Woman* (London: Virago, 1980: 2000), pp. 11–12; Hoggart, *The Uses of Literacy* (London: Penguin books in association with Chatto and Windus, 1957, 1962), p. 326.

28 Hoggart, *A Local Habitation*, p. 111.

29 Hoggart, *The Uses of Literacy*, pp. 294–5, 298.

30 Hoggart, *A Local Habitation*, pp. 29, 86–8, 101, 124, 156.

31 *Ibid.*, p. 172. Hoggart's family did not acquire a radio until 'quite late'.

32 Hoggart, *The Uses of Literacy*, p. 50.

33 A. Horn, *Juke Box Britain: Americanisation and Youth Culture, 1945–60* (Manchester: Manchester University Press, 2009).

34 S. Todd, 'Flappers and factory lads: youth and youth culture in inter-war Britain', *History Compass*, 4:4 (2006), p. 723.

35 For the shifting relationship between masculinity and femininity, see J. Tosh, 'What should historians do with masculinity?' in R. Shoemaker and M. Vincent (eds) *Gender and History in Western Europe* (Cambridge: Cambridge University Press, 1998).

36 D. Thom, 'The healthy citizen of empire or juvenile delinquent? Beating and mental

health in the UK', in M. Gijswijt-Hofstra and H. Marland (eds), *Cultures of Child Health in Britain and the Netherlands in the Twentieth Century* (Amsterdam and New York: Rodopi, 2003), pp. 192, 193.

37 *Ibid.*, pp. 195, 196.

38 The use of corporal punishment by magistrates' courts was declining. About 2,000 cases per year before the First World War had fallen to about 170 per year before the Second World War. H. Cunningham, *The Invention of Childhood* (London: BBC Books, 2006), p. 201. In 1948, magistrates lost the power to inflict the birch. J. Middleton, 'The experience of corporal punishment in schools, 1890–1940', *History of Education*, 37:2 (2008), 253–75; Rose, *Intellectual Life*, p. 168.

39 *The Boy* (February 1928), pp. 5, 22; *ibid.* (April 1929), p. 88; A. Briggs, *The History of Broadcasting in the United Kingdom*, Vol. 1, *The Birth of Broadcasting* (Oxford: Oxford University Press, 1995), p. 236; see D. Cardiff, 'The serious and the popular: aspects of the evolution of style in the radio talk 1928–1939', *Media, Culture and Society*, 2:29 (1980), 29–47. The politicising effects of the Depression, unemployment, the rise of fascism, distrust in capitalism and interest in Marxism are apparent in students who went to university between 1932 and 1939, whom Simon describes as a 'very specific generation'. B. Simon, 'The student movement in England and Wales during the 1930s', *History of Education*, 16:3 (1987), 189–203, republished in B. Simon, *The State and Educational Change: Essays in the History of Education and Pedagogy* (London: Lawrence and Wishart, 1994), pp. 109, 111.

40 Madge et al., *To Start You Talking*, p. 5.

41 The main reception area for Radio Normandie (set up in 1931) was in southern England. Radio Luxembourg (established in 1933) attracted most listeners in working-class areas of North-East England and Wales. J. J. Nott, *Music for the People: Popular Music and Dance in Inter-war Britain* (Oxford: Oxford University Press, 2002), p. 73; R. McKibbin, *Classes and Cultures: England 1918–51* (Oxford: Oxford University Press, 1998), p. 463; A. Crisell, *An Introductory History of British Broadcasting* (London: Routledge, 2002), pp. 51–2.

42 D. Hebdige, *Hiding in the Light: On Images and Things* (London: Routledge, 2002), p. 55; Horn, *Juke Box Britain*, pp. 50, 83, 188–9. The BBC's inflexibility and the dominance of major record labels on Radio Luxembourg's post-war broadcasting schedules encouraged the emergence of commercial off-shore 'pirate' radio stations, such as Radio Caroline in 1964. J. Curran, *Media and Power* London: Routledge, 2002, p. 21.

43 Nott, *Music*, p. 225.

44 *Ibid.*, pp. 213, 233. A Jewish East-Ender who grew up in the inter-war years professed to have changed his name from 'Kominsky', which the English 'could never bloody spell!', to 'Kaye' because of his admiration for the film star Danny Kaye. Danny Kaye's birth name was Daniel David Kaminski. For the appeal of Jewish film stars among Jewish cinema-goers, see G. Toffell, ' "Come and see, and hear, the mother tongue!" Yiddish cinema in inter-war London', *Screen*, 50:3 (2009), pp. 281–2.

45 Nott, *Music for the People*, pp. 216, 234.

46 *Ibid.*, pp. 202, 209, 211, 225, 233.

47 Richards and Sheridan, *Mass-Observation*, pp. 34, 43, 47, 73, 79, 81, 83–4, 85, 87, 89.

48 Hinton, 'The "class" complex', p. 106; Richards and Sheridan, *Mass-Observation*, pp. 48, 63, 64, 86, 87.

49 J. Hinton, 'The "class" complex': Mass-Observation and cultural distinction in pre-war Britain', *Past and Present*, 199:1 (2008), pp. 213–14, 219–20; MOA File Report 11A November 1939 'Jazz and Dancing', p. 2; Nott, *Music*, p. 199; S. Frith, *Performing Rites: On the Value of Popular Music* (Oxford: Oxford University Press, 1996), p. 34.

50 Nott, *Music for the People*, p. 37; R. Reitz, 'Hot snow: Valaida Snow (queen of the trumpet sings and swings)', *Black American Literature Forum*, 16:4 (1982), pp. 158–9.

51 George Harrison's father was on the White Star Line and brought back Jimmie Rodgers records and record players. John Lennon's father also brought back records. E-mail communication with Dave Cotterill of Souled Out Films, Liverpool, 12 April 2010. For these transatlantic links during and after the Second World War see D. Cotterill, M. Morris and I. Lysaght (dirs), *Liverpool's Cunard Yanks*, DVD (Souled Out Films, 2007).

52 D. Fowler, *Youth Culture in Modern Britain, c. 1920–c. 1970* (Basingstoke: Palgrave Macmillan, 2008), pp. 5, 6; Ministry of Education, *The Purpose and Content of the Youth Service. A Report of the Youth Advisory Council appointed by the Minister of Education in 1943* (London: HMSO, 1945), p. 5.

53 K. Boyd, *Manliness and the Boys' Story Paper in Britain: A Cultural History, 1855–1940* (Basingstoke: Palgrave Macmillan, 2003), p. 102; S. Todd, 'Young women, work and leisure in inter-war England', *The Historical Journal*, 49:3 (2005), p. 803. The expanding market aimed at young females similarly distinguished the lifestyles of young women from those of younger schoolgirls.

54 B. Naughton, *Neither Use nor Ornament: A Memoir of Bolton: 1920s* (Newcastle upon Tyne: Bloodaxe Books, 1995), p. 110; A. J. Hammerton, 'The English weakness? Gender, satire and "moral manliness" in the lower middle class, 1870–1920', in A. Kidd and D. Nicholls (eds), *Gender, Civic Culture and Consumerism: Middle-Class Identity in Britain, 1800–1940* (Manchester: Manchester University Press, 1999), pp. 167, 170, 176.

55 McKibbin, *Classes and Cultures*, pp. 73, 264, 265. See also, Rose, *Intellectual Life*. Some 40 per cent of grammar school pupils were working-class, although this was a very small minority of their class as a whole and middle-class children benefited far more.

56 P. Ayers, 'The making of men: masculinities in inter-war Liverpool', in M. Walsh (ed.), *Working Out Gender: Perspectives from Labour History* (Aldershot: Ashgate, 1999), pp. 17, 20, 26, 75.

57 The imaginative use of archive film may yield new insights into movement, posture, physique and dress.

58 M. Childs, *Labour's Apprentices: Working Class Lads in Late Victorian and Edwardian England* (London: The Hambledon Press, 1992), p. xiv; L. Davidoff, M. Doolittle, J. Fink and K. Holden, *The Family Story: Blood, Contract and Intimacy, 1830 –1960* (Longman: London and New York, 1999), p. 13.

59 D. C. Jones, *The Social Survey of Merseyside*, 3 vols (Liverpool: Liverpool University Press, 1934), Vol. III, pp. 274–8, 292–3, 295; Dennis Houlston, oral history transcript, CCINTB Archive; Todd, 'Flappers and factory lads', p. 722.

60 Ayers, 'The making of men', pp. 17, 20, 26, 75.

61 Contemporary youth researchers frequently observe a difference between what boys tell in collective settings and what is revealed on their own, when less consensual

views sometimes challenge what is said in the larger group. Inter-war youth workers were also sensitive to these differences. B. L. Q. Henriques, *Club Leadership* (London: Oxford University Press, 1933, 1943), pp. 53–9. See also, M. Peel, B. Caine and C. Twomey, 'Masculinity, emotion and subjectivity: introduction', *The Journal of Men's Studies*, 15:3 (2007), p. 247, and Frank Mort's observations on relationships between interviewers and groups of young men in F. Mort, 'Boy's own? Masculinity, style and popular culture', in R. Chapman and J. Rutherford (eds), *Male Order: Unwrapping Masculinity* (London: Lawrence & Wishart, 1988, 1996), pp. 216–18.

Bibliography

Primary sources

Burnett Archive of Working-Class Autobiographies, University of Brunel

Armitage, J. H., *The Twenty Three Years, Or the Late Way of Life – And of Living. By The Exile*

Baker, E., *Untitled*

Beeston, R., *Some of my Memories of and about Uley Until About 1930*

Bold, E., *The Long and short of it. Being the Recollections and Reminiscences of Edna Bold*

Dorrell, H., *Falling Cadence: An Autobiography of Failure*

Edmonds, J., *The Lean Years*

Fagan, H., *An Autobiography*

Flintoff, T. R., *Friday the Thirteenth of May*

Foley, S., *Asphalte*

Gill, H., [Untitled]

Goss, F., *My Boyhood at the Turn of the Century*

Hansford, C. L., *Memoirs of a Bricklayer*

Harris, H. J., *Autobiographical Letters*

Hughes, G. C., *Shut the Mountain Gate*

Jacobs, A. P., *Just Take a Look at These!*

Loftus, J., *Lee Side.*

Martin, E., *The Best Street in Rochdale*

Mountford, S., *A Memoir*

Metcalfe, S., *One Speck of Humanity*

Rice, S., *The Memories of a Rolling Stone: Times and Incidents Remembered*

Vere, P. (pseud. of H. V. Smith), *The Autobiography of a Working Man*

Waddicor, T., *Memories of Hightown and Beyond*

Ward, J. R., *Low Street Boy*

Ward, R., *A Lancashire Childhood*

Ward, W., *Fit For Anything*

The Cinema Culture in 1930s Britain (CCINTB) Archive, University of Lancaster

Oral history transcripts:

Bird, Ashley

Godbold, E. J. Born 1918, Stowmarket, Suffolk

Hart, Raphael. Born 1921, Golders Green, London

Houlston, Dennis. Born 1917, Levenshulme, Manchester

MacDonald, Norman. Born 1915, Glasgow

McGoran, Thomas. Born 1927, Glasgow

McWinnie, Sheila. Born 1919, Glasgow
Turner, George
Venis, Anthony. Born 1924, Wembley, London.

Government reports and parliamentary debates
Board of Education, *The Youth Service After the War. A report of the Youth Advisory Council appointed by the President of the Board of Education in 1942 to advise him on questions relating to the Youth Service in England* (London: HMSO, 1943)
Census Report, 1931: classification of occupations (London: HMSO, 1934)
Education in 1935. Cmnd 5290 (London: HMSO, 1936)
Ministry of Education, *The Purpose and Content of the Youth Service. A Report of the Youth Advisory Council appointed by the Minister of Education in 1943* (London: HMSO, 1945)
Hansard House of Commons Debates, 30 March 1938, Vol. 333, cc. 2007–11
Hansard House of Commons Debates, 3 November 1938, Vol. 340
Hansard House of Commons Debates, 16 December 1938, Vol. 342, cc. 2420–38

Mass Observation Archive
MOA File Report 11A, November 1939, 'Jazz and Dancing'

Official publications
British Tutorial Institutes Ltd *Opportunities in the Police Force*, London, 1936
Griffin, F. W., 'The Club Boy', Being an address delivered by Dr. F. W. Griffin (author of 'The Quest of the Boy') at the Experimental Training Course held on February 28, 1931 (London: National Association of Boys' Clubs, n.d.)
National Association of Boys' Clubs, Annual Report and Balance Sheet, 1928–9
National Association of Boys' Clubs, *Fourteen to Eighteen: The Critical Years of Boyhood*, Annual Report, 1930–1
National Association of Boys' Clubs, *Opening Doors*, Annual Report, 1932–3
National Association of Boys' Clubs, *Years of Experiment*, Annual Report, 1933–4
National Association of Boys' Clubs, *Youth and the Future*, Annual Report, 1934–1935
National Association of Boys' Clubs, Annual Report, 1936–7
National Association of Boys' Clubs, Annual Report and Balance Sheet, 1938
National Association of Boys' Clubs, *The Club or the Street? Training Boys for Citizenship* (London: National Association of Boys' Clubs), 1937
National Association of Boys' Clubs, *Principles and Aims of the Boys' Club Movement* (London: National Association of Boys' Clubs, 1936, 1938)

Newspapers, journals and magazines
British Medical Journal
Chronicle and Echo (Northampton)

Cinema Theatre Association Bulletin
Contemporary Review
Daily Dispatch
Daily Express
Daily Mail
Daily Mirror
Everybody's Weekly
Lansbury's Labour Weekly
Manchester Evening News
Manchester Guardian
Melody Maker
Millgate Monthly
Modern Woman
New Statesman
News of the World
Northern Voice
Picture Post
Sunday Dispatch
The Boy (Magazine of the National Association of Boys' Clubs)
The Confederate (Magazine of the Birmingham and District Federation of Boys Clubs)
The Dancing Times
The Miner
The Times
Woman
Woman's Home Companion
Woman's Magazine
Woman's Outlook
Woman's Own
Woman's Weekly

The British Universities Newsreel Database (BUND)
Mussolini calls to youth (1930)
Drill for Il Duce. Italy's rising generation (1932)
The new Germany. Hundreds of thousands of boys and girls in great demonstration of youth (1933)
How Mussolini catches 'em young (1935)
Russian youth keeps fit. Thousands take part in spectacular mass drill (1935)
Mussolini reviews fascist youth (1935)
Balilla review by King of Italy (1936)
Hitler Youth in Italy (1936)
Soviet youth stages parade in Red Square (1936)
Young Italy learns art of war (1937)
Youth rally. Huge gymnastic display in Nuremberg arena (1938)

Hitler Jugend in Japan (1938)
Fascist youth on parade (1939)

North West Film Archive, Manchester Metropolitan University
Film No 120, 'Glimpses of a Manchester Popular Rendezvous – The Piccadilly Restaurant and Dance Salon', Gaumont, for Charles Ogden Cinema Circuit, 1924
Film No 541, 'Over and Over!', A dance demonstration by the Apache Speciality Dancer, Miss Constance Evans, Eves Film Review, 1927

Oral history collections
Centre for North West Regional Studies, University of Lancaster
Manchester Studies Tapes, Tameside Local Studies and Archives Unit, Tameside Library
Northampton Borough Council Oral History Project
Tameside Local Studies and Archives Unit, Tameside Library

Printed primary sources

Abrams, M., *The Teenage Consumer* (London: London Press Exchange, 1959)
The Advertiser's Annual and Convention Year Book, 1925–6 (London: Business Publications Ltd, 1926)
The Advertiser's Annual and Convention Year Book, 1930 (London: Business Publications Ltd, 1930)
Andrews, B., *Don't Fret My Lad: An Ashton Boyhood* (Manchester: Neil Richardson, 1987)
Atkinson, M. 'Sex education of the young', in W. A. Lane (ed.), *The Golden Health Library: A Complete Guide to Golden Health for Men and Women of all Ages* (London: Collins, [1929])
The Bennett College (Ltd), Sheffield: History of the Bennett College (n.d.)
Benson, T. P., *As I Return to Yesteryear* (Owen Sound, Ont.: T. P. Benson, 1983),
Bernstein, H., *The Invisible Wall* (London: Hutchinson, 2007)
Blake, J., *Memories of Old Poplar* (London: Stepney Books Publications, 1977)
Bowen, M., *Making Our Boys Effeminate* (London: 1927)
Bowley, A. L. and M. Hogg, *Has Poverty Diminished?* (London: P. S. King & Son Ltd., 1925)
Bowley, R., 'Amusements and entertainments', in H. L. Smith (ed.), *The New Survey of London Life and Labour*, Vol. IX, *Life and Leisure* (London: P. S. King & Son Ltd., Westminster, 1935)
Boys' Club Handbook, No. 1 (London: National Association of Boys' Clubs, reprinted March 1936, reprinted June 1938)
Brereton, W., *Salford Boy. The Illustrated Memories of Wallace Brereton* (Manchester: Neil Richardson, 1985; first published by Salford Local History Society, 1977)

Brooke, J., *The Dukinfield I Knew, 1906–1930* (Manchester: Neil Richardson, 1987)

Bryan, H. S., *The Troublesome Boy* (London: C. Arthur Pearson Ltd., 1936)

Burgess, A., *Little Wilson and Big God* (New York: Grove Weidenfeld)

Burnett, J. (ed.), *Destiny Obscure: Autobiographies of Childhood, Education and Family from the 1820s to the 1920s* (London: Routledge, 1994)

Burt, C., *The Young Delinquent* (London: University of London Press, 1925, 1931)

Butterworth, J., *Clubland* (London: The Epworth Press, 1932)

Bygraves, M., *I Wanna Tell You a Story* (London: W. H. Allen, 1976)

Calder-Marshall, A., *The Changing Scene* (London: Chapman and Hall, 1937)

Cameron, C., A. Lush and G. Meara, *Disinherited Youth* (Edinburgh: Carnegie United Kingdom Trust, 1943)

Caradog Jones, D. (ed.), *The Social Survey of Merseyside*, 3 vols (Liverpool: Liverpool University Press, 1934)

Carley, J., *Old Friends, Old Times, 1908–1938: Manchester Memories from the Diaries of Joe Carley* (Manchester: Neil Richardson, 1990)

Carrington, C., *Soldier from the Wars Returning* (Barnsley: Pen and Sword Books Limited, 2006; first published in 1965 by Hutchinson & Co.)

Chadwick, H., *Childhood Memories of Gorton in the Nineteen Twenties* (Manchester: Neil Richardson, 1994)

Chesser, E., *The Sexual, Marital and Family Relationships of the English Woman* (London: Hutchinson's Medical Publications, 1956)

Clephane, I., *Towards Sex Freedom* (London: John Lane, 1935)

Coué, E., *Self-Mastery by Conscious Auto-Suggestion* (New York: Kessinger Publishing, 1922)

Cox, G. M., *Youth, Sex, and Life* (London: George Newnes Limited, 1935)

Critchlow, D., *'Dear Jane Dawson . . .'* (London: Robert Hale Limited, 1977)

Currie, S., *How to Make Friends Easily* (London: W. Foulsham & Co., Ltd., [1939])

Davenport, K., *Some Oldham Times* (Manchester: Neil Richardson 1985)

Dudley, E., *The Leakage: Cause and Remedy'* (Catholic Truth Society: London, 1931)

Durant, H. W., *The Problem of Leisure* (London: George Routledge and Sons, 1938)

Eagar, W. McG. and H. A. Secretan, *Unemployment Among Boys* (London: J. M. Dent, 1925)

Edynbry, E., *Real Life Problems and Their Solution* (London: Odhams Press, 1938)

Eyles, L., *Women's Problems of To-Day* (London: Labour Publishing Co., 1926)

Eyles, L., *Common Sense about Sex* (London: Victor Gollancz, 1936).

Eyles, L., *The Ram Escapes: The Story of a Victorian Childhood* (London: Peter Nevill, 1953)

Ford, P., *Work and Wealth in a Modern Port: An Economic Survey of Southampton* (London: Allen & Unwin Ltd., 1934)

Ford, R., *Children in the Cinema* (London: Allen & Unwin, 1939)

Furniss, T., *The Walls of Jericho: Slum Life in Sheffield between the Wars* (Sheffield: Rebel Press, 1979)

Gallichan, W. M. *How to Love. The Art of Courtship and Marriage* (London: C. Arthur Pearson, 1915)

Gallichan, W. M., *A Text-Book of Sex Education for Parents and Teachers* (London: T. Werner Laurie, 1919)

Gallichan, W. M., *Letters to a Young Man on Love and Health* (London: T. Werner Laurie, 1919)

Gallichan, W. M., *Youth and Maidenhood, or Sex Knowledge for Young People* (London: Health Promotion, 1920)

Gallichan, W. M. *The Poison of Prudery: An Historical Survey* (London: T. Werner Laurie Ltd., 1929)

Glasser, R., 'Growing up in the Gorbals', in *The Ralph Glasser Omnibus* (Edinburgh: Black and White Publishing, 2006; first published by Chatto and Windus, 1986)

Glasser, R., 'Gorbals Boy at Oxford', in *The Ralph Glasser Omnibus* (Edinburgh: Black and White Publishing, 2006; first published by Chatto and Windus, 1988)

Glasser, R., 'Gorbals Voices, Siren Songs', in *The Ralph Glasser Omnibus* (Edinburgh: Black and White Publishing, 2006; first published by Chatto and Windus, 1990)

Gollan, J., *Youth in British Industry: A Survey of Labour Conditions To-day* (London: Gollancz, 1937)

Gorer, G., *Exploring English Character* (London: Cresset Press, 1955)

Gosling, R. *Personal Copy: A Memoir of the Sixties* (London: Faber and Faber, 1980)

Gray, A. H., *Sex Teaching* (London: National Sunday School Union, [1929])

Griffin, F. W., 'The Club Boy', an address delivered at the experimental training course held on 28 February 1931 (London: National Association of Boys' Clubs, n.d.)

Griffiths, B., *Growing Up in Manchester* (Manchester: Didsbury Press, 1991)

Hague, E., *Streets away from Paradise: Reminiscences of a Stalybridge Lad* (Manchester: Neil Richardson, 1987)

Haire, N., with A. Costler, A. Willy et al. (eds), *Encyclopaedia of Sexual Knowledge* (London: Francis Aldor, 1934)

Hall, G. S., *Adolescence*: *Its Psychology and Its Relations to Physiology, Anthropology, Sociology, Sex, Crime, Religion, and Education*, 2 vols (London: Sidney Appleton, 1904)

Halliwell, L., *Seats in All Parts: Half a Lifetime at the Movies* (London: Granada, 1985)

Hatton, S. F., *The Yarn of a Yeoman* (London: Hutchinson, 1930)

Hatton, S. F. *London's Bad Boys* (London: Chapman & Hall Ltd., 1931)

Haworth, D., *Figures in a Bygone Landscape* (London: Methuen, 1986)

Henriques, B. L. Q., *Club Leadership* (London: Oxford University Press, 1933, 1943)

Henriques, B. L. Q., *The Indiscretions of a Warden* (London: Methuen & Co. Ltd., 1937)

Hinson, M., *Mary Ann's Girl. Memories of Newbridge Lane* (Stockport: Metropolitan Borough of Stockport Recreation and Culture Division, 1984)

Hoggart, R., *A Local Habitation*, Vol. 1, *Life and Times 1918–40* (Oxford: Oxford University Press, 1989)

Hutchinson, E. D., *Creative Sex* (London: Allen & Unwin, 1936)

Jackson, J., *Under the Smoke. Salford Memories, 1922–1941* (Manchester: Neil Richardson, 1990)

Jacobs, J., *Out of the Ghetto: My Youth in the East End. Communism and Fascism 1913–1939* (London: Janet Simon, 1978)

James, N., *A Derbyshire Life. Autobiography of a South Normanton Woman* (South Normanton: Post Mill Press, 1981)

Jenkinson, A. J., *What Do Boys and Girls Read?* (London: Methuen & Co. Ltd., London, 1940)

Jennings, H. and W. Gill, *Broadcasting in Everyday Life: A Survey of the Social Effects of the Coming of Broadcasting* (London: BBC, 1939)

Jephcott, A. P., *Girls Growing Up* (London: Faber and Faber, 1942)

Jephcott, J., *Some Young People* (London: George Allen & Unwin, 1954)

Jones, D. C., *The Social Survey of Merseyside*, 3 vols (Liverpool: Liverpool University Press, 1934), Vol. III

Jordan, M., *Hulme Memories* (Manchester: Neil Richardson 1989)

Kay, J., *The Chronicles of a Harpurhey Lad* (Manchester: Neil Richardson, 1990)

Kenyon, N., *I Belong to Bolton* (Manchester: Neil Richardson, 1989)

Lestrange, W. F., *Wasted Lives* (London: George Routledge & Sons Ltd., 1936)

London County Council, Education Committee, *School Children and the Cinema*, (London: London County Council, 1932)

Lynd, R. S. and H. M. Lynd, *Middletown: A Study in Contemporary American Culture* (New York: Harcourt, Brace and Company, 1929)

Mackie, J. (ed.), *The Edinburgh Cinema Enquiry: Being an Investigation Conducted in to the Influence of the Film on Schoolchildren and Adolescents in the City* (Edinburgh: Edinburgh City Library, 1933)

Makins, P., *The Evelyn Home Story* (London: Collins, 1975)

Marks Northampton Directory, 1929

Mayer, J. P., *British Cinemas and their Audiences* (London: Dennis Dobson Ltd., 1948)

Moore, A., *Ballroom Dancing* (London: Pitman, 1936)

Morgan, A. E., *The Needs of Youth. A Report Made to King George's Jubilee Trust Fund* (Oxford: Oxford University Press, 1939)

Morgan, A. E., *Young Citizen* (Harmondsworth: Penguin, 1943)

Moss, P., *Manchester's Dancing Years* (Manchester: Neil Richardson, 1996)

Moss, P., *True Romances at Manchester's Dances* (Manchester: Neil Richardson, 1998)

National Association of Boys' Clubs, *The Club or the Street? Training Boys for Citizenship* (London: National Association of Boys' Clubs, 1937)

Naughton, B., *Neither Use nor Ornament: A Memoir of Bolton, 1920s* (Newcastle upon Tyne: Bloodaxe Books, 1995)

Naughton, B., *On the Pig's Back* (Oxford: Oxford University Press, 1988)

Naughton, B., *Saintly Billy: A Catholic Boyhood* (Oxford: Oxford University Press, 1989)

Nestle, J., *A Restricted Country: Essays and Short Stories* (London: Sheba Feminist, 1988)

The Northampton County Borough Directory, 1936

Northampton Official Handbook, 1936

Opportunities in the Police Force (London: British Tutorial Institutes Ltd., 1936)

Paterson, A., *The Doctor and the OMM* (London: Oxford Medical Mission, 1910)

Paterson, A., *Across the Bridges* (London: Edward Arnold, 1912)

Pettigrew, E., *Time to Remember: Growing up in Liverpool from 1912 onwards* (Liverpool: Toulouse, 1989)

Preston, J., *Memoirs of a Salford Lad* (Manchester: Neil Richardson, undated)

Priestley, J. B., *English Journey* (London: Heinemann/Gollancz, 1934)

Principles and Aims of the Boys' Club Movement (London: National Association of Boys' Clubs, 1930)

Pritchard, F., *My Manchester* (Manchester: Neil Richardson, 1986)

Pritchard, F., *Dance Band Days around Manchester* (Manchester: Neil Richardson, 1988)

Pritchard, F., *East Manchester Remembered* (Manchester: Neil Richardson, 1989)

Read, C. S., 'The adolescent boy', in W. A. Lane (ed.), *The Golden Health Library: A Complete Guide to Golden Health for Men and Women of All Ages* (London: Collins, [1929])

Read, D., *A Manchester Boyhood in the Thirties and Forties – Growing up in War and Peace* (Lewiston, NY: Lampeter: The Edwin Mellen Press, c. 2003)

Reed, B. H., *Eighty Thousand Adolescents: A Study of Young People in the City of Birmingham by the Staff and Students of Westhill Training College for the Edward Cadbury Charitable Trust* (London: George Allen & Unwin Ltd., 1950)

Richardson, P. J. S., *A History of English Ballroom Dancing 1910–1945: The Story of the Development of the Modern English Style* (London: Herbert Jenkins Ltd., 1945)

Roberts, R., *A Ragged Schooling: Growing Up in the Classic Slum* (Glasgow: Fontana/Collins, 1978; first published 1976)

Roker, P. and H. Crawford Scott, 'Juvenile unemployment in West Ham', *Economica*, 16 March 1926, pp. 58–77

Roof, M., *Youth and Leisure. A Survey of Girls' Organisations in England and Wales* (Edinburgh: Carnegie United Kingdon Trust, 1935)

Rowntree, B. S., *Poverty and Progress: A Second Social Survey of York* (London: Longmans, Green and Co., 1941)

Rowntree, B. S. and G. R. Lavers, *English Life and Leisure: A Social Study* (London: Longmans, Green and Co, 1951)

Royden, A. M., *Sex and Common-Sense* (London: Hurst and Blackett, [1922])

Royle, C., *This Was My Village: Boyhood Recollections of Flixton 1922–1938* (Manchester: Neil Richardson, 1994)

Russell, C. E. B., 'City Lads', *Child* (April 1911)

Russell, C. E. B. and L. M. Russell, *Lads' Clubs: Their History, Organisation and Management* (London: A. & C. Black Ltd., 1932)

Scott, B., *Heaton Norris Boy* (Stockport: Metropolitan Borough of Stockport, Leisure Services Division, 1987)

Seabrook, J., *Mother and Son* (London: Victor Gollancz, 1979)

Secretan, H. A., *The Yarn of a Yeoman* (London: Hutchinson, 1930)

Secretan, H. A., *London below Bridges* (London: Geoffrey Bles, 1931)

Shephard, E., *A Sergeant-Major's War: From Hill 60 to the Somme*, ed. Bruce Rosser and Richard Holmes (Marlborough, Wiltshire: The Crowood Press, 1987)

Silvester, V., *Modern Ballroom Dancing* (London: Herbert Jenkins, 1928)

Silvester, V., *Dancing Is My Life* (London: Heinemann, 1958)

Slawson, J., *Hopwood, Heywood and Me* (Manchester: Neil Richardson, 1986)

Stebbing, L. *The Stebbing System of Height Increase* (n.p., 1930)

Steedman, C., *Landscape for a Good Woman* (London: Virago, 1986)

Stopes, M. C., *Sex and the Young* (London: G. P. Putnam and Sons, 1926, 1929)

Stovin, H., *Totem: The Exploitation of Youth* (London: Methuen, 1935)

Summerskill, D., *Happy Lad: Reminiscences of a Lancashire Childhood* (Skipton: Katharine Cheney, 2009)

Sutton, L., *Mainly about Ardwick* (Manchester, 1977)

Temple, A., *Good or Bad – It's Life* (London: Nicholson & Watson, 1944)

Terry, E., *Etiquette for All: Man, Woman or Child* (London: Foulsham & Co. Ltd., 1925)

Tildsley, D., *Remembrance, Recollections of a Wartime Childhood in Swinton, Incorporating a Roll of Honour for the Borough* (Manchester: Neil Richardson, 1985)

Tucker T. F. and M. Pout, *Awkward Questions of Childhood. A Practical Handbook on Sex Education for Parents and Teachers* (London: Gerald Howe Ltd., 1934)

Vaughan, B., *Growing up in Salford, 1919–1928* (Manchester: Neil Richardson, 1983)

Walton, E., *From Hepthorne Lane to Rangoon . . . and Back* (Alfreton: Higham Press, n.d.)

Watkin, H., *From Hulme All Blessings Flow* (Manchester: Neil Richardson, 1985)

Weatherhead, L. D., assisted by Dr Marion Greaves, *The Mastery of Sex through Psychology and Religion* (London: Student Christian Movement Press, 1931)

Woodruff, W., *Billy Boy: The Story of a Lancashire Weaver's Son* (Halifax: Ryburn Publishing, 1993); also published as *The Road to Nab End: An Extraordinary Northern Childhood* (London, Abacus Books, 2003)

Wynne, J., *Where's Mi Chunks, Mam? The Childhood of a Nobody in Particular. Salford Memories, 1930–38* (Manchester: Neil Richardson, 1997)

Secondary sources

Abrams, L., '"There was nobody like my daddy": fathers, the family and the marginalisation of men in modern Scotland', *Scottish Historical Review*, 78 (1999), 218–42

Abramson, P. L., *Sob Sister Journalism* (Westport, CT.: Greenwood Press, 1990)

Adams, M. L., '"Death to the prancing prince": effeminacy, sport discourses and the salvation of men's dancing', *Body and Society*, 11:4 (2005), 63–86

Albright, A. C., *Choreographing Difference: The Body and Identity in Contemporary Dance* (Hanover NH.: Wesleyan University Press, 1997)

Aldrich, R., *A Century of Education* (Falmer: Routledge, 2002)

Alexander, S., 'Becoming a woman in London in the 1920s and 1930s', in D. Feldman and G. Stedman Jones (eds), *Metropolis London: Histories and Representations since 1800* (London: Routledge, 1989)

Alexander, S., 'The mysteries and secrets of women's bodies: sexual knowledge in the first half of the twentieth century', in M. Nava and A. O'Shea (eds), *Modern Times: Reflections on a Century of English Modernity* (London: Routledge, 1996)

Alexander, S., 'Men's fears and women's work: responses to unemployment in London between the wars', *Gender and History*, 12:2 (2000), 401–25

Andrews, G. J., R. A. Kearns, P. Kontos and V. Wilson, '"Their finest hour": older people, oral histories and the historical geography of social life', *Social and Cultural Geography*, 7:2 (2006), 154–77

Attfield, J., *Wild Things: The Material Culture of Everyday Life* (London: Berg, 2000)

Austin, V. A. 'The céilí and the public dance halls act, 1935', *Eire–Ireland*, 28:3 (1993), 7–16

Ayers, P., 'The making of men: masculinities in interwar Liverpool', in M. Walsh (ed.), *Working Out Gender: Perspectives from Labour History* (Aldershot: Ashgate, 1999)

Baade, C. (2006) '"The dancing front": dance music, dancing, and the BBC in World War II', *Popular Music*, 25:3 (2006), 347–68

Back, L., 'Gendered participation: masculinity and fieldwork in a south London adolescent community', in D. Bell, P. Caplan and W. J. Karim (eds), *Gendered Fields: Women, Men and Ethnography* (London: Routledge, 1993)

Bailey, V., *Delinquency and Citizenship: Reclaiming the Young Offender, 1914–1948* (Oxford: Clarendon, 1987)

Baines, D. and P. Johnson, 'In search of the "traditional" working class: social mobility and occupational continuity in interwar London', *Economic History Review*, 52:4 (1999), 692–713

Baker, A. P., 'Pringle, John Christian (1872–1938)', *Oxford Dictionary of National*

Biography (Oxford: Oxford University Press, 2004), www.oxforddnb.com/
view/article/69003 (accessed 20 August 2007)

Banes, S., *Dancing Women: Female Bodies on Stage* (London: Routledge, 1998)

Banks, I., 'Education and debate. No man's land: men, illness and the NHS',
British Medical Journal, 3 November 2003, pp. 1058–60

Baron, B., *The Doctor. The Story of John Stansfeld of Oxford and Bermondsey*
(London: Edward Arnold, 1952)

Barton, S., *Working-Class Organizations and Popular Tourism, 1840–1970*
(Manchester: Manchester University Press, 2005)

Barty-King, H., *Expanding Northampton* (London: Secker and Warburg, 1985)

Baxendale, J., ' "... into another kind of life in which anything might happen
...": Popular music and late modernity, 1910–1930', *Popular Music*, 14:2
(1995), 137–54

Beasley, M. H., 'Elizabeth M. Gilmer as Dorothy Dix: a woman journalist
rewrites the myth of the southern lad', paper presented at the Dorothy Dix
Symposium, Woodstock Mansion, Todd County, Kentucky, 27 September
1991, http://library.apsu.edu/Dix/kanervo.htm (accessed 7 February 2007)

Beaven, B., *Leisure, Citizenship and Working-Class Men in Britain* (Manchester:
Manchester University Press, 2005)

Beetham, M., *A Magazine of Her Own? Domesticity and Desire in the Woman's
Magazine, 1800–1914* (London and New York: Routledge, 1996)

Belford, B., *Brilliant Bylines: A Biographical Anthology of Notable
Newspaperwomen in America* (New York: Columbia University Press, 1986)

Benjamin, D. K. and L. A. Kochin, 'What went right in juvenile unemployment
policy between the wars: a comment', *Economic History Review*, 32:4 (2008),
523–28

Bennett, A., M. Cieslik and S. Miles, *Researching Youth* (London: Palgrave
Macmillan, 2003)

Benninghaus, C., 'Mothers' toil and daughters' leisure: working-class girls and
time in 1920s Germany', *History Workshop Journal*, 50 (2000), 45–72

Benson, J., *Affluence and Authority: A Social History of 20th Century Britain*
(London: Hodder Arnold, 2005)

Bet-El, I. R., 'Men and soldiers: British conscripts, concepts of masculinity, and
the Great War', in B. Melman (ed.), *Borderlines: Genders and Identities in
War and Peace, 1870–1930* (New York and London: Routledge)

Bill, K., 'Attitudes towards women's trousers: Britain in the 1930s', *Journal of
Design History*, 6:1 (1993), 45–53

Bingham, A., *Gender, Modernity and the Popular Press in Britain* (Oxford:
Oxford University Press, 2004)

Bingham, A., *Family Newspapers? Sex, Private Life and the British Popular Press,
1918–1978* (Oxford: Oxford University Press, 2009)

Binnie, J., J. Holloway, S. Millington and C. Young, 'Mundane geographies:
alienation, potentialities and practice', *Environment and Planning A*, 39:3
(2007), 515–20

Binnie, J., T. Edensor, J. Holloway, S. Millington and C. Young, Editorial, 'Mundane mobilities, banal travels', *Social and Cultural Geography*, 8:2 (2007), 165–74

Black, J. A., '"Who dies if England live?" Masculinity, the problematics of "Englishness" and the image of the ordinary soldier in British war art, c. 1915–28', in S. Caunce, E. Mazierska, S. Sydney-Smith and J. K. Walton (eds), *Relocating Britishness* (Manchester: Manchester University Press, 2004)

Blanch, M., 'Imperialism, nationalism and organised youth', in J. Clarke, C. Critcher and R. Johnson (eds), *Working Class Culture: Studies in History and Theory* (Birmingham: Centre for Cultural Studies, 1979)

Blokland, T., 'Bricks, mortar, memories: neighbourhood and networks in collective acts of remembering', *International Journal of Urban and Regional Research*, 25:2 (2001), 268–83

Boddy, W., 'Archaeologies of electronic vision and the gendered spectator', *Screen*, 35:2 (1994), 105–22

Bourke, J., *Working-Class Cultures in Britain, 1890–1960: Gender, Class and Ethnicity* (London: Routledge, 1994)

Bourke, J., *Dismembering the Male: Men's Bodies, Britain and the Great War* (London: Reaktion Books, 1996)

Bourke, J., 'Fragmentation, fetishization and men's bodies in Britain, 1890–1939', *Women: A Cultural Review*, 7:3 (1996), 240–9

Boyd, K., 'Knowing your place: the tension of manliness in boys' story papers, 1918–39', in M. Roper and J. Tosh (eds), *Manful Assertions: Masculinities in England since 1800* (London: Routledge, 1991)

Boyd, K., 'Exemplars and ingrates: imperialism and the boys' story paper, 1880–1930', *Historical Research*, 67:163 (1994), 143–55

Boyd, K., *Manliness and the Boys' Story Paper in Britain: A Cultural History, 1855–1940* (Basingstoke: Palgrave Macmillan, 2003)

Branson, N. and M. Heinemann, *Britain in the Nineteen Thirties* (London: Weidenfeld and Nicolson, 1971)

Braybon, G. and P. Summerfield, *Out of the Cage: Women's Experiences in Two World Wars* (London: Pandora Press, 1987)

Brennan, T., 'History, family, history', in H. Kean, P. Martin and S. J. Morgan (eds), *Seeing History. Public History in Britain Now* (London: Francis Boutle Publishers, 2000)

Breward, C., *The Hidden Consumer: Masculinities, Fashion and City Life in 1860–1914* (Manchester: Manchester University Press, 1999)

Brewer, C., 'Style and subversion: postwar poses and the neo-Edwardian suit in mid-twentieth century Britain', *Gender and History*, 14:3 (2002), 560–83

Briggs, A., *The History of Broadcasting in the United Kingdom*, Vol. 1 *The Birth of Broadcasting* (Oxford: Oxford University Press, 1995)

Brooke, S., 'A new world for women? Abortion law reform in Britain during the 1930s', *The American Historical Review*, 106:2 (2001), 431–59

Brown, C., *Northampton 1935–1985: Shoe Town, New Town* (Chichester: Phillimore, 1990)

Brown, P., *Schooling Ordinary Kids: Inequality, Unemployment, and the New Vocationalism* (London: Tavistock, 1987)

Browning, B., *Samba: Resistance in Motion* (Bloomington: Indiana University Press, 1995)

Bruce, L. W., 'Creating a socialist scout movement: the woodcraft folk, 1924–1942', *History of Education*, 13:4 (1984), 299–311

Bunce, M., *The Countryside Ideal: Anglo-American Images of Landscape* (London: Routledge, 1994)

Bunn, G. C., G. Richards and A. D. Lovie (eds), *Psychology in Britain: Historical Essays and Personal Reflections* (Leicester: BPS Books, 2001)

Burchardt, J., *Paradise Lost: Rural Idyll and Social Change since 1800* (London and New York: I. B. Tauris, 2002)

Burgess, A., *Little Wilson and Big God* (New York: Grove Weidenfeld, 1986)

Burgess, K., 'Youth unemployment policy during the 1930s', *Twentieth Century British History*, 6:1 (1995), 23–55

Burman, B., 'Pocketing the difference: gender and pockets in nineteenth century Britain', in B. Burman and C. Turbin, *Material Strategies: Dress and Gender in Historical Perspective* (Oxford: Blackwell Publishing, 2003)

Burt, R., *The Male Dancer: Bodies, Spectacle, Sexualities* (London: Routledge, 1995)

Butler, J., 'Performative acts and gender constitution: an essay in phenomenology and feminist theory', in S. E. Case (ed.), *Performing Feminisms: Feminist Critical Theory and Theatre* (Baltimore, MD: Johns Hopkins University Press, 1990)

Butterfield, M. and J. Spence, 'The transition from girls' clubs to girls' clubs and mixed clubs: UK youth, 1934–1944', in R. Gilchrist, T. Jeffs, J. Spence and J. Walker (eds), *Essays in the History of Youth and Community Work: Discovering the Past* (Lyme Regis, Dorset: Russell House Publishing, 2009)

Cadogan, M., *Richmal Crompton: The Woman behind Just William* (London: Allen & Unwin, 1986, 2003)

Canning, K., 'Feminist history after the linguistic turn: historicizing discourse and experience', *Signs: Journal of Women in Culture and Society*, 19:2 (1994), 368–404

Canning, K., 'The body as method? Reflections on the place of the body in gender history', *Gender and History*, 11:3 (1999), 499–513

Capps, D., 'From masturbation to homosexuality: a case of displaced moral approval', *Pastoral Psychology*, 51:4 (2003), 249–72

Carden-Coyne, A., *Reconstructing the Body: Classicism, Modernism, and the First World War* (Oxford: Oxford University Press, 2009)

Cardiff, D., 'The serious and the popular: aspects of the evolution of style in the radio talk 1928–1939', *Media, Culture and Society*, 2:29 (1980), 29–47

Carrington, C., *Soldier from the Wars Returning* (Barnsley: Pen and Sword Books Limited, 2006; first published 1965 by Hutchinson & Co.)

Childs, M., *Labour's Apprentices: Working Class Lads in Late Victorian and Edwardian England* (London: The Hambledon Press, 1992)

Christie, D. and R. Viner, 'Clinical review: ABC of adolescence. Adolescent development', *British Medical Journal* (5 February 2005), 301–4

Chuppa-Cornell, K., 'Filling a vacuum: women's health information in *Good Housekeeping*'s articles and advertisements, 1920–1965', *The Historian*, 67:3 (2005), 454–73

Classen, C., D. Howes and A. Synnott, *Aroma: The Cultural History of Smell* (London: Routledge, 1994)

Coffield, F., C. Borrill and S. Marshall, *Growing Up at the Margins: Young Adults in the North East* (Milton Keynes: Open University Press, 1986)

Cohen, P., 'Historical perspectives on the youth question especially in Britain', in D. Dowe (ed.), *Jugendprotest und Generationenkonflikt in Europa im 20. Jahrhundert: Deutschland, England, Frankreich und Italien im Vergleich* (Bonn: Verlag Neue Gesellschaft, 1986), pp. 241–59

Cohen, S., *Folk Devils and Moral Panics: The Creation of the Mods and Rockers* (London: MacGibbon and Kee, 1972)

Cole, S., *'Don We Now Our Gay Apparel': Gay Men's Dress in the Twentieth Century* (Oxford: Berg, 2000)

Collins, M., *Modern Love: An Intimate History of Men and Women in Twentieth-Century Britain* (London: Atlantic Books, 2003)

Collins, T., 'Review article: Work, rest and play: recent trends in the history of sport and leisure', *Journal of Contemporary History*, 42:2 (2007), 397–410

Colls, R., 'When we lived in communities: working class culture and its critics', in R. Colls and R. Rodger (eds), *Cities of Ideas, Governance and Citizenship in Urban Britain, 1800–2000* (Aldershot: Ashgate, 2005),

Conboy, K., N. Medina and S. Stanbury (eds), *Writing the Body: Female Embodiment and Feminist Theory* (New York: Columbia University Press, 1997)

Conboy, M., *The Press and Popular Culture* (London: Sage Publications, 2002)

Connell, R. W., *Masculinities* (Cambridge: Polity Press, 1995)

Cook, H., *The Long Sexual Revolution: English Women, Sex, and Contraception* (Oxford: Oxford University Press, 2005)

Cook, M., 'Queer conflicts: love, sex and war, 1914–1967', in M. Cook (ed.), with R. Mills, R. Trumbach and H. G. Cocks, *A Gay History of Britain: Love and Sex between Men since the Middle Ages* (Oxford and Westport, CT: Greenworld Publishing, 2007)

Cook, M., 'Review article: Twentieth-century masculinities', *Journal of Contemporary History*, 43:127 (2008)

Cook, R. L., 'Dancing in the thirties – short story', *Contemporary Review*, 1 July 1999

Cooks, S., 'Passionless dancing and passionate reform: respectability, modernism, and the social dancing of Irene and Vernon Castle', in W. Washabaugh (ed.), *The Passion of Music and Dance: Body, Gender and Sexuality* (Oxford: Berg, 1998)

Corns, C. and J. Wilson, *Blindfold and Alone: British Military Executions in the First World War* (London: Cassell, 2005)

Cotterill, D., M. Morris and I. Lysaght (dirs) *Liverpool's Cunard Yanks*, DVD (Souled Out Films, 2007)

Counihan, C. and P. Van Esterik, *Food and Culture: A Reader* (London: Routledge, 1997)

Cox, P. and H. Shore, *Becoming Delinquent: British and European Youth, 1650–1930* (Aldershot: Ashgate, 2002)

Creeber, G., 'Dennis Potter and Richard Hoggart, scholarship boys', in V. W. Gras and J. R. Cook (eds), *The Passion of Dennis Potter: International Collected Essays* (ew York: St. Martin's Press, 2000)

Cresswell, T., ' "You cannot shake that shimmie here": producing mobility on the dancefloor', *Cultural Geographies*, 13:1 (2006), 55–77

Crisell, A., *Understanding Radio* (London: Methuen, 1986)

Crisell, A., *An Introductory History of British Broadcasting* (London: Routledge, 2002)

Croll, A., 'Street disorder, surveillance and shame: regulating behaviour in the public spaces of the late Victorian British town', *Social History*, 24:3 (1999), 250–68

Crook, D., 'Wood, Sir Robert Stanford (1886–1963)', *Oxford Dictionary of National Biography* (Oxford: Oxford University Press, 2004), www.oxforddnb.com/view/article/37004 (accessed 9 February 2008).

Cross, G. (ed.), *Worktowners at Blackpool: Mass Observation and Popular Leisure in the 1930s* (London: Routledge, 1990)

Crossley, C., Review of John Neubauer, *The Fin-de-Siècle Culture of Adolescence* (New Haven, CT: Yale University Press, 1992) in *The Journal of Modern History*, 67:1 (1995), 115–16

Crowther, B., 'The partial picture: framing the discourse of sex in British educative films of the early 1930s', in L. D. H. Sauerteig and R. Davidson, *Shaping Sexual Knowledge. A Cultural History of Sex Education in Twentieth Century Europe* (London and New York: Routledge, 2009)

Cunningham, H., *The Invention of Childhood* (London: BBC Books, 2006)

Curran, J., *Media and Power*, London: Routledge, 2002

Curtin, A. and D. Linehan, 'Where the boys are – teenagers, masculinity and a sense of place', *Irish Geography*, 35:1 (2002), 63–74

Darby, W. J., *Landscape and Identity: Geographies of Nation and Class in England* (Oxford and New York: Berg, 2000)

Das, S., *Touch and Intimacy in First World War Literature* (Cambridge: Cambridge University Press, 2005)

Davidoff, L., M. Doolittle, J. Fink and K. Holden, *The Family Story: Blood, Contract and Intimacy, 1830–1960* (London and New York: Longman, 1999)

Davidson, J. and C. Milligan, 'Embodying emotion, sensing space: introducing emotional geographies', *Social & Cultural Geography*, 5:4 (2004), 523–32

Davies, A., *Leisure, Gender and Poverty* (Buckingham and Philadelphia: Open University Press, 1992)

Davies, A., 'Street gangs, crime and policing in Glasgow in the 1930s: the case of the Beehive Boys', *Social History*, 23:3 (1998), 251–68

Davies, A., 'Youth gangs, masculinity and violence in late Victorian Manchester and Salford', *Journal of Social History*, 32:2 (1998), 364–5

Davies, A., '"These viragoes are no less cruel than the lads": young women, gangs and violence in late Victorian Manchester and Salford', *British Journal of Criminology*, 39:1, Special Issue (1999), 72–89

Davies, A., *The Gangs of Manchester: The Story of the Scuttlers, Britain's First Youth Cult* (Preston: Milo Books, 2008)

Davies, A. and S. Fielding (eds), *Workers' Worlds: Cultures and Communities in Manchester and Salford 1880–1939* (Manchester: Manchester University Press, 1992)

Davies, B., *A History of the Youth Service in England*, Vol. 1, *1939–1979* (Leicester: Youth Work Press, 1999)

Davies, J. A., 'Working-class women, Liverpool 1910–1940: social life, courtship marriage and motherhood. An oral history', in J. E. Hollinshead and F. Pogson (eds), *Studies in Northern History* (Liverpool: Liverpool Hope Press, 1997)

Davin, A., 'Flight to the centre. Winnie Gonley, 1930s colonial cosmopolitan', unpublished paper, 2000

Davis, F., *Fashion, Culture and Identity* (Chicago and London: University of Chicago Press, 1992)

Davis, J., *Youth and the Condition of Britain. Images of Adolescent Conflict* (London: Athlone Press, 1990)

Davis. M. D. and E. Lapovsky Kennedy, *Boots of Leather, Slippers of Gold: The History of a Lesbian Community* (New York and London: Routledge, 1993)

Dawes, F., *A Cry from the Streets. The Boys' Club Movement in Britain from the 1850s to the Present Day* (Hove, Sussex: Wayland Publishers, 1975)

Dawson, G., *Soldier Heroes: British Adventure, Empire and the Imagining of Masculinity* (London: Routledge, 1994)

De Certeau, M., *The Practice of Everyday Life*, trans. S. F. Rendall (Berkeley: University of California Press, 1984)

Dedman, M., 'Baden-Powell, militarism, and the "invisible contributors" to the Boy Scout Scheme, 1904–1920', *Twentieth Century British History* 4:3 (1993), 201–23

Dekkers, O., 'Walter Matthew Gallichan: fiction and freethought in the 1890s', *English Studies*, 83:5 (2002), 406–22.

Dickie, M., 'Town patriotism and the rise of labour: Northampton 1918–1939', PhD, University of Warwick, 1987

Doan, L., 'Passing fashions: reading female masculinities in the 1920s', *Feminist Studies*, 24:3 (1998), 663–700

Drotner, K., 'Schoolgirls, madcaps, and air aces: English girls and their magazine reading between the wars', *Feminist Studies*, 9:1 (1983), 33–52

Drotner, K., *English Children and Their Magazines, 1751–1945* (New Haven, CT and London: Yale University Press, 1988)

Dyck, N. and E. P. Archetti, *Sport, Dance and Embodied Identities* (Oxford: Berg, 2003)

Dyer, R., ' "I seem to find the happiness I seek": heterosexuality and dance in the musical', in H. Thomas (ed.), *Dance, Gender and Culture* (New York: St. Martin's Press, 1993)

Dyhouse, C., *Girls Growing Up in Late Victorian and Edwardian England* (London: Routledge and Kegan Paul, 1981)

Eagar, W. M., *Making Men: The History of Boys' Clubs and Related Movements in Great Britain* (London: University of London Press, 1953)

Eason, A. V., *'Remember now Thy Creator': A History of the Boys' Brigade in and around Northampton, Being a Record of its Activities in the Promotion of Christian Manliness* (Northampton: Boys' Brigade, Northampton Battalion, 1982)

Eavis, M., 'The picture palaces of Northampton, with particular reference to the Exchange and the Savoy', *Cinema Theatre Association Bulletin*, 9:4 (1975)

Edensor, T., 'Walking in the British countryside: reflexivity, embodied practices and ways to escape', *Body and Society*, 6:81 (2000), 81–106

Edwards, E. 'Photographs as object of memory', in M. Kwint, C. Breward, and J. Aynsley (eds), *Material Memories: Design and Evocation* (Oxford: Berg, 1999)

Eichengreen, B., 'Juvenile unemployment in twentieth century Britain: the emergence of a problem', *Social Research*, 54:2 (1987), 273–301

Elliot, R., ' "Everybody did it" – or did they? The use of oral history in researching women's experiences of smoking in Britain, 1930–1970', *Women's History Review*, 15:2 (2006), 297–322

Erenberg, L. A., 'Everybody's doin' it: the pre-World War I dance craze, the Castles, and the modern American girl', *Feminist Studies*, 3:1/2 (1975), 155–70

Exell, A., 'Morris Motors in the 1930s', *History Workshop Journal*, 6 (1978), 52–78

Farnell, B., 'Ethno-graphics and the moving body', *Man*, 29:4 (1994), 929–74

Fincham, B., 'Bicycle messengers and the road to freedom', *Sociological Review*, 54:1 (2006), 208–22

Fisher, K., *Birth Control, Sex and Marriage in Britain, 1918–1960* (Oxford: Oxford University Press, 2006)

Fisher, T., 'Fatherhood and the British fathercraft movement, 1919–39', *Gender and History*, 17:2 (2005), 441–62

Foster, S. (ed.), *Corporealities: Dancing Knowledge, Culture and Power* (London: Routledge, 1996)

Fowler, D., 'Teenage consumers? Young wage-earners and leisure in Manchester, 1919–1939', in A. Davies and S. Fielding (eds), *Workers' Worlds: Culture and Communities in Manchester and Salford, 1880–1939* (Manchester: Manchester University Press, 1992)

Fowler, D., *The First Teenagers. The Lifestyle of Young Wage Earners in Interwar Britain* (London: Woburn Press, 1995)

Fowler, D., *Youth Culture in Modern Britain c. 1920–c. 1970* (London: Palgrave Macmillan, 2008)

Francis, M., 'The domestication of the male? Recent research on nineteenth and twentieth century British masculinity', *The Historical Journal*, 45:3 (2002), 637–52

Franko, M., *Dancing Modernism/Performing Politics* (Bloomington: Indiana University Press, 1995)

Frith, S., *Performing Rites: On the Value of Popular Music* (Oxford: Oxford University Press, 1996)

Frosh, S., A. Phoenix and R. Pattman, *Young Masculinities: Understanding Boys in Contemporary Society* (London: Palgrave Macmillan, 2001)

Fussell, P., *The Great War and Modern Memory* (Oxford: Oxford University Press, 1975, 1977)

Gardiner, M. E., *Critiques of Everyday Life* (London and New York: Routledge, 2000)

Garside, W. R., 'Juvenile unemployment statistics between the wars', *Bulletin of the Society for the Study of Labour History*, 33 (1976), 38–46

Garside, W. R., 'Juvenile unemployment and public policy between the wars', *Economic History Review*, 30:2 (1977), 322–39

Garside, W. R., 'Juvenile unemployment between the wars: a rejoinder', *Economic History Review*, 32:4 (1979), 529–32

Garside, W. R., 'Youth unemployment in 20th century Britain: protest, conflict and the labour market', in D. Dowe (ed.), *Jugendprotest und Generationenkonflikt in Europa im 20. Jahrhundert: Deutschland, England, Frankreich und Italien im Vergleich* (Bonn: Verlag Neue Gesellschaft, 1986)

Gilbert, S. M., Review of Das, *Touch and Intimacy*, *The Review of English Studies*, 57:232 (2006), 849–51

Giles, J., '"Playing hard to get": working class women, sexuality and respectability in Britain, 1918–40', *Women's History Review*, 1:2 (1992), 239–55

Giles, J., '"You meet 'em and that's it": working class women's refusal of romance between the wars in Britain', in L. Pearce and J. Stacey (eds), *Romance Revisited* (London: Lawrence and Wishart, 1995)

Giles, J., *Women, Identity and Private Life in Britain, 1900–1950* (London: Macmillan Press Ltd, 1995)

Gillis, J. R., *Youth and History: Tradition and Change in European Age Relations, 1700–Present* (New York and London: Academic Press, 1974)

Gillis, J. R., *For Better, for Worse. British Marriages, 1600 to the Present* (New York and Oxford: Oxford University Press, 1985)

Gillis, J. R., *A World of Their Own Making: Myth, Ritual and the Quest for Family Values* (Cambridge, MA: Harvard University Press, 1996)

Gittins, D., 'Married life and birth control between the wars', *Oral History, Family History Issue*, 3:2 (1975), 53–64

Gittins, D., *Fair Sex, Family Size and Structure 1900–1939* (London: Hutchinson, 1982)

Glancy, M., 'Temporary American citizens? British audiences, Hollywood films and the threat of Americanization in the 1920s', *Historical Journal of Film, Radio and Television* (2006), 26:4, 461–84

Gomersall, M., *Working Class Girls in Nineteenth-Century England: Life, Work and Schooling* (Basingstoke: Macmillan, 1997)

Goodall, H., 'Telling country: memory, modernity and narratives in rural Australia', *History Workshop Journal*, 47 (1999), 160–90

Gough, K. V. and M. Franch, 'Spaces of the street: socio-spatial mobility and exclusion of youth in Recife', *Childrens' Geographies*, 3:2 (2005), 149–66

Grant, J., 'A "real boy" and not a sissy: gender, childhood and masculinity, 1890–1940', *Journal of Social History*, 37:4 (2004), 829–51

Gray, F., *Designing the Seaside: Architecture, Society and Nature* (London: Reaktion, 2006)

Greenall, R., *A History of Northamptonshire and the Soke of Peterborough* (Chichester: Phillimore, 1979)

Greenall, R. L., *Northamptonshire Life, 1914–39. A Photographic Survey* (Northampton: Northamptonshire Libraries, 1979)

Greenfield, J., S. O'Connell and C. Reid, 'Fashioning masculinity: *Men Only*, consumption and the development of marketing in the 1930s', *Twentieth Century British History*, 10:4 (1999)

Griffin, C., *Representations of Youth: The Study of Youth and Adolescence in Britain and America* (Cambridge: Polity Press, 1993)

Gruneberg, M. and P. Morris, *Aspects of Memory*. Vol. 1, *The Practical Aspects* (London and New York: Routledge, 1978, 1992)

Gudelunas, D., *Confidential to America: Newspaper Advice Columns and Sexual Education* (New Brunswick and London: Transaction Publishers, 2008)

Gullace, N., 'White feathers and wounded men: female patriotism and the memory of the Great War', *Journal of British Studies*, 36:2 (1997), 178–206

Hagerty, B., *Read All About It! 100 Sensational Years of the Daily Mirror* (Lydney, Gloucestershire: First Stone Publishing, 2003)

Haine, W. S., 'The development of leisure and the transformation of working-class adolescence, Paris 1830–1940', *Journal of Family History*, 17:4 (1992), 451–76

Haines, R., '"Dressing to impress"? Seaside fashion and the cult of respectability in inter-war Wales', paper presented at Recording Leisure Lives: Holidays and Tourism in 20th Century Britain, University of Bolton, March 2010

Hall, L., *Sex, Gender and Social Change in Britain since 1880* (London: Palgrave Macmillan, 2000)

Hall, R. (ed.), *Dear Dr Stopes: Sex in the 1920s* (Harmondsworth: Penguin Books, 1978)

Hall, S. and T. Jefferson (eds), *Resistance through Rituals: Youth Subcultures in Post-war Britain* (London: Hutchinson in association with the Centre for Contemporary Cultural Studies, University of Birmingham, 1976)

Hall, T. et al., *Locality, Biography and Youth in a Transforming Community*, full research report, ESRC end of award report, RES-000-23-0878, www.esrc. ac.uk/my-esrc/grants/RES-000-23-0878/read/reports (accessed January 2009)

Hallam E. and J. Hockey, *Death, Memory and Material Culture* (Oxford: Berg, 2001)

Hammerton, A. J. 'The English weakness? Gender, satire and "moral manliness" in the lower middle class, 1870–1920', in A. Kidd and D. Nicholls (eds), *Gender, Civic Culture and Consumerism: Middle-class Identity in Britain, 1800–1940* (Manchester: Manchester University Press, 1999)

Hammerton, A. J., 'Pooterism or partnership? Marriage and masculine identity in the lower middle class, 1870–1920', *Journal of British Studies*, 38:3 (1999), 291–321

Hammerton, A. J., Review Essay, 'Forgotten People? Marriage and Masculine Identities in Britain', *Journal of Family History*, 22:1 (1997), 110–13

Hanawalt, B. A., 'Historical descriptions and prescriptions for adolescence', *Journal of Family History*, 17:4 (1992), 241–51

Hanna, J. L., *Dance, Sex and Gender: Signs of Identity, Dominance and Desire* (Chicago: Chicago University Press, 1988)

Hantover, J. P., 'The Boys Scouts and the validations of masculinity', *Journal of Social Issues*, 34:1 (1978), 184–95

Harley, J. L., 'Report of an enquiry into the occupations, further education and leisure interests of a number of girl wage-earners from elementary and central schools in the Manchester district, with special reference to the influence of school training on their use of leisure', MEd dissertation, University of Manchester (1937)

Harrison, P. 'Making sense: embodiment and the sensibilities of the everyday', *Environment and Planning D: Society and Space*, 18:4 (2000), 497–517

Haste, C., *Rules of Desire: Sex in Britain; World War One to the Present* (London: Chatto and Windus, 1992)

Heaven, P. C. L., *The Social Psychology of Adolescence* (Basingstoke: Palgrave, 1994, 2001)

Hebdige, D., *Subculture: The Meaning of Style* (London: Methuen, 1979)

Hebdige, D., *Hiding in the Light: On Images and Things* (London: Routledge, 2002)

Hendrick, H., *Images of Youth. Age, Class, and the Male Youth Problem, 1880–1920* (Oxford: Clarendon Press, 1990)

Heron, C., 'Boys will be boys: working class masculinities in the age of mass production', *International Labor and Working-Class History*, 69:1 (2006), 6–34

Heward C., *Making a Man of Him: Parents and Their Sons' Education at an English Public School, 1929–50* (London: Routledge, 1988)

Higgins, N., 'The changing expectations and realities of marriage in the English working class, 1920–1960' (PhD thesis, University of Cambridge, 2002)

Hiley, N., ' "Let's go to the pictures": the British cinema audience in the 1920s and 1930s', *Journal of Popular British Cinema*, 2 (1999), 39–53

Hill, J., *Sport, Leisure and Culture in Twentieth Century Britain* (Basingstoke: Palgrave, 2002)

Hilton, M., *Smoking in British Popular Culture, 1800–2000* (Manchester: Manchester University Press, 2000)

Hinton, J., 'The "class" complex': Mass-Observation and cultural distinction in pre-war Britain', *Past and Present*, 199:1 (2008), 207–36

Hoggart, R., *The Uses of Literacy* (London: Penguin books in association with Chatto and Windus, 1957, 1962)

Holt, J., *Public School Literature, Civic Education and the Politics of Male Adolescence* (Aldershot: Ashgate, 2008)

Holt, R., *Sport and the British: A Modern History* (Oxford: Clarendon Press, 1989)

Honeyman, K., 'Following suit: men, masculinity and gendered practices in the clothing trade in Leeds, England, 1890–1940', *Gender and History*, 14:3 (2002), 426–46

Honeyman, K., 'Style monotony and the business of fashion: the marketing of menswear in inter-war England', *Textile History*, 34:2 (2003), 171–91

Hood, R. and K. Joyce, 'Three generations: oral testimonies on crime and social change in London's East End', *British Journal of Criminology*, 39:1, Special Issue (1999), 136–60

Horn, A., *Juke Box Britain: Americanisation and Youth Culture, 1945–60* (Manchester: Manchester University Press, 2009)

Horwood, C., ' "Girls who arouse dangerous passions": women and bathing, 1900–1939', *Women's History Review*, 9:4 (2000), 653–73

Houlbrook, M., ' "Lady Austin's camp boys": constituting the queer subject in 1930s London', *Gender and History*, 14:1 (2002), 31–61

Houlbrook, M., 'Soldier heroes and rent boys: homosex, masculinities, and Britishness in the Brigade of Guards, circa. 1900–1960', *Journal of British Studies*, 42:3 (2003), 351–88

Houlbrook, M., *Queer London: Perils and Pleasures of the Sexual Metropolis, 1918–1957* (Chicago: University of Chicago Press, 2005)

Houlbrook, M., ' "The man with the powder puff" in interwar London', *The Historical Journal*, 50:1 (2007), 145–71.

Humphries, S., *Hooligans or Rebels? An Oral History of Working-Class Childhood and Youth, 1889–1939* (Oxford: Basil Blackwell, 1981)

Humphries, S., *A Secret World of Sex: Forbidden Fruit: The British Experience, 1900–1950* (London: Sidgwick and Jackson, 1988)

Humphries, S. and P. Gordon, *A Man's World. From Boyhood to Manhood, 1890–1960* (London: BBC Books, 1996)

Hunt, F. (ed.), *Lessons for Life: The Schooling of Girls and Women* (Oxford: Basil Blackwell, 1987)

Hustwitt, M., ' "Caught in a whirlpool of aching sound": the production of dance music in Britain in the 1920s', *Popular Music*, Producers and Markets Special Issue, 3 (1983), 7–31

Hynes, S., *A War Imagined: The First World War and English Culture* (New York: Athenaeum, 1990)

Jackson, L., 'Childhood and youth', in H. G. Cocks and M. Houlbrook (eds), *The Modern History of Sexuality* (Basingstoke: Palgrave Macmillan, 2006)

Jacobs, I., 'Social organisations for adolescent girls', in H. L. Smith (ed.), *The New Survey of London Life and Labour*, Vol. IX, *Life and Leisure* (London: P. S. King & Son Ltd., Westminster, 1935)

James, H. E. O., and F. T. Moore, 'Adolescent leisure in a working class district: Part I', *Occupational Psychology*, 14:3 (1940), 132–45

James, H. E. O. and F. T. Moore, 'Adolescent leisure in a working class district: Part II', *Occupational Psychology*, 18:1 (1944), 24–34

Jephcott, P., *Some Young People* (London: George Allen & Unwin, 1954)

Jo, Y., 'Murrell, Christine Mary (1874–1933)', *Oxford Dictionary of National Biography* (Oxford: Oxford University Press, 2004), www.oxforddnb.com/view/article/54293 (accessed 20 October 2009)

Joannou, M., *'Ladies, Please Don't Smash These Windows': Women's Writing, Feminist Consciousness and Social Change, 1918–38* (Oxford: Berg, 1995)

Johnston, R. and A. McIvor, 'Dangerous work, hard men and broken bodies: masculinity in the Clydeside heavy industries, c. 1930–1970s', *Labour History Review*, 69:2 (2004), 135–51

Jones, E., 'The psychology of killing: the combat experience of British soldiers during the First World War', *Journal of Contemporary History*, 41:2 (2006), 229–46

Jones, M., 'What should historians do with heroes? Reflections on nineteenth and twentieth century Britain', *History Compass*, 5:2 (2007), 439–54

Jones, S. G., *Workers at Play: A Social and Economic History of Leisure, 1918–39* (London: Routledge and Kegan Paul, 1986)

Kane, H. T. with E. B. Arthur, *Dear Dorothy Dix: The Story of a Compassionate Woman* (New York: Doubleday & Company, Inc., 1952)

Kanervo, E., T. Jones and J. White, 'One hundred years of advice: an analysis of the style and content of Dear Abby and Dorothy Dix', paper presented at the Dorothy Dix Symposium, Woodstock Mansion, Todd County, Kentucky, 27 September 1991, http://library.apsu.edu/Dix/kanervo.htm (accessed 7 February 2007)

Kean, H., 'East End stories: the chairs and the photographs', *International Journal of Heritage Studies*, 6:2 (2000), 111–27

Kean, K., *London Stories. Personal Lives, Public Histories: Creating Personal and Public Histories of Working Class London* (London: Rivers Oram Press, 2004)

Kent, R., *Aunt Agony Advises: Problem Pages through the Ages* (London: W. H. Allen, 1979)

Kent, S. K., 'Gender reconstruction after the First World War', in H. L. Smith (ed.), *British Feminism in the Twentieth Century* (Amherst: University of Massachusetts Press, 1990)

Kent, S. K., 'Remembering the Great War', *Journal of British Studies*, 37:1 (1998), 105–10

Kent, S. K., *Gender and Power in Britain, 1640–1990* (London: Routledge, 1999)

Kett, J., *Rites of Passage: Adolescence in America, 1790 to the Present* (New York: Basic Books, 1977)

King, N., *Memory, Narrative and Identity: Remembering the Self* (Edinburgh: Edinburgh University Press, 2000)

King, P., 'The rise of juvenile delinquency in England, 1780–1840: changing patterns of perception and prosecution', *Past and Present*, 160:1 (1998), 116–66

King, P. and J. Noel, 'The origins of the problem of juvenile delinquency: the growth of juvenile prosecutions in London in the late eighteenth and early nineteenth centuries', *Criminal Justice History*, 14 (1993), 17–41

Kirkham, P., 'Dress, dance, dreams and desire: fashion and fantasy in dance hall', *Journal of Design History*, 8:3 (1995), 195–214

Koven, S., 'From rough lads to hooligans: boy life, national culture and social reform', in A. Parker, M. Russo, D. Somer and P. Yaeger (eds), *Nationalisms and Sexualities* (New York and London: Routledge, 1992)

Koven, S., 'Remembering and dismemberment: crippled children, wounded soldiers and the Great War in Great Britain', *The American Historical Review*, 99:4 (1994), 1167–202

Kramer, S., 'The fragile male', *British Medical Journal*, December 2000, 1609–12

Kuhn, A., *Cinema, Censorship and Sexuality, 1909–1925* (London: Routledge, 1988)

Kuhn, A., *An Everyday Magic: Cinema and Cultural Memory* (London and New York: I. B. Tauris, 2002)

Langhamer, C., *Women's Leisure in England, 1920–1960* (Manchester: Manchester University Press, 2000)

Langhamer, C., 'Love and courtship in mid-twentieth century England', *The Historical Journal*, 50:1 (2007), 173–96

Latham, E., 'The Liverpool Boys' Association and the Liverpool Union of Youth Clubs: youth organisations and gender, 1940–70', *Journal of Contemporary History*, 35:3 (2000), 423–37

Leed, E., *No Man's Land: Combat and Identity in World War One* (Cambridge,: Cambridge University Press, 1979)

Lefebvre, H., 'The everyday and everydayness', trans. Christine Levich, with Alice Kaplan and Kristin Ross, *Yale French Studies*, 73 (1987), 7–11

LeMahieu, D., *A Culture for Democracy: Mass Communications and the Cultivated Mind in Britain between the Wars* (Oxford: Clarendon Press, 1988)

Lesko, N., *Act Your Age! A Cultural Construction of Adolescence* (New York and London: Routledge Falmer, 2001)

Levi, G. and J.-C. Schmitt (eds), *A History of Young People*, vol. 1: *Ancient and Medieval Rites of Passage*, trans. C. Naish (Cambridge, MA: Harvard University Press, 1997)

Levsen, S., 'Constructing elite identities: university students, military masculinity and the consequences of the Great War in Britain and Germany', *Past and Present*, 198:1 (2008), 147–83

Life in Old Northampton (Northampton: Northamptonshire Libraries, 1976)

Light, A., *Forever England: Femininity, Literature and Conservatism between the Wars* (London: Routledge, 1991)

Loewe, L. L., *Basil Henriques. A Portrait Based on his Diaries, Letters and Speeches as Collated by his Widow Rose Henriques* (London: Routledge and Kegan Paul, 1976)

Lowndes, G. A. N., *The Silent Revolution: An Account of the Expansion of Public Education in England and Wales, 1896–1965* (Oxford: Oxford University Press, 1969)

Mac an Ghaill, M., *The Making of Men: Masculinities, Sexualities and Schooling* (Milton Keynes: Open University Press, 1994)

McBee, R. D., *Dance Hall Days: Intimacy and Leisure among Working-Class Immigrants in the United States* (New York: New York University Press, 2000)

McCabe, S., 'Henriques, Sir Basil Lucas Quixano (1890–1961), rev., *Oxford Dictionary of National Biography* (Oxford: Oxford University Press, 2004), www.oxforddnb.com/view/article/33821 (accessed November 2007)

McCormack, D., 'Diagramming practice and performance', *Environment and Planning D: Society and Space*, 23:1 (2005), 119–47

Macdonald, M., *Representing Women: Myths of Femininity in the Popular Media* (London: Edward Arnold, 1995)

MacDonald, R. H., 'Reproducing the middle-class boy: from purity to patriotism in the boys' magazines, 1892–1914', *Journal of Contemporary History*, 24:3 (1989), 519–39

MacDonald, R. H., *Sons of the Empire: The Frontier and the Boy Scout Movement, 1890–1918* (Toronto: University of Toronto Press, 1993)

MacKian, S., 'Mapping reflexive communities: visualizing the geographies of emotion', *Social and Cultural Geography*, 5:4 (2004), 615–31

McKibbin, R., *Classes and Cultures: England, 1918–51* (Oxford: Oxford University Press, 1998)

Madge, C., A. W. Coysh, G. Dixon and I. Madge, *To Start You Talking* (London: The Pilot Press, 1945)

Magarey, S., 'The invention of juvenile delinquency in early nineteenth century England', *Labour History*, 34 (1978), 11–27

Malone, K., 'Street life: youth, culture and competing uses of public space', *Environment and Urbanization*, 14:2 (2002), 157–68

Mangan, J. A. and J. Walvin (eds), *Manliness and Morality: Middle-class Masculinity in Britain and America 1800–1940* (Manchester: Manchester University Press, 1987)

Martino, M. and M. Pallotta-Chiarolli, *So What's a Boy? Addressing Issues of Masculinity and Schooling* (Maidenhead: Open University Press, 2003)

Marwick, A., 'Youth in Britain, 1920–60: detachment and commitment', *Journal of Contemporary History*, 5:1 (1970), 37–45

Matthews, H. and M. Limb, *Exploring the 'fourth environment': young people's use of place and views on their environment: full report on research activities and results*, SN 4076, www.esds.ac.uk/findingData/snDescription.asp?sn=4076 (accessed January 2009)

Matthews, J. J., 'They had such a lot of fun: the Women's League of Health and Beauty between the wars', *History Workshop Journal*, 30 (1990), 22–54

Matthews, J. J., 'Stack, Mary Meta Bagot (1883–1935)', *Oxford Dictionary of National Biography* (Oxford: Oxford University Press, 2004), www.oxforddnb.com/view/article/45797 (accessed 12 July 2009)

Matthews, J. J., *Dance Hall and Picture Palace: Sydney's Romance with Modernity* (Sydney: Currency Press, 2005)

Matthews, W., *British Diaries: An Annotated Bibliography of British Diaries Written Between 1442 and 1942* (Berkeley: University of California Press, 1950)

Mauss, M., 'Techniques of the body', *Economy and Society*, 2:1 (1973), 70–88

May, M., 'Innocence and experience: the evolution of the concept of juvenile delinquency in the mid-nineteenth century', *Victorian Studies*, 17:1 (1973), 2–29

Mayne, A. and S. Lawrence, 'Ethnographies of place: a new urban research agenda', *Urban History*, 26:3 (1999), 325–48

Melman, B., *Women and the Popular Imagination in the Twenties: Flappers and Nymphs* (New York: St Martin's, 1988)

Middleton, J., 'The experience of corporal punishment in schools, 1890–1940', *History of Education*, 37:2 (2008), 253–75

Mitterauer, M., *A History of Youth* (Oxford: Blackwell, 1986, 1992)

Moores, S., '"The box on the dresser": memories of early radio and everyday life', *Media, Culture, Society*, 10:23 (1988), 23–40

Morris, B., 'What we talk about when we talk about "walking in the city"', *Cultural Studies*, 18:5 (2004), 675–97

Morris, G., *Moving Words: Re-writing Dance* (London: Routledge, 1996)

Mort, F., 'Boy's own? Masculinity, style and popular culture', in R. Chapman and J. Rutherford (eds), *Male Order: Unwrapping Masculinity* (London: Lawrence and Wishart, 1988, 1996)

Mort, F., *Cultures of Consumption: Masculinities and Social Space in Late Twentieth-Century Britain* (London: Routledge, 1996)

Mort, F. and P. Thomson, 'Retailing, commercial culture and masculinity in 1950s Britain: the case of Montague Burton, the Tailor of Taste', *History Workshop Journal*, 38 (1994), 106–27.

Mosse, G., *Fallen Soldiers: Reshaping the Memory of the World Wars* (Oxford: Oxford University Press, 1990)

Mowat, C. L., *Britain between the Wars, 1918–40* (London: Methuen, 1955)

Murfin, L., *Popular Leisure in the Lake Counties* (Manchester: Manchester University Press, 1990)

Musgrove, F., *Youth and the Social Order* (Bloomington: Indiana University Press, 1964)

Muus, R. E., *Theories of Adolescence* (New York: Random House, 1962, 1988)

Nellis, M., review of W. J. Forsythe, *Penal Discipline, Reformatory Projects and the English Prison Commission 1895–1939* (Exeter: University of Exeter Press, 1990), in *British Journal of Criminology*, 34:3 (1994), 403–6

Nicholson, V., *Singled Out: How Two Million Women Survived Without Men after the First World War* (London: Penguin Books, 2008)

Norris, S., 'Mass Observation at the dance hall: a democracy of fashion?' in R. Snape and H. Pussard (eds), *Recording Leisure Lives: Histories, Archives and Memories of Leisure in 20th Century Britain* (Eastbourne: Leisure Studies Association, University of Brighton, 2009)

Nott, J. J., *Music for the People: Popular Music and Dance in Interwar Britain* (Oxford: Oxford University Press, 2002)

Novack, C. J., 'The body endeavours as cultural practices', in S. L. Foster (ed.), *Choreographing History* (Bloomington: Indiana University Press, 1995)

O'Brien, M., *Framing Memories: Experiences of Picture Going and Working in Cinemas in South London between the 1920s and the 1950s*, an oral history research project undertaken for the Research and Information Division of the British Film Institute, April 1992

O'Connell, S., 'Smoking in British popular culture', review of M. Hilton, *Smoking in British Popular Culture, 1800–2000* (Manchester: Manchester University Press, 2000), Reviews in History, Institute of Historical Research, www.history.ac.uk/reviews/paper/oconnellS.html, (accessed November 2007)

O'Connor, B., 'Sexing the nation: Discourses of the dancing body in Ireland in the 1930s', *Journal of Gender Studies*, 14:2 (2005), 89–105

O'Donnell, M., and S. Sharpe, *Uncertain Masculinities: Youth, Ethnicity, and Class in Contemporary Britain* (London: Routledge, 2000)

Oliver, E., 'Liberation or limitation? A study of women's leisure in Bolton, c. 1919–1939', PhD dissertation, University of Lancaster, 1997

Oram, A., 'Feminism, androgony and love between women in *Urania*, 1916–1940', *Media History*, 7:1 (2001), 57–70

Osborne, C. A., 'Presumptuous pinnacle ladies? The development of independent climbing for women during the inter-war years', paper presented at Women's History Network (Midlands Region) conference, 'Women, Sport and Leisure', Worcester University, May 2007

Osborne, C. A., 'An extraordinary Joe? The emergence of the working class climber as hero', paper presented at British Society of Sports History conference, University of Stirling, August 2007

Osgerby, B., 'From the roaring twenties to the swinging sixties: continuity and change in British youth culture, 1929–59', in B. Brivati and H. Jones (eds), *What Difference Did the War Make?* (Leicester: Leicester University Press, 1993)

Osgerby, B., *Youth in Britain since 1945* (Oxford: Blackwell, 1998)

Osgerby, B., *Playboys in Paradise: Masculinity, Youth and Leisure-Style in Modern America* (Oxford: Berg, 2001)

Parratt, C. M., *More than Mere Amusement: Working-Class Women's Leisure in England, 1750–1914* (New York: St. Martin's Press, 2001)

Parsonage, C., *The Evolution of Jazz in Britain, 1880–1935* (Aldershot: Hampshire: Ashgate, 2005)

Passerini, L., *Fascism in Popular Memory: The Cultural Experience of the Turin Working Class* (Cambridge: Cambridge University Press, 1987)

Pearson, G., *Hooligan: A History of Respectable Fears* (London: Macmillan, 1983)

Pearson, G., 'Perpetual novelty: a history of generational conflicts in Britain', in D. Dowe (ed.), *Jugendprotest und Generationenkonflict in Europa im 20. Jahrhundert: Deutschland, England, Frankreich und Italien im Vergleich* (Bonn: Verlag Neue Gesellschaft, 1986), pp. 165–77

Peel, M., B. Caine and C. Twomey, 'Masculinity, emotion and subjectivity: Introduction', *The Journal of Men's Studies*, 15:3 (2007), 247–49

Pegg, M., *Broadcasting and Society, 1918–1939* (London: Croom Helm, 1983)

Perry, G., 'The great British PICTURE SHOW', in B. Waites, T. Bennett and G. Martin (eds), *Popular Culture: Past and Present* (London: Croom Helm in association with the Open University Press, 1982)

Phillips, A., 'Advice columnists', in B. Franklin (ed.), *Pulling Newspapers Apart: Analysing Print Journalism* (London: Routledge, 2008)

Pilcher, J., 'Sex in health education: official guidance for schools in England, 1928–1977', *Journal of Historical Sociology*, 17:2/3 (2004), 185–208

Pittock, M., 'Richard Hoggart and the Leavises', *Essays in Criticism*, 60:1 (2010), 51–69

Pomfret, D. M., *Young People and the European City: Age Relations in Nottingham and Saint-Etienne, 1890–1940* (Aldershot: Ashgate, 2004)

Pooley, C., J. Turnbull and M. Adams, 'The impact of new transport technologies on intra-urban mobility: a view from the past, *Environment and Planning A*, 38:2 (2006), 253–67

Porter, R. and L. Hall, *The Facts of Life. The Creation of Sexual Knowledge in Britain, 1650–1950* (New Haven, CT: Yale University Press, 1995)

Power, R., 'Healthy motion. Images of "natural" and "cultured" movement in early twentieth-century Britain', *Women's Studies International Forum*, 19:5 (1996), 551–65

Powys, J. C. and L. Marlow, *Letters of John Cowper Powys to Louis Wilkinson, 1935–1956* (London: Macdonald, 1958)

Powys, L., *Still the Joy of It* (London: Macdonald, 1956)

Proctor, T. M., '(Uni)forming youth: girl guides and boy scouts in Britain, 1908–39', *History Workshop Journal*, 45 (1998), 103–34

Proctor, T. M., *On My Honour: Guides and Scouts in Interwar Britain* (Philadelphia: American Philosophical Society, 2002)

Proctor, T. M., 'Scouts, Guides and the fashioning of empire, 1919–1939', in W. Parkins (ed.) *Fashioning the Body Politic: Gender, Dress, Citizenship* (Oxford: Berg, 2002)

Proctor, T. M., '"Something for the girls": Girl Guides and emerging youth cultures, 1908–1939', in C. Benninghaus, M. J. Mayne, and B. Søland (eds), *Secret Gardens, Satanic Mills: Placing Girls in Modern European History* (Bloomington: Indiana University Press, 2005)

Proctor, T. M., '"Gone home": Boy Scouting and the writing/re-writing of the war in Britain, 1914–1920s', www.inter-disciplinary.net/ptb/wvw/wvw3/proctor%20paper.pdf (accessed 12 January 2007)

Prynn, D., 'The woodcraft folk and the Labour movement 1925–70', *Journal of Contemporary History*, 18:1 (1983), 79–95

Pugh, M., *We Danced All Night: A Social History of Britain between the Wars* (London: Vintage, 2009)

Pumphrey, M., 'The flapper, the housewife and the making of modernity', *Cultural Studies*, 1:2 (1987), 179–94

Puuronen, V., 'Youth research at the beginning of the new millenium', in V. Puuronen (ed.), *Youth on the Threshold of the Third Millennium* (Joensuu: Karelian Institute, University of Joensuu, 2001)

Pyke, S., 'The popularity of nationalism in the early British Boy Scout movement', *Social History*, 23:3 (1998), 309–24

Reed, S. A., 'The politics and poetics of dance', *Annual Review of Anthropology*, 27 (1998), 503–32

Register, W., *The Kid of Coney Island: Fred Thompson and the Rise of American Amusements* (New York: Oxford University Press, 2003)

Reitz, R., 'Hot snow: Valaida Snow (queen of the trumpet sings and swings)', *Black American Literature Forum*, 16:4 (1982), 158–60

Richards, G., 'Britain on the couch: the popularization of psychoanalysis in Britain, 1918–1940', *Science in Context*, 13:2 (2000), 183–230

Richards, J., *The Age of the Dream Palace: Cinema and Society in Britain 1930–39* (London: Routledge and Kegan Paul, 1984)

Richards, J., '"Passing the love of women": manly love and Victorian society', in J. A. Mangan and J. Walvin (eds), *Manliness and Morality: Middle-class Masculinity in Britain and America 1800–1940* (Manchester: Manchester University Press, 1987)

Richards, J. and D. Sheridan (eds), *Mass-Observation at the Movies* (London and New York: Routledge and Kegan Paul, 1987)

Richardson, A., 'Rolfe, Sybil Katherine Neville- (1885–1955)', *Oxford Dictionary of National Biography* (Oxford: Oxford University Press, 2004), www.oxforddnb.com/view/article/76744 (accessed 24 April 2007)

Rickwood, P. W., 'Public enjoyment of the open countryside in England and Wales, 1919–1939', PhD thesis, University of Leicester, 1973

Roberts, E., *A Woman's Place: An Oral History of Working-Class Women, 1890–1940* (Oxford: Basil Blackwell, 1984)

Roberts, R., *The Classic Slum: Salford Life in the First Quarter of the Century* (London: Penguin Books, 1971, 1990)

Robinson, J.A., 'Autobiographical memory', in M. Gruneberg and P. Morris (eds), *Aspects of Memory* (London and New York, 1978, 1992)

Roper, M., 'Between manliness and masculinity: the "war generation" and the psychology of fear in Britain, 1914–1950', *Journal of British Studies*, 44:2 (2005), 343–62

Roper, M., *The Secret Battle: Emotional Survival in the Great War* (Manchester and New York: Manchester University Press, 2009)

Rose, J., *The Intellectual Life of the British Working Classes* (New Haven, CT and London: Yale Nota Bene, 2002)

Rosenthal, M., *The Character Factory: Baden-Powell and the Origins of the Boy Scout Movement* (New York: Pantheon Press, 1986)

Ross, E., 'Women's neighbourhood sharing in London before World War One', *History Workshop Journal*, 15:1 (1983), 4–28

Ross, E., *Love and Toil: Motherhood in Outcast London, 1870–1918* (New York and Oxford: Oxford University Press, 1993)

Rowbotham, S., 'New entry points from USA women's labour history', in M. Walsh (ed.), *Working Out Gender: Perspectives from Labour History* (Aldershot: Ashgate, 1999)

Russell, D., *Football and the English* (Lancaster: Carnegie Publishing Ltd., 1997)

Rust, F., *Dance in Society: An Analysis of the Relationship between Dance and Society in England from the Middle Ages to the Present Day* (London: Routledge and Kegan Paul, 1968)

Samuel, R., 'Doing the Lambeth Walk', in *Theatres of Memory: Past and Present in Contemporary Culture* (London: Verso, 1994)

Samuel, R., *Theatres of Memory: Past and Present in Contemporary Culture* (London: Verso, 1994)

Sarsby, J., *Missuses and Mouldrunners: An Oral History of Women Pottery-Workers at Work and Home* (Milton Keynes: Open University Press, 1988)

Sauerteig, L. D. H. and R. Davidson, 'Shaping the sexual knowledge of the young', in L. D. H. Sauerteig and R. Davidson, *Shaping Sexual Knowledge: A Cultural History of Sex Education in Twentieth Century Europe* (London and New York: Routledge, 2009)

Savage, J., *Teenage: The Creation of Youth, 1875–1945* (London: Chatto and Windus, 2007)

Scarry, E., *The Body in Pain: The Making and Unmaking of the World* (Oxford: Oxford University Press, 1987)

Schilpp, M. G. and S. M. Murphy, *Great Women of the Press* (Carbondale, IL: Southern Illinois Press, 1983)

Schuyf, J., '"Trousers with flies!" The clothing and subculture of lesbians', *Textile History*, 24:1 (1993), 61–73

Scott, D. B., 'Silvester, Victor Marlborough (1900–1978)', *Oxford Dictionary of National Biography* (Oxford: Oxford University Press, September 2004), www.oxforddnb.com/view/article/31685 (accessed 7 June 2007)

Seabrook, J., 'The New Statesman essay – goodbye to provincial life', *New Statesman*, 129:18 (December 2000), pp. 33–4

Sedgwick, J., *Popular Filmgoing in the 1930s: A Choice of Pleasures* (Exeter: University of Exeter Press, 2000).

Sedgwick, J., 'Regional distinctions in the consumption of films and stars in mid-1930s Britain', Institute of Historical Research, Electronic Seminars in History presentation (1998), www.history.ac.uk/resources/e-seminars/sedgewick-paper (accessed December 2009)

Selleck, R. J., *English Primary Education and the Progressives, 1914–1939* (London: Routledge and Kegan Paul, 1972)

Shaw, J., 'Winning territory: changing place to change pace', in J. May and N. Thrift (eds), *Timespace: Geographies of Temporality* (London: Routledge, 2001)

Shields, R., *Places on the Margin: Alternative Geographies of Modernity* (London: Routledge, 1991)

Shore, H., *Artful Dodgers: Youth and Crime in Early 19th-Century London* (Woodbridge: Boydell and Brewer, 1999, 2002)

Shore, H., 'Cross coves, buzzers and general sorts of prigs: juvenile crime and the criminal "underworld" in the early nineteenth century', *British Journal of Criminology*, 39:1 (1999), 10–24

Shore, H., 'The trouble with boys: gender and the "invention" of the juvenile offender in the early nineteenth century', in M. Arnot and C. Usborne (eds), *Gender and Crime in Modern Europe* (London: UCL Press, 1999), pp. 75–92

Signorielli, N. D., *Women in Communication: A Biographical Sourcebook* (Westport, CT: Greenwood Press, 1996)

Simey, M., 'D'Aeth, Frederic George (1875–1940)', *Oxford Dictionary of National Biography* (Oxford: Oxford University Press, 2004), www.oxforddnb.com/view/article/54584 (accessed 9 February 2008).

Simon, B., 'The student movement in England and Wales during the 1930s', *History of Education*, 16:3 (1987), 189–203, republished in B. Simon, *The State and Educational Change: Essays in the History of Education and Pedagogy* (London: Lawrence and Wishart, 1994)

Smith, C. 'Paterson, Sir Alexander Henry (1884–1947)', *Oxford Dictionary of National Biography* (Oxford: Oxford University Press, 2004), www.oxforddnb.com/view/article/35405 (accessed 24 June 2006).

Smith, H. L. (ed.), *The New Survey of London Life and Labour*, Vol. IX, *Life and Leisure* (London: P. S. King & Son Ltd., Westminster, 1935)

Smith, M. K. (2002) 'James Butterworth, Christian youth work and Clubland', The Encyclopedia of Informal Education, www.infed.org/thinkers/butterworth.htm (accessed January 2006)

Smith, S. J., *Children, Cinema and Censorship: From Dracula to the Dead End Kids* (London and New York: I. B. Tauris, 2005)

Smyth, J., 'Dancing, depravity and all that jazz: the public halls dance act of 1935', *History Ireland*, 1:2 (1993), 51–4

Snell, K. D. M., 'Gravestones, belonging and local attachment in England, 1700–2000', *Past and Present*, 179:1 (2003), 97–179

Spence, J., 'Youth work and gender', in T. Jeffs and M. Smith (eds), *Young People, Inequality and Youth Work* (London: Macmillan, 1990)

Springhall, J., 'Lord Meath, youth and empire', *Journal of Contemporary History*, 5:4 (1970), 97–111

Springhall, J., 'The Boy Scouts, class and militarism in relation to British youth movements, 1908–30', *International Review of Social History*, 16 (1971), 121–58

Springhall, J., *Youth, Empire and Society: British Youth Movements, 1883–1940* (Beckenham: Croom Helm, 1977)

Springhall, J., *Sure and Steadfast: A History of the Boys' Brigade, 1883–1993* (London: Collins, 1983)

Springhall, J., *Coming of Age: Adolescence in Britain, 1860–1960* (Dublin: Gill and Macmillan, 1986)

Springhall, J., 'Young England, rise up and listen! The political dimensions of youth protest and generation conflict in Britain, 1919–1939', in D. Dowe (ed.), *Jugendprotest und Generationenkonflikt in Europa im 20. Jahrhundert: Deutschland, England, Frankreich und Italien im Vergleich* (Bonn: Verlag Neue Gesellschaft, 1986)

Springhall, J., 'Building character in the British boy: the attempt to extend Christian manliness to working class adolescents, 1880–1914', in J. A. Mangan and J. Walvin (eds), *Manliness and Morality: Middle-class Masculinity in Britain and America, 1800–1940* (Manchester: Manchester University Press, 1987)

Springhall, J., *Youth, Popular Culture and Moral Panics: Penny Gaffs to Gangsta Rap, 1830–1966* (London: Macmillan Press Ltd, 1998)

Stacey, J., 'Desperately seeking difference', in L. Gamman and M. Marshment (eds), *The Female Gaze: Women as Viewers of Popular Culture* (London: Women's Press, 1988)

Stanley, L., 'Women have servants and men never eat: issues in reading gender, using the case study of Mass Observation's 1937 day-diaries', *Women's History Review*, 4:1 (1995), 95–102

Stearns, P. N., 'Girls, boys, and emotions: redefinitions and historical change', *The Journal of American History*, 80:1 (1993), 36–74

Stearns, P. N., Review essay, 'Informalization and contemporary manners: the Wouters studies', *Theory and Society*, 36:4 (2007), 373–9

Steele, V., *Fashion and Eroticism: Ideals of Feminine Beauty from the Victorian Era to the Jazz Age* (New York and Oxford: Oxford University Press, 1985)

Steele, V., 'Letter from the editor', *Fashion Theory: The Journal of Dress, Body and Culture*, 1:4 (1997), 337–38

Stevenson, J., *British Society, 1914–45* (Harmondsworth: Penguin, 1984, 1990)

Susman, W., *Culture as History: The Transformation of American Society in the Twentieth Century* (New York: Pantheon Books, 1984)

Susman, W., 'Personality and the making of twentieth-century culture', in W. Susman, *Culture as History: The Transformation of American Society in the Twentieth Century* (New York: Pantheon Books, 1984), essay available on www.h-net.org/~hst203/readings/susman2.html (accessed November 2009).

Swiencicki, M. A., 'Consuming brotherhood: men's culture, style and recreation as consumer culture, 1880–1930', *Journal of Social History*, 31:4 (1998), 773–809

Symes, C., 'Chronicles of labour: a discourse analysis of diaries', *Time and Society*, 8:2 (1999), 357–80

Taylor, D. J., *Bright Young People: The Rise and Fall of a Generation, 1918–1940* (London: Vintage, 2008)

Taylor, H., *A Claim on the Countryside: A History of the British Outdoor Movement* (Edinburgh: Keele University Press, 1997)

Taylor, J., 'Sex, snobs and swing: a case study of Mass-Observation as a source for social history', Mass-Observation Online, British Social History, 1937–1972, University of Sussex

Taylor, M., 'Round the London ring: boxing, class and community in interwar London', *The London Journal*, 34:2 (2009), 139–62

Tebbutt, M., *Women's Talk? A Social History of 'Gossip' in Working Class Neighbourhoods, 1880 – 1960* (Aldershot: Scolar Press, 1995)

Tebbutt, M., 'Rambling and manly identity in Derbyshire's Dark Peak, 1880s–1920s', *Historical Journal*, 49:4 (2006), 1125–53

Tebbutt, M., 'Exhibition and inhibitions: new narratives of working-class boys and leisure in the 1920s and 1930s', in R. Snape and H. Pussard (eds), *Recording Leisure Lives: Sports, Games and Pastimes in 20th Century Britain* (Eastbourne: Leisure Studies Association, 2010)

Teo, H.-M., 'Women's travel, dance, and British metropolitan anxieties, 1890–1939', *Gender and History*, 12:2 (2000), 366–400

Thom, D., 'The healthy citizen of empire or juvenile delinquent? Beating and mental health in the UK', in M. Gijswijt-Hofstra and H. Marland (eds), *Cultures of Child Health in Britain and the Netherlands in the Twentieth Century* (Amsterdam and New York: Rodopi, 2003)

Thompson, F. M. L. (ed.), *The Cambridge Social History Of Britain, 1750–1950* (Cambridge: Cambridge University Press, 1993)

Thompson, P., 'The war with adults', *Oral History*, 3:2 (1975), 29–38

Thrift, N. and S. French, 'The automatic production of space', *Transactions of the Institute of British Geographers*, 27:3 (2002), 309–35

Tinkler, P., 'An all-round education: the Board of Education's policy for the leisure-time training of girls, 1939–1950', *History of Education*, 23:4 (1994), 385–403

Tinkler, P., *Constructing Girlhood, Popular Magazines for Girls Growing Up in England, 1920–1950* (London: Taylor and Francis, 1995)

Tinkler, P., 'Sexuality and citizenship; the state and girls' leisure provision in England, 1939–45', *Women's History Review*, 4:2 (1995), 193–217

Tinkler, P., 'At your service: the nation's girlhood and the call to service in England, 1939–1950', *European Journal of Women's Studies*, 4 (2001), 353–77

Tinkler, P., 'English girls and the international dimensions of British citizenship in the 1940s', *European Journal of Women's Studies*, 8:1 (2001), 103–27

Tinkler, P., 'Rebellion, modernity and romance: smoking as a gendered practice in popular women's magazines, Britain 1918–1939', *Women's Studies International Forum*, 24:1 (2001), 111–22

Tinkler, P., '"Red tips for hot lips": advertising cigarettes for young women in Britain, 1920–1970', *Women's History Review*, 10:2 (2001), 249–72

Tinkler, P., 'Cause for concern: young women and leisure, 1930–1950', *Women's History Review*, 12:2 (2003), 233–60

Tinkler, P., 'Refinement and respectable consumption: the acceptable face of women's smoking in Britain, 1918–1970', *Gender and History*, 15:2 (2003), 342–60

Tinkler, P., 'Advertising', in J. Goodman (ed.) *Tobacco in History and Culture: An Encyclopedia* (Farmington Hills, MI: Charles Scribner's Sons, 2004)

Tinkler, P., 'Sexual politics', in J. Goodman (ed.) *Tobacco in History and Culture: An Encyclopedia* (Farmington Hills, MI: Charles Scribner's Sons, 2004)

Tinkler, P., *Smoke Signals: Women, Smoking and Visual Culture* (Oxford and New York: Berg, 2006)

Tinkler, P., 'Sapphic Smokers and English Modernities', in L. Doan and J. Garrity (eds), *Sapphic Modernities* (London: Palgrave, 2007)

Tinkler, P., 'Youth', in F. Carnevali and J. Strange (eds), *Twentieth Century Britain: Economic, Cultural and Social Change* (Harlow: Pearson Longman, 2007)

Todd, S., '"Boisterous workers": young women, industrial rationalization and workplace militancy in interwar rural England', *Labour History Review*, 68:3 (2003), 293–310

Todd, S., 'Poverty and aspiration: young women's employment in inter-war England', *Twentieth Century British History*, 15:2 (2004), 119–42

Todd, S., 'Young women, work and family in interwar rural England', *Agricultural History Review*, 52:1 (2004), 83–98

Todd, S., *Young Women, Work, and Family in England, 1918–1950* (Oxford: Oxford University Press, 2005)

Todd, S., 'Young women, work and leisure in interwar England', *The Historical Journal*, 49:3 (2005), 789–809

Todd, S., 'Flappers and factory lads: youth and youth culture in interwar Britain', *History Compass*, 4:4 (2006), 715–30

Toffell, G., ' "Come and see, and hear, the mother tongue!" Yiddish cinema in interwar London', *Screen*, 50:3 (2009), 277–98

Tosh, J., Review of J.A. Mangan and James Walvin (eds), *Manliness and Morality: Middle-Class Masculinity in Britain and America 1800–1940*, in *History Workshop Journal*, 29 (1990), 187–8

Tosh, J., 'What should historians do with masculinity?' in R. Shoemaker and M. Vincent (eds), *Gender and History in Western Europe* (Cambridge: Cambridge University Press, 1998)

Tosh, J., 'Masculinities in an industrializing society: Britain, 1800–1914', *Journal of British Studies*, 44:2 (2005), 330–42

Travell, J. C., *Doctor of Souls: A Biography of Leslie Dixon Weatherhead* (Cambridge: Lutterworth Press, c.1999)

Turner, B. S., 'Introduction: bodily performance: on aura and reproducibility', *Body and Society*, 11:4 (2005), 1–17

Ugolini, L., 'Clothes and the modern man in 1930s Oxford', *Fashion Theory*, 4:4 (2000), 427–46

Ugolini, L., *Men and Menswear: Sartorial Consumption in Britain, 1880–1939* (Aldershot: Ashgate, 2007)

Ugolini, L., 'Autobiographies and menswear consumption in Britain, c. 1880–1939', *Textile History*, 40:2 (2009), 202–11

Urry, J., *The Tourist Gaze: Leisure and Travel in Contemporary Societies* (London: Sage Publications, 1990)

Vanderbeck, R. M., 'Masculinities and fieldwork: widening the discussion', *Gender, Place and Culture*, 12:4 (2005), 387–402

Vincent, D., *Bread, Knowledge and Freedom. A Study of Nineteenth Century Working Class Autobiography* (London and New York: Methuen, 1981)

Vincenzi, P., 'Obituary: Marjorie Proops', *Independent* (12 November 1996).

Voeltz, R., 'The antidote to "khaki fever"? The expansion of the British Girl Guides during the First World War', *Journal of Contemporary History*, 27 (1992), 627–38

Walton, J. K., *The Blackpool Landlady* (Manchester: Manchester University Press, 1979)

Walton, J. K., 'Afterword: Mass-Observation's Blackpool and some alternatives', in G. Cross (ed.), *Worktowners at Blackpool: Mass-Observation and Popular Leisure in the 1930s* (London: Routledge, 1990)

Walton, J. K., *Fish and Chips and the British Working Class, 1870–1940* (Leicester: Leicester University Press, 1994)

Walton, J. K., *Blackpool* (Edinburgh: Edinburgh University Press, 1998)

Walton, J. K., *The British Seaside: Holidays and Resorts in the Twentieth Century* (Manchester: Manchester University Press, 2000)

Walton, J. K., 'Beaches, bathing and beauty: health and bodily exposure at the British seaside from the eighteenth century to the twentieth', *Revue Française de Civilisation Britannique*, 14:2 (2007), 119–36

Ward, A. 'Dancing in the dark: rationalism and the neglect of social dance', in H. Thomas (ed.), *Dance, Gender and Culture* (London: Macmillan, 1993)

Ward, C. and D. Hardy, *Goodnight Campers! The History of the British Holiday Camp* (London and New York: Mansell Publishing Limited, 1986)

Warren, A., 'Citizens of the empire: Baden-Powell, Scouts and Guides, and an imperial ideal', in J. Mackenzie (ed.), *Imperialism and Popular Culture* (Manchester: Manchester University Press, 1986)

Warren, A., 'Sir Robert Baden-Powell, the scout movement, and citizen-training in Britain, 1900–1920', *English Historical Review*, 101:399 (1986), 376–98

Warren, A., 'Baden-Powell: a final comment', *English Historical Review*, 102:405 (1987), 948–50

Warren, A., 'Popular manliness: Baden-Powell, scouting and the development of manly character', in J. A. Mangan and J. Walvin (eds), *Manliness and Morality: Middle-class Masculinity in Britain and America, 1800–1940* (Manchester: Manchester University Press, 1987)

Warren, A., 'Mothers for the empire? The Girl Guide Association in Britain, 1909–1939', in J. A. Mangan (ed.), *Making Imperial Mentalities: Socialisation and British Imperialism* (Manchester, Manchester University Press, 1990)

Warren, A., 'Sport, youth and gender in Britain, 1880–1940', in J. C. Binfield and J. Stevenson (eds), *Sport, Culture and Politics* (Sheffield: Sheffield Academic Press, 1993)

Warwick, L. and A. Burman, *Northampton in Old Picture Postcards* (Zaltbommel: European Library, 1989)

Waters, C., 'Representations of everyday life: L. S. Lowry and the landscape of memory in postwar Britain', *Representations*, 65 Special Issue: New Perspectives in British Studies (1999), 121–50

Waters, C., 'Autobiography, nostalgia, and the practices of working-class selfhood', in G. Behlmer and F. Leventhal (eds), *Singular Continuities: Tradition, Nostalgia, and Society in Modern Britain* (Stanford: Stanford University Press, 2000)

Weatherspoon, E., 'Beloved consolation: the life of Dorothy Dix', paper presented at the Dorothy Dix Symposium, Woodstock Mansion, Todd County, Kentucky, September 27 1991, http://library.apsu.edu/Dix/kanervo.htm (accessed 7 February 2007)

Webster, W., 'There'll always be an England: representations of colonial wars and immigration, 1948–68', paper given at 'Relocating Britishness' conference, University of Central Lancashire, Preston, 22–24 June 2000

White, J., *The Worst Street in North London: Campbell Bunk, Islington, between the Wars* (London: Routledge and Kegan Paul, 1986)

White, R. and J. Why, 'Youth agency and social context', *Journal of Sociology*, 34:3 (1998), 314–27

Wilkinson, P., 'English youth movements, 1908–30', *Journal of Contemporary History*, 4:2 (1969), 3–23

Willcock, H. D. and Mass Observation, *Report on Juvenile Delinquency* ([S. I.]: Falcon Press, 1949)

Williams, D., *Ten Lectures on the Theories of the Dance* (Metuchen, NJ.: The Scarecrow Press, 1991)

Wills, A., 'Delinquency, masculinity and citizenship in England, 1950–1970', *Past and Present*, 187:1 (2005), 157–85

Winlow, S., *Badfellas: Crime, Tradition and New Masculinities* (Oxford: Berg, 2001)

Winter, J., *Sites of Memory, Sites of Mourning: The European War in European Cultural History* (Cambridge: Cambridge University Press, 1995)

Woodward, K. (ed.) *Identity and Difference* (London: Sage, 1997)

Wouters, C., *Sex and Manners: Female Emancipation in the West, 1890–2000* (London: Sage Publications, 2004)

Wouters, C., *Informalization: Manners and Emotions since 1890* (London: Sage Publications, 2007)

Wulff, H., 'Memories in motion: the Irish dancing body', *Body and Society*, 11:4 (2005), 45–62

Yeo, E. J., '"The boy is the father of the man": moral panic over working-class youth, 1850 to the present', *Labour History Review*, 69:2 (2004), 185–99

Youngran, J. 'Murrell, Christine Mary (1874–1933)', *Oxford Dictionary of National Biography* (Oxford: Oxford University Press, 2004), www.oxforddnb.com/view/article/54293 (accessed 20 October 2009)

Zimring, R., '"The dangerous art where one slip means death": dance and the literary imagination in inter-war Britain', *Modernism/Modernity*, 14:4 (2007), 707–27

Zweiniger-Bargielowska, I., 'Building a British superman: physical culture in interwar Britain', *Journal of Contemporary History*, 41:4 (2006), 595–610

Internet resources

British Pathé, www.britishpathe.com/

The Encyclopaedia of Informal Education, www.infed.org/archives/nayc/index.htm (accessed May 2008)

Imperial Society of Teachers of Dancing, www.istd.org/main.html (History) (accessed 27 April 2007)

International Lyrics Playground, http://lyricsplayground.com/index.html (accessed February 2010)

Radio Caroline, www.radiocaroline.co.uk/#home.html

The Old Corral, www.surfnetinc.com/chuck/hgibson.htm (accessed March 2009)

Index